LAW IN POLITICS, POLITICS IN LAW

A great deal has been written on the relationship between politics and law. Legislation, as a source of law, is often highly political, and is the product of a process or the creation of officials often closely bound into party politics. Legislation is also one of the exclusive powers of the state. As such, legislation is plainly both practical and inevitably political; at the same time most understandings of the relationship between law and politics have been overwhelmingly theoretical. In this light, public law is often seen as part of the political order or as inescapably partisan. We know relatively little about the real impact of law on politicians through their legal advisers and civil servants. How do lawyers in government see their roles and what use do they make of law? How does politics actually affect the drafting of legislation or the making of policy?

This volume will begin to answer these and other questions about the practical, day-to-day relationship between law and politics in a number of settings. It includes chapters by former departmental legal advisers, drafters of legislation, law reformers, judges and academics, who focus on what actually happens when law meets politics in government.

Volume 3 in the series Hart Studies in Constitutional Law

Hart Studies in Constitutional Law

Law in Politics, Politics in Law

Edited by
David Feldman

·HART·
PUBLISHING
OXFORD AND PORTLAND, OREGON
2013

Published in the United Kingdom by Hart Publishing Ltd
16C Worcester Place, Oxford, OX1 2JW
Telephone: +44 (0)1865 517530
Fax: +44 (0)1865 510710
E-mail: mail@hartpub.co.uk
Website: http://www.hartpub.co.uk

Published in North America (US and Canada) by
Hart Publishing
c/o International Specialized Book Services
920 NE 58th Avenue, Suite 300
Portland, OR 97213-3786
USA
Tel: +1 503 287 3093 or toll-free: (1) 800 944 6190
Fax: +1 503 280 8832
E-mail: orders@isbs.com
Website: http://www.isbs.com

British Library Cataloguing in Publication Data
Data Available

ISBN: 978-1-84946-473-4

Typeset by Hope Services, Abingdon
Printed and bound in Great Britain by
TJ International Ltd, Padstow, Cornwall

Preface

This volume is largely based on papers presented at two events in 2011. One was the Annual Conference of the Society of Legal Scholars (SLS), the learned society of university lawyers in the United Kingdom and Ireland, which took place at Downing College and the Faculty of Law, University of Cambridge, from 5th to 8th September 2011. A distinguished collection of speakers discussed their experiences as lawyers in and around politics and the civil service. Professor Elizabeth Cooke, Sir Ross Cranston, David Howarth, Sir Stephen Laws, Professor Hector MacQueen, Matthew Parish and Sir Philip Sales subsequently revised their presentations or prepared new material for this collection. The other event was a seminar marking the centenary of the Parliament Act 1911, which was organised for the University of Cambridge Centre for Public Law (CPL) and held at the Canary Wharf offices of Clifford Chance LLP, generous and long-standing supporters of the CPL, on 22nd November 2011. Of the eminent participants, Dr Chris Ballinger, Daniel Greenberg, Professor Lord Norton of Louth, Professor Dawn Oliver and Dr Rhodri Walters kindly wrote up their presentations or offered new work to afford readers of this volume a range of perspectives on the interaction of law and politics in the planning, enactment and implementation of the 1911 Act and its amending Act of 1949, a case-study of the relationships between law and politics. Three speakers, the Right Hon Theresa Villiers MP, Professor Vernon Bogdanor and Professor Rodney Brazier, kindly took part in the conference or the seminar and greatly enhanced the discussion, but were unable to contribute to this volume. I am grateful to all of them for the illumination they offered, and am particularly indebted to the authors for translating their presentations into the form in which they appear here and for their patience and flexibility in responding to editorial demands.

The authors of two chapters did not take part in those events. Matthew Windsor arrived serendipitously in Cambridge in 2012 to undertake research on legal ethics in relation to lawyers advising governments on international law, and generously allowed himself to be persuaded to add the writing of a chapter on legal ethics to the other, more pressing demands on his time. The late Alan Rodger, Lord Rodger of Earlsferry, in a way laid the groundwork for this book by opening my eyes to aspects of its subject in his Presidential Address to the Holdsworth Club in the University of Birmingham in 1998. Then and subsequently, he showed me great professional and personal consideration and kindness. In 2009 we discussed the plans for the 2011 SLS Annual Conference and the possibility of a book such as this, and he delighted me by agreeing in principle to allow his 1998 Presidential Address to be included in any collection which might emerge from the Conference. His death in June 2011 deprived the legal world of a great gentleman, a fine lawyer and legal historian, an elegant, entertaining speaker and writer, and a delightful, inspiring companion.

Two chapters, or versions of them, are published elsewhere. I am grateful to the following for permission to use material in this book:

Dr Christine Rodger, the Holdsworth Club of the University of Birmingham and its Vice-President, Mr George Applebey, Dr Ludwig Burgmann and Löwenklau Gesellschaft eV, Frankfurt am Main, for chapter four, 'The Form and Language of Legislation' by Lord

Rodger of Earlsferry, previously published by the Holdsworth Club (Birmingham, 1998), and, in a revised and updated version, in (1999) 19 *Rechtshistorisches Journal*, 601–35;

Mr Nicolas Besly, Editor of *The Table: The Journal of the Society of Clerks at the Table of Commonwealth Parliaments*, and the Society of Clerks-at-the-Table in Commonwealth Parliaments, for chapter thirteen, 'The Impact of the Parliament Acts 1911 and 1949 on a Government's Management of its Legislative Timetable, on Parliamentary Procedure and on Legislative Drafting', published in *The Table*, vd 80, 201: pp 11–16.

Many people have developed my own interest in the relationship between politics and law over 40-odd years. I owe special debts to Dr Stephen Cretney, my tutor, ex-colleague and friend, and to Professor Richard Hodder-Williams and Dr Hugh Rawlings, sometime colleagues in the University of Bristol, who organised an annual Law & Politics Colloquium in the 1970s and 1980s.

Finally, I acknowledge my gratitude and sense of obligation to several other people and organisations for making this book possible. The SLS honoured me by electing me as its President for 2010–11, allowing me to place law and politics at the heart of its Annual Conference in 2011. Professor John Bell, Director of the CPL, played a major part in organising the seminar on the Parliament Act 1911, and offered his customarily erudite and wholehearted support to the project. Mrs Felicity Eves-Rey, of the University of Cambridge Faculty of Law, provided valuable administrative backing and keen organisational skills for the Conference, seminar and book. I benefited from Richard Hart's encouragement of this project as I have for projects for more than a quarter of a century. For Hart Publishing, the perceptive copy-editor, Victoria Broom, ensured that many errors could be corrected and ambiguities resolved. It has been a pleasure to work with Rachel Turner, Mel Hamill and Tom Adams, whose efficiency and patience ensured that the various papers were smoothly moulded into a book at a particularly busy time for any academic publisher. And at home, Jill continued to tolerate me and my preoccupations and make everything seem worthwhile, as she has for 30 years.

David Feldman
Comberton, 29th August 2013

Contents

List of Authors

Dr Chris Ballinger is the Academic Dean and an Official Fellow of Exeter College, Oxford.

Elizabeth Cooke is Professor of Law in the University of Reading and a member of the Law Commission.

Sir Ross Cranston, FBA, is a Judge of the High Court of Justice of England and Wales, and was previously a Labour MP for Dudley North, Solicitor General, and a professor of law.

David Feldman, QC (Hon), FBA, is the Rouse Ball Professor of English Law in the University of Cambridge and a Fellow of Downing College, Cambridge, and was previously Legal Adviser to the Joint Committee on Human Rights in the UK Houses of Parliament.

Daniel Greenberg is Parliamentary Counsel, Berwin Leighton Paisner LLP; Editor of *Craies on Legislation*; and Visiting Professor of Legislation in the University of Derby.

David Howarth is a Reader in Private Law in the University of Cambridge, a Fellow of Clare College, Cambridge, and former Liberal Democrat leader of Cambridge City Council and MP for Cambridge.

Sir Stephen Laws, KCB, QC (Hon), now retired, was previously First Parliamentary Counsel.

Hector MacQueen, FBA, FRSE, is Professor of Private Law in the University of Edinburgh and a member of the Scottish Law Commission.

Philip Norton, Lord Norton of Louth, is Professor of Politics at the University of Hull and takes the Conservative whip in the House of Lords.

Dawn Oliver, QC (Hon), FBA, is Emeritus Professor of Constitutional Law at University College, London.

Matthew Parish is a partner with the law firm Holman Fenwick Willan in Geneva, and was previously legal counsel to the World Bank and, from 2005 to 2007, the Chief Legal Adviser to the International Supervisor of Brčko.

The late Alan Rodger, Lord Rodger of Earlsferry (1944–2011) was Solicitor General for Scotland and Lord Advocate (Conservative), Lord Justice General and Lord President of the Court of Session in Scotland, a Lord of Appeal in Ordinary, and a Justice of the Supreme Court of the United Kingdom.

Sir Philip Sales is a Judge of the High Court of Justice of England and Wales.

David Seymour, now retired, was the Legal Adviser to the UK Government's Home Office.

Dr Rhodri Walters is Reading Clerk in the House of Lords in the UK Parliament.

Matthew Windsor is a PhD candidate in the Faculty of Law, University of Cambridge, and a WM Tapp Scholar at Gonville and Caius College, Cambridge.

Sir Michael Wood is a barrister in private practice at 20 Essex Court, London, and was previously the Legal Adviser to the UK Government's Foreign and Commonwealth Office.

Table of Cases

INTERNATIONAL

International Arbitration

International Centre for Settlement of Investment Disputes (ICSID)

International Court of Justice (ICJ)

International Criminal Court (ICC)

UN Commission on International Trade Law (UNCITRAL)

EUROPEAN

European Court of Human Rights

European Court of Justice

DOMESTIC

Australia

New Zealand

United Kingdom

United States

Table of Legislation

DOMESTIC

Statutory Instruments

United States

Part 1

Introduction

1

Beginning at the Beginning: The Relationships between Politics and Law

DAVID FELDMAN*

I THE NATURE OF THE ENTERPRISE

W E ARE CONCERNED in this collection with the interaction of law and politics. It is important to make clear the scope and limits of our purpose. We are interested first in how lawyers who work as or with politicians see their roles, and particularly how their legal expertise affects them in their political roles, how politics affects the way they view law, and how legal advisers accommodate political goals in their work. Our contributors include people who have served in different roles and institutions as politicians, legal civil servants, advisers and judges, as well as academics with distinctive expertise in aspects of the subject. They write about how their legal responsibilities interact with government and politics, and how politics affects their views of law. This is related to the issue of legal ethics: first, are lawyers who work for government subject to the same ethical code as lawyers in private practice? If not, what ethical standards (if any) apply to them? Secondly, we want to see how the stuff of law is shaped to advance politicians' aims, and how the need to transform party policies into the formal structure and language of legislation may work. Thirdly, we seek to understand how politicians' differing political priorities can affect the content of legislative proposals, whether from government or the Law Commissions for England and Wales and Scotland, and their chance of being passed into law.

There are a number of matters which could usefully be examined but which are outside the remit which we have set ourselves in this book. First, we are not looking at public administration as such. Several of the lawyers whose work is discussed were civil servants, and that inevitably affects the ways they used law and how their political clients used their advice and expertise. Nevertheless, we do not look at their roles as administrators as such, but rather at the practical effects of law and legal advice on policy development by politicians. Indeed, apart from managing other lawyers, legal advisers in the UK's civil service these days are rather separated from mainstream administration in their departments of state. Lawyers in government in the UK have become specialists advising generalists, rather than generalists with special expertise who regularly move to the top of the administrative stream in the civil service. Professor Terence Daintith and Professor Alan Page noted that

* I am grateful to the contributors, and particularly to Chris Ballinger and Sir Michael Wood, for helpful comments on a draft of this chapter.

at the beginning of the twentieth century three of the four top civil servants in the Home Office were legally trained, but that this had fallen to one by 1913, although as late as 1931 the Royal Commission on the Civil Service still thought that a tactful legal adviser could exercise considerable influence over policy.[1] By 1989, the Government Legal Service (GLS) was seen as having an identity which cut across the departmental divisions of government, and the Treasury Solicitor became Head of the GLS and acquired managerial responsibilities not just for the Treasury Solicitor's Department but for the whole of the GLS. In 1996, the Treasury Solicitor's Department was hived off as an agency, charging departments for legal work, but the Treasury Solicitor continued to operate as Head of the GLS.[2]

Secondly, we are not looking at the effect of courts and tribunals on politics and administration, or of politics or administration on courts and tribunals. There is much valuable work on that subject, as there is on the interaction of law and administrators and administration, but that is not our focus.[3] We accept, however, that it is not possible to draw a clear line between administration and policy-making. Administrators and their procedures can facilitate or inhibit certain policy choices. The importance of not divorcing administrative law from administrative values and practices has long been stressed by Professor Carol Harlow and Professor Richard Rawlings,[4] and Dr Eoin Carolan has drawn attention to the importance of accommodating the roles of administrators and regulators in making, steering or otherwise influencing policy within the conceptual structure of the separation of powers.[5] These and related matters are important, but they lie outside the purview of this collection, which focuses on law and the process of politics rather than on the impact of administration on policy-making.

II VARIETIES OF CONNECTION BETWEEN POLITICS AND LAW

We can think about the relationship between politics and law in several ways. First, there are the people of politics and law. It is common for the same people to operate as politicians and as lawyers, either at the same time or moving from one role to the other. There is a long history of lawyer-politicians.[6] Some offices are specifically designed for people who function as both at the same time. In the UK, examples include the Law Officers (for example the Attorney General and Solicitor General in England and Wales and Northern

---

[1] Terence Daintith and Alan Page, *The Executive in the Constitution: Structure, Autonomy, and Internal Control* (Oxford, Oxford University Press, 1998) 210–11; see also Royal Commission on the Civil Service (Chairman: Lord Tomlin), *Report* (Cmd 3909, 1931).

[2] Daintith and Page (n 1) 218–19.

[3] See, eg, Simon Halliday, *Judicial Review and Compliance with Administrative Law* (Oxford, Hart Publishing, 2004); Mark Hertogh and Simon Halliday (eds), *Judicial Review and Bureaucratic Impact: International and Interdisciplinary Perspectives* (Cambridge, Cambridge University Press, 2004); Robert Thomas, *Administrative Justice and Asylum Appeals* (Oxford, Hart Publishing, 2011); Maurice Sunkin, Kerman Calvo and Lucinda Platt, *Does Judicial Review Influence the Quality of Local Authority Services?* (ESRC Public Services Programme Discussion Paper Series No 801, 2008); Varda Bondy and Maurice Sunkin, 'Settlement in Judicial Review Proceedings' [2009] *Public Law* 372–79; Maurice Sunkin, Lucinda Platt and Kerman Calvo, 'The Positive Effect of Judicial Review on the Quality of Local Government' (2010) 15 *Judicial Review* 337–42; Maurice Sunkin and Varda Bondy, *The Dynamics of Judicial Review Litigation: The Resolution of Public Law Challenges Before Final Hearing* (London, Public Law Project, 2009).

[4] Carol Harlow and Richard Rawlings, *Law and Administration* (London, Weidenfeld & Nicolson, 1981; 2nd edn, London, Butterworths, 1997; 3rd edn, Cambridge, Cambridge University Press, 2009).

[5] Eoin Carolan, *The New Separation of Powers* (Oxford, Oxford University Press, 2009) especially chs 4–7.

[6] See Ross Cranston in ch 2 of this volume.

Ireland, and the Lord Advocate in Scotland), who are typically members of one of the Houses of Parliament (although the role of the Lord Advocate has changed since devolution to Scotland took effect), and act as legal advisers to the Government of the day, and are responsible to Parliament for aspects of government.[7] The Lord Chancellor was, until fairly recently, another example, being a politician and lawyer whose tasks included presiding over the House of Lords, acting as head of the judiciary, and acting as a Minister of the Crown with special responsibility for the judicial system. The Constitutional Reform Act 2005 separated these roles from each other and made it possible for someone who was neither a peer nor a lawyer to become Lord Chancellor. It was only in 2007, however, that a commoner, Jack Straw MP, first served as Lord Chancellor, without power to sit as a judge. He and his successor, the Conservative Kenneth Clarke QC, MP, were both barristers, although Mr Straw had practised for only a short time, more than 30 years earlier.[8] In 2012, the first non-lawyer became Lord Chancellor (Christopher Grayling MP). For these officers, their task is one of special delicacy, reconciling party loyalty and (in the case of the Attorney General and the Lord Chancellor) collective ministerial responsibility with giving objectively rational legal advice and supporting the rule of law and the judicial system. It is difficult to avoid the suspicion that having as Lord Chancellor a person with neither legal nor wide governmental experience, and the old Lord Chancellor's Department becoming (via the Department for Constitutional Affairs) a Ministry of Justice with responsibility for a range of non-judicial administrative fields acquired from the Home Office, have widened the gap between the Government and the legal professions and judges.[9]

In the past, people regularly moved from political to judicial office.[10] Lord Reid went directly from the Scottish Bar to the House of Lords in 1948, having served as Solicitor General for Scotland and Lord Advocate. He sat until 1974, playing a large part in shaping the development of common law, particularly administrative law. Lord Rodger of Earlsferry, one of our contributors (though sadly a posthumous one), started as a legal academic before going to the Scottish Bar in 1974, served as Solicitor General for Scotland and then Lord Advocate between 1989 and 1995, then was appointed head of the Scottish judiciary as Lord Justice General and Lord President of the Court of Session in 1996, becoming a Lord of Appeal in Ordinary sitting in the House of Lords in 2001 and one of the first Justices of the Supreme Court in 2009. Reginald Manningham-Buller was a barrister who was elected to Parliament as a Conservative in 1943, became Solicitor General in 1951 and served as Attorney General between 1954 and 1962, became Lord Chancellor from 1962 until the Conservatives lost office in 1964, but was appointed a Lord of Appeal in Ordinary by a Labour Lord Chancellor in 1969, serving until 1980. He was the last Lord Chancellor to be appointed a Lord of Appeal in Ordinary, never having sat in lower courts.

It used to be common for Attorneys General to move to the High Court bench.[11] Some politicians have become Lord Chief Justice. Rufus Isaacs, Liberal MP for Reading, became Attorney General in the Liberal administration from 1910 to 1913 (during which time he

---

[7] J Ll J Edwards, *The Law Officers of the Crown* (London, Sweet & Maxwell, 1964); J Ll J Edwards, *The Attorney General, Politics and the Public Interest* (London, Sweet & Maxwell, 1984); Daintith and Page (n 1) 231–38; Ross Cranston in ch 2 of this volume.

[8] Jack Straw, *Last Man Standing: Memoirs of a Political Survivor* (London, Pan Books, 2013). I am grateful to Chris Ballinger for pointing this out to me.

[9] Chris Ballinger has suggested to me that the shape of the new Ministry of Justice may be more significant in this respect than the change in the character and function of the Lord Chancellor.

[10] See Ross Cranston in ch 2 of this volume.

[11] ibid.

was the first Attorney General to be a member of the Cabinet), from which he was appointed directly to the office of Lord Chief Justice as Lord Reading. Sir Ross Cranston, a former law professor, was elected MP for Dudley North (1997–2005). He was Solicitor General (1998–2001), returned to a professorship at the London School of Economics in 2005, but was appointed to the High Court bench in 2007. Nor is this a purely British phenomenon. In Australia, Lionel Murphy became a Justice of the High Court after being Attorney General in a Labour government. In the Constitutional Court of Bosnia and Herzegovina, on which I served for several years, it was common for politicians who were lawyers to be elected to the Constitutional Court.

This has benefits and disadvantages, as Sir Ross Cranston and David Howarth discuss in their respective chapters in this book. One benefit is to ensure that courts understand the business of politics from which much law emerges. A disadvantage is that it can lead outside observers to doubt the independence and impartiality of politician-judges, at least when they deal with issues on which they expressed views when in politics. It seems that moving from politics to the Bench in this country is becoming rare, and that has implications for the relationship between politics and law. David Howarth also draws attention to the declining number of legally qualified MPs in the House of Commons. Legal expertise in the House of Lords, too, has suffered since the abolition of Lords of Appeal in Ordinary when the Supreme Court came into operation in 2009, and the resulting prohibition on Justices of the Supreme Court who are peers from participating in the parliamentary activities of the House of Lords.[12]

By contrast, there has never been a major tradition of moving from bureaucratic positions to the judiciary or into politics (except when former civil servants receive peerages on retiring). This may explain a relative lack of understanding of administration on the part of politicians and many lawyers. Lawyer-civil servants are also rare; as noted above, lawyers in the civil service are mainly professional legal advisers who work with, advise and act for other civil servants and ministers. These legal advisers have several functions which overlap with politics.[13] They advise on the legal implications of proposed policies. In so doing, they may be instrumental, directly or indirectly, in formulating a government's policies. Parliamentary Counsel draft legislation on instructions from departments, turning government policy into the stuff of law. Lawyers in government also advise on litigation involving governmental bodies and officers, and may conduct litigation on behalf of departments and ministers. At the same time, they are dealing with a host of legal matters which are not directly political but affect governmental bodies in their day-to-day work, such as conveyancing, employment matters, public procurement, and so on. Other lawyers advise parliamentary select committees in the course of their work scrutinising government departments and legislation. Sometimes lawyers move from one role to another. For example, Sir James Nursaw was Legal Adviser to the Home Office and the Northern Ireland Office from 1983 to 1988, when he became Treasury Solicitor. In 1993, after his retirement from the Treasury Solicitor's Department, he was appointed Counsel to the Lord Chairman of Committees in the House of Lords, advising committees and their chairmen in their work, a role he filled until 2002. Some might regard this as a poacher turning game-keeper, although others would say the reverse.

---

[12] Chris Ballinger has also pointed out to me that, whilst former Justices of the Supreme Court may resume membership of the House of Lords on retiring from the Supreme Court, Justices appointed since 2009 are not peers and might not receive life peerages on retirement.

[13] See Stephen Laws, ch 5 of this volume; David Seymour, ch 6; and Michael Wood, ch 7.

That is not to say that it is impossible for government legal advisers to move into judicial posts. In New Zealand, Sir Kenneth Keith was at different times a government lawyer and a university law professor before being appointed to the High Court and later Supreme Court, from which he was elected a Judge of the International Court of Justice. The boundary between government legal posts and judicial appointments seems to be particularly porous in the field of international law: Legal Advisers at the Foreign Office who have gone on to hold international judicial offices include Sir JES (James) Fawcett (Assistant Legal Adviser, Foreign and Commonwealth Office, 1945–50; General Counsel to the International Monetary Fund, 1955–60; member of the European Commission of Human Rights, 1960–84 and President, 1972–81) and Sir Gerald Fitzmaurice (Legal Adviser to the Foreign and Commonwealth Office, 1953–60; Judge of the International Court of Justice, 1960–73; Judge of the European Court of Human Rights, 1974–80). Sir Franklin Berman, Legal Adviser to the Foreign and Commonwealth Office from 1990 to 1999, has been an arbitrator in many cases, as well as an ad hoc judge of the International Court of Justice.

In short, there is a good deal of overlap between the *dramatis personae* of politics and that of law. As already mentioned, this ensures that the courts have an understanding of the political world. It also ensures that politicians do not lose sight of the values of the rule of law, which ultimately depends in part on governments internalising them and being loyal to them. The idea that lawyers have a duty to instil the values of good government and the rule of law is respectably ancient. For centuries the Lord Chancellor was described as the keeper of Her (or His) Majesty's conscience, perhaps because they were often clerics alongside their political, administrative and judicial duties. Mixing functions can be useful from a practical angle; a separation of powers, if too complete, weakens institutions' understanding of each other when they come in contact.

From this perspective, signs of a growing separation between politicians and lawyers give cause for concern, as David Howarth and Sir Ross Cranston argue in their chapters in this book. Yet, if we regard lawyers in government and public administration as principally either politicians or technocrats, we will not understand the tensions which arise from the fact that these people have dual roles and to some extent dual personalities. This prompts us to consider the special challenges facing lawyers in government, which distinguish them from lawyers in private practice. Sir Michael Wood reflects on this in chapter seven, and Matthew Windsor in chapter eight analyses the special problems for legal ethics which the combination of political and legal responsibilities pose for governmental legal advisers. There is rarely time in the rush of day-to-day events for the actors to reflect on the ethical challenges they face, but they are sometimes intense; in the field of international law and international relations, as Sir Michael writes, the archive of the Chilcot Inquiry into the background to the invasion of Iraq in 2003 is a rich source of information. It is important to think about the special ethical position of governmental legal advisers in view of their functions in a political sphere, as Matthew Windsor does.

Turning from the personnel of law and politics to their substance, there is an obvious link between legislation as a source of law and the political process which produces legislation. At some level, all legislation is political; that fact is both an explanation for its controversial character and a source of its legitimacy. As a general proposition, as Sir Stephen Laws points out in chapter five, legislation is usually needed only in order to change the law. The change is normally desired by the Government in order to further its political, and often party-political, aims and interests. But developments in the common law are equally generated by a desire for change, although the mechanism is different and the motivation is generally less to give effect to a government's policies and more to give effect to judicial principles. The common law usually moves incrementally, by analogy, rather than making clear breaks, although sometimes changes mark a decisive break from the past rather than a development from it.

This links politics to law at an abstract, metaphysical level, quite different from officers' multiple roles (either concurrently or sequentially). Two bodies of scholarship link the ideas of politics and law. The first is political theory, particularly the theory of the state. The other builds on sociology or social psychology to identify particular political standpoints or preferences with legal officials (especially judges). Both are important, although neither in itself forms a major focus of the contributions to this book.

The realm of political theory can illuminate the role of politics and law in establishing, legitimating and operating states and similar structures. For example, Professor Martin Loughlin has undertaken the huge task of explaining what makes public law, placing it in an historical and philosophical framework which takes account of theories of the state alongside the history of ideas, particularly about authority, legitimacy, and sovereignty. In the course of this, he has analysed politics as operating at several levels. The first order of politics is the idea of 'the political' itself. Essentially, Loughlin argues, it stems from conflicts between groups of people.[14] The distinctive role of the state is to contain or channel those conflicts. Second-order distinctions, between, for example, governors and governed and government and opposition, constitute the state.[15] The job of the state is to manage, not eliminate, conflict. It is likely to facilitate this task if the state can maintain a public sense of its even-handedness, in order to foster public acceptance of its actions and support for its institutions. This is the task of constitutional law, which operates as what Loughlin calls 'the third order of the political'.[16] It legitimises the power of the state and bolsters its authority by constraining its capacity for arbitrariness or oppressiveness.[17]

Loughlin's analysis is helpful, for our current purposes, in that it offers a model of the relationship between public law and politics which, if we adopt it, can help lawyers in politics and lawyers who advise politicians to clarify their essential functions in the life of the state. It is only one of several possible models. Following Carl Schmitt, Loughlin's view of people's motivations in creating states is based in social conflict. States are a rational response on the part of a dominant people or group to fear of other peoples or groups.[18] Once up and running, states' governors (a term which encompasses politicians, lawyers and administrators in state institutions) must engage in Macchiavellian statecraft to shore up the authority of their institutions or offices in order to provide conditions in which they can govern effectively. But even if one inclines more towards a model of the state as an instrument for building a sense of social solidarity and community, the value of statecraft remains, and the actions of lawyers in state institutions will take account of it.

Alongside political theory, but separate from it, there is a body of scholarship concerned with the attitudes of the personnel of law. Studies in the 1970s and 1980s argued

---

[14] Martin Loughlin, *The Idea of Public Law* (Oxford, Oxford University Press, 2003) 33–34.

[15] ibid 37.

[16] ibid 42.

[17] See also Martin Loughlin, *Foundations of Public Law* (Oxford, Oxford University Press, 2010) ch 6.

[18] Carl Schmitt (1888–1985) was a German legal theorist who provided much of the theoretical justification for Nazi ideas of constitutionalism and the responsibility of the State to oppose, if necessary by force, those who are popularly regarded as unacceptable, regardless of the morality or goodness of their philosophies and conduct. See C Schmitt, *The Concept of the Political* (expanded edn, 1932, trans G Schwab, Chicago, University of Chicago Press, 2007).

that judges were, by virtue of their backgrounds and experiences, inherently likely to feel more sympathy with individualism than with collectivism, or with Conservative Party policies than with Labour Party policies. They also advanced the view that case law demonstrated that this was indeed so.[19] Advocates for these views advanced them forcefully and to some degree persuasively. Yet, there were three weaknesses in the argument. The first was methodological. Professor John Griffith's work depended on selecting certain cases as being typical from among a mass of different decisions. Taking a different selection could produce very different results.[20] Secondly, the critique was external, taking little account of the constitutional obligations which should, and in the UK normally do, inform judges' behaviour.[21] Thirdly, the critiques were, by their nature, aimed at contingent rather than inherent features of the judiciary. Experience of the judges' response to Conservative Party dominance during the 1980s and early 1990s indicated that the judiciary was inclined to test the limits of governments' powers whatever the political complexion of the Government for the time being was. Administrative law principles were developed greatly during this time, to the annoyance of the Conservative Government. Indeed, over the course of Conservative governments between 1979 and 1997, Labour governments between 1997 and 2010, and a Conservative-Liberal Democrat coalition government after 2010, it became clear that the judges' constitutional role is to provide a check on the work of government whatever the political complexion of that government and regardless of the social and economic circumstances. Over the period, the reach of and grounds for judicial review of administrative and executive action expanded. More and more types of decisions and decision-makers came to be treated as judicially reviewable. Tests for standing to bring a claim became more flexible. Politicians and campaigners increasingly used judicial review as one instrument in political campaigns.[22]

Three factors have added to the risk of collisions between ministers and judges. First, immigration and asylum policies have become increasingly restrictive and repressive, but many people have become frustrated at long delays in removing from the UK people whose immigration or asylum claims have been rejected. Part of the reason for the delay is that would-be immigrants challenge their removal in tribunals and courts where judges have to give effect to relevant law. Secondly, at the same time the Human Rights Act 1998, which came into force fully on 2 October 2000, required UK judges to subject public authorities to constraints of Convention rights under the ECHR, including rights of would-be immigrants and asylum-seekers. Thirdly, counter-terrorism powers, which had been scaled back following the decline in terrorism related to the affairs of Northern Ireland at the end of the 1990s, were renewed and increased from 2001 in response to terrorist attacks by Al-Qaida and other groups. This increased the number of occasions on which the judiciary appeared to parts of the press and public to be interfering with the efforts of politically accountable decision-makers.

These are particular pressures giving rise to a certain tension between lawyers and politicians, and, more acutely, between judges and governments. But even without them there

---

[19] See eg JAG Griffith, *The Politics of the Judiciary* (London, Fontana, 1977; 4th edn, 1997); Patrick McAuslan, 'Public Law and Public Choice' (1988) 51 *Modern Law Review* 681–705.

[20] David Feldman, 'Public Law Values in the House of Lords' (1990) 106 *Law Quarterly Review* 246–76.

[21] For a full discussion of this, see Roger Cotterrell, *The Sociology of Law*, 1st edn (London, Butterworths, 1984) 245–249.

[22] Carol Harlow and Richard Rawlings, *Pressure Through Law* (Abingdon, Pearson, 1992).

would inevitably be tension. Judges and governments have different constitutional roles. When they collide, ministers tend to see the constitutional role of judges as interference in the political sphere, or as an illegitimate restriction of the exercise of power by a democratically accountable legislature and government. That misconception has soured relations between the two institutions, as ministers have tried to treat judges as if the judges' function is to act as an arm of the civil service, giving effect to government policy, rather than a check on governmental compliance with rule of law principles. Frustration on each side at what appears to each to be the other's misunderstanding of what they are doing can spill over into damaging confrontation. Where human rights are in issue, UK politicians are particularly likely to engage in rancorous, generally ill-informed attacks on judges at home and in the European Court of Human Rights, despite the legal obligation of ministers and others under the Constitutional Reform Act 2005 to preserve the independence of the judiciary (international as well as national).

Politicians' attacks on judges are usually concerned both with the merits of individual cases and with a sense that by their decisions judges are interfering with the legislative sovereignty of the Queen in Parliament. That perception often seems to arise from a misunderstanding of both the UK's constitution and the relationship between the UK and international tribunals. As regards the European Court of Human Rights, it is too rarely understood that it operates on the international plane and cannot affect, and does not claim to alter, the UK's internal, constitutional, institutional arrangements. It deals with acts of the state. This does not infringe national sovereignty, since the authority of the Court was granted by treaties to which the UK was a party. The Court operates by virtue of an exercise by the UK of its national sovereignty to enter into treaties which, like any other treaty, may require legislative action in order to implement it within the UK. The relationship between the Court and the High Contracting Parties to the Convention is complex, and there are good reasons for the Court sometimes to take account of national, constitutional values and structures when making its decisions. Nevertheless, it is misleading to characterise the decisions of the Court, or some of them, as an attack on either national sovereignty or parliamentary sovereignty. Different institutions operate in their own parts of the ocean, and their activities create ripples which sometimes makes the water choppy in other areas.[23] As Sir Philip Sales argues, despite the tensions, the European Court of Human Rights can be seen as acting to uphold democratic ideals through its work in protecting Convention rights under the European Convention on Human Rights.

Nevertheless, some tension is inevitable and proper. Sir John Laws[24] has pointed out the importance of members of all institutions recognising and giving due weight to the fact that each institution has its own morality – he identifies particularly the morality of government and the morality of adjudication – but the fact remains that each institution properly operates according to its own, distinctive morality. It is improper for a court to try to adopt the morality of government. Two of the grounds for a court's legitimacy, whether in national or international spheres, are the moral quality of its decisions and the public justifications which it offers for them in its judgments. The tension which the independent exercise of courts' constitutional jurisdiction creates is desirable in a constitutional democracy. It helps to ensure that each institution is regularly reminded that its morality and

---

[23] See David Feldman, 'Sovereignties in Strasbourg' in Richard Rawlings, Peter Leyland and Alison Young (eds), *Sovereignty and the Law: Domestic, European and International Perspectives* (Oxford, Oxford University Press, 2013).

[24] John Laws, 'The Good Constitution' [2012] *Cambridge Law Journal* 567–82.

values can claim no monopoly of respect within the state. Only in that way can the rule of law and democracy, both of which are fragile, survive. As the late Lord Bingham observed, there are countries where the Government approves of every judicial decision, but those are not places where one would want to live.[25]

III LAW AS A TOOL OF POLITICIANS

There is a further point to be made about the relationship between law and politics. Politicians often rely on law in order to pursue their political aims. Politicians typically want to improve society, and they use law as an instrument of change. Law is a powerful tool, but, like any tool, it has inherent limitations. First, law is not self-executing. It needs to be implemented. Governments and legislatures need to have regard to political and social practicalities. If a measure proves too unpopular or too complicated to be made to work, the resulting damage is not confined to the Government's reputation for competence, although the political damage may be considerable, as the attempt by Mrs Thatcher's government to replace domestic rates with the community charge (or poll tax) showed.[26] It also chips away at the underpinning of consent on which the legislative authority of the Queen in Parliament depends; parliamentarians' claim to unlimited legislative power cannot retain public acceptance if too many pieces of legislation call into question the grasp of social reality.

A related problem arises when legislation imposes burdens of compliance on regulators and the regulated, or on taxpayers and tax collectors, which make it too burdensome on all concerned to establish exactly what liabilities people have as a matter of law, making it efficient for state bodies to reach negotiated settlements with people and corporations in the light of, but not dictated by, relevant legal rules. This can give rise to suspicions (whether or not they are well founded) that too close a relationship may develop between state agencies and those with whom they have to deal, resulting in the former becoming over-reliant on the latter, leading to what has been called 'agency-capture'. Concern of this kind was triggered by the move of the former Head of HMRC, David Hartnett, to the tax accountancy firm Deloitte, with whose senior British partner, David Cruickshank, he had previously negotiated settlements on behalf of HMRC of the tax liabilities of many of Deloitte's major clients.[27]

Legislation which is unduly complex, or poorly aimed or formulated, and in consequence produces results which people regard as unfair or silly weakens the authority of both government and Parliament. Complaints about the amount of tax paid by international corporations and wealthy individuals, when they arrange their affairs within the law to minimise their tax liabilities, are of this kind. Politicians may seek to cast blame on companies or on tax officials, but corporations owe a duty to their shareholders to minimise their tax liabilities, and officials have to consider the cost of fully investigating taxpayers' affairs when deciding how to maximise the chance of optimising tax yield. Lawmakers who claim very extensive legislative power but exercise it in ways which fail to achieve their objectives cannot fairly complain when others use the law for their own benefit.

[25] Tom Bingham, *Lives of the Law* (Oxford, Oxford University Press, 2011) 146.

[26] David Butler, Andrew Adonis and Tony Travers, *Failure in British Government: Politics of the Poll Tax* (London, Oxford Paperbacks, 1994).

[27] Simon Neville, 'Deloitte Appoints Official Criticised Over "Sweetheart" Tax Deals', *The Guardian*, 27 May 2013, online at www.guardian.co.uk/business/2013/may/27/deloitte-appoints-dave-hartnett-tax.

The reality is that the law, while a powerful tool, like any other instrument imposes its own limits on what can be achieved. To be effective, it must be reasonably comprehensible, general, and normally prospective only, and must not make excessive demands of people or offend important values and interests (including vested interests) in ways which will either undermine the legitimacy of the law itself or threaten the ability of law-enforcers to make it effective. The first three are characteristics of law which derive from its law-ness;[28] they are related to what Lon L Fuller called the 'inner morality of law', the largely formal qualities with both moral and functional importance: using the wrong type of rule can compromise its success.[29] The others are concerned with the substance of the law, the obligations it imposes and elements affecting the chances of the law being obeyed voluntarily or, if violated, effectively enforceable. In chapter four, the late Lord Rodger reflects on the interaction of political aims, legislative procedures, and the language and structure of legislation. Sir Stephen Laws explores the implications of these matters in chapter five, from the point of view of a highly experienced drafter of legislation and legal civil servant.

The relationship between the generation of law and political circumstances is the subject of Part four of the book. In chapter nine, Professor Elizabeth Cooke and Professor Hector MacQueen offer an inside view of how the outcome of the Law Commissions' law reform programmes, despite stemming from independent, advisory bodies, is affected by the political milieu which legislation inhabits. Much legislation is affected by, and may even be lost as a result of, political cross-currents flowing from issues which have nothing to do with the matter at hand but have the effect of driving a wedge between those who would normally have been willing to support the proposals. As Professor Dawn Oliver observes in chapter sixteen, inter-party friction between the coalition partners, the Conservative and Liberal Democrat parties, over another bill was one factor (but not the only one) leading to the downfall of the House of Lords Reform Bill in 2012. Legislating is nearly always an inescapably political activity, even when the subject matter of a bill is relatively uncontroversial in party-political terms. When the irritant of political tribalism divides parties or groups of parliamentarians, as was the case there, the outcome becomes uncertain.

With this in mind, chapters ten to thirteen offer a case study of the making and operation of two highly politically charged Acts, the Parliament Act 1911 and the Parliament Act 1949. Professor Lord Norton uncovers the political alignments and purposes behind the 1911 Act, and Dr Chris Ballinger does the same for the amending Act of 1949. The cross-cutting politics of the Acts can be seen in the significance of Irish home rule to the different sides when the Parliament Act 1911 was being debated, and in the way the 1949 Act materialised as a preventative measure to ensure that the Labour Government would be able to push through its bill to nationalise the iron and steel industries before the end of the Parliament. Turning to the way in which the Act works, Daniel Greenberg and Dr Rhodri Walters, in chapters twelve and thirteen respectively, illuminate aspects of the procedural implications of the Acts for the legislative process and for relations between the two Houses of Parliament from the perspectives of a legislative draftsman and an Officer of the House of Lords. The whole of this Part reveals, I think, the complex interplay of politics, parliamentary procedure, the use of law as a political tool and the need for ways around inconvenient legal technicalities, and also the importance of the officials who have to make the whole process work.

---

[28] Lon L Fuller, *The Morality of Law*, revised edn (New Haven, Yale University Press, 1969).
[29] Robert Baldwin, *Rules and Government* (Oxford, Clarendon Press, 1995); Julia Black, '"Which Arrow?" Rule Type and Regulatory Policy' (1995) *Public Law* 94–117.

IV LAW, POLITICS, THE STATE AND THE 'INTERNATIONAL COMMUNITY'

In the final part of the book, we turn our attention outwards and upwards. In chapter fourteen, Matthew Parish reflects on the experience of trying to make international law work when it is in danger of being disrupted by political manoeuvring between great powers, and asks whether it is right to speak of international law as law at all. At the level of relations between a state – the UK – and an international body – the European Court of Human Rights – Sir Philip Sales in chapter fifteen focuses on relations between the national and international spheres of action and the contribution of human rights, and the European Court of Human Rights, to democratic politics in the area of the Council of Europe. In chapter sixteen Professor Dawn Oliver then brings us home to the UK by exploring the interplay of political and constitutional ideals and political realities in the context of what she calls 'constitutional moments' in the UK. These chapters complement each other by illuminating the connections between law, constitutional theory and practice, and international relations, showing that each in practice demands attention to the interweaving of politics and law or law-like activity. The various tensions do not operate in the same way at all times or in different legal and political spheres. Nevertheless, their interactions are constant.

The better we understand the roles, aspirations and motivations of actors, and the better they understand each other, the more likely it is that the tensions between them will be constructive, not destructive. The best understanding is likely to be achieved by listening to what people say about their own experiences, and to the history and sociology of the relationships between ideas and institutions. Those, at any rate, are the hypotheses and hopes on which this book is based.

Part 2

Lawyer-Politicians

2

Lawyers, MPs and Judges

ROSS CRANSTON

I INTRODUCTION

T HIS IS LARGELY a people piece. It seeks to throw light on some aspects of the relationship between law and politics by using the experiences and views of a number of
MPs who were lawyers (and in a few cases became judges) and of some leading common law judges. The first part of the chapter explains the nineteenth and twentieth century
institutional context which enabled lawyers to play such a prominent part in Parliament, or
at least the House of Commons. In recent decades the institutional context has changed. So
quite apart from the nature of politics in a media driven and celebrity conscious age, a partial explanation for the declining importance of lawyers in the House of Commons lies in
the way it operates and the expectations placed on its members. The second part turns to the
importance to our constitutional arrangements in particular of the principle of mutual
respect between Parliament, the executive and the judiciary. Mutual respect is essential if the
machinery of the state is to work as smoothly as possible given the inevitable clashes which
occur. At one time that principle was underpinned by the practice of MPs (often ministers)
becoming judges. That is no longer the case and we need to foster other mechanisms to
enhance understanding between the three branches of government. The final part explores,
in outline, the judicial philosophies of three leading common law judges who sought to
rationalise the accommodation of judicial to political power. The need for this has become
more acute in Britain with the enactment of the Human Rights Act 1998.

II LAWYERS AS MPS

In the introductory survey to his magisterial history of the House of Commons in the late
fourteenth and early fifteenth centuries, JS Roskell notes the passage of an ordinance forbid-
ding the election as shire knights of 'gentz de ley' engaged in business in the King's courts
on behalf of clients who had retained them for that purpose.[1] The Commons themselves
had petitioned for the ordinance, since they objected to the way lawyers had exploited
their membership of the Lower House to promote their clients' petitions. When Henry IV
summoned the Coventry Parliament in 1404, he forbade the return of lawyers. But this form

---

[1] JS Roskell, L Clark and C Rawcliffe, *The House of Commons 1386-1421* (Stroud, Alan Sutton for the History of
Parliament Trust, 1993) 56–57.

of royal interference was never repeated. Professor Blair Worden's history of the Rump Parliament records the demands for the exclusion of lawyers from it – 'verminous caterpillars' was one description – because in what he describes as an extraordinarily litigious era they were seen as taking from people's pockets and because, when acting as MPs, many were perceived as obstructive to reform.[2] That view of MPs is echoed in a contemporary view, albeit of lawyers in the House of Lords: '[T]he eminent left-wing lawyers who graced the Upper House, whose radicalism extended to everything but their own profession, about which they were dyed-in-the-wool reactionaries'. That sentiment, of Nigel (now Lord) Lawson would be shared, I am sure, more widely.[3] So the point to appreciate from the outset is that the participation of lawyers in politics has never been universally perceived as good.

The second point relates to the number of lawyer-MPs. Professor Michael Rush and Dr Nicholas Baldwin penned a helpful survey, covering the centuries, in which they reported that the number of MPs with legal backgrounds generally seems to have been in double figures, at times over 20 per cent, until dipping to just below 10 per cent in the 1830s.[4] Then as the law became an avenue to social mobility in the rapidly expanding economy of the nineteenth century the number increased, reaching 20 per cent again, a pattern which continued until the Second World War. There was a decline after that, and a sharp fall in 1997, partly because the number of lawyers in the Labour Party never matched that in the old Liberal Party. As regards the branch of the profession from which they came, barristers always seem to have dominated, perhaps when it was still possible to run a practice at the Bar and attend the House.

In 2011 the House of Commons library brought the Rush/Baldwin figures up to date.[5] Since the 1997 election, the proportion of barristers in the Commons has been at five to six per cent, the number of solicitors increasing at each election, from 4.5 per cent in 1997 to 6.1 per cent in 2010. That meant that in 2010 the number of solicitors exceeded the number of barristers for the first time. Overall, lawyers are the largest category of professionals in the House of Commons by a long way. However, those with business backgrounds constitute a quarter of members in the current Parliament and 'professional politicians' now comprise some 14.5 per cent of members, up from 3.4 per cent in 1997. Politics as a career choice has troubling aspects, not the least being the obvious lack of experience of the outside world. The other side of the coin is that someone like Bill Clinton, who trained as lawyer, but spent most of his adult life in politics, can emerge as a most impressive political leader.

So why so many lawyers? The usual rationalisation is that lawyers understand legislation and law-making and that legal skills are readily transferable to Parliamentary work, notably, analysing issues, marshalling arguments and, in the barrister's case, oral advocacy. At least these were the responses when the magazine *The Lawyer* interviewed prospective Parliamentary candidates in the run up to the 2010 election.[6] The capacity to cope with late nights and heavy workloads were also explanations given for the advantages which these lawyers thought they would be able to bring to the job. As *The Economist* expressed in an

---

[2] Blair Worden, *The Rump Parliament, 1648-1653* (London, Cambridge University Press, 1974) 110, 115.

[3] Nigel Lawson, *The View From No. 11: Memoirs of a Tory Radical* (London, Corgi, 1992) 620.

[4] M Rush and N Baldwin, 'Lawyers in Parliament' in D Oliver and G Drewry (eds), *The Law and Parliament* (London, Butterworths, 1998) 156–58.

[5] R Cracknell and F McGuinness, 'Social Background of Members of Parliament' *House of Commons Library Standard Note*, 4 November 2011, 7–8.

[6] Gavriel Hollander, 'Focus: Lawyer Parliamentary Candidates - Win Some, Lose Some' *The Lawyer* (17 May 2010).

article in 2009: '[T]he law deals with the same sort of questions as politics: what makes a just society; the balance between liberty and security, and so on.'[7]

All this is too simplistic. In its very helpful comparative survey *The Economist* correctly contended that history, culture, and economy all have a bearing on the occupational back-grounds of legislators. For its legislators Brazil likes doctors, South Korea, civil servants, Egypt, academics and China, engineers. Indeed in many communist countries engineers were frequently prominent as legislators. Engineering and science were lauded and for stu-dents, these subjects were far less contentious than some other disciplines. Since the fall of communism in Eastern Europe and Russia, businesspeople have risen to prominence as politicians in these countries. The explanation offered in a study of the 247 businesspeople who stood as candidates in 259 gubernatorial elections in Russia between 1991 and 2005 was that when institutions such as a free media are strong, businessmen are not inclined to run for office. When institutions which hold elected officials to account are weak, however, businessmen seek elected office to avoid the cost of lobbying elected officials, even though without it they can still subvert democratic systems. In those regions professional polit-icians crowd out businesspeople when the rents from office are especially large.[8] Lawyers do not feature in the analysis.

But even in our own system there are issues of causation. Lawyer-MPs have not neces-sarily been devoted to the law, but have chosen it as an avenue to politics. John (later Viscount) Simon, Home Secretary and Foreign Secretary in the 1930s, and Lord Chancellor from 1940 to 1945, had a large practice at the Bar when he entered the House of Commons in 1906. He did not see law as falling within the higher ranges of human achievement, but simply as 'just a way of earning one's living'.[9] That was put starkly to me by Kenneth Clarke QC MP, then the Secretary of State for Justice and Lord Chancellor, when I interviewed him for the London School of Economics' Legal Biography project in December 2011. Clarke decided on a political career when at school. He had been admitted to Cambridge University to read history but changed his mind over the summer before arriving. He explained the background to his decision.

> My interest in history has remained. [T]hen I got very utilitarian. . . . I decided it would be easier to be a politician if I became a lawyer because most politicians were lawyers, so I decided I might like to be a lawyer. Once I made some money working in a brewery – I left school at Easter – I then took an unpaid place in a solicitors' office [in Nottingham] to see whether I liked the law and whether it would actually suit me. I acted as a kind of office boy and they used to send me to sit behind counsel in the courts. . . . I decided I quite liked this solicitors' office but I would prefer to be a barrister. I rather liked the appearing in court and the advocacy. So I determined that I would probably go the Bar. . . .[10]

A similar point is made by Jack Straw MP, who explains how he sought the advice of the head of his chambers, a Conservative MP, Edward Gardner QC, when he was offered a position of political adviser to Barbara Castle MP in 1974 when she became a member of the Cabinet. Gardner asked him whether in 20 years' time he wanted to be in the Cabinet

---

[7] 'Selection Bias in Politics. There Was a Lawyer, an Engineer and a Politician . . . Why Do Professional Paths to the Top Vary So Much?' *The Economist* (16 April 2009).

[8] S Gehlbach, K Sonin, E Zhuravskaya, 'Businessman Candidates' (2010) 54 *American Journal of Political Science* 718, 732.

[9] Viscount Simon, *Retrospect* (London, Hutchinson, 1952) 61.

[10] There is a podcast of the interview on the Legal Biography website. See also M Balen, *Kenneth Clarke* (London, Fourth Estate, 1994) 24.

or on the High Court Bench, to which he replied the former.[11] Straw relinquished his legal practice and took the job. Later, he succeeded Barbara Castle to her Parliamentary seat and eventually became Home Secretary, Foreign Secretary and Secretary of State for Justice and Lord Chancellor.

Until relatively recently it was possible to combine a career at the Bar (and other occupations as well) with being an MP. Constituency duties were light or non-existent and Parliamentary hours and pay contemplated other employment. Thus before World War I those like HH Asquith (later Prime Minister), Richard Haldane (later Secretary of State for War and Lord Chancellor), Rufus Isaacs (later Lord Chief Justice and Viceroy of India), FE Smith (later, as Lord Birkenhead, Lord Chancellor) John Simon and Gordon Hewart (later Lord Chief Justice) had large practices at the Bar while in the House. Asquith became an MP in 1886 but it was after this that his career at the Bar took off and he took silk in 1890. After being Home Secretary between 1892 and 1895 he returned to his practice at the Bar (while still an MP) to keep his wife, Margot, in the style to which she was accustomed – they had a house in Cavendish Square with 14 servants and entertained lavishly – which he only relinquished when he became Chancellor of the Exchequer in 1905.[12] While an MP in the 1890s and early 1900s, Haldane conducted a heavy appellate court practice.[13] Rufus Isaacs was already in silk when he became MP for Reading in 1904. During the day he was in court or in chambers. In the evening, when at the House of Commons, if not in the Chamber he would be in the library working on his briefs. He said of this period: 'I was tired out when I got to the House.'[14] On entering the Commons, Simon's earnings fell for the first time and he 'had to be more assiduous than ever in the Temple in the interval until two years later, in 1908, I took silk'.[15] FE Smith built up a practice in London after moving from Liverpool when elected to the House of Commons in 1906. Despite quickly establishing his political reputation he was also busy at the Bar, spending a great deal of his life on trains.[16] The Director of Public Prosecutions continued to brief Gordon Hewart on important cases on the Northern circuit, including murders, after his election in 1913.[17]

The same applied in the interwar and post-World War II years. Stafford Cripps built up a large practice at the Bar in the 1920s and entered the House of Commons after being appointed Solicitor-General in the 1930 Labour Government. He was one of the relatively few Labour members who survived the 1931 election. While following a bizarre political trajectory in the 1930s, which eventually led to his expulsion from the Labour Party, he kept up an important practice as a barrister, of potential financial benefit to the party.[18] Norman Birkett (later Birkett J and LJ) was a leading King's Counsel while he sat as a Liberal MP, receiving criticism from his Conservative opponent for a consequent

---

[11] Jack Straw, *Last Man Standing, Memoirs of a Political Survivor* (Basingstoke, Macmillan, 2012) 94–95.

[12] R Jenkins, *Asquith* (London, Collins, 1964) 38, 48, 50, 90–92; S Koss, *Asquith* (London, Allen Lane, 1976) 26, 29, 43–44, 74.

[13] R Heuston, *Lives of the Lord Chancellors 1885-1940* (Oxford, Clarendon, 1964) 195–97.

[14] H Montgomery Hyde, *Lord Reading* (London, Heinemann, 1967) 61.

[15] Viscount Simon, *Retrospect* (n 9) 47.

[16] J Campbell, *FE Smith* (London, Jonathan Cape, 1983) 162.

[17] R Jackson, *The Chief* (London, George G Harrap, 1959) 66.

[18] See S Burgess, *Stafford Cripps* (London, Victor Gollancz, 1999) 72, 87. The law reports of that decade record appearances mainly in intellectual property and employment cases and in Privy Council appeals. In *James v Commonwealth of Australia* [1936] AC 578 (PC), a case involving s 92 of the Australian Constitution, he appeared for the winning side against the Australia's Attorney General, and later Prime Minister, RG Menzies – who is discussed further later in the chapter.

lack of attention to his Parliamentary duties.[19] DN Pritt was a King's Counsel when he entered the House of Commons in 1935 at the age of 48. He was to be an MP until 1950, although he was expelled from the Labour Party in 1940. He later said that he combined his large practice with his Parliamentary duties by packing three days' work into every one.[20] Quintin Hogg, later Viscount Hailsham LC, who had won a controversial by-election in Oxford in 1938, tells of how he stood down from the front bench and resumed practice at the Bar after the Conservative Party defeat in 1945. 'I simply had to earn my living . . .'.[21] He soon built up a substantial practice although it became increasingly difficult to combine the travel involved in a circuit practice 'with the demands of the Whips at Westminster'.[22] In his London School of Economics interview, Ken Clarke told me how he continued his practice in the 1960s and 1970s, even though it was based in Birmingham.

> I must be one of the last who really did it. I combined being on circuit with being a Member of Parliament. . . . [The courts] would typically sit at half ten, usually go on until 4. Off to New Street station [Birmingham], down to London, I would go to the House of Commons. The House of Commons in the evening used to sit on until 10, at least usually. The midnight train from London was where I usually wound up. I did have a place to stay in London. If I was busy at work I would travel north, either to return to a trial I was in or to read a brief when I was back home and go to court in the morning. It was pretty strenuous. . . . [I]n those days you could control your time as a Member of Parliament and with the help of the clerk – I had a very helpful and supportive clerk – he controlled quite a bit the listing of your cases in the courts. . . . If I had a committee I had to do as shadow spokesman I would tell the clerk I couldn't be in court on Tuesdays, or whatever it was, and try to get him to move the significant cases so I could do them.

At the very least law meant the capacity to earn an additional income when Parliamentary salaries were non-existent or low.[23] Up until World War II, being an MP was attractive as a career for a lawyer for the reason that it could be a road to professional prominence. That was certainly the perception, and to an extent the reality, in the nineteenth century.[24] Thus it was possible for any MP who was a barrister to become a King's Counsel or Queen's Counsel ('Parliamentary silk'), even though his or her practice would not otherwise justify it. Being an MP was also a route to judicial appointment. When he was Prime Minister, Lord Salisbury said that there was no clearer statute in the unwritten law than the rule that party claims should always weigh very heavily in the disposal of the highest legal appointments.[25] It became something of a scandal when Lord Halsbury was Lord Chancellor and appointed a number of party hacks to the High Court bench, which attracted public censure at the time.[26] Lord Devlin says that it was still the case until the middle of the last century that

---

[19] H Montgomery Hyde, *Norman Birkett* (London, Hamish Hamilton, 1964) 322.

[20] DN Pritt, *From Right to Left* (London, Lawrence & Wishart, 1965) 87.

[21] Lord Hailsham, *A Sparrow's Flight* (London, Collins, 1990) 241. See also G Lewis, *Lord Hailsham* (London, Jonathan Cape, 1997) 107–09.

[22] ibid 245–46.

[23] Payment for MPs was first introduced in 1911. The £400 per annum remained unchanged until 1937, after which it rose at irregular intervals. As a result of the recommendations of the Lawrence Committee, the salary of an MP was increased in 1964 from £1,500 to £3,250 a year. In 1975, as a result of the Senior Salaries Review Body, it went from £4,500 to £5,750. By 1997 it was £43,860: see House of Commons, Committee on Members' Expenses, *The Operation of the Parliamentary Standards Act 2009* (HC 2011, 1484) 8–11.

[24] D Duman, *The Judicial Bench in England 1727-1875* (London, Royal Historical Society, 1982) 75–78.

[25] R Andrews, *Lord Salisbury: Political Titan* (London, Weidenfeld & Nicolson, 1999) 684.

[26] R Heuston, *Lives of the Lord Chancellors 1885-1940* (n 13) 40–63; J Hostettler, *Lord Halsbury* (Chichester, Barry Rose, 1998) 110–12.

a brief Parliamentary career, during which political strings were pulled, was one of the quickest ways onto the bench.[27]

Practising law while an MP is no longer possible with constituency duties taken more seriously (generally speaking rightly so, albeit that MPs are often treated as glorified social workers) and the Parliamentary hours making a day in court or chambers followed by the evening in the House impractical. At the beginning of the 1997 Parliament, the hours were 2.30–10.30pm (but with no guarantee that proceedings would finish at 10.30pm). To make the hours more 'family friendly', from 1999 Thursday sittings began at 11.30am and finished at 7pm. From 2003, 11.30am became the starting time for Tuesday and Wednesday as well.[28] In addition select committees, which might commence at 9.30am, became a more established outlet for the ambitious back-bencher. While it might be possible for someone at the Bar to keep up a paper practice, a litigation practice seems out the question if the MP is to participate in ordinary Parliamentary business. As for Parliamentary silk, Lord Mackay as Lord Chancellor discontinued the practice in the 1990s. Judicial appointments were largely divorced from party politics in the post-World War II era.[29] Since 2007 they are no longer in political hands but are made by the Judicial Appointments Commission.

Once elected to the House of Commons, lawyer-MPs have not necessarily engaged in law related debates or committees or sought ministerial office related to law. In some respects this may simply have been a lack of opportunity. In other cases, however, it was deliberate choice since it was political, not legal, advancement which was sought. Law was simply the means to an end. Thus, John Simon explains how he sought to avoid appointment as Solicitor General in 1910, for he wanted a political career in a broader sense. For the same reason he avoided the Woolsack (Lord Chancellor) in 1915, although it was on offer.[30] For Rufus Isaacs law was utilitarian even though he became Lord Chief Justice. When he was later appointed Viceroy of India, he said: 'I will never look at a law report again if I can help it!'[31] In the interview mentioned earlier, Ken Clarke explained his approach.

> You chose a different path. I was quite determined not to become a political lawyer. . . . I was quite interested in the generality of politics. I kept law and politics apart. My legal practice was in the West Midlands; my political activities were in the East Midlands. Birmingham for the law; Nottingham for politics. . . . I decided that if I wished for a wholly legal career there was no point in going into politics. Why just not stick to the bar? So I went into politics precisely because my interests were much wider than the law. When I was a backbencher, I didn't advertise the fact that I'd been a lawyer. I made a point of not speaking on legal issues.

Not all lawyers abandon their profession with such alacrity. In 1905 Haldane greatly desired the Woolsack but had to make do with the War Office.[32] In his early years as an MP, FE Smith intervened in some important legal debates – not in the partisan way which was to become characteristic – on matters such as the establishment of a court of criminal

---

[27] Patrick Devlin, *Taken at the Flood* (Privately printed, 1996) 152. See also R Stevens, *The Independence of the Judiciary* (Oxford, Clarendon, 1993) 83.

[28] R Kelly, 'Sitting hours', *House of Commons Library Standard Note*, 18 July 2012.

[29] D Woodhouse, *The Office of Lord Chancellor* (Oxford, Hart Publishing, 2001) 140–42; K Malleson, 'Appointments to the House of Lords: Who Goes Upstairs?' in L Blom-Cooper, Brice Dickson and G Drewry, *The Judicial House of Lords 1876-2009* (Oxford, Oxford University Press, 2009) 119. But see J Griffith, *The Politics of the Judiciary*, 5th edn (London, Fontana, 1997) 17.

[30] Viscount Simon, *Retrospect* (n 9) 75, 103.

[31] Montgomery Hyde, *Lord Reading* (n 14) 327.

[32] S Koss, *Lord Haldane. Scapegoat for Liberalism* (New York, Columbia University Press, 1969) 35–36.

appeal, family law reform and international law.[33] Rush and Baldwin tried to measure the role of lawyer-MPs by looking at Parliamentary activity such as questions, speeches and committee participation. The raw numbers did not uncover significant differences although further analysis for the 1994–45 session revealed that lawyer-MPs were over-represented in standing committees considering law reform Bills and in debates on matters of interest to lawyers.[34] Nothing surprising there: debates on education attract teachers, agriculture, farmers, and dental services, dentists. Of course these subjects will also see a participation by others, although in the past the sheer number of lawyers might have squeezed out the non-lawyers when legal topics were discussed.

Qualitatively, have lawyers brought anything special to the consideration of law-related issues? One view is that they may bring nothing but self-interest, and that in spades. This is unduly cynical. However, it would be wrong to think that it is only the lawyer who brings to politics a refined concern for matters such as civil liberties, human rights and the power of executive government. Importantly, a concern for rights is to an extent institutionalised in Parliament. At present, for example, there is the role of the Joint Committee, and the House of Commons Select Committee, on Statutory Instruments, and more importantly, the Joint Select Committee of Human Rights. The former undertake the mundane but important task of scrutinising statutory instruments to determine whether they contain provisions excluding challenge in the courts; have retrospective effect where the parent statute confers no express authority for this; are intra vires; or make some unusual or unexpected use of the powers conferred by the statute under which they are made.[35] Of more recent origin, the Joint Committee on Human Rights has a specific remit to review remedial orders under the Human Rights Act 1998 but in its numerous reports has considered a range of matters concerning human rights, in particular the compatibility of proposed legislation with Convention rights.[36] The membership of these committees is by no means confined to lawyers.

In government, these matters fall specifically within the remit of the law officers – for England and Wales, the Attorney General and the Solicitor General. These ministers are Parliamentarians and at least one will sit in the House of Commons. (Until 1997 both law officers did; that practice has been revived since 2010.) Before being presented to Parliament, all Bills must be approved by what is now called the Parliamentary Business and Legislation Committee, which is chaired by the Leader of the House of Commons and has the Attorney General as a member. For that, committee Bills must be accompanied by a memorandum on the European Convention of Human Rights implications which has been submitted by departmental lawyers to the law officers to ensure the analysis is comprehensive and contains credible arguments.[37] The law officers must also approve retrospective clauses in Bills and early commencement provisions. They will give close attention to what were at one time known as 'law officer points', such as the ambit of the power to make delegated legislation set out in a Bill.[38]

---

[33] Campbell, *FE Smith* (n 16) 169.
[34] Rush and Baldwin, 'Lawyers in Parliament' (n 4) 160–62.
[35] *Standing Orders of the House of Commons* (Public Business, London, 2012) r 151.
[36] ibid r 152B. see eg, J Hiebert, 'Governing Under the Human Rights Act' [2012] *Public Law* 27, 37–41.
[37] Cabinet Office, *Guide to Making Legislation*, April 2013, 11.13.
[38] ibid 12.9; House of Commons, Constitutional Affairs Committee, *Constitutional Role of the Attorney General* (HC 2007, 306) Ev 60; J Edwards, *The Law Officers of the Crown* (London, Sweet and Maxwell, 1964) 147–48); J Edwards, *The Attorney General, Politics and the Public Interest* (London, Sweet and Maxwell, 1984) 186–87.

III MPS AND JUDGES

In early 2011 the Prime Minister was asked at Prime Minister's Questions about a decision of the Supreme Court regarding the sex offenders' register. The Supreme Court had unanimously upheld a declaration that parts of the Sexual Offences Act 2003 were incompatible with Article 8 of the European Convention on Human Rights in imposing indefinite notification requirements on sex offenders without a future mechanism for individual review.[39] The Prime Minister said:

> My hon. friend speaks for many people in saying how completely offensive it is, once again, to have a ruling by a court that flies in the face of common sense. Requiring serious sexual offenders to sign the register for life, as they now do, has broad support across this House and across the country. I am appalled by the Supreme Court ruling. We will take the minimum possible approach to this ruling . . . [I]t is about time we ensured that decisions are made in this Parliament rather than in the courts.[40]

Mr Cameron has expressed similar views on the decision of the European Court of Human Rights about votes for prisoners.[41] These sentiments cannot be easily dismissed, nor can the resonance they have with significant sections of the public. It is not a sufficient explanation in the context of the European Convention on Human Rights to respond that, after all, Parliament has conferred powers on the courts to give effect to the Convention rights it contains, when there can be different readings of what these rights mean in particular situations. Nor is it adequate to distinguish between, say, the power the courts have under the Human Rights Act 1998 to declare legislation incompatible with Convention rights from the power to strike it down, a power which, unlike the courts in places like the United States and Australia, British courts do not have. The political reality is that once a court makes a declaration of incompatibility, the pressures on government to change the relevant statute are considerable. Thus the Prime Minister raised a legitimate concern about the role of courts in a democratic society even if his answer could have been better phrased. Parliament has debated the issue of prisoner votes with a degree of maturity which cynics might not have expected.[42]

In this area there are at least three constitutional principles of fundamental significance. The first is the principle of democratic accountability; the second, of judicial independence; and the third, of mutual respect between the three branches of government. The first principle does not appear sufficiently prominently in constitutional tomes, although the successful struggle for a representative democracy over a period of centuries was a distinguishing feature of our constitutional history compared with that of most of our European partners. A more detailed discussion is for another day. The second principle, that of judicial independence, is crucial to the role of the judiciary in society and to the

---

[39] *R (on the application of F) v Secretary of State for the Home Department* [2010] UKSC 17, [2010] AC 331.

[40] HC Deb 16 Feb 2011, vol 523, col 955. See also Mr Cameron's comment: 'The judges are creating a sort of privacy law, whereas what ought to happen in a parliamentary democracy is parliament – which you elect and put there – should decide . . .': *The Guardian*, 21 April, 2011.

[41] *Hirst v United Kingdom (No 2)* [2005] ECHR 681, (2006) 42 EHHR 41. See Prime Minister's Questions, HC Deb 24 October 2012, cols 922–23.

[42] See D Nicol, 'Legitimacy of the Commons Debate on Prisoner Voting' [2011] *Public Law* 681; S Fredman, 'From Dialogue to Deliberation: Human Rights Adjudication and Prisoners' Rights to Vote' [2013] *Public Law* 292.

general acceptance of judicial rulings. The third principle recognises the sometimes delicate balance between Parliament, the executive and the courts.

In some countries the assumption is that just as one buys goods and services, especially those with designer labels, one does the same with judges, who are also in the pocket of the Government. By comparison we are lucky. Judicial independence is entrenched in our constitution. The Constitutional Reform Act 2005 now imposes a special responsibility on the Lord Chancellor to uphold judicial independence: he (or she) must have regard to the need to defend that independence; the need for the judiciary to have the support necessary to enable them to exercise their functions; and the need for the public interest with regard to matters relating to the judiciary and the administration of justice to be properly represented in decisions affecting those matters.[43] However, the Act also imposes the duty to uphold judicial independence on other ministers of the Crown 'and all with responsibility for matters relating to the judiciary or otherwise to the administration of justice'.[44] Importantly, the Cabinet Manual interprets that phrase as including MPs.[45]

Since 2007 the Lord Chancellor has sat in the House of Commons and since 2012 has not been a lawyer. There is nothing wrong with that. However, the developing office of Secretary of State for Justice means that the Lord Chancellor is becoming more political. The office is now for those on the up, not just for those at the end of the road (Jack Straw, Lord Chancellor 2007–10 and Kenneth Clarke, Lord Chancellor 2010–12 fell into the latter category). The upshot may be that it will be the law officers who, as ministers, will become major protectors in practice of judicial independence.[46] The current Attorney General, Dominic Grieve QC MP, seems to be playing that role, to an extent, over Britain's obligation under the European Convention on Human Rights to implement the prisoner votes decision. If this were to be the case it would be a natural addition to the law officers' quasi-judicial functions. Indeed these quasi-judicial functions relate to judicial independence.[47] That quasi-judicial role of the law officers is mainly in relation to prosecutions and was underlined by the criticism in the 1920s – misdirected in Professor Edward's view if the practice of other Attorneys General such as Lords Hewart and Birkenhead (as they subsequently became) were to be considered – about the Labour Cabinet's role in the dropping of the prosecution for sedition of the editor of *Workers Weekly*.[48]

Mutual respect between the three arms of government manifests itself in a number of practices and conventions such as the notion of judicial deference (perhaps wrongly labelled, but nonetheless crucial) and what should be the caution which MPs and ministers exhibit when they are confronted with an adverse judicial decision. There is the rule of parliamentary procedure inhibiting members from commenting on judicial decisions or

---

[43] Section 3(6).

[44] Constitutional Reform Act 2005, s 3(1).

[45] *The Cabinet Manual*, 1st edn, October 2011, 638.

[46] Another possibility would be to separate the positions of Secretary of State for Justice and Lord Chancellor with the latter a more neutral position but not a complete reversion to the former role.

[47] Edwards, *The Law Officers of the Crown* (n 38) 6.

[48] Edwards, *The Attorney General, Politics and the Public Interest* (n 38) 317. Acting in a quasi-judicial manner the law officers are agents of the public interest in other ways as well: for example in exercising the power to bring proceedings for contempt of court; to bring proceedings to restrain vexatious litigants; to bring or intervene in certain family law and charity proceedings; and most importantly, to bring or intervene in other legal proceedings in the public interest. None of these are major in themselves, but they underline that in important respects the law officers are not, and do not act, in a party partisan manner.

criticising judges.[49] However, there is nothing comparable, as there is in the New Zealand Cabinet Manual, for ministers speaking outside Parliament.[50] Mutual respect is enhanced by a knowledge of the tasks of the other institutions. On occasions judges appear before Parliamentary committees to give evidence and that helps the Parliamentary understanding. However, that is generally in relation to specific topics, and the present guidance to the judiciary is that it should be exceptional.[51] Moreover, the current guidance to judges about giving evidence before select committees is that they should not comment on the merits of individual cases; on serving judges, politicians, or other public figures, and more generally on the quality of appointments; on the merits or likely effect of provisions in any Bill; and on government policy, which is the subject of government consultation on which the judiciary are intending to make a formal response. All this is relatively restrictive but the rationale is to ensure the impartiality of the judiciary and to uphold judicial independence.

Mutual respect – and democratic accountability – might be enhanced if MPs had a role in senior judicial appointments. As an MP I expressed the view that there needed to be a greater degree of democratic accountability, especially in the appointment of judges of the Supreme Court. At the time of the passage of the Constitutional Reform Bill I was critical of the Government's decision that the appointment commission should be able to put forward the name of only one nominee to the Lord Chancellor, rather than the three names originally proposed.[52] In debate I also drew attention to the 'cult of the non-political', the delusion that politics can be taken out of important decisions by entrusting them to quangos. In several debates I invoked Professor Robert Hazell's critique, that judicial appointments are too important to be left to the judges and that there are very real dangers if judges are perceived as a self-appointing oligarchy.[53] But relevant for present purposes I also raised the possibility of nominees for the Supreme Court appearing before a parliamentary committee, along the lines of the practice for those appointed to the Monetary Policy Committee of the Bank of England, who appear before the Treasury Select Committee of the House of Commons. The principle of mutual respect meant that judges had little to fear from such an experience.[54]

What about the other side of the coin, judicial understanding of government and Parliament? In her ethnographic study of judges, Penny Darbyshire found a readiness on the part of her judges to blame government for particular problems.[55] She does not explain if there was an appreciation among them of resource priorities and the legitimacy of political choice. Treasury counsel, the barristers who regularly represent the Government in court, do obtain valuable insights into governmental decision-making. At one time they had what was effectively a right to be appointed to the bench, although that is no longer guaranteed after the establishment of the Judicial Appointments Commission. In recent times, ex-Treasury counsel such as Lord Woolf, Lord Brown, Laws LJ, Stephen Richards LJ, Charles J and Sales J have played an important role as judges in administering public law.

---

[49] *Standing Orders of the House of Commons, Public Business*, London, 2012, Appendix 1, Matters sub judice; *Erskine May's Parliamentary Practice*, 24th edn (London, Lexis Nexis, 2011) 444.

[50] See House of Lords, Select Committee on the Constitution, *Relations between the Executive, the Judiciary and Parliament: Follow up Report*, 11th Report of Session 2007-08, para 8.

[51] Judicial Executive Board, 'Guidance to Judges on Appearances before Select Committees', 2012.

[52] House of Commons, Constitutional Affairs Committee, *Judicial Appointments and Supreme Court*, First Report of Session 2003–04, vol 1, 63–64.

[53] See HC Deb 27 May 2004, vol 1 col 499WH; 17 Jan 2005, cols 589–594.

[54] See A Horne, *The Changing Constitution: A Case for Judicial Confirmation Hearings?* (The Study of Parliament Group Paper No I, 2010).

[55] P Darbyshire, *Sitting in Judgment. The Working Lives of Judges* (Oxford, Hart Publishing, 2011) 140–41.

But knowledge of government and Parliament will not come from more direct experience. I am the first former MP and government minister in some 40 years to be appointed to the High Court bench in England and Wales.[56] At one time this was a well-trodden route. Of the judges appointed between 1727 and 1760, 25 or 57 per cent sat in Parliament; from 1760–90, 16 judges or 50 per cent were MPs; from 1790–1820, 17 judges or 59 per cent were MPs; from 1820–50, 23 judges or 52 per cent were MPs.[57] Of the 139 judges appointed between 1832 and 1906, 80 were MPs at the time of appointment and 11 others had been candidates, sometimes on more than one occasion. Of the 80, 63 were appointed when their own party was in power and 33 had been law officers.[58]

The process continued after 1906, as with some of those already mentioned. Thus, Rufus Isaacs was Solicitor General for six months in 1910, then Attorney General until his appointment as Lord Chief Justice in 1913 at the age of 53. (He spent a great deal of his time as Chief Justice as an unofficial adviser to government both during the war and after.) Isaacs' appointment as Lord Chief Justice was one example of the 'orderly advancement' principle enunciated by Francis Bacon. Under 'orderly advancement' the Attorney General could claim the office of Lord Chief Justice, the Solicitor General other high appointment, such as head of a division or membership the Court of Appeal. This right to succession for the Attorney General was strongly supported by Lord Birkenhead in 1922 at the time that Sir Gordon Hewart, the Attorney General, sought to become Lord Chief Justice, ultimately successfully.[59] Bacon's expression of the principle was part of his own scheming for high office, and Edwards' view is that Birkenhead's support for the right of the Attorney General to the office of Lord Chief Justice was because of his close friendship with Hewart, possibly also coloured by an exaggerated belief in the importance of maintaining the perquisites of an office he had once occupied.[60]

In the post-World War II period the number of MPs becoming judges began to decline. There are four examples of law officers becoming judges: James Reid had been Lord Advocate and became a law lord in 1948; Reginald Manningham-Buller (Viscount Dilhorne) had been Solicitor General and Attorney General and, after being Lord Chancellor, was appointed a law lord[61]; Lynn Ungoed-Thomas had been Solicitor General for only six months prior to Labour's defeat in October 1951 and was appointed a judge of the Chancery division in 1962[62]; and Jocelyn Simon (Lord Simon of Glaisdale) had been

---

[56] Scotland has done slightly better: of current judges in the Court of Session, Lord Mackay of Drumadoon was Lord Advocate from 1995 to 1997, although not an MP; Lady Clark of Calton was an MP from 1997 to 2005 and Advocate General for Scotland from 1999 to 2006; and although not an MP, Lord Boyd was Solicitor General for Scotland (for the UK Government from 1997 to 1999, for the Scottish Executive in 1999) and Lord Advocate from 2000 to 2006.

[57] Dunman, *The Judicial Bench in England 1727–1875* (n 24) 78.

[58] H Laski, *Studies in Law and Politics* (London, George Allen & Unwin, 1932) 168.

[59] Jackson, *The Chief* (n 17) 127–30.

[60] Edwards, *The Law Officers of the Crown* (n 38) 328.

[61] R Heuston, *Lives of the Lord Chancellors 1940–1970* (Oxford, Clarendon, 1987): R Stevens, *Law and Politics* (London, Weidenfeld & Nicolson, 1979) 426ff. Manningham-Buller would never have won a popularity contest. His combative style led to his nickname Reginald Bullying-Manner. His role in collecting cabinet opinion on Macmillan's successor in October 1963, and the basis on which he reported that the preponderant opinion was for Alex Douglas-Home, was savagely criticised within the Conservative Party. And the well-respected law lord, Lord Devlin, famously said that while the ordinary careerist makes himself agreeable, falsely or otherwise, 'Reggie' achieved advancement by making himself disagreeable.

[62] Ungoed-Thomas had been offered appointment as a High Court judge by the Labour Lord Chancellor, Jowitt, but declined on the basis that he would not create a by-election when the party was at such a low ebb: Heuston, *Lives of the Lord Chancellors 1940–1970* (n 61). A notable careerist himself, Jowitt must have been bemused by an expression of such scruples.

Solicitor General and was appointed President of the Probate, Admiralty and Divorce division in 1962 and later a law lord. In addition to these law officers, there are three examples of backbench MPs being appointed to the High Court bench: Terence Donovan, who sat as a Labour MP and eventually rose to become a law lord[63]; Basil Nield, a Conservative MP, who became a High Court judge via the circuit bench and whose claim to fame was that he presided at all 61 assize towns in England and Wales before abolition of the system; and Gerald Howard, Conservative MP for Cambridgeshire, who was appointed to the Queen's Bench division in 1961.[64] One striking feature is that judicial preferment for four of seven – Donovan, Reid, Ungoed-Thomas and Manningham-Buller – came not from their own party but from the other side of the House. That is strong support for the largely non-partisan nature of judicial appointments under the Lord Chancellors of the post-World War II era. Attlee has perhaps the most notable record for non-partisan appointments: he appointed James Reid as a law lord; Donald Somervell, a Conservative law officer of the 1930s, to the Court of Appeal in 1946; and a former Conservative parliamentary candidate, Rayner Goddard, as Lord Chief Justice in 1946.

Is there anything we can learn from the experiences of these MP-judges? Lords Reid and Simon deserve closer attention. After Cambridge, followed almost immediately by four years away on active service during World War I, Reid started to build up a reputable, but not huge, practice at the Edinburgh Bar. Some of his spare time was spent as a legal author. Active in Conservative politics in Scotland in the 1920s, he was elected in 1931 as MP for Stirling and Falkirk. He lost the seat in 1935, but came in again at a by-election as member for Hillhead in 1937. Professor TB Smith has commented that Reid's career illustrates in striking fashion that eminence at the Scottish Bar and a political career cannot be satisfactorily combined.[65] Nonetheless, Reid was Solicitor General for Scotland from 1936 to 1941 (when first appointed he was not in the Commons) and Lord Advocate from 1941 to 1945. In Opposition after 1945, Reid became a formidable critic of the Attlee Government in the House of Commons. Many of his colleagues were tired out by the years in office and the war and few were able to assimilate the details of Labour's legislative avalanche. Perhaps that makes the offer in 1949 of direct appointment as a law lord all the more surprising. After checking with his party, and not receiving encouragement about preferment should it return to office, Reid accepted Attlee's offer.

Reid made a significant and well-known contribution to English common law. Until his retirement at the end of 1974, he sat on some 500 appeals during his time as a law lord. He gave judgment in the majority of these appeals, often the main judgment. After he became senior law lord in 1962, he was the most influential judge in the court, with a creativity and sophistication of method few could match.[66] His influence on principled developments in the law is evidenced by judgments still cited – *Ridge v Baldwin*,[67] *Hedley Byrne v Heller and Partners Ltd*[68], and *Heron II* to name three from the areas of public law, tort and damages.[69]

---

[63] On Donovan, see Stevens, *Law and Politics* (n 61) 520–23.
[64] See B Nield, *Farewell to the Assizes* (London, Garnstone, 1972).
[65] TB Smith, Oxford Dictionary of National Biography.
[66] Stevens, *Law and Politics* (n 61) 468ff.
[67] *Ridge v Baldwin* [1964] AC 40.
[68] *Hedley Byrne v Heller and Partners Ltd* [1964] AC 465.
[69] *Heron II* [1969] 1 AC 350.

Lord Reid himself was proudest of the first of these.[70] Reid's account of judicial method is well known.[71] At first instance, said Reid, 90 per cent of the time judges spend deciding the facts, upon which in most cases the law becomes clear. At the appellate level, however, judges inevitably make law. There is no golden rule of judicial law-making: law is as much an art as a science. What the judge must have regard to is commonsense, legal principle and public policy in that order. Commonsense is not static, and what was plain good sense in the nineteenth century could be nonsense today. As for legal principle, that can offer consistency but rigid adherence to precedent has to be avoided. Finally public policy, in Reid's characterisation, keeps the law in step with movements of public opinion.

If Lord Reid is the most distinguished of the MP-judges of the post-World War II period, Lord Simon of Glaisdale is possibly the most interesting. Jocelyn Simon began at the Bar in 1934, served in the War, including Burma, and became MP for Middlesbrough West in 1951. In the years 1957 to 1959 he was a junior minister at the Home Office and then Financial Secretary to the Treasury. In 1959 he became Solicitor General and remained in that office until he left Parliament in 1962, on his appointment as President of the Probate, Divorce and Admiralty Division of the High Court. This is the last example which provided some support for the law officers' 'right' to judicial preferment. Simon left a considerable legacy as a senior judge. He was prepared expressly to mould the common law to the realities of changing social conditions and to address issues of public policy.[72] Simon expressed himself beautifully. His background as a politician also made him acutely aware of the need for the courts and Parliament to respect each other.[73]

Shortly before his death, Lord Bingham noted that the earlier era, where the law lords had members with political backgrounds, was unlikely to be repeated in the future. He regretted the absence of experience in public administration among members of the highest tribunal. '[I]ts deliberations would be enriched if some of its members had direct personal experience of the democratic and bureaucratic process . . .'[74] Reid and Simon are good examples of what judges with a political background can bring to the bench. On his retirement, Reid echoed Bingham's sentiment that former politicians serving as law lords knew how the machinery of government worked and were able to understand issues concerning the administration.[75] Reid also demonstrated a fine sense of the importance as a judge of knowing the experiences of ordinary people. Referring no doubt to his service during the World War I and his years as an MP, Reid said the following in his account of judicial law-making:

> If the law is to keep in step with movements of public opinion then judges must know how ordinary people of all grades of society think and live. You cannot get that from books or courses of study. You must have mixed with all kinds of people and got to know them. If you only listen to those who hit the headlines you get quite the wrong impression. If we are to remain a democratic people those who try to be guided by public opinion must go to the grass roots. That is why it is so valuable for a judge to have given public service of some kind in his earlier days.[76]

---

[70] See L Blom-Cooper and G Drewry, 'Towards a System of Administrative Law: The Reid and Wilberforce Era, 1945-82', in Blom-Cooper, Brice Dickson and Drewry (n 29) 219–20.

[71] Lord Reid, 'The Judge as Lawmaker' (1972) 12 *Journal of the Society of Public Teachers of Law* 22.

[72] Stevens, *Law and Politics* (n 61).

[73] The best example is *British Railways Board v Pickin* [1974] AC 765.

[74] T Bingham, 'The Law Lords: Who Has Served' in Blom-Cooper, Brice Dickson and Drewry (n 29) 125.

[75] M Berlins, 'The One Judge We Will Really Miss' *The Times*, 14 January 1975.

[76] Lord Reid, 'The Judge as Lawmaker' (n 71) 27.

Both Reid and Simon also had a developed sense of the boundaries of judicial law-making, the need to leave certain matters to Parliament because of their greater institutional competence and the importance of respect for the work of other arms of the Government.[77]

IV JUDGES AND POLITICS[78]

Constitutional courts have power to thwart democratically elected governments. Consequently, they have had to grapple with the issue of how the exercise of that power is to be exercised, explained and justified both to the politicians and the public. Historically, the constitution of the United Kingdom has not conferred on the courts a comparable power. The growth of judicial review from the 1960s led to some discussion about the appropriate role for the courts in upsetting the plans of executive government. In his Hamlyn Lectures in 1990, Lord Woolf acknowledged the dangers which could result from an over-invasive use of judicial review, the need to strike a balance and the safeguards against abuse such as the flexible nature of the remedies.[79] There has been a great deal of writing since about judicial deference to legislative and executive power.[80]

With the Human Rights Act 1998, the issue has been placed very firmly centre stage. The courts' role in giving force to the European Convention on Human Rights has become a matter of acute public debate. It is not simply a matter of what the European Court of Human Rights does. Our courts are implicated as well. So how can judicial power be successfully accommodated to that of democratically elected politicians?

On 21 April 1952, one of the great common lawyers of the last century, Sir Owen Dixon, was sworn in as Chief Justice of the High Court of Australia, the country's highest court. He had been a judge of the High Court for almost a quarter of a century, although he had taken time out from his judicial tasks, notably to serve during World War II as Australia's Ambassador to the United States. He had a close, if not always a smooth, relationship, with RG Menzies, who dominated the Australian political scene for many years.[81] At the swearing in ceremony, Dixon set out his conception of the judicial function in deciding disputes under the Australian constitution:

> [T]he court's sole function is to interpret a constitutional description of power or restraint upon power and say whether a given measure falls on one side of a line consequently drawn or the other. . . . [I]t has nothing whatever to do with the merits of demerits of the measure. . . .[C]lose adherence to legal reasoning is the only way to maintain the confidence of all parties in Federal conflicts. It may be that the court is thought to be excessively legalistic. I should be sorry to think that it is anything else. There is no other safe guide to judicial decisions in great conflicts than a strict and complete legalism.[82]

---

[77] See Stevens, *Law and Politics* (n 61) 474, 574; A Paterson, *The Law Lords* (London, Macmillan, 1982) 178, 197–98.

[78] This part draws on my 2012 Law and Society lecture at Queen Mary, University of London.

[79] Sir Harry Woolf, *The Protection of the Public-The New Challenge* (London, Stevens, 1990).

[80] For eg A Kavanagh, 'Defending Deference in *Public Law* and Constitutional Theory' (2010) 126 *Law Quarterly Review* 222; J King, 'Institutional Approaches to Judicial Restraint' (2008) 28 *Oxford Journal of Legal Studies* 409. For the views of the current Master of the Rolls, Lord Dyson, 'Some Thoughts on Judicial Deference' [2006] *Judicial Review* 103.

[81] Menzies had been Dixon's pupil at the Bar.

[82] (1952) 85 CLR xiv. See P Lane, 'High Court Techniques' (169) 43 *Australian Law Journal* 172; L Zines, *The High Court and the Constitution*, 3rd edn (Sydney, Butterworths, 1993) 340ff.

When Dixon made these remarks he had in mind the recent public criticism of the Court's decision in what became known as the Communist Party Case (*Australian Communist Party v Commonwealth*).[83] There the Court had struck down the Government's Communist Party Dissolution Act 1950 on constitutional grounds. That legislation had proscribed the Communist Party and enabled the executive to decide whether individuals and organisations were associated with it and threatened the country's defence. The Court had reasoned that the legislation had purported to declare conclusively that the party was prejudicial to the country's defence; that it had sought to punish citizens, not for objective acts, but because of their association; and that it was not justified under the Federal Government's power to legislate for defence. After the Court's decision, the Government called an election which it won, but it lost the subsequent referendum to change the constitution to enable it to ban the party and deal with its members.[84]

The High Court's decisions, some years earlier, in *Australian National Airways Pty Ltd v Commonwealth*[85] and *Commonwealth v Bank of New South Wales*[86] had been just as controversial. In the first, the Labour Government attempted to establish a government airline with a monopoly on interstate travel. The Court held that although under the constitution a government airline was authorised, section 92 forbade conferring a monopoly on it.[87] The second was even more controversial. Section 46 of the Banking Act 1947 empowered the Federal Government to prohibit any private bank from continuing in business. The banks mobilised a widespread campaign against the legislation which was a major element in the defeat of the Labour Government in 1949 and the return to power of RG Menzies as Prime Minister.[88] The Privy Council upheld the majority decision of Australia's High Court, that the power in section 46 was an infringement of the freedom of interstate trade contained in section 92 of the constitution.

So Dixon's legalism was an attempt to justify judicial decisions taken in areas which were highly political. In an address at Yale Law School in 1955, Dixon developed at greater length what he conceived to be the correct approach to judicial method.[89] (He said that he was not primarily concerned with constitutional decisions but with common law decision-making in the higher courts. Constitutional interpretation, he said, was not 'capable of the objective treatment characteristic of the administration by courts of private law'.) In Dixon's view the law provided a body of doctrine which governed decisions in particular cases. Decisions would be 'correct' or 'incorrect', 'right' or 'wrong' as they conformed to ascertained legal principles and were applied according to a standard of reasoning which was not personal to the judges themselves. The judge could not disregard the external standard provided by legal doctrine because of dissatisfaction with the outcome in a particular case. Dixon recalled Maitland's historical description of the common law method as one of strict logic and high technique.[90] Although Dixon conceded that that might not be a

[83] *Australian Communist Party v Commonwealth* (1951) 83 CLR 1. See P Ayres, *Owen Dixon* (Melbourne, Miegunyah Press, 2003) 233. See also DP Derham, 'The Defence Power' in R Else-Mitchell (ed), *Essays on the Australian Constitution* (Sydney, Law Book Co, 1961) 177–81.

[84] J Molony, *History of Australia* (Ringwood, Victoria, Penguin, 1987) 305.

[85] *Australian National Airways Pty Ltd v Commonwealth* (1945) 71 CLR 29.

[86] *Commonwealth v Bank of New South Wales* (1949) 79 CLR 497 (PC). The Privy Council purported to apply, inter alia, *James v Commonwealth of Australia* (n 18).

[87] S Brogden, *Australia's Two-Airline Policy* (Melbourne, Melbourne University Press, 1968) 58–65.

[88] R May, *The Battle for the Banks* (Sydney, Sydney University Press, 1968); LF Crisp, *Ben Chifley* (Croydon, Victoria, Longmans, 1961) 338–40).

[89] Sir Owen Dixon, 'Concerning Judicial Method' (1956) 29 *Australian Law Journal* 468.

[90] ibid 469.

completely accurate description in the modern age, he believed that there had been no sharp break from that tradition.

Dixon acknowledged that legalism might not respond sufficiently to an ever-changing legal order. But he believed that an express change of legal doctrine by legal innovators was forbidden.[91] However, Dixon asserted that the common law method, as he conceived it, did not inhibit legal change, albeit that change had to be limited to what was necessary to decide the instant case. But it was wrong for a judge, discontented with a result held to flow from a long accepted legal principle, 'deliberately to abandon the principle in the name of justice or of social necessity or of social convenience'. At his swearing in address as Chief Justice, it will be recalled, Dixon stressed the importance of legalism to public confidence. In his Yale lecture Dixon said that deliberate judicial innovation usurped authority. Caution in making change was not a sign of timidity but rather of wisdom in the light of the limited capacity of the judge to foresee its implications.

Legalism has cast a long shadow over Australian legal method. It means a mastery of authority and a close attention to the text. It has the benefit of stability and offers a justification of the courts' power. But there is a downside. The critics have long suggested that Dixon's method masked the application of values as the neutral application of established principle.[92] In the 1980s, a time of social change in Australia, there was a change of course.[93] Judges of the High Court of Australia became more open about values. A number had been taught by Professor Julius Stone at the University of Sydney and imbibed the notion that in judicial decision-making there are what Stone called 'leeways of choice'.[94] Sir Anthony Mason, a member of the Court from 1972 and Chief Justice from 1987 to 1995, said that the Court's constitutional role was impossible without taking values into account, not the values of the judges themselves but community values. The judges, he also asserted, have authority to make law as an incident of their power to adjudicate. '[T]here can be no brightline distinction between legislative and judicial law-making'.[95] The creative role of the judge was eloquently espoused by a prominent member of the Court, Michael Kirby, when he gave the Hamlyn Lectures in 2003.[96]

Leading decisions of the High Court during this period discovered a right to free political discussion in the constitution and to native title to land in the common law.[97] There was intense public controversy. Judges sympathetic to acknowledging the Court's law-making role saw the danger of intruding into the legislative sphere. In this category was Mary Gaudron, the first woman member of the High Court. In her view if the case for change was pragmatic, rather than principled, it was more appropriate to leave the matter to the legislature. In *Breen v Williams* she and McHugh J said that advances in the common

---

[91] ibid 472. We know from his private correspondence that this was a reference to Lord Denning: Ayres, *Owen Dixon* (n 83) 253.

[92] B Galligan, *Politics of the High Court* (St Lucia, Qld, University of Queensland Press, 1986) 32–33, 40–41, 232; F Carrigan, 'A Blast From The Past: The Resurgence of Legal Formalism' (2003) 27 *Melbourne University Law Review* 163, 172–73.

[93] M Coper, 'Concern About Judicial Method' (2006) 30 *Melbourne University Law Review* 554, 565–66.

[94] J Stone, *Legal System and Lawyers' Reasoning* (London, Stevens, 1964) 274–76. See Justice Michael Kirby, 'Julius Stone and the High Court of Australia' (1997) 20 *University of New South Wales Law Journal* 239.

[95] Sir Anthony Mason, 'Legislative and Judicial Law-Making: Can We Locate an Identifiable Boundary?' (2003) 24 *Adelaide Law Review* 15.

[96] Justice Michael Kirby, *Judicial Activism* (London, Sweet & Maxwell, 2004): See also AJ Brown, *Michael Kirby* (Sydney, Federation Press, 2011) 209–10, 359–75.

[97] See eg *Australian Capital Television Pty Ltd v Commonwealth* (1988) 165 CLR 360; *Mabo v Queensland* (1992) 175 CLR 1.

law had to proceed by conventional methods of legal reasoning and that it was a serious constitutional mistake to think that the common law courts had the authority to 'provide a solvent' for every social, political or economic problem: 'In a democratic society, changes in the law that cannot logically or analogically be related to existing common law rules and principles are the province of the legislature'.[98] Not surprisingly there was a political reaction against the High Court in this open and activist phase.[99] That was most evident in the conscious policy of the then Australian Government of appointing judges, expressing a less activist philosophy. There has been a partial reversion amongst some of the judges to Dixonian legalism.[100]

Probably the most famous judge in United States history is Oliver Wendell Holmes. In the opening passage of his book, *The Common Law*, Holmes encapsulated his philosophy in a famous passage, that the common law is more besides logic.

> The life of the law has not been logic: it has been experience. The felt necessities of the time, the prevalent moral and political theories, intuitions of public policy, avowed or unconscious, even the prejudices which judges share with their fellow-men, have had a good deal more to do than the syllogism in determining the rules by which men should be governed.[101]

So the common law had not developed through logic and technique alone, as Dixon asserted. Its content at any particular time corresponded closely to what was convenient for a society's needs. Logic was an element, as Holmes acknowledged, but judges sometimes exercise discretion and respond to community values. Holmes developed his concept of judicial method primarily from an exhaustive study of the case law he undertook to prepare the twelfth edition of Kent's Commentaries, an American legal encyclopaedia.[102] He did this while practising law in Boston and teaching, to a limited extent, at Harvard Law School. Holmes was part of a philosophical group, some of whom were later characterised as the American pragmatists. Holmes had little affinity with the positivism of Langdell, Dean of Harvard Law School from the 1870s, who conceived of law as a science and saw the ultimate source of all legal knowledge in the cases, which could be used inductively to discover legal principles to be applied in future decisions.[103]

In 1881, at the age of 41, Holmes was appointed to the Supreme Judicial Court of Massachusetts, and refined his approach, but still primarily in the context of common law cases. In his writings, Holmes advanced as a merit of the common law that it is made through resolving concrete disputes. Cases are decided one at a time, Holmes argued, but at some point it becomes necessary to formulate a doctrine or principle to reconcile the

---

[98] *Breen v Williams* (1996) 186 CLR 71. On Gaudron, see P Burton, *From Moree to Mabo* (Perth, U Western Australia Publishing, 2010) 296. For McHugh, see his 'The Law-Making Function of the Judicial Process' (1988) 62 *Australian Law Journal* 15 (Pt1), 116 (Pt2). No doubt Gaudron and McHugh with more working class backgrounds would have regarded themselves as better barometers of community values than the more patrician Mason.

[99] See J Pierce, *Inside the Mason Court Revolution* (Carolina Academic Press, 2006).

[100] eg Justice Dyson Heydon, 'Judicial Activism and the Death of the Rule of Law' (2003) 47(1) *Quadrant* 9; (Chief Justice) AM Gleeson, 'Individualised Justice – The Holy Grail' (1995) 69 *Australian Law Journal* 421; Justice K Hayne, 'Concerning Judicial Method-Fifty Years On' (2006) 32 *Monash University Law Review* 223. See also F Wheeler and J Williams, 'Restrained Activism in the High Court of Australia' in Brice Dickson (ed), *Judicial Activism in Common Law Supreme Courts* (Oxford, Oxford University Press, 2007) 30–32.

[101] Oliver Wendell Holmes, *The Common Law* (London, Macmillan, 1882) 1.

[102] S Novick, *Honorable Justice. The Life of Oliver Wendell Holmes* (New York, Dell, 1989) 121–22.

[103] See B Kimball, *The Inception of Modern Professional Education: C C Langdell 1826–1906* (Chapel Hill, University of North Carolina Press, 2009).

discrete decisions in a particular area. The principle therefore evolves and is based on the work of a number, indeed of many, minds. If the decisions have been developing in different directions it becomes necessary to choose the shape and direction of the principle. This might be done in an apparently arbitrary manner. That is not the end of the matter, since further cases may raise new issues not contemplated by the principle, which must be modified in the light of them. Community standards play a large part in the law's development as judges and juries make decisions in the context of concrete disputes. Community standards are a cause of judicial restraint in the common law. If questions of policy arise, Holmes said, they are legislative questions.[104]

In 1897, while still a judge of the Supreme Judicial Court of Massachusetts, Holmes gave a lecture at Boston University, 'The Path of the Law',[105] which was still being discussed a century later.[106] In one part of the lecture Holmes turned to the basis for judicial restraint. Judges failed to adequately recognise, he said, their duty of weighing considerations of what he called social advantage, the public policy behind a rule. Judicial aversion to do so left the foundation of judgments inarticulate and often unconscious. Thus judges made choices which they thought were natural but in fact represented their own social preferences. Holmes said that he suspected that a fear of socialism had influenced judicial action both in the United States and in England, albeit not consciously. That had also led people who could not control the legislatures to look to the courts for favourable decisions based on principles to be discovered in the Constitution. Holmes continued that if lawyers considered public policy more explicitly, they would sometimes hesitate where now they were confident, and would see that they were 'taking sides upon debatable and often burning questions'.[107]

After his appointment to the Supreme Court in 1902, Holmes used this insight as a philosophy for constitutional restraint. Constitutional decisions should not embody views of public policy which are contested, he believed, but only those which have already prevailed. In his first opinion written for the Court, concerning a Californian constitutional restriction on the forward sale of securities, Holmes first commented that general propositions, for example, the need for a provision to bear a reasonable relation to the evil sought to be cured, did not carry the analysis very far.[108] Holmes then said that while the courts must exercise a judgment of their own, it was by no means true that every law was void which might seem to the judge to be excessive, unsuited to its ostensible end, or based upon conceptions of morality with which they disagreed. Considerable latitude had to be allowed for differences of view as well as for possible peculiar conditions which the Court could know imperfectly, if at all. Otherwise a constitution, instead of embodying only relatively fundamental rules of right, as generally understood by all English-speaking communities, would become the partisan of a particular set of ethical or economical opinions, by no means held universally.[109]

---

[104]   F Kellogg, *Oliver Wendell Holmes Jr, Legal Theory, and Judicial Restraint* (New York, Cambridge University Press) 27–31, 58, 76.

[105]   Oliver Wendell Holmes, 'The Path of the Law' (1897) 10 *Harvard Law Review* 457. See also his 'Privilege, Malice, and Intent' (1894) 8 *Harvard Law Review* 1; 'Law in Science and Science in Law' (1899) 12 *Harvard Law Review* 443.

[106]   Symposium, 'The Path of the Law After One Hundred Years' (1997) 110 *Harvard Law Review* 989.

[107]   Wendell Holmes, 'Privilege, Malice, and Intent' (n 105) 467–68.

[108]   *Otis v Parker* 187 US 606 (1903).

[109]   ibid 609.

Still cited today, Holmes' dissent in *Lochner v New York*[110] embodied his philosophy of judging. There under the due process clause in the fourteenth amendment to the constitution, the majority struck down New York legislation which imposed a 10 hour day, 60 hour week for bakers. The issue posed by Peckham J for the majority was whether the legislation was

> a fair, reasonable and appropriate exercise of the police power of the State, or . . . an unreasonable, unnecessary and arbitrary interference with the right of the individual . . . to enter into those contracts in relation to labor which may seem to him appropriate.[111]

The fourteenth amendment protected the right to contract in relation to a person's business. Bakers could protect themselves, without the interference of the state. Moreover, the trade was not especially unhealthy so as to justify legislative action under the police power.[112] Holmes' dissent was short:

> This case is decided upon an economic theory which a large part of the country does not entertain. If it were a question whether I agreed with that theory, I should desire to study it further and long before making up my mind. But I do not conceive that to be my duty, because I strongly believe that my agreement or disagreement has nothing to do with the right of a majority to embody their opinions in law . . . [A] constitution is not intended to embody a particular economic theory, whether of paternalism and the organic relation of the citizen to the State or of laissez faire . . . It is made for people of fundamentally differing views, and the accident of our finding certain opinions natural and familiar or novel and even shocking ought not to conclude our judgment upon the question whether statutes embodying them conflict with the Constitution of the United States . . . I think that the word liberty in the Fourteenth Amendment is perverted when it is held to prevent the natural outcome of a dominant opinion . . .[113]

During his 30 years on the Supreme Court, Holmes' judicial method continued along the lines expressed in these early cases.[114] Holmes' legacy has been considerable. The constrained pragmatism of Judge Richard Posner of the 7th Circuit Court of Appeals and the University of Chicago Law School, the most cited legal scholar of his generation, is influenced by it.[115] So was Sandra Day O'Connor, the first woman member of the Supreme Court and during her 25 years on the Court until her retirement in 2006 often the swing vote between the liberal and non-liberal blocs.[116] Justice O'Connor sat on the Supreme Court in an era when the constitutional focus was on issues quite different from Holmes' day. A key constitutional issue for Holmes was, as in *Lochner*, whether economic regulation was constitutionally valid. From the 1950s, the constitutional issues tended to revolve around individual and social, not economic, rights. *Brown v Board of Education*[117] requiring the desegregation of schools,

---

[110] *Lochner v New York* 198 US 45 (1905).

[111] ibid 56.

[112] This approach presaged to an extent what was later called substantive due process which struck at state regulation and came to an end during the New Deal era of the 1930s: see GE White, *The Constitution and the New Deal* (Cambridge, Massachusetts, Harvard University Press, 2000) 245–53 on the complexities of the story.

[113] *Lochner v New York* (n 110) 75–76.

[114] S Novick, *Honorable Justice* (n 102) 298, 327, 352, 456–57, 463. See also GE White, *The American Judicial Tradition*, 3rd edn (New York, Oxford University Press, 2007) 134; GE White, *Patterns of American Legal Thought* (New Orleans, Quid Pro Books, 2010) 135–36.

[115] Richard Posner, *How Judges Think* (Cambridge, Massachusetts, Harvard University Press, 2008. See also C Sunstein, *One Case at a Time. Judicial Minimalism on the Supreme Court* (Cambridge, Massachusetts, Harvard University Press, 1999).

[116] W Huhn, 'The Constitutional Jurisprudence of Sandra Day O'Connor' (2006) 39 *Akron Law Review* 373, 379.

[117] *Brown v Board of Education* 347 US 483 (1954).

was the first major example, but there followed a series of decisions striking at laws and legal instruments relating to a wide range of matters such as voting, school prayers, contraception, free speech and abortion. Such decisions produced reactions, both political and intellectual. One strand in the sphere of legal method was the call for neutral principles, enunciated in Professor Herbert Wechsler's Oliver Wendell Holmes lecture at Harvard in 1959, neutral principles being those which would lead to reasoning and analysis transcending the immediate result.[118] Another strand was John Hart Ely's notion of limiting constitutional activism to promote democratic processes.[119] Yet another strand was that closely associated with Justice Scalia of the Supreme Court, who contends that courts interpreting constitutional and statutory provisions must focus on the text.[120]

Rather than addressing individual and social rights through American eyes, let me turn to Lord Bingham, the outstanding British judge of his generation. Bingham was successively Master of the Rolls, Lord Chief Justice of England and Wales and, from 2000 to 2008, senior law lord. Along with the rest of the judiciary, but very much as a leader, Bingham had to address the transformation of jurisprudence wrought by the Human Rights Act 1998. Bingham's judicial method was what can be described as English pragmatism. It began with a rejection of what he variously described as the declaratory theory or the traditional school of judging. Bingham associated these with Viscount Simonds, who had dominated the House of Lords for the two decades until his retirement in 1962, and with Sir Owen Dixon. Here Bingham followed in the footsteps of those such as Lord Reid, who had described the declaratory theory of law as a fairy tale. Bingham rejected the traditional school that judges have no role as lawmakers, because it did not offer an adequate explanation of judging experienced by judges, particularly at the appellate level, whose experience was that the cases which came before them did not in the main turn on sections of statutes which were clear and unambiguous in their meaning.[121]

At the other end of the spectrum from Simonds and Dixon was Lord Denning. Denning was appointed a judge at a relatively young age in the 1940s and quickly established himself as a legal innovator. Denning's judicial philosophy was clear and simple: judges were there to use the authority of the law to do justice. In his book *The Road to Justice*, which in 1955 collected a number of his addresses,[122] Denning said that in too many respects the law was inadequate for the needs of modern society. Some lawyers cared too much for law and too little for justice; they had become technicians spelling out the meaning of words instead of making the law fit for the times. For Denning the road to justice meant that precedents could be discarded, common law presumptions had to be made to fit with the times and statutes were to be read purposively to fill gaps and carry out the Parliamentary intention.[123]

Bingham greatly admired Denning but, like many, found him frustrating. He recounted that one of the times he appeared in Denning's court as counsel he was relying heavily on an observation of Lord Simon, giving the unanimous judgment of the House of Lords, but was interrupted by Denning who said: 'Oh, but Lord Simon was very sorry he ever said

[118] Herbert Wechsler, *Principles, Politics and Fundamental Law* (Cambridge, Massachusetts, Harvard University Press, 1961) 3ff.

[119] John Hart Ely, *Democracy and Distrust* (Cambridge, Massachusetts, Harvard University Press, 1980).

[120] Antonin Scalia, *A Matter of Interpretation. Federal Courts and the Law* (Princeton, Princeton University Press, 1997).

[121] T Bingham, *Lives of the Law* (Oxford, Oxford University Press, 2011) 130–33.

[122] Lord Denning, *The Road to Justice* (London, Stevens, 1955).

[123] See C Stephens, *The Jurisprudence of Lord Denning* (Newcastle, Cambridge Scholars Publishing, 2009) vol 3, 73–86.

that. He told me so.'[124] Bingham rejected Denning's assertion that the law-making role of judges could be pursued whenever established law impeded the doing of justice in an individual case; first, if judges were too free with existing law, or too neglectful of precedent, the law could become reprehensibly uncertain and unpredictable; secondly, too much would depend on the temperament and predilections of individual judges; thirdly, judges working to an agenda cannot respond to the merits of the case before them; and finally, judges are not, by and large, equipped to be law reformers.[125]

Bingham preferred what he saw as the majoritarian school in England and Wales, that judges did sometimes make law and that this was an entirely proper judicial function, so long as it was within boundaries. Writing before the Human Rights Act 1998, Bingham identified five possible boundaries, either not to be crossed or to be crossed with care: first, when reasonable people had ordered their affairs on the basis of a certain understanding of the law; secondly, where the law was defective but its reform demanded research or consultation of a type a court could not undertake; third, where there was no consensus within the community about an issue; fourthly, when a matter was the subject of current Parliamentary activity; and finally where the subject was far removed from ordinary judicial experience. Bingham also cautioned that in some cases judges might think that they were required to elect between different legal solutions and, in effect, create new law, but that usually the question would be which of the established legal principles applied. Even where judges engaged in balancing exercises – this was written before the Human Rights Act 1998 – discretion had nothing to do with it because the matters which went with the balance were established, although different judges might attach to the factors different weight. However, the inescapable fact to Bingham was that judges had to make a choice sometimes and unless superseded by legislation that choice determined what the law should be.

To Bingham the principles governing constitutional interpretation, including interpretation of human rights instruments, were in one sense the same as those applying to statutory construction. In another sense they were different in as much as constitutional provisions were expressed in broader terms, and because their context and application changed over time. The judicial task was also similar as with any other type of case. Facts had to be found, the text and authorities examined, and a reasoned judgment produced. The difference lay in the type of decision being made which, although not unfamiliar in domestic law, was of a more evaluative kind. In Bingham's view there were limits to judicial law-making. He very firmly rejected the idea that the common law placed limits on Parliamentary sovereignty.[126] In relation to claims under the Human Rights Act 1998, Bingham thought the scope for law-making small. The courts had to give effect to the text of the European Convention on Human Rights, and that has to mean the same in all Convention states. Judges had to be sure that their judgments reflected a Council of European consensus. There was clear authority that courts must comply with the Strasbourg jurisprudence. There was no licence to freewheel.

This approach is evident in Bingham's jurisprudence.[127] A major concern articulated was institutional competence. That is evident in *A v Secretary of State for the Home Department*

---

[124] T Bingham, *The Business of Judging* (Oxford, Oxford University Press, 2000) 411.

[125] ibid 32–33.

[126] T Bingham, *The Rule of Law* (London, Allen Lane, 2010) 167.

[127] See R Clayton and H Tomlinson, 'Lord Bingham and the Human Rights Act 1998' in M Andenas and D Fairgrieve (eds), *Tom Bingham and the Transformation of the Law* (Oxford, Oxford University Press, 2009).

(the Belmarsh case),[128] which was the successful challenge to the detention of foreign nationals, who could not be removed from the United Kingdom for safety or other reasons, but whom the Secretary of State regarded as a threat to national security and terrorists. The Government had laid an order whereby the United Kingdom would derogate from Article 5(1) of the European Convention on Human Rights so that the nine appellants could be detained. It did so on the basis that there was a public emergency threatening the life of the nation within the meaning of Article 15 of the Convention. The House of Lords upheld the derogation. However, the Court made a declaration of incompatibility under the Human Rights Act 1998 as regards the statutory provision, section 23 of the Anti-Terrorism, Crime and Security Act 2001, which authorised the appellants' detention; it unjustifiably discriminated against them but made no provision for United Kingdom nationals who presented the same threat. Bingham said:

> [29] . . . The more purely political (in a broad or narrow sense) a question is, the more appropriate it will be for political resolution and the less likely it is to be an appropriate matter for judicial decision. The smaller, therefore, will be the potential role of the court. It is the function of political and not judicial bodies to resolve political questions. Conversely, the greater the legal content of any issue, the greater the potential role of the court, because under our constitution and subject to the sovereign power of Parliament it is the function of the courts and not of political bodies to resolve legal questions. The present question seems to me to be very much at the political end of the spectrum . . .

V   CONCLUSION

Lawyers in our system have always been a significant force in politics. That for some has been a matter of regret, since their contributions have sometimes been seen to be open to self-interest and special pleading. While there is some truth in this, lawyers have played a valuable role in Parliament. However, it is the height of folly to assume that lawyer-MPs have been better at scrutinising legislation and guarding civil liberties and human rights than others. In the past one explanation for lawyers' prominence in the House of Commons was that legal practice, especially at the Bar, could be combined with a political career. That was the path taken by at least one Prime Minister (Asquith) and by any number of Lord Chancellors, Home Secretaries and law officers. That is no longer the case with the Parliamentary hours and the demands of Parliamentary and constituency business. One corollary has been the rise of the professional politician who enters Parliament at a relatively early age and knows only politics as a career. That is not as bad as is sometimes portrayed but too many professional politicians, unleavened by those with experience of the outside world, would not be an unalloyed good.

David Feldman has argued that their different standpoints mean that Parliament, the executive and the judiciary have different visions of our constitutional arrangements. There is a consequent need to accommodate the conflicts.[129] Unlike the nineteenth and twentieth centuries the bench is now bereft of judges with a political background. There is nothing to prevent the Judicial Appointments Commission appointing ex-MPs (or local councillors) to the higher courts but that requires a supply of applicants. One consequence

---

[128]   *A v Secretary of State for the Home Department* [2005] 2 AC 68.
[129]   D Feldman, 'None, One or Several? Perspectives on the UK's Constitution(s)' [2005] *Cambridge Law Journal* 329.

is that the judiciary is robbed of those with first-hand experience of, as Lord Bingham put it, the democratic and bureaucratic processes. More importantly, it means that there is one less institutional mechanism contributing to the mutual respect between the three branches of government, necessary as they accommodate the inevitable conflicts. There are other mechanisms contributing to mutual respect, such the role judges play in presenting evidence before Parliamentary Select Committees. These other mechanisms are unable to carry much weight. There is building to be done.

Common law judges have developed methods to accommodate the political implications of their decisions. In routine cases Dixonian legalism is a satisfactory and accurate explanation. Judges apply, indeed must apply, established principle. That is the case even at the appellate level, where judges cannot ignore principle to pursue their own agendas. They apply principle in a manner well known to first year law students, who are told when answering problem questions to apply the law to the facts. While not properly described as logical, the method is formal in character, principle being applied in a particular context and reasoned to a defensible conclusion. There is no doubt that as with any profession it is possible to say that some analysis and reasoned outcomes are better than others. But Dixon was wrong in denying the law-making function of judges and the role of values in that. As Bingham explained, the inescapable fact is that judges have to make a choice sometimes and unless superseded by legislation that choice determines what the law should be. Values entered into this, the experience to which Holmes referred in his famous aphorism. As Holmes put it, these values may be inarticulate or unconscious to the judge. Holmes' contention was that the judge must strive to uncover any values they may bring to decision-making, so as not to assume that their choices are somehow natural. Not to be aware of the values bearing on a decision could mean the taking of sides, as Holmes put it, upon debatable and often burning questions.

It is at this point that the boundaries to judicial decision-making enter. Dixon did not identify boundaries but assumed that public confidence would derive from an acceptance of the consequences flowing from the logic and technique of his judicial method. That was not the reality at the time and has become less so as public knowledge has increased and deference declined. Holmes' view, expressed in *Lochner*, was that a constitutional instrument is made for a diverse people and the majority has a right to embody its opinion in law. That idea has faced challenge in an era of individual and social rights. The ever present temptation for majorities to disadvantage, even oppress, minorities founds a protective function in the courts under the common law and the European Convention on Human Rights. But as Bingham correctly asserted, certain decisions are intrinsically political, where courts must not venture, even if individual rights are involved. The balance will come down in favour of upholding Parliamentary and executive action. It is simply a mistake to think that the courts can solve all problems and that the often hard grind of politics can be avoided by appealing to them to act.

3

Lawyers in the House of Commons

DAVID HOWARTH

THE RELATIONSHIP BETWEEN law and politics is complex. It contains a set of legal issues (what is the law about politics?), a set of questions of descriptive political science (which types of decision does a particular political system leave to the law?), a set of normative problems (to what extent should political issues be decided by legal processes?) and a set of conceptual questions (is law a subset of politics, an input into it, a process within it or an output of it?). It is also a relationship between two sets of people and two sets of institutions, between lawyers and politicians. This chapter will concentrate on this final aspect of the relationship. It examines the intersection between the world of lawyers and the world of politicians, in particular those lawyers who take a direct part in British politics by becoming or attempting to become members of the House of the Commons.

I LAWYERS IN THE MODERN HOUSE OF COMMONS

Max Weber once observed, 'Modern democracy has been inextricably linked to the modern advocate.'[1] Nearly a century later, Weber's hypothesis has become conventional wisdom. Comments of the sort 'most MPs are lawyers' or 'most of the House is composed of those who have served either as barristers or as solicitors' are commonplace. Indeed, a Google search on the phrase 'most MPs are lawyers' returns more than 1400 results. Nor is that view restricted to the often delusional world of internet commentary. If one asks groups of students, even of students interested in British politics, what proportion of British members of parliament are lawyers, one frequently hears estimates of 60 per cent or more.

The truth is different. Lawyers are a minority in British national politics. In the House of Commons elected in 2005, 11.7 per cent of members had practised as barristers or solicitors. In the House elected in 2010, the figure crept up to 13.8 per cent.[2] One might pad the numbers a little by adding legal academics who never practised (six in the 2005 Parliament, three in 2010)[3] and those who hold law degrees but who neither practised nor taught (eight in 2005, 12 in 2010, although, in the reverse direction, a third of the House's lawyers are

---

[1] Max Weber, *Politik als Beruf* (Munich and Leipzig, Duncker & Humblot, 1919) 24.
[2] See Feargal McGuinness, *Social Background of MPs* – Standard Note SN/SG/1528 (London, House of Commons Library, 2010) (based on Byron Criddle's counts for Philip Cowley and Dennis Kavanagh, *The British General Election of 2010* (Basingstoke, Palgrave Macmillan, 2010)).
[3] These figures are culled from MPs' entries in *Who's Who* and *Dods*. Both are self-reports (subjects write their own entries and update them at regular intervals), which makes them equivalent to surveys.

not law graduates), but the brute fact of the matter is that, far from being a majority, lawyers are outnumbered in Britain's primary legislative chamber by more than five to one.

Nor is the overall picture altered by considering the upper House. One estimate of the size of the legal element in the House of Lords puts it at 10 per cent.[4] Some of the lawyers from the Lords have come to prominence as Law Officers, but that merely emphasises the lack of lawyers in the Commons. Until 1997, the Law Officers had been drawn exclusively from the lower House, but so few barristers were available in the Parliamentary Labour Party after 1997 that for all but the first two years of the 1997–2010 Labour Government, the Attorney-General was chosen from the Lords, and for nearly half of that period the post of Solicitor-General was occupied by lawyers who were not barristers.[5]

Part of the explanation for the popular exaggeration of the proportion of lawyers in Parliament might be that in 21 of the 31 years preceding the 2010 election, the Prime Minister was a lawyer and several leading cabinet members were lawyers, including three Chancellors of the Exchequer, five Home Secretaries, and even three Foreign Secretaries. Since 2010, however, the situation has changed. The first Coalition cabinet contained only three lawyers out of 28 members. The second Coalition cabinet, in office from September 2012, saw a slightly higher proportion of lawyers (five out of 31) but is also notable for the fact that none of the highest offices – Prime Minister, Deputy Prime Minister, Chancellor of the Exchequer, Foreign Secretary, Home Secretary and even Justice Secretary and Lord Chancellor – was entrusted to a lawyer. At the level of the cabinet, lawyers are no longer dominant.[6]

Of course, popular opinion is not entirely wrong. The proportion of lawyers in the House of Commons is very much larger than in the UK's working population as a whole. Under 0.5 per cent of the working population practice law. Even if we control for the fact that MPs are largely drawn from the most highly educated part of the workforce,[7] the picture changes only a little. There are still about 10 times more lawyers in the House than one would expect if the House were broadly representative solely of the professional and higher managerial segment of the population. Lawyers are not under-represented. They are, however, far from the dominant force often imagined.

Moreover, the most striking fact about the proportion of lawyers in the Commons is that it is declining. The trend is not a new one. It was noticed by David Podmore in the 1970s. Podmore brought together research carried out in the 1940s by JFS Ross[8] and the work of the post-1945 Nuffield British General Election Studies to provide a figure for the percentage of lawyers elected at each of the general elections from 1918 to the second

[4] Meg Russell and Meghan Benton, *Analysis of Existing Data on the Breadth of Expertise and Experience in the House of Lords* (London, University College London, 2010) 16 (on a slightly different basis).

[5] At the start of the 2005 Parliament, of the 14 barristers in the Parliamentary Labour Party, five, including Tony Blair, were already Cabinet ministers, three were newly elected, one had practised mainly in France in the 1970s, one had only three years' legal experience (of which one was in California), one was called only to the Scottish Bar and one was an inveterate troublemaker.

[6] The proportion of lawyers in the US Congress is much higher than in Parliament, especially in the Senate, where lawyers have sometimes outnumbered non-lawyers (and might explain some of the confusion in Britain) but even in Congress, it is not as high as popularly believed – in 2012, it was 38% of the Senate and 24% of the House. See R Eric Petersen, *Representatives and Senators: Trends in Member Characteristics since 1945* (Washington DC, Congressional Research Service, 2012) 22. Similarly in the Netherlands the proportion of lawyers in the legislature seems to have been much higher than in the UK throughout the last 100 years but has also been falling. See M Bovens and A Wille, 'The Dominance of the Well-educated in the Dutch Political Elite', Paper for the Politicologenetmaal 2010, Leuven, 27–28 May 2010 (http://soc.kuleuven.be/web/files/11/72/W02-28.pdf) 10–11.

[7] Of the 2005 and 2010 House, 78% and 79% respectively were university graduates, which is more than three times the national average (ONS News Release, 24 Aug 2011).

[8] JFS Ross, *Parliamentary Representation* (London, Eyre and Spottiswoode, 1943) 58–77.

election of 1974. Eight general elections have occurred since Podmore's research and, for-tunately, the Nuffield General Election Studies have also continued, using broadly consist-ent definitions. As a result, we can plot that data onto the end of Podmore's series to generate Figure 1.

Figure 1 suggests a downward long-term trend of the percentage of lawyers in the Commons. Admittedly, it is not a simple linear trend. The percentage drifted downwards before the Second World War, rose again after 1945, peaking in the early 1960s, before dropping through the 1970s, 80s and 90s, reaching a nadir in 1997 before drifting back up in the early twenty-first century.[9] The curve around the trend looks like an oscillating wave whose wavelength is around 60 years and whose amplitude is falling over time. It is as if every half century or so the political system reaches a limit for its tolerance of lawyers and starts to expel them. After two generations it rediscovers its need for lawyers and starts to readmit them, and the process starts again. Crucially, however, the percentage of lawyers that triggers the system's loss of patience and the point at which the system realises that it needs lawyers are both falling, the former faster than the latter.

Podmore, however, was not convinced that the decline in the percentage of lawyers in the Commons was real. Drawing on work on Danish and German lawyers in politics, he suggested that the apparent fall could be explained by the rise of the Labour Party.[10]

Figure 1: Lawyers Elected at UK General Elections 1918–2010

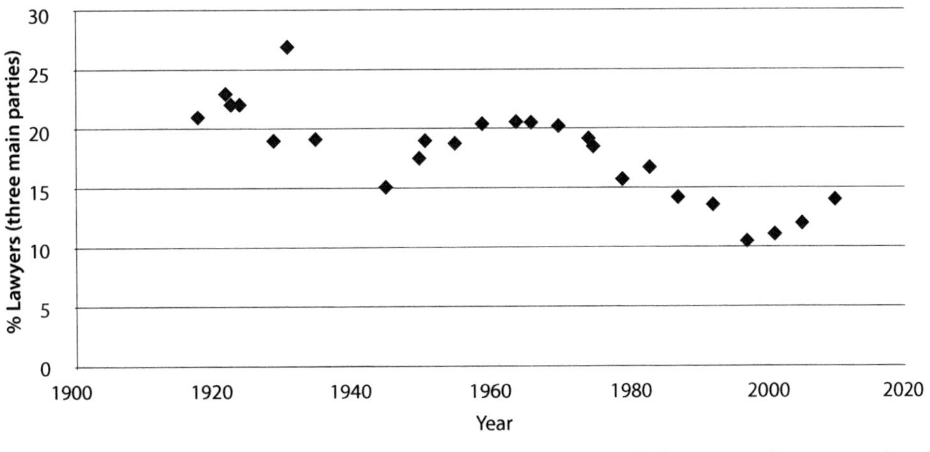

Source: Podmore (1997) (based on Ross (n 8), the Nuffield General Election Studies 1945–74) and McGuinness (n 2) (based on counts by Byron Criddle for the Butler, Kavanagh et al, *General Election Studies* 1979–2010

---

[9] A linear fit can be done, resulting in a coefficient of -0.1145 and an R2 of 63.43%. The curve looks far from linear, however. Calculating the autocorrelation and partial autocorrelation functions using the NumXL program (with straight-line interpolations – not necessarily the right approach) suggests a decaying oscillating wave with many significant lags – in particular positive ones around 60 years and negative ones at 73 and 85 years.

[10] See D Podmore, 'Lawyers and Politics' (1977) 4 (2) *British Journal of Law and Society* 155–85, 183 and David Podmore, *Solicitors and the Wider Community* (London, Heinemann, 1980) 187 (citing MN Pederson, 'Lawyers in Politics: the Danish Folketing and United States Legislatures' in SC Patterson and J Cork (New York, Wiley, 1972) and D Rueschemeyer, *Lawyers and their Society* (Cambridge, Harvard University Press, 1973)).

Labour's class-based politics, the thesis went, was hostile to lawyers, because lawyers were associated with the rich and with attacks on trade unions. Labour was also more likely than the other parties to select candidates from a broader base of occupations, including working-class occupations, thereby leaving less room for lawyers. The proportion of lawyers in the parliamentary Labour Party was indeed consistently lower than that in the Conservatives and Liberals. The theory was that as the proportion of Labour MPs in the House steadily rose in the years after 1918 (the first election in which Labour was a serious independent contender), the proportion of lawyers in the House fell.

Does Podmores's explanation stand in the light of the additional data? With more data points we can apply statistical tests with a little less apprehension than in 1980. Admittedly, the 25 data points we now have are not quite enough to be confident that the assumptions of ordinary statistical analysis apply, that, for example, the variables are normally distributed,[11] but they are not so few that one would expect to find no significant effects regardless of whether such effects were really there. A simple regression of the relationship between the percentage of Labour MPs and the percentage of lawyer MPs at any given general election would have serious methodological problems.[12] We can, however, examine the changes in those percentages election-on-election – that is whether a correlation exists between changes in the percentage of Labour MPs between one election and the next and the equivalent changes in the percentage of lawyers.[13] That relationship is indeed negative and statistically significant.[14] It does not, however, explain anything near the whole of the variance[15] and other factors are clearly in play. For one thing, the percentage of lawyers in the Parliamentary Labour Party, for which we have data from 1945, itself changed, including a constant and precipitate drop from 16.3 per cent in 1970 to 6.3 per cent in 1992.[16] For another, if we ignore Labour MPs and look at only Conservative and Liberal/Alliance/Liberal Democrat MPs, for which we also have data for the period from 1945, the trend is downward, especially after 1966.[17]

The decline in the total percentage of lawyers, however, is not the end of the story. If we divide lawyers into barristers and solicitors (for which we have consistent data since 1945) another very striking pattern emerges (see Figure 2).

The percentage of solicitors has not been falling. If anything it has been rising – although again not in an entirely linear way. There seems to be an oscillation about five elections

---

[11] They look consistent with normality when plotted and formal tests for normality do not reject the hypothesis that they are normal, although that is perhaps not surprising.

[12] Regressing two non-stationary time series variables (ie ones whose real variance and mean are changing over time) produces a great risk of spuriously high R^2s and spuriously low p values (see C Granger and P Newbold, 'Spurious Regressions in Econometrics' (1974) 2(2) *Journal of Econometrics* 111–20). The Durbin-Watson statistic for the residuals of the regression of the percentage of Labour MPs against the percentage of lawyers is 0.399551, meaning that a problem of this kind is highly likely.

[13] For this 'first differencing' method, see ibid 118.

[14] F= 30.119, p>0.0001. Durbin-Watson= 1.997, ie probably no autocorrelation problem.

[15] R^2= 57.79%.

[16] Over the period from 1945–2010 there is a linear fit y = -0.1116x + 231.55, R^2 = 48.81%, but since the percentage generally rises from 1945 to 1970, falls constantly from 1970 to 1992 and then rises constantly to 2010, a linear model is probably not the best. There is, for example, a cubic equation that produces an R^2 of 89.13%.

[17] The percentage of lawyers among Conservative-plus-Liberal, etc MPs rises from 1945 to 1966 and then falls. There is a linear fit of y = -0.1335x + 285.15, R^2 = 56.16%, although a better fit exists using quadratics, eg y = -0.0038x2 + 15.015x – 14689, R^2 = 71.21%. One other point to mention, although not overly to rely upon, is that a multiple regression across the whole period from 1918 using the percentage of Labour MPs and the passage of time itself as independent variables gives a coefficient for time of -0.09 (p= 0.0003) (ie the percentage of lawyers drops about 1% per decade even controlling for how many Labour MPs were elected). The problem is that the Durbin-Watson statistic for this regression is 0.900573, so that the p-value probably means very little.

long. The percentage of barristers, however, rose to a peak in 1959 and then levelled out and subsequently fell, at first gradually and then precipitously, recovering slightly after 2001. That year also marks the first time the percentage of solicitors surpassed that of barristers. What needs to be explained is not just a gradual overall fall in the number of lawyers in the Commons but also two other changes: a sudden and severe fall in the proportion of barristers and a change in ratio of barristers to solicitors in favour of the latter.

It would be very difficult for the fortunes of the Labour Party to explain both a falling and rising trend. Indeed, to the extent that we can draw any conclusions from 18 data points, election-on-election changes in Labour's representation explain part of the changes in the proportion of barristers, but not the rise of solicitors.[18] Moreover, the period also saw great changes in the proportion of barristers within the Parliamentary Labour Party, rising from 6.9 per cent in 1945 to 11.8 per cent in 1970 and then back down to 2.8 per cent in 2005, in a pattern similar to that for barristers as a whole. Moreover, changes in the percentage of Labour MPs elected do not explain changes in the percentage of barristers specifically in the Parliamentary Labour Party.[19]

Figure 2: Barristers and Solicitors in the Commons 1945–2010

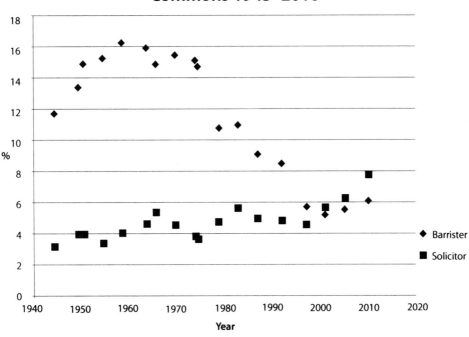

Source: Podmore (n 10) McGuinness (n 2).

---

[18] A regression of election-on-election changes in the percentage of Labour MPs on the same changes in the percentage of barristers is statistically significant at $p<0.05$, but the R^2 is only 23.95% (Durbin Watson= 1.634 – probably no problem). No significant result emerges for solicitors.

[19] F=2.222, p= 0.1567 (and the coefficient is in any case very low).

II DEMOGRAPHIC AND ECONOMIC CHANGE

If the decline in lawyers in general and in barristers in particular cannot be explained solely by variations in the success of the Labour Party, can it be explained by changes in the number of lawyers in society or in the structure of the economy? That seems unlikely. Both branches of the legal profession have grown rapidly. In 1978 there were 4,263 barristers in private practice in England and Wales and 33,864 practising solicitors.[20] In 2010, there were 12,420 barristers in private practice and 117,862 practising solicitors.[21] In 1978 barristers constituted 0.016 per cent of the UK's economically active population and solicitors 0.129 per cent;[22] in 2010 the corresponding figures were 0.039 per cent and 0.374 per cent, a rate of growth faster than that of the professional, technical and scientific sector as a whole.[23] The number of lawyers has risen five times faster than the number of workers in information and communications technology and more than five times faster than the number of workers in finance and insurance.[24]

Could the shift towards solicitors nevertheless reflect changes in the profession? Again that is unlikely. The ratio of barristers to solicitors did shift in favour of solicitors, but nothing like the change in Parliament. In 1978, there were about eight practising solicitors for every barrister in private practice. In 2010 there were about 9.5.

III IF NOT BARRISTERS, WHO?

If fewer barristers are being elected to Parliament, who else is being elected? The House of Commons elected in 1979 provides some clues as to what has happened in British politics over the past 35 years. One can readily find more than a dozen instances of seats held by barristers in October 1974 being transferred to a non-barrister of the same party in 1979. On the Conservative side, David Renton, barrister MP for Huntingdon, was replaced by the future Prime Minister, John Major, a banker. The seat held in 1974 by the venerable barrister and farmer Jasper More found itself represented by Eric Cockeram, a property manager. The Chipping Barnet seat of the disgraced minister and barrister, Reginald Maudling, went to an architect, Sydney Chapman. On the Labour side, one can find barristers replaced by trade union officials, a social worker, a local government officer and a local councillor.

One can see an even better clue in the new MPs of 1979 as a whole, about 150 in total, who included seven marketing or advertising executives (all Conservatives), three television presenters (one Labour, two Conservatives) and nine whose working life largely or wholly consisted of employment by a political party, by a member of Parliament or by a minister. By 2010, these trends had firmed up, so that, in the new intake of that year, a

---

[20] *Royal Commission on Legal Services* (Cmnd 7648-1, 1979/80) (Benson Committee) Final report, vol 2, 46. There were also 3000 barristers 'employed or abroad' – not only a suspiciously round number but incapable of being compared with later figures, which give the number of employed barristers but not the number practising in another country.

[21] Bar Council Statistics www.barcouncil.org.uk/about-the-bar/facts-and-figures/statistics/#AllBarStats and Law Society, *Trends in the Solicitors' Profession Annual Statistical Report 2010*.

[22] Calculated from Labour Force Survey data available from the UK Office of National Statistics (ONS) (series MGSF). These figures are slight underestimates since they count lawyers in only England and Wales.

[23] Calculated from UK Workforce data, available from ONS (series JWS9).

[24] Calculated from UK Workforce data, available from ONS (series JWS6 and JWS7).

record 232, 41 (17.7 per cent) reported that they had worked in public relations, marketing or advertising – far more than all the lawyers in the new class.[25] A similar number, 39 (16.8 per cent), reported that they had been employed by a political party, for example in its Research Department or as a full-time agent. In addition, 57 (24.6 per cent) – more than four times the proportion of barristers – had worked for a politician as a special adviser, researcher or assistant, and 50 (21.6 per cent) had worked in lobbying ('public affairs'), political campaigning or as a political or national officer of a trade union.[26] If one takes a broad view, 27.6 per cent of the class of 2010 had worked in some capacity in media-related jobs (PR, marketing, advertising, journalism, TV and radio production, management of media companies and acting as a press officer) and 45.3 per cent in politics broadly defined (employed by a party, special advisers, researchers, members of the European Parliament and devolved assemblies, employees of political think-tanks and denizens of the world of quangos and politically appointed government jobs).[27] Some lawyer-MPs had also worked in such jobs, but 60 per cent had not.

IV THE PRODUCTION OF MPS

The replacement of barristers by others, especially by media and political professionals, raises further questions about both politics and lawyers. To understand what is happening we need to look more closely at how MPs are produced.

The process can be conceived of as a set of filters. We begin with the entire eligible population. The first filter is that some of that population, but not others, offer themselves for acceptance by a political party on its list of approved candidates.[28] The second filter is that, of those who offer themselves, some succeed and some fail in gaining approval by a party at national level.[29] The third filter is selection as a prospective candidate by a particular constituency. Finally the electorate has its say. Some selected candidates win a seat in the Commons and some do not.

---

[25] These counts are also drawn from *Who's Who* and *Dods.* They differ from those used by Podmore and McGuinness in one very important respect. Their counts are based on the Nuffield General Election Studies, which took the view that MPs could be classified according to a single prior occupation or group of occupations. If one reads the CVs of more recent MPs, however, it quickly becomes clear that the idea of a single prior 'vocation' is untenable. The same person might have worked as an MP's researcher, in public relations and in finance or have served in the army and then become a journalist and a lobbyist. The best way to preserve the full richness of the data is to let the MPs speak for themselves, so that any job they consider important enough to mention in *Who's Who* or *Dods,* as long as it is not plainly a voluntary position, is here taken as worth counting. *cf* P Cairney, 'The Professionalisation of MPs: Refining the "Politics-Facilitating" Explanation' (2007) 60 *Parliamentary Affairs* 2, 212–33 (adopting a similar multi-occupation approach). The result, however, is that the counts are not necessarily cumulative,

[26] Counting trade union officials has created some difficulty in the literature about MPs' backgrounds. See eg Cairney (n 25). The answer depends on the purpose of the study. If, as here, one wants to distinguish political from non-political jobs, only those officials whose jobs included lobbying or campaigning should count. If, however, the purpose is broader, a different approach might be appropriate.

[27] That figure rises to over 50% if one includes the rather elusive category of full-time local councillors – those who have lived off their allowances as elected officials without any other visible, or at least plausible, means of support.

[28] The processes adopted by the three main parties in the period were essentially similar. See P Norris and J Lovenduski, *Political Recruitment: Gender, Race and Class in the British Parliament* (Cambridge, Cambridge University Press, 1995) and Rhys Williams and Akash Paun, *Party People: How Do – and How Should – British Political Parties Select their Parliamentary Candidates?* (London, Institute for Government, 2011).

[29] This part of the process is now effectively both authorised and required by ss 22 and 24 of the Political Parties and Referendums Act 2000 (requiring political parties to appoint nominating officers and disqualifying election nominations from party candidates not endorsed by that officer).

The filtering process can be conceived of as a string of conditional probabilities: what is the probability of putting oneself forward given that one is eligible? What is the probability of being approved nationally given that one has put oneself forward? What is the probability of being selected for a seat given that one has been approved? And finally, what is the probability of being elected given that one has been selected?

One way of further breaking down the process is to distinguish between processes relevant to the 'supply' of candidates and those relevant to the 'demand' for them.[30] Supply-side explanations focus on why participation in politics is easier – in a sense of being less costly – for some people than others. This is not just a matter of opportunity cost – the difference between what people can earn in their occupations and what they can earn in politics. It is also a matter of differences in what might be thought of as the costs of production. One such cost is the cost of searching for political opportunities. Researchers, special advisers and party employees are, for example, better placed than outsiders to know whether incumbents are deciding to stand down. Another is the cost of commitment to a political career, including the ability to continue with one's outside career while in office and to return to it without much penalty if the electorate decides to interrupt one's political career. Conventionally that category is thought to include lawyers, who are believed to be, unlike for example production managers in factories, far from indispensable to the working lives of others, so that they can take time out of their careers, or out of their working day, to pursue political projects. Another part of that type of cost is the cost of training oneself or acquiring skills. If one can acquire skills relevant to politics in the course of training for another job, one faces much lower costs of acquiring those skills if one moves to a political career. Even better, if one continues to use those skills in politics, the costs of returning to the outside career will also be lower. Public relations practitioners, for example, acquire skills highly relevant to politics and then continue to exercise skills relevant to public relations when they are in politics.

Supply decisions occur at every stage. Eligible people must decide whether to offer themselves; after being approved, a candidate must decide whether to bear the cost of fighting a local selection battle; after being selected, a candidate must decide whether to contest the election; and after being elected, the candidate must decide whether to serve. But since normally anyone elected will serve and nearly everyone selected will contest the seat, supply considerations are usually thought of as applying only to the first two stages – coming forward in the first place and fighting local selection battles.

Demand-side explanations focus on the relative attractiveness of candidates to those who decide who should become members of Parliament. That means, roughly, three groups of people: members of national party committees or national party officials who control the approved lists; the local 'selectorates' (which vary enormously from party to party, and even, since the Conservatives started to experiment with primary elections, within parties); and, finally, the electorate at large. The first two groups have incentives to authorise or select candidates for whom the third group, the electorate, will vote, but

---

[30] See eg Norris and Lovenduski (n 28) 14ff and 'If Only More Candidates Came Forward': Supply Side Explanations of Candidate Selection in Britain' (1993) 23(3) *British Journal of Political Science* 373, 408. See also Cairney (n 25). These writers further distinguish between 'brokerage' and 'instrumental' occupations, both of which are said to 'facilitate' politics, but in different ways – the former giving better chances for time off to do politics and the latter providing 'stepping stones' in political careers. That distinction, however, conflates supply-side and demand-side advantages. Furthermore, the advantages of a 'politics-facilitating' occupation might appear at some stages and disappear at others. These terms are thus somewhat confusing and are not used here.

electability is not their only concern. The national party will also want candidates who will cause no trouble for the leadership if elected, who, as a group, rather than individually, will give the right impression of the party (for example in terms of gender and ethnicity) and who might effectively fulfil national roles, such as minister or shadow minister. The local selectorate might include those for whom ideological concerns, or concerns about securing the seat for a member of a particular interest group – such as a trade union – might weigh more importantly than the attractiveness of the candidate to the electorate.

Every factor is subject to change, both on the supply side and the demand side. To switch the analogy from economics to ecology, the process is similar to natural selection, in which the environment affects the chances that particular characteristics of organisms will survive. Changes in the environment can alter the chances that a characteristic is favoured or disfavoured.

V LAWYERS IN THE PRODUCTION PROCESS

What do we know about how lawyers as a group fare at the various stages of the filtering process? We know less and less the further back we go. We know far more about election than selection, more about selection than national approval and more about national approval than about those who offer themselves for approval. It might be argued that we should start as far back as possible, since the output of each filter constitutes the input for the next filter and the conditional probabilities are conditional on all the previous stages. But it also makes sense to move from what we do know to what we do not. We therefore start with the final stage, election.

A Lawyers in Elections

The data we have about the professions of candidates and whether they succeeded in being elected have been compiled over the decades by Byron Criddle for the Nuffield British General Election series. Podmore found that from 1950 to 1974, lawyers of both the Labour and Conservative parties had a better than evens chance of being elected.[31] That pattern seems largely to have continued. In every election since 1974 except one, lawyers have had a better chance of being elected than candidates as a whole.[32] The exception is 1997, which was a bad year for lawyers in many ways.

But what of the difference between barristers and solicitors? We can also calculate for each election the chance a barrister would be elected, the chance a solicitor would be elected and the chance any candidate would be elected. Using those probabilities we can further calculate by how much the chance of a barrister and the chance of a solicitor being elected differed from the chance of any selected candidate being elected. The results for the most relevant period can be seen in Figure 3.

---

[31] Podmore (n10) 160–62.
[32] Author's own calculations from Criddle's data.

Figure 3: Barristers and solicitors election chances 1974–2010

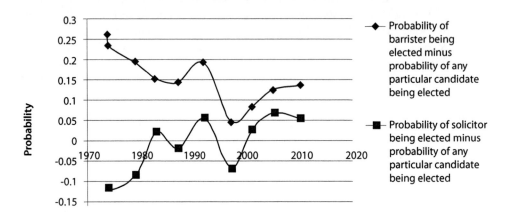

Source: Author's own calculations from data collected by Byron Criddle for the Nuffield General Election Series 1974–2010 .

The electorate maintained a positive view of barristers throughout the whole period, in the sense that the probability of a barrister being elected was always higher than the probability of the average candidate being elected. The position for solicitors was different. Until 1983, solicitors lagged behind the average candidate and fell behind again in 1987 and in 1997 (a year in which the chance of both kinds of lawyer fell sharply but that of barristers fell slightly more than that of solicitors). Although no statistically significant difference between the parties emerges, Conservative lawyers of both types fared better than Conservative candidates as a whole in every election in the period, whereas Labour's barristers fell behind Labour's average on three occasions (1997, 2001 and 2005) and their solicitors lagged the party's candidates as a whole in a majority of the elections from 1974 to 2010.

We can also calculate the gap between the chance of a barrister being elected and the chance of a solicitor being elected. The result for the most relevant period can be seen in Figure 4. Although the chance that a barrister would be elected exceeded the chance that a solicitor would be elected for the whole of the relevant period, the gap between the two narrowed considerably.[33]

Conventional wisdom among political scientists is that, apart perhaps from incumbency and some social characteristics, the nature of the candidate makes very little difference to election results.[34] But that conventional wisdom should perhaps be reconsidered. The success rate of barristers was statistically significantly higher than the success rate of solicitors

---

[33]   As a linear fit, y = -0.0083x + 16.618. R² = 0.7996. Usual caveats apply.

[34]   See eg B Criddle, 'Candidates' in David Butler and Dennis Kavanagh, *British General Election of 1987* (Basingstoke, Macmilllan, 1988). Incumbency and small effects around gender, race and ideology were observed in eg Pippa Norris, Elizabeth Vallance and Joni Lovenduski, 'Do Candidates Make a Difference? Gender, Race, Ideology and Incumbency' (1992) 45(4) *Parliamentary Affairs* 496–517, but even incumbency advantages have been doubted: see Brian Gaines, 'The Impersonal Vote? Constituency Service and Incumbency Advantage in British Elections 1950-92' (1998) 23(2) *Legislative Studies Quarterly* 167–95. Growing variation in results in different constituencies, however, provides evidence that local campaigning has some significance.

Figure 4: Difference between the probability of election of barristers and solicitors 1974–2010

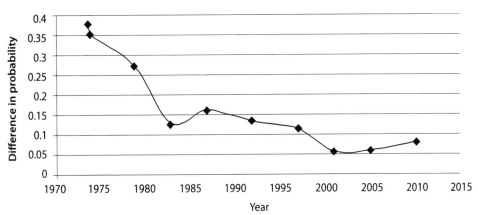

Source: See Figure 3.

in the 1970s and 1980s, but ceased to be so in later decades.[35] At the very least we can say that whether a candidate was a barrister as opposed to a solicitor made a difference in the 1970s and 1980s and that whatever caused that difference no longer applies.[36]

Less clear is how and why. Research in the area of candidate efficacy is in its infancy – largely because of the conventional wisdom that candidates make little difference. A positive relationship has emerged, however, between electoral success and some measures of candidate quality. In particular Silvester and Dykes have found that scoring highly in a critical thinking test predicts a better result, in terms not just of percentage vote (which might be the result of selection for better seats rather than better election performance) but also in terms of swing.[37] The mechanism might not, of course, be that the electorate directly perceives the candidate's superior intellectual powers. Instead the ability to think critically might allow the candidate to make good decisions about campaign messages and resource deployment. However the process works, the result suggests that one reason for the gap closing between barristers and solicitors is that the two branches of the profession have converged in terms of their members' intellectual abilities.

Another possibility, albeit one for which less evidence exists, is that the electorate has become less deferential, and thus less likely to see any difference between the higher status branch of the profession and the lower.[38] Another is, more simply, that solicitors, especially those in the City, gained prestige from the rise of their clients in financial services, a

---

[35] Taking $p<0.05$ (two-tailed) as the criterion, the differences are statistically significant in every election from February 1974 until 1987 and not significant in every subsequent election.

[36] Absence of significance is not the same as significance of absence, but given the clear downward trend of the difference (p(trend) on a runs test=0.0266) we can be reasonably confident that something has happened.

[37] J Silvester and C Dykes, 'Selecting Political Candidates: A Longitudinal Study of Assessment Centre Performance and Political Success in the 2005 UK General Election' (2007) 80 (1) *Journal of Occupational and Organizational Psychology* 11–25.

[38] A decline in social deference in Britain is often asserted (see eg David Cannadine, *Class in Britain* (London, Penguin 2000) ch 4 Parts III and IV) but, rather like Samuel Beer's claims about a populist revolt, the evidence seems impressionistic.

gain in which barristers, associated in the public mind mostly with criminal trials, failed to share.

Figure 4 contains another important point. Barristers' chances always exceeded those of solicitors. That means that one cannot explain the whole of the turnaround between the two branches of the profession by these changes alone. For that we need to look at the previous stages.

B Lawyers in Selections

Political scientists tend now to play down demand-side factors in explaining the composition of the House of Commons not just in elections, where the process is largely demand-side, but also in selections, where some combination of demand and supply factors operate. For example, Norris and Lovenduski, who studied a large sample of non-incumbent candidates for the 1992 general election, concluded that party selectorates 'did not choose candidates on the basis of education, social class, trade-union membership, financial resources, ambition or support networks', and any bias about occupation could be explained by supply-side factors alone.[39] The sample they collected, however, identified a number of barristers and solicitors and it is possible to make some further calculations that suggest that demand-side effects should not be ruled out. With regard to barristers, Norris and Lovenduski's data imply that, confining ourselves to the Labour and Conservative parties,[40] the chance of a barrister being selected to fight a seat having been approved as a potential candidate at national level was 53.3 per cent, whereas the chance of a solicitor being selected to fight a seat having been approved at national level was 40.1 per cent. The probability of any nationally approved Labour or Conservative candidate, lawyer or not, being selected to fight a seat was 43.8 per cent.[41] Since the sample picked up very few lawyers on the Labour side, we should also record the probabilities for Conservatives alone: the chance of being selected given that one was a Conservative barrister was 60.2 per cent, of being selected given that one was a Conservative solicitor was 46.6 per cent, and of any approved Conservative being selected was 49.5 per cent.

[39] P Norris and J Lovenduski, '"If Only More Candidates Came Forward": Supply-Side Explanations of Candidate Selection in Britain' (1993) 23(3) *British Journal of Political Science* 373–408, 405–06.

[40] Norris and Lovenduski's data includes other parties' selected candidates, but, unfortunately, only Labour and Conservative Party candidates who were not selected. The analysis therefore has to be confined to the candidates of those two parties. The data are published at www.esds.ac.uk/.

[41] The derivation of these probabilities depends on Bayes' Theorem, namely:

$$p(A|X) = \frac{p(X|A)^*p(A)}{p(X|A)^*p(A) + p(X|{\sim}A)^*p({\sim}A)}$$

That is, we are looking for the probability of being selected given that one is a barrister or given that one is a solicitor $(p(A \mid X))$. We can infer the probability of being selected or not selected overall $(p(A)$ and $p({\sim}A))$ from Norris and Lovenduski (1993) 377 and 408. On p 377 they give the number of candidates each party eventually selected. On p 408 they say that they chose 656 names of unselected applicants by adding one in three from the Labour lists of such candidates to one in two from the equivalent Conservative list. If we assume that the intention was to identify the same number from each party, we can infer from this the total number of unselected candidates, and thus the probability of being selected. We can establish the probabilities of being a barrister or a solicitor given that one has been selected $(p(X \mid A))$ by observing the number of barristers and solicitors who appear in Norris and Lovenduski's sample of selected Labour and Conservative candidates. Finally, we can establish the probabilities of being a barrister or a solicitor given that one has not been selected $(p(X \mid {\sim}A))$ by observing how many barristers and solicitors appear among Norris and Lovenduski's sample of approved but non-selected candidates.

Can we dismiss these differences by reference to supply-side factors? The only supply-side factors relevant to candidate selection itself are those that affect a candidate's willingness to campaign in the selection battle, such as job flexibility and dispensability, and not broader factors that might affect willingness to come forward at an earlier stage. One can see how a junior barrister with a failing practice might have more time on his or her hands to devote to campaigning than an overworked City of London solicitor, but nearly all the solicitors in Norris and Lovenduski's samples, both the successful and the unsuccessful, describe themselves as 'self-employed' or 'partners' in their firms, and one suspects they would have enjoyed no less flexibility than barristers. One possibility is that younger barristers have less to lose by taking time off since their earning power is not very high and possibly less than solicitors of the same age, a situation that reverses itself as both groups age, but in Norris and Lovenduski's data, the average age of selected barristers is if anything slightly higher than that of unselected barristers, and only marginally higher than that of selected solicitors.

Another theory might be disposed of at this point. Was the bias towards barristers confined to safe seats? If so, it might explain some of the differential electoral success of barristers. Selectorates might, for example, consider barristers good prospective MPs but less good campaigners. In Norris and Lovenduski's sample, however, there was no significant difference in the proportion of barristers selected in seats candidates thought they would win easily and seats candidates judged to be close or where the situation was unclear.[42] Again we have no time series to help us understand what happened previously. Subsequently, however, we know, for example, that in 2010 barristers were selected for 5.6 per cent of the safe seats open to new candidates and 8.0 per cent of the successful marginals.[43] The selectorate's bias in favour of barristers does not come from any obvious differential preference for them in safe seats.

The main puzzle of these results is how they accord with a decline in the number of barristers in the Commons. The idea, for example, that Margaret Thatcher's Conservative Party moved against 'posh' candidates such as barristers is not borne out by a finding that just after her retirement local parties were far more likely to select a barrister than a solicitor.[44] Norris and Lovenduski themselves report remarks by Conservative regional agents to the effect that local parties (under the agents' guidance) would begin by ruling out 'London barristers' only in the end to select one,[45] which might indicate anti-barrister pressure from the national party not working. Unfortunately, we have no comparable data about selection for the period preceding 1991 and data for subsequent periods seem publicly unavailable.[46] Were local parties perhaps even more favourable to barristers in the preceding years? One untested possibility is that selectorates reflect electoral success but with considerable lags, so that a decline in barristers' electoral appeal beginning in the 1970s (and the improvement of that of solicitors) would only show up in selections later.

We should particularly notice something in the data about the Labour Party. Very few barristers appeared on the Labour side in 1991–92 (only 1.5 per cent of Labour's selected

---

[42] In 'win easily' seats, 5.2% of the candidates were barristers, in other seats, 5.4%. There was also no difference for solicitors.

[43] Based on the Electoral Reform Society's classification of safe seats published online by *The Guardian* www.guardian.co.uk/news/datablog/2010/apr/07/election-safe-seats-electoral-reform.

[44] See eg Eric Evans, *Thatcher and Thatcherism* (London, Routledge, 2004) 49.

[45] Norris and Lovenduski (n 28) 43.

[46] The British Representation Studies of, for example, 1997, 2001, 2005 and 2010.

non-incumbent candidates and none of the sample of non-selected candidates). It is entirely possible that Labour selectorates took a very different view of barristers in the immediately preceding period from that of Conservative selectorates. Although we cannot rule out the possibility that there was an equivalent fall in the number of barristers coming forward for selection, so that the rate of selection of barristers might not itself have fallen, some effect at the level of constituency parties is not implausible. In support of that hypothesis, we also know that during that period the Labour Party was experiencing considerable conflict at constituency level between the party establishment and various leftist factions, including the Militant Tendency.[47] One of themes of Militant was workerism, the belief that political virtue lies exclusively in members of the working class and that intellectuals are not to be trusted.[48] When we see in 1979 a number of Labour barristers being replaced on their retirement by trade union officials, we might be seeing the first fruits of such developments. One might further speculate that solicitors, especially those with union connections, might have been less adversely affected.

C Lawyers in Approval Systems

The stage before selection is gaining entry to a party's national list of approved candidates. This is an important stage, although precisely how important is not entirely clear. Norris and Lovenduski estimated that in the Conservative Party about 750 to 800 candidates were approved out of 2000 applicants.[49] Another indication is that out of the 415 applicants who attended the assessments observed by Silvester and Dykes, only 106 went on to be candidates, although that number fails to include those approved but not selected. We lack data not only about the probability for all candidates of getting through a national assessment but also about the characteristics of those who succeed and those who fail.

We do, however, possess evidence about the criteria the parties now use, which may or may not indicate the criteria used previously. The Conservatives and Liberal Democrats have similar lists of characteristics desirable in a parliamentary candidate.[50] Both require communication skills across a wide variety of media, leadership qualities, including the capacity to motivate others, intellectual skills (called 'strategic thinking and judgment' by the Liberal Democrats), resilience, being able to relate to different kinds of people and, of course, political commitment to the values of the party and the ability to convey political convictions.[51] These criteria have been generated and formalised in the last decade, as the parties professionalised their assessment processes,[52] although they might have become important earlier.

Several of these national criteria disadvantage lawyers, especially barristers. We might allow that lawyers have intellectual skills and some might be resilient, but motivating teams

---

[47] See eg Norris and Lovenduski (n 28) 67–68. The number of de-selections was small, but that does not rule out considerable leftist influence over the selection of new candidates.

[48] See eg John Callaghan, 'The Politics of the Militant Tendency' (1982) (August) *Marxism Today* 18, 19. Other leftist factions active in constituencies have attracted the label 'workerist', for example Labour Briefing (see eg Leo Panitch and Colin Leys, *The End of Parliamentary Socialism: From New Left to New Labour* (London, Verso, 2001) 343).

[49] Norris and Lovenduski (n 39) 377.

[50] J Silvester, 'Recruiting Politicians: Designing Competency Based Selection for UK Parliamentary Candidates' in A Weinberg (ed), *The Psychology of Politicians* (Cambridge, Cambridge University Press, 2012).

[51] Labour's criteria seem similar. See Williams and Paun (n 28) 32.

[52] See Silvester (n 50) and Williams and Paun (n 28).

and being able to relate to different kinds of people are not obviously strong suits for barristers (although solicitors might do better). As for communications skills, barristers' proficiency at oral presentation might be an advantage, but only in the traditional context of a formal speech. In the television and radio studio, very different standards of rhetoric apply. As for written communication skills, lawyers of both kinds are unlikely to excel at writing pithy political leaflets or headline grabbing press releases. More generally, modern political communication is increasingly done in pictures – on TV, on YouTube, in photographs – a world as alien to the discursive world of lawyering as it is familiar to the world of PR, marketing and advertising.

D Lawyers Entering Politics

Finally we reach the start of the process, the flow of citizens into politics. This is fundamentally a supply-side question about which we have little direct evidence. One can say, however, that, given the great increases in the numbers of both barristers and solicitors, if lawyers' propensity to enter politics had merely remained the same, a much larger number of lawyers would have been presenting themselves for national approval as candidates. Since those who study these processes fail to mention the parties being overwhelmed by lawyer applicants, we might reasonably suspect that no such increase has happened, so that some decline in the propensity of lawyers to offer themselves must have occurred. How big that decline is, however, cannot easily be estimated.

One supply-side factor we can probably exclude, however, is change in the relative earnings of barristers and MPs. The Benson Committee found that in 1976, the median barrister earned £8,715 per year net (that is after costs such as Chambers rent), which was 143 per cent of the salary of MPs at that time (£6,062).[53] In 2012 the Bar Council, in an internal consultation document, estimated median earnings before costs as under £100,000.[54] The Jackson Review of Civil Costs estimated barristers' costs around the same time as in the range of 13–15 per cent, rather lower than the 34 per cent found by the Benson Committee.[55] Applying the minimum figure for costs, in 2012 the median barrister was earning 132 per cent of an MP's salary, 11 percentage points less than in the 1970s.[56]

Another possibility is that the relative non-pay benefits of law and politics have changed. In particular, at a time when members of Parliament are despised, one might wonder why members of any respectable profession should enter politics. Both legal professions provide high status jobs whereas members of Parliament are treated as lower than vermin. The problem with this as an explanation of the decline in the number of barristers in the Commons, however, is that little evidence exists that the situation has changed across the relevant period. In 1983, a MORI poll found that 18 per cent of the electorate trusted MPs

---

[53] Benson Committee (1978/80) Final Report vol 2, 590.

[54] Stephen Collier, *Practising Certificate Fee Consultation* (London, Bar Council, 2012) 4.

[55] Rupert Jackson, *Review of Civil Litigation Costs: Preliminary Report* (London, The Stationery Office, 2009) vol 1, 84.

[56] Finding equivalent figures for solicitors is difficult. The Benson Committee gave no global figure for solicitors' earnings, estimating median net profits per partner at £11,686 (vol 2, 507) and the median salary of other qualified lawyers at £4,346 (p 505). It also estimated there to be 2.5 times more partners than other lawyers, which implies an overall median similar to that of barristers, a surprising result. In 2007, when, incidentally, the ratio of partners to other lawyers had precisely reversed itself, the Law Society said that the median was £50,000 (ie 81% of an MP's salary at the time). See Jackson, *Preliminary Report* (n 55) 79–80.

to tell the truth, a figure that drifted up to 22 per cent in 2004 before falling to its post-expenses crisis level of 13–14 per cent. That is not massively less than its 1980s levels. Although we have no equivalent series for lawyers, we do have a proxy, namely judges, trust in whom to tell the truth, albeit much higher than for MPs (in the high 70s), has also not moved since the early 80s.[57]

Another supply-side possibility is that barristers might have found more difficulty in combining service as an MP with continuing to practice. Some point, for example, to changes in the House of Commons' hours. The Commons used to sit every day except Fridays (which were for private members' business only) at 2.30pm with the main debate starting no earlier than 3.30pm. That allowed barristers to devote a full day in court before repairing to the House. The House now sits regularly in the morning, starting between 9.30 and 11.30 on all days except Mondays. The trouble with this explanation, however, is that, apart from an experiment of holding debates without votes on Wednesday mornings, which ran from 1995 to 1999,[58] no major changes to the hours of the House occurred between 1974 and 1999, the period of the dramatic fall in the proportion of barristers. In fact, no major change in hours occurred until 2003,[59] after which, paradoxically, the proportion of barristers in the House rose a little.

Search costs are also unlikely to provide an explanation. If large numbers of MPs continue to practice as barristers, information about political opportunities might conceivably be imparted in the margins of legal activity – in the corridors of the courts and at dinners of the Inns of Court, for example – and if barristers' numbers decline, so would that flow of information. But that increase in search costs would be a consequence of the fall in barristers' numbers, not a cause of it. As for dispensability, one might plausibly claim that barristers' work has become more connected with the requirements of business and less arranged solely for the convenience of barristers themselves. The difficulty is that such changes occurred even more markedly for solicitors. Similarly, the growth of the legal sector might plausibly have given rise to greater specialisation so that diversifying into politics might be seen not just as unnecessary but also as positively harmful to one's legal career. The problem is that barristers and solicitors would have been equally affected by increasing specialisation.

A related explanation, however, might have more traction. Perhaps the problem in the supply of barristers to the House of Commons lies not so much in the acquisition of legal skills as in their maintenance. For practitioners of PR or marketing, and even more for political professionals, politics contains opportunities to exercise professional skills, but is the same still true for barristers? If we assume that barristers ply their trade mostly in the courts, the question arises as to whether barrister-MPs can use opportunities in their life as MPs to maintain their court-room skills. The answer is not as obvious as some might think. Barristers have two modes of argument: one, their usual one, is for judges; the other, used more rarely and increasingly only by specialists, is for juries. The former assumes a shared technical vocabulary with the judge and a shared set of standard techniques. The latter assumes that listeners are passive recipients of arguments they will only hear once. Neither

---

[57] IPSOS-MORI Research Archive. We also know from a different IPSOS-MORI poll running from the late 1990s to the early 2000s that results for judges and lawyers differ little on the question 'how satisfied are you with the way the following are doing their job?' (The proportion of the electorate 'very dissatisfied' with parliamentarians was 16% and 3.5% for lawyers).

[58] HC Library Research Paper 02/41, 23–26.

[59] HC Library Standard Note SN/PC/06380 (18 July 2012) 6.

of these situations obtains in the House of Commons. Barristers in their 'legal' mode usually strike the House as narrow and largely irrelevant, but in their 'jury' mode they can be easily undermined by the tendency of the Commons to answer back, to challenge and to remember the member's previous speeches. Moreover, even if parliamentary speeches were good practice for court, an MP's life is less and less about speeches. In 2011, a survey of new MPs suggested that they spend only a fifth of their time in the Chamber.[60] Half of their time, about 35 hours a week, is spent on constituency business. That was not the situation in the early 1970s, when the estimate for the time taken by MPs on constituency work was 11 hours.[61] The mass of a modern MP's work thus offers little to barristers hoping to combine political activity with maintaining legal skills. In contrast, solicitors might find that they can practice some of their professional skills concurrently while serving as MPs, especially extracting relevant information from lay people who do not understand the rules of the system, interacting with recalcitrant bureaucracies and maintaining contact with potential clients.

Some evidence of the problem of skill maintenance, though not from the most relevant period and pertaining as much to solicitors as to barristers, is visible in what happens when lawyer MPs lose their seats. If one looks, for example, at the 20 lawyers who left the House of Commons in 2010, there are certainly some who were able to return to full-time legal practice – notably Douglas Hogg and Bob Marshall-Andrews, barristers practising mainly criminal law, both of whom had continued to take cases while serving in the Commons. One or two, including the former Solicitor-General Mike O'Brien, even launched new legal careers. But most did not return to the law. Some quickly returned to electoral politics, as London Assembly members or Police and Crime Commissioners. Others took jobs in political campaigning or lobbying – for example one became Chief Executive Officer of the Independent Pharmacists' Federation, another Head of Policy at the Chartered Institute of Environmental Health. Others still, usually those who had attained high office, took business jobs. But some took quite humble roles, for example as a regional organiser for a trade union or a visiting lecturer in politics, roles much less remunerative than practising law. Another perhaps longer term indicator is whether law firms show that they value political experience by recruiting solicitors who are former MPs. One might expect political experience to be very highly valued, especially in the large City firms, given that many of them devote considerable resources to influencing legislation on their clients' behalf. In the London 'Magic Circle' firms, however, it is very difficult to find a single partner who used to be a member of the UK Parliament. One or two former members of other legislatures (the Belgian Senate, for example, or the Landtag of Bavaria) appear in the lists of partners or consultants in offices elsewhere, but at their London offices, political experience seems not to be prized at all.

Another supply-side factor might have been important, namely access to judgeships. If one looks at the current UK higher judiciary, only one, Ross Cranston, is a former MP. It is difficult to find many judges who will confess publicly, in their *Who's Who* entry, to any kind of previous political career. Two confess to having stood for Parliament, one served as a Belfast City Councillor, and two retired members of the Court of Appeal served as district councillors in the 1960s. Otherwise, the judiciary is a politics-free zone, or at least wants to portray itself as such.

---

[60] Hansard Society, *A Year in the Life* (Hansard Society, 2011).
[61] See Philip Norton, 'The Growth of the Constituency Role of the MP' (1994) 47 *Parliamentary Affairs* 705–20, 711–12 and P Norton and D Wood, 'Constituency Service by Members of Parliament: Does it Contribute to a Personal Vote?' (1990) 43 *Parliamentary Affairs* 196–208, 199.

In past decades, it was perfectly possible for members of Parliament to be plucked from their political careers and appointed directly to the judicial bench. There was a recognised convention, for example, that if the post of Lord Chief Justice of the King's Bench became vacant, the job would be offered to the Attorney-General of the day (by the nineteenth century a political appointee chosen almost invariably from among sitting MPs).[62] Between the 1830s and the 1960s, more than 100 MPs resigned their seats to take up immediate high judicial office, without counting those who left the Commons to become Lord Chancellor.[63] They include some well-known judicial figures. George Jessel was the member for Dover on his appointment as Master of the Rolls in 1873. The first Lord Russell of Killowen was the member for Hackney South on his appointment as a Law Lord and Lord Chief Justice in 1894. Others include HH Cozens-Hardy, Gordon Hewart, William Watson (Lord Thankerton), James Reid, Terence Donovan, JT Wheatley and Jocelyn Simon.[64]

Since 1962, however, there have been no appointments of sitting members of Parliament directly to the higher judiciary. The last such elevation was that of the Labour MP Lynn Ungoed-Thomas (Donovan's successor as member for Leicester North-East) to the Chancery Division. The nearest since then was the elevation of Ronald King Murray to the Court of Session very soon after his retirement as the member for Edinburgh, Leith at the general election of 1979.

The immediate causes of the decline in judicial appointments from the House of Commons are not entirely clear. They cannot include, as is sometimes suggested, that the quality of judges chosen from the Commons was unsatisfactory. The list includes some of the most esteemed judges of the twentieth century, especially Lord Reid. Two more theories were proposed by Lord Bingham: the increased difficulty of combining high level careers in both representative politics and the law and the introduction of apolitical methods of judicial appointment.[65] The former has some purchase, a result not least of the skill-maintenance problem. The problem with the latter, however, is that, at least in formal terms, it comes too late – the Judicial Appointments Commission was established in 2005, well after the decline set in. The causes might instead have been political, for example that after the Orpington by-election of 1962, a spectacular Liberal victory over the ruling Conservatives, all reasons for voluntary by-elections became less acceptable, or they might have been ideological – a growing concern that the judiciary should be seen to be outside politics, particularly after the revival of judicial review of administrative action following the cases of *Ridge v Baldwin* in 1964 and *Padfield v Minister of Agriculture, Fisheries and Food* in 1968.[66]

---

[62] The convention was well-known enough that in 1913 it caused a serious political problem. Just after the Marconi Scandal, in which the incumbent Attorney-General, Rufus Isaacs, had been embroiled, Viscount Alverstone (himself previously an MP and Attorney-General) retired from the Lord Chief Justiceship. Isaacs wanted to continue in politics, but Asquith believed that if Isaacs were not appointed to the Bench, public opinion would conclude that Asquith suspected Isaacs of impropriety. Isaacs was therefore elevated, and his political career ground, temporarily, to a halt. See Dennis Judd, *Lord Reading* (London, Weidenfeld and Nicolson, 1982).

[63] I am grateful to Eve Samson for letting me have the fruits of her research into this question. The original list was prepared, at her suggestion, by Andrew Parker and Richard Kelly of the House of Commons Library.

[64] All three main parties provide examples: Jessel, Russell, Cozens-Hardy and Hewart were Liberals, Watson, Reid and Simon Conservatives, and Donovan and Wheatley Labour members. Moreover, governments of all three parties made such appointments, and they did not always appoint members of their own party – for example Reid was appointed by a Labour government.

[65] See Tom Bingham, 'The Law Lords: Who Has Served?' in Louis Blom-Cooper, Brice Dickson and Gavin Drewry, *The Judicial House of Lords: 1876-2009* (Oxford, Oxford University Press, 2009) 122–27, 125.

[66] *Ridge v Baldwin* [1964] AC 40, *Padfield v Ministry of Agriculture, Fisheries and Food* [1968] AC 997.

The possibility of a judgeship would have been an incentive for barristers to become MPs, effectively a reduction in the cost of serving in the Commons, or an increase in its rewards. Those incentives have now disappeared. Indeed, political experience seems to have become a positive disadvantage for those seeking senior judicial office. No such problems affected solicitors at the time, since they were largely ineligible for judicial appointment, and even now that solicitors are eligible, the effects are less important in a profession in which judicial appointment is still a rarity and presumably not an important incentive to enter the profession or to excel in it.

VI SUMMARY OF THE CAUSES OF THE DECLINE

The causes of the decline of lawyers, and in particular the decline of barristers, are not entirely clear. Some of the variation results from the fate election-on-election of the Labour Party, but other explanations are needed for the extent of the fall, especially that of barristers since the 1970s. Contrary to conventional wisdom, strong evidence exists of the importance of demand-side factors, certainly at the level of the electorate, possibly at the level of the selectorate, particularly on the Labour side, and conceivably at the level of the national assessment of candidates. What drove down demand for barristers is itself largely a matter for conjecture, but plausible candidates include a decline in the intellectual superiority of the Bar, a decline in deference (perhaps not shared by the Conservative selectorate), outbreaks of workerism in the Labour Party and a lack of fit between what the parties are looking for in candidates and the skills and attributes typical of barristers, in particular barristers' lack of experience with the media and visual culture and their isolation from much of ordinary life. Less direct evidence exists for supply-side effects, largely because we have little data about the stage at which they are most likely to operate, namely at the initial stage of entering the political world, but there is a plausible problem about whether barristers, unlike PR and marketing practitioners and long-term political professionals, are able to maintain their professional skills while practising politics and another in the closure of the conduit from the Commons to the judicial bench.

VII THE SEPARATION OF LAW AND POLITICS

The decline in the number of lawyers in the Commons constitutes a separation of law and politics. It stands beside more formal examples of such a separation, such as the severance of the Supreme Court from the House of Lords, the transformation of the office of Lord Chancellor from one that combined judge, cabinet minister and legislative presiding officer into one that consists entirely of being a minister and the diminution of the role of ministers in the appointment of judges through the creation of the Judicial Appointments Commission.[67] These developments share with the decline of lawyers in the Commons the characteristic that they involve breaking network connections and heightening personal distance between lawyers and politicians.

---

[67] See Parts 2, 3 and 4 of the Constitutional Reform Act 2005.

The formal part of the process of separation of law and politics rests in part on a conception of the separation of powers, according to which an individual should not exercise judicial power concurrently with executive or legislative power.[68] That conception fails, however, fully to explain the degree of separation now being developed, namely that those who exercise judicial power should never in the past have exercised executive or legislative power. The underlying idea seems to be that politics is a kind of pollution and that anyone involved in it becomes, ipso facto, incapable of objective, non-partisan judgement. One can even plausibly claim that the identification of 'political' with 'untrustworthy' is now part of the law itself. Examples include the exclusion of anyone who has taken part in 'inappropriate' political activity from serving on the Judicial Appointments Commission or any of its panels, or as Judicial Appointments and Conduct Ombudsman.[69] It is perhaps not surprising that involvement in politics counts for many as stigmatising in an era of anti-political populism – the belief that 'the people' are always pure and 'politicians' always corrupt,[70] but it is surprising that its effects should reach so deeply into the legal system that, for example, ex-MPs on the bench are very rare indeed and ex-MPs in the City law firms are non-existent.

Other political changes are important. An increasingly mediatised politics, in which moving images are central, both in their conventional form on television and on the internet, is not the kind of politics in which lawyers are comfortable. Lawyers like clear structures and process. Increasingly, politics rejects both. Political authority rests less on formal structures and more on the ephemera of media reputation and on fame itself.[71] A significant shift came with the appointment as Lord Chancellor of someone who is not only a non-lawyer but is also a former TV producer and a marketing manager for a PR and lobbying organisation. Moreover, policymakers are turning to methods, such as behavioural 'nudges', which might be characterised as 'alegal'; not unlawful but eschewing the use of regulation and independent of specific legal authorisation.

It is also arguably a more lawless politics in other ways. At one stage, political attacks on the judiciary became commonplace.[72] Powerful actors, especially those who work in large media corporations, apparently have come to feel that legal obligation is for other people[73] and those who operate in the new politics of the internet have become convinced that the legal system cannot, and should not, affect them.[74] Alongside declining respect for law lies

---

[68] *cf* Robert Hazell, 'The Continuing Dynamism of Constitutional Reform' (2007) 60(1) *Parliamentary Affairs* (2007) 3–25, 17.

[69] Constitutional Reform Act 2005 s 12(11))(c), schedule 12, para 10(3)(c) and schedule 13, para 1(3)(c).

[70] *cf* Daniele Albertazzi and Duncan McDonnell, 'Introduction: The Sceptre and the Spectre' in Daniele Albertazzi and Duncan McDonnell (eds), *Twenty-First Century Populism The Spectre of Western European Democracy* (London, Palgrave, 2008) 1–11, 3.

[71] See David Howarth, 'In the Theatre State' *Times Literary Supplement*, 11 March 2011 23. See also HC Deb 20 Oct 2009, vol 497 col 828.

[72] See eg Jason Pierce, 'Conflicts with Courts in Common Law Countries' in Bruce Peabody, *The Politics of Judicial Independence: Courts, Politics, and the Public* (Baltimore, JHU Press, 2010). See further Shami Chakrabarti, 'Rights and Rhetoric: The Politics of Asylum and Human Rights Culture in the United Kingdom' (2005) 32(1) *Journal of Law and Society* 131–47.

[73] See Leveson Report (An Inquiry into the Culture, Practices and Ethics of the Press) (London, The Stationery Office, 2012) 719 ('many have also argued that elements of the press in this country have acquired a sense of impunity, of being above the law, because they have become too powerful, their economic and social power having become concentrated into too few hands'). Leveson does not specifically endorse that suggestion but it is difficult to read the preceding section of his Report without concluding that it is correct. See especially media contempt for the law exemplified at 536–37, 591–655, 682–83, 703.

[74] Leveson (n 73) 175. See further Report of the Joint Committee on Privacy and Injunctions (HL Paper 273/HC 1443, 2012) vol 2, 1080 (prominent political blogger declaring he would not obey any privacy law, even if contained in a specific statute).

a tendency in politics to treat legislation itself as a form of press release, for example the legislative creation of unenforceable standards and targets.[75]

Although some lawyers have looked for ways to accommodate their work to these new conditions,[76] many others find this new world unsettling and alien. Lawyers are repelling politics at the same time as politics is repelling lawyers.

VIII CONSEQUENCES AND REMEDIES

In practical terms, a reduction in the number of lawyers in the Commons, or even their complete disappearance, might have a smaller effect on the content of legislation than one might imagine. The Government keeps a very tight grip on the process of legislative drafting.[77] The only effect might be a further weakening of the already somewhat perfunctory control the Commons exercises over what legislation actually says. One can even argue that the replacement of barristers by solicitors might be helpful for the influence of lawyers within the political system, since it might help to shift thinking about law away from the litigation-obsessed world of barristers and towards the more creative, problem-solving world of solicitors.[78] But as part of a wider disengagement between law and politics, the decline of lawyers in Parliament, and the accompanying lack of people with political experience in the legal system, is a seriously disturbing development.

As Lord Bingham commented, specifically in regard to the Supreme Court, but with wider applicability:[79]

> While the independence of the judges is rightly regarded in this country as fundamental, the absence of experience in public administration among members of the highest tribunal must be regretted: its deliberations would be enriched if some of its members had direct personal experience of the democratic and bureaucratic process as of the civil and criminal trial.

That is, it would be helpful if judges understood democracy. One can go further. Courts consisting of lawyers who have never participated in politics risk adopting the very anti-political populism that is helping to create such courts in the first place. In *R v Chaytor*,[80] the case about parliamentary privilege arising out of the expenses crisis, the Supreme Court interpreted the Speaker of the House of Commons' failure to defend the House's exclusive jurisdiction over implementation of its internal spending decisions as evidence that the House accepted that no such jurisdiction could ever exist. No one with the slightest understanding of the state of British politics at the time could have made such a statement. Anyone then appearing to suggest limits to the guilt of MPs would have seen their career instantly terminated by the media. It is risky to interpret silence as consent at the best of times. In these times, it was obtuse. The Court no doubt felt highly satisfied with itself for deciding *Chaytor* in the direction demanded by public opinion, that thieving MPs should not escape justice, but the conclusion that exclusive jurisdiction could never apply in these

---

[75] eg Warm Homes and Energy Conservation Act 2000, Fiscal Responsibility Act 2010, Child Poverty Act 2010 (see further Jill Rutter and William Knighton, *Legislated Policy Targets: Commitment Device, Political Gesture or Constitutional Outrage?* (London, Institute for Government, 2012).

[76] See notably, Stephen Laws, 'Giving Effect to Policy in Legislation: How to Avoid Missing the Point' (2011) 32 *Statute Law Review* 1–16.

[77] See Office of Parliamentary Counsel, *Working with Parliamentary Counsel* (London, Cabinet Office, 2011).

[78] See David Howarth, *Law as Engineering: Thinking About What Lawyers Do* (Cheltenham, Elgar, 2013) 207–09.

[79] Bingham (n 65) 125.

[80] *R v Chaytor* [2010] UKSC 52, [2011] 1 AC 684.

circumstances (as opposed to saying, for example, that it could apply, but could be waived by resolution of the House) constitutes overreaching.

More generally, there is a danger that judges who lack political experience will not understand the deep frustrations democratic politicians feel in the face of the juridification of political problems.[81] Equally, such a judiciary might not correctly identify situations in which intervening in a paralysed political situation would be wise. Many fundamental constitutional problems – including what should lie within the exclusive jurisdiction of the legislature – have no final answer. A politically sophisticated court, as Alexander Bickel pointed out half a century ago, will respond by seeking to keep open a colloquy or dialogue with the other branches.[82] In contrast, a politically unsophisticated court will be in constant danger of prematurely closing off that dialogue.

The problem is most acute in the interpretation of the Human Rights Act. The immense difficulties of amending the European Convention on Human Rights mean that Bickel's 'counter-majoritarian difficulty' is at its zenith. Bingham's own remarks in *R (Ullah) v Secretary of State for the Home Department*[83] that UK courts should 'follow' Strasbourg jurisprudence, not just take it into account, as the Act requires, constitute a case in point. The subsequent scramble to explain them away might not have been necessary had the Court been in a better position to think through their anti-democratic implications.[84]

Just as judges should understand democratic politics, politicians should understand the rule of law. Most lawyers, from their education and training, have at least some insight into the inherent difficulty of the position of the judge – the necessity to decide, the importance of fidelity to law, the hierarchy of authority. Many, including, one would hope, those with reputable law degrees, might even have acquired some respect for the rule of law itself, or at least have intuited the existence of virtues inherent in law as a method of government – the openness of the incentives it creates, its commitment to rationality, its universality. The decline in the number of lawyers in the Commons makes such understanding in politics less likely. Of course, one should not take this too far. Lawyers were, for example, no less likely than other MPs to vote to defy the European Court of Human Rights on the issue of prisoner votes.[85] Moreover, some of the politicians indulging in attacks on the judiciary have themselves been lawyers. But one hopes that a lawyer would not have acted with the brutal disregard for all procedural fairness displayed by Ed Balls, Secretary of State for Children, Schools and Families at the time of the events of *R (Shoesmith) v Ofsted*,[86] when Balls peremptorily ordered the replacement of a senior social services official who had fallen foul of a media campaign to remove her because an infamous child abuse case had fallen within her jurisdiction.

The central point is that if courts and legislatures are to engage in a constructive constitutional dialogue, rather than hurl anathemas at one another, each must understand the world

---

[81] See eg Pierce (n 72), who attributes political attacks on the judiciary to this frustration, although other factors are relevant in British politics, for example anti-Europeanism.

[82] See Alexander Bickel, *The Least Dangerous Branch* (New York, Bobbs-Merrill, 1962), especially ch 4, 'The Passive Virtues'. See also Guido Calabresi, *A Common Law for the Age of Statutes* (Cambridge, Massachusetts, Harvard University Press, 1982) ch 3 and Trevor Allan, 'Constitutional Dialogue and the Justification for Judicial Review' (2003) 23 *Oxford Journal of Legal Studies* 563–84.

[83] *R (Ullah) v Secretary of State for the Home Department* [2004] UKHL 26 [20].

[84] See eg *R v Horncastle (Michael Christopher)* [2009] UKSC 14, [2010] 2 AC 373; *Manchester City Council v Pinnock* [2010] UKSC 45, [2010] 3 WLR 1441; and *Cadder v HM Advocate (Scotland)* [2011] UKSC 43.

[85] See HC Deb 10 Feb 2011,vol 523 col 584–86.

[86] *R (Shoesmith) v Ofsted* [2011] EWCA Civ 642.

as it looks to the other. As those worlds separate, communication and understanding become harder and miscommunication and misunderstanding more likely. Instead of seeing themselves as different parts of the same structure, judges and parliamentarians might come to see themselves as belonging to separate structures: judges in a structure focussed on other judicial bodies such as the European Court of Human Rights and the European Court of Justice; parliamentarians in a structure that contains only other major political actors. Some might see such a development as a positive, or at least an inevitable, consequence of the separation of powers. That view, however, assumes an essentialist view of the separation of powers in which it has no purpose beyond itself, rather than a pragmatic view in which its purpose is either to help government avoid mistakes by requiring dialogue or to preserve liberty by undermining excessive concentrations of power in particular people.

Further separation of law and politics is not, however, inevitable. Some aspects of it are amenable to change through conscious policy-making. For example, we could restore political experience as a positive advantage in judicial appointment, both for its direct effects on the judiciary and for its longer term indirect effects on the supply of lawyers into politics. As for other aspects, although little can be done to affect underlying trends in the nature of politics, we can at least recognise the risks and attempt to mitigate them. One possibility is to create institutions that involve lawyers in politics in new ways, for example a Council of State to review the drafting of legislation before its submission to Parliament. Another is to involve lawyers more in existing political institutions, for example by making legal drafting advice available to opposition and backbench MPs and making it easier for law graduates to enter the civil service not as specialists but in the policy fast stream.

Perhaps the most important long term measure we might take to prevent further separation, however, is an intellectual one, namely to challenge the populist assumption that politics is a form of pollution. Law is not hermetically sealed from politics but instead a specific way of achieving political goals, one that carries with it specific virtues (and some vices). Lack of understanding of law arguably makes a politician technically and morally defective, but lack of political experience in a lawyer makes that lawyer not a purer person but merely a worse lawyer.

4

The Form and Language of Legislation

LORD RODGER OF EARLSFERRY[1]

I T IS NO mere conventional platitude if I say that I greatly appreciate the honour of being elected President of the Holdsworth Club, although I find it daunting to follow so many distinguished predecessors, not least the Master of the Rolls, Lord Woolf. The fact that it is 'the Holdsworth Club' is especially attractive to me, since I have always been interested in history generally and enjoy reading about developments in English Law, especially those which have affected the history of Scots Law.

I intend to discuss the form and language of statutes. What I have to say has been influenced, I suppose, by two aspects of my life, neither of which has much to do with being a judge. The first is that I have spent a long time – many would say much too long a time – studying Roman Law. Now I know that Roman Law is not taught in Birmingham and so I thought it right to warn you straightaway that I shall now mention this forbidden topic. Rest assured, I shall not hand out Roman Law tracts nor actively seek to convert you to the study. I shall not even go into any of its doctrines. My examples will, for the most part, be drawn from current statutes. Nevertheless, I do not disguise the fact that much of what I have to say stems from things which I have noted and which have puzzled me when looking at Roman Law texts. Why such instructive legal materials are now deliberately kept from law students is a mystery. The second experience which has a bearing on my remarks is my time as Solicitor General for Scotland and later as Lord Advocate when I was the minister having formal responsibility of the draftsmen who prepare Scottish legislation.

Though these experiences have helped shape what I have to say, in one sense my interest in the topic really goes back to a remark of Sir Otto Kahn-Freund to a group of Family Law tutors in Oxford more than 25 years ago. It was a time when the law had recently been reformed in a series of statutes, the Family Law Reform Act 1969,[2] the Divorce Reform Act 1969[3] and the Matrimonial Proceedings and Property Act 1970.[4] Under Sir Otto's kindly but watchful eye the tutors were discussing how their tutorials were going. Gradually there

---

[1] This is a revised version of a lecture given on 6 March 1998 at the Faculty of Law, University of Birmingham. I was more than grateful to the members of the Holdsworth Club for their warm welcome on that occasion and for the hospitality shown to me. As so often, I should like to thank the Hon Lord Davidson for reading the text and making a number of suggestions. John McCluskie, QC, Legal Secretary and First Scottish Parliamentary Counsel, and Gregor Clark, Assistant Legal Secretary and Assistant Scottish Parliamentary Counsel, were both kind enough to read the text and make a number of most useful observations which I have taken into account in revising the lecture for publication. The views expressed are my own, however.

[2] Cap 46.
[3] Cap 55.
[4] Cap 45.

emerged a hint that not all were going particularly well. The trouble was that the new legis-lation had resolved many of the old problems which might have been discussed in tutorials and the undergraduates found this nice new polished legislation, well, just a trifle dull and certainly not particularly interesting. At this Kahn-Freund cried out in exasperation, 'But students *should* be interested in legislation!' And so they should. Equally you may say that children *should* like salads and reject burgers and fries, but we know that in practice it is often the other way round. Kahn-Freund, who had been educated in Germany and who had done so much for the study of the codified French Law, found the undergraduates' attitude very disappointing.

And when I say 'the undergraduates' attitude', I should perhaps simply say 'my attitude', for I at least was blaming the undergraduates for what were really my own failings. It was I, of course, who found the material somewhat dull and it was I who yearned for the open spaces of the older law where the accretion of case law to the original statutes meant that there were anomalies to unearth and decisions to distinguish. The plain text of the statutes seemed lifeless by comparison. And I suppose that this has continued to be my attitude. Like so many lawyers I still tend to find the opinions of the judges more interesting than the productions of Parliament.

Partly at least I think this stems from my particular cast of mind, about which I can do little. I have always enjoyed reading stories and waste a huge amount of my time – as one of my judicial colleagues would put it – reading fiction. By contrast, when required to do so, I found little pleasure in studying axioms in geometry. In the same way I understand an area of law better when I read about it in judges' opinions, setting out a story and reasoning based on that story, than when it is set down somewhat clinically in sections and subsec-tions, schedules and paragraphs. Presumably, supporters of codification have the opposite experience.

I INDIVIDUALITY IN DRAFTING

I doubt if this is the complete explanation. Part of the problem seems to me to lie in the fact that statutes are so often discussed in somewhat arid terms. When we study the cases in a common law system we can see doctrines apparently being developed by the judges down the ages. The contributions and styles of individual judges can be identified and assessed. By contrast when we look at Acts of Parliament, we tend to approach them as if they had indeed all been written somewhat mechanically by a body called Parliament which had remained the same and had written in the same way over the years. At the very least, we tend to regard the draftsmen rather as Savigny regarded ancient Roman jurists, as 'fungible persons',[5] ie as persons who all belonged to a group and who were so lacking in individual characteristics as to be virtually interchangeable. That was, of course, not really true for Roman jurists and it is certainly wrong for modern draftsmen. As you would soon discover if you were to visit their lairs in 36 Whitehall and 2 Carlton Gardens, draftsmen and drafts-

---

[5] FC von Savigny, *Vom Beruf unsrer Zeit für Gesetzgebung und Rechtswissenschaft*, 1st edn (Heidelberg, Mohr und Zimmer,1814) 157 in J Stern, *Thibaut und Savigny* (Berlin, F Vahlen, 1914) 163: 'man könnte (mit einem Kunstausdruck der neueren Juristen) sagen, dass damals die einzelnen Juristen fungible Personen waren'. See F Schulz, *Principles of Roman Law* (translated by M Wolff, Oxford, Clarendon Press, 1936) 106 et seq. where the passage is translated 'one might say (using a technical term employed by modern jurists) that at that time the individual jurists were fungible personalities'.

women are all different and I have little doubt that one could, with patience, detect different hands at work in our statute book.

Two simple illustrations can be given. A widely held view among experts in drafting is that, since legislation is 'always speaking', it should be expressed in the present tense rather than in the future tense.[6] So you should say, for instance, that a schedule 'has effect' rather than that it 'shall have effect'. The draftsman of section 22 of the Social Security Administration (Fraud) Act 1997[7] follows that precept and writes 'Schedule 1 . . . and Schedule 2 have effect', while the draftsman of section 1(9) of the Sex Offenders Act 1997[8] spurns such guidance and writes 'Schedule 1 to this Act . . . shall have effect'. Meanwhile, over in the Lord Advocate's Department the Scottish draftsman throws caution to the wind and writes in section 5 that schedule 2 to the Local Government and Rating Act 1997[9] 'is to have effect'. We are dealing with three individuals, all of whom, no doubt, would vigorously defend their particular style. Similarly – and here I turn to the second example – one can tell something about the draftsman of the Prescription and Limitation (Scotland) Act 1973[10] from looking at its provisions: the draftsman actually understood Latin. A person who knew no Latin might have written section 5(2) which speaks of a deed being '*ex facie* invalid', but only a person who actually understood the Latin words could have referred to a title being exempt from challenge 'on the ground that the deed is invalid *ex facie* or was forged'.[11]

You may dismiss these as nothing more than small variations in language. The modern study of Roman Law depends to a large extent, however, on paying attention in this way to the details of the form and language of the texts. Most of our information about Roman Law comes from the Digest, a huge book, roughly one and a half times as long as the Bible, which was compiled at the beginning of the sixth century AD. The book was not written by one person. Rather, it preserves thousands of short, some very short, excerpts from a large number of different books on law written by many lawyers over a period of roughly 400 years. Happily, just to make the mixture more difficult to understand, the excerpts were altered, to a greater or lesser extent, by the sixth-century lawyers who compiled the Digest. In addition to the Digest we have short excerpts from rulings on various points of law given by the emperors when acting as a kind of Privy Council. Finally there are various fragments of ancient laws which have turned up in inscriptions which archaeologists or, equally importantly, people with metal detectors have found. The crucial point is that all these materials on ancient Roman Law are incomplete. Those who want to build up a picture of the system and its history must therefore scrutinise the pieces of text which we have in order to try to deduce from them things which they do not tell us directly. For this purpose modern scholars have devised a variety of techniques, but common to them all is that they depend to a large extent on studying not only *what* the text says but *how* it says it. For these purposes, for example, the order in which items occur in a text may be a clue as to their relative dating, while any disruption in the grammatical structure of the text may indicate that the text was altered at the point where the disruption occurs. In such studies inconsistencies and grammatical infelicities are to be welcomed as clues, rather than to be deplored as signs of slipshod work.

[6] GC Thornton, *Legislative Drafting*, 4th edn (London, Butterworth, 1996) 103 (hereinafter 'Thornton').
[7] Cap 47.
[8] Cap 51.
[9] Cap 29.
[10] Cap 52.
[11] Section 1(1). See also ss 2(1) and 3(1).

It is by using such techniques that Professor Honoré has been able to identify the styles of different draftsmen of the Emperors' legal decisions,[12] just as I suggested that you could identify the hands of different draftsmen in our statute book.

Precisely because we have so much material to study in modern law, however, we tend not to devote the same minute attention to our texts as scholars of Roman Law devote to theirs. Nonetheless, close attention to form and style might well pay dividends in our understanding of our system.

A Judges' Opening Lines

Judges' opinions are, of course, the most obvious area for examining individual style.[13] It is well known that the form of Lord Denning's judgments is often as important a reason for their impact as is their content. Lord Denning says as much in one of his autobiographical writings[14] and, 20 years ago at least, law students were well aware of this. When drink had been taken, many a law society dinner was enlivened by recitations of some of Lord Denning's more famous opening lines, such as 'It was bluebell-time in Kent' from *Hinz v Berry*.[15] Without their opening lines, these judgments of Lord Denning would be as bereft as *Pride and Prejudice* without 'It is a truth universally acknowledged'.

Lord Denning is only the most famous example. There are many others. You would have to be blind to all sense of style, for instance, not to notice that Lord Devlin begins his speech in the famous contract case of *McCutcheon v David MacBrayne Ltd*,[16] with a very deliberately crafted sentence: 'When a person in the Isle of Islay wishes to send goods to the mainland, he goes into the office of Macbrayne (the respondents) in Port Askaig, which is conveniently combined with the local post office.' The fact that the office is combined with the post office is of no legal significance, of course. Why then does Lord Devlin mention it? Assuredly, so that the reader immediately understands the simple Highland setting in which the company are trying to argue that Mr McCutcheon should have solemnly read through the conditions behind which MacBraynes were trying to escape liability for destroying his car when their shop sank due to negligent navigation.[17] If we knew what the case was about but had nothing more than this opening sentence, not only could we see that Lord Devlin writes elegant English[18] but we could make a fair guess at his decision. By the end of the first paragraph, with its references to the 'three or four thousand words' and 'the twenty-seven paragraphs' making up 'this formidable contract', the company's fate is sealed. If we had that paragraph and nothing more, we could easily deduce that MacBraynes were going to lose. The opening paragraphs of the other speeches in the House of Lords are strikingly different. So, anyone interested in the attitudes of the Lords of Appeal to their

---

[12] T Honoré, *Emperors and Lawyers*, 2nd edn (Oxford, Clarendon Press, 1994).

[13] On judges' styles generally see RA Posner, *Law and Literature* (revised edition, Cambridge, Mass., Harvard University Press, 1998) ch 8 with references; RA Posner, *Cardozo: A Study in Reputation* (Chicago, University of Chicago Press, 1990) ch 6.

[14] Lord Denning, *The Family Story* (London, Butterworths, 1981) 206–14.

[15] *Hinz v Berry* [1970] 2 QB 40, 39, [1964] 1 WLR 125, 132.

[16] *McCutcheon v David MacBrayne Ltd* 1964 SC (HL) 28, 39, [1964] 1 WLR 125, 132.

[17] After the lecture George Appleby told me that the ship, the 'Lochiel', ended its days as a restaurant in Bristol harbour, and was visited by student members of the Holdsworth Club in 1991. It was finally broken up in 1996.

[18] I would wager a fair sum that Lord Devlin thought long and hard before inserting '(the respondents)', which impairs the flow of the sentence.

judicial task could learn quite a lot simply from studying them and reflecting on why their Lordships, who all agreed on the result, should have approached the matter so differently.

II HOW STATUTES BEGIN

Just as the openings of judges' opinions repay study, so also do the opening provisions of Acts of Parliament. They too vary considerably. According to some theories,[19] among the earliest provisions in an Act should be commencement and extent sections and definitions so that the reader can see immediately whether the Act applies to him and what the terms used in it mean. That is indeed the very rational practice followed in some countries. Nowadays, however, it is unusual for a United Kingdom statute to start in that way and readers are expected to go through the text and check to see whether there are any helpful definitions tucked away at the end. Occasionally, however, the pattern is broken. And when the usual pattern is broken, we should be on the alert. So, for instance, the Environmental Protection Act 1990[20] begins with a whole series of definitions. It is not immediately obvious why, but it would be foolish indeed to assume that the departure from normal practice was accidental. There will undoubtedly have been a reason for it. While I do not know for sure, I suspect that in this case the unusual positioning of the definitions is a sign that the draftsman himself realised just how complex and abstruse the provisions in the first Part of the Act would be for an uninstructed reader. By putting the definitions at the front the draftsman is warning of the problems and difficulties which lie ahead and is suggesting that the reader would be well advised to study the definitions before going any further. Certainly anyone who has to apply Part I of the Act soon becomes aware of just how important the definitions are.

When a statute begins with definitions, it is like a speaker clearing his throat before launching on his speech. Sometimes, however, things begin quite deliberately with a bang. The bang can even occur in the Short Title. Michael Forsyth, the Scottish Secretary in the last government, is a highly political animal. It can have been no accident therefore that one of the Acts for which he was responsible is called the 'Crime and Punishment (Scotland) Act 1997'.[21] The name, with its particular resonances, gives a good indication of the flavour of the legislation or at least of how the Government hoped that it would be perceived. Similarly, in 1987, when reforming the system of local government finance in Scotland, the Government of the day hoped (in vain) that people would remember the good news, the abolition of domestic rates, rather than the bad news, the introduction of the community charge (or 'poll tax'). Hence the statute, which effected both changes, was called the Abolition of Domestic Rates Etc. (Scotland) Act 1987 and the abolition of domestic rates was given pride of place in section 1. Much political trouble lay stored up in that abbreviation 'Etc.'.

A classic example of a spectacular opening provision is to be found in the Scotland Bill which is currently before Parliament and which is designed, of course, to effect a major constitutional reform by introducing a system of devolution. Clause 1(1) reads 'There shall be a Scottish Parliament'. That is an opening worthy of any great stylist, designed for maximum

---

[19] For example, Thornton (n 6) 190 et seq, but the question has long been discussed. See, for instance, Sir Henry Thring, *Practical Legislation* (London, John Murray, 1877, reprinted 1904) 38.

[20] Cap 43.

[21] Cap 48.

dramatic effect. I do not know whether Donald Dewar, the present Secretary of State for Scotland, had any hand in it, but he certainly saw its potential for having a political impact. I first learned of the wording of the clause via a satellite BBC television news programme when, lying half awake in bed in India, I heard Donald Dewar read it out and add with tremendous enthusiasm, 'I like that!'. The words of the clause and his comment, I subsequently discovered, were widely reported in the Scottish newspapers the following day, sometimes in block capitals. There can be little doubt therefore that the opening words were carefully chosen to have an effect. If you question that, you need only imagine the Secretary of State's consternation if the draftsman had come to him at the last moment and announced that they were going to reorder the clauses and begin with a definition clause instead. From a legal point of view, it would have made no difference. From a political point of view, however, the effect would have been wholly different. And for the Secretary of State at that stage the politics of the Bill would, quite properly, be at least as important as, if not more important than, the convenience of those who will one day have to interpret it. I shall have more to say at the end about the importance of political considerations for the form of legislation.

A   Preambles

Sometimes it may be felt that no provision in the body of the Act itself would be adequate to convey the significance of what is being enacted. Then, just as when we go to a wedding we get dressed up in the kinds of clothes which our ancestors wore, so in much the same way on very solemn occasions Parliament may use a device which was once quite common but is now used only rarely, the preamble. For instance, when King Edward VIII abdicated on 10 December 1936, the following day Parliament passed the final Act of his reign, His Majesty's Declaration of Abdication Act 1936.[22] This opens with two preambular paragraphs, the first reciting the King's irrevocable renunciation of the Throne and the second referring to the consents of the Dominions, before proceeding, 'Be it therefore enacted by the King's most Excellent Majesty' and so forth. The preambles are testimony to the solemn, irrevocable and far-reaching nature of the step to which Parliament was giving effect. We learned recently[23] that Her Majesty The Queen had signified that she would be content for an Act to be passed to abolish the rule of male primogeniture in relation to the succession to the Crown. If such an Act were passed, I should be by no means surprised to find that it began with a preamble. When President Kennedy was assassinated in 1963, it was decided to create a memorial to him in the United Kingdom. In due course, a site at Runnymede was chosen and transferred from the Crown Estate to the ownership of the United States in his memory. The formalities were accomplished by the John F Kennedy Memorial Act 1964[24] and again the high purpose and significance of what was being done were emphasised by three preambular paragraphs before the formula of enactment.

---

[22]   1 Edw 8 & 1 Geo 6. Cap 3.
[23]   Reply by Lord Williams of Mostyn, Parliamentary Under-Secretary of State, Home Office to Second Reading Debate on Lord Archer of Weston-Super-Mare's Succession to the Crown Bill, 27 February 1998, *Official Report House of Lords*, vol 586, cols 916–17. See also statement by the Lord Privy Seal (Lord Richard), 2 March 1998, *Official Report House of Lords*, vol 586, cols 954–58.
[24]   Cap 85.

B Formal Language[25]

If we move on into a statute, then we soon discover that both its use of language and its structure are fairly distinctive. If we look first at the language which is used, the most obvious distinguishing characteristic is that it frequently expresses an obligation. Only very rarely, of
course, does Parliament actually address the reader of a statute directly and impose an obligation on him by telling him what to do. This makes it all the stranger for a lawyer, drowsing
peacefully over section 1(3) of the Copyright, Designs and Patent Act 1988, to find himself
suddenly commanded by Parliament to 'see section 153 and the provisions referred to
there'.[26] Presumably the cross-references are meant to make it easier for a lay user of the Act
to find his way about. Similarly, in section 50(1)(a) of the Drug Trafficking Act 1994,[27]
Parliament refers to a drug trafficker and (shades of Ethel Merman) commands the reader to
'call him "A"'. The equivalent Scottish provision says more prosaically that the trafficker is
'referred to as "A"'.[28] Usually indeed obligations are imposed in the third person and this
makes for one of the characteristics of legislative style, the repeated use of 'shall' to express an
obligation[29]: 'A life prisoner subject to a licence shall comply with such conditions . . . as may
for the time being be specified in the licence',[30] or 'The Board shall appoint a person to be
known as the Registrar of Architects'.[31] If you found a scrap of paper with just a small frag-
ment of an Act on it, you would readily guess from this feature alone what kind of text it was.
In much the same way in Roman statutes third person future imperatives (*esto, facito* etc),
which are used to express obligation, are one of the hallmarks of legislative style.[32]

The language of legislation is often criticised as stilted, archaic and somewhat pompous.
There are populist calls for the use of plain English and these seem to be having some effect.
Indeed, the author of one recent textbook tells draftsmen that they have 'a special obligation'
to avoid archaic words. The phrase immediately makes me wonder why the obligation on
parliamentary draftsmen is supposed to be 'special', but the point appears to be considered
self-evident.[33] The author declares poor old 'hereby' to be 'fusty'[34] and in this modern world
the inoffensive 'foregoing' is to be eliminated as 'pretentious and pompous'.[35] Great emphasis
is laid on the principle that draftsmen should not deviate from commonly used language
except for good reason.[36]

---

[25] On written legal language generally see D Crystal and D Davy, *Investigating English Style* (Harlow, Longmans, 1969) ch 8.

[26] Cap 48. The device is found in a number of other sections, eg, s 9(2)(b) and s 16(1). Direct imperatives addressed to the reader may also be found in schedules relating to the drafting of documents. See, for instance, the schedules to the Titles to Land Consolidation (Scotland) Act 1868 (31 & 32 Vict Cap 101).

[27] Cap 37; originally s 24(1)(a) of the Drug Trafficking Offences Act 1986 (Cap 32).

[28] Section 38(1) of the Criminal Law (Consolidation)(Scotland) Act 1995 (Cap 5); originally s 43(1) of the Criminal Justice (Scotland) Act 1987 (Cap 41).

[29] Thornton (n 6) 103.

[30] Crime (Sentences) Act 1997 (Cap 43), s 31(2).

[31] Architects Act 1997 (Cap 22), s 2(1).

[32] See the influential discussion in R von Jhering, *Geist des römischen Rechts* 4th edn (Leipzig, Druck und Verlag und von Breitkopf und Härtel, 1883) vol II 2, 604 et seq.

[33] Thornton (n 6) 91.

[34] ibid 93.

[35] ibid – presumably not the kind of reference which would find favour with the author.

[36] ibid 91. The desirability of using simple expressions has often been stressed. See, for example, G Coode, *Legislative Expression; or the Language of the Written Law*, 2nd edn (London, Thomas Turpin and James Ridgway, 1852), reproduced conveniently as Appendix I to EA Driedger, *The Composition of Legislation*, 2nd edn (Ottawa, Department of Justice, 1976) 376–77. Coode's work appeared originally in 1843 as part of an Appendix to the Report of the Poor Law Commissioners on Local Taxation. Coode was Secretary to the Commissioners.

Doubtless this is all well-meant advice, along the same lines as the recommendations for the rewriting of the Prayer Book or the Lord's Prayer. Rather than indulge in the judges' bad habit of simply adding to the criticisms of traditional drafting style, I should prefer to ask why legislation has been drafted in this more formal and complex style. It is certainly not an isolated British phenomenon. We find exactly the same kind of thing in ancient Roman statutes.[37] Although the earliest Roman statute, dating perhaps from the fifth century BC, appears to have been written in very simple Latin, the language of later statutes was somewhat archaic and formal. Indeed, so old-fashioned and unusual were some of the expressions which the legislator used that the workmen who engraved the bronze plates on which the legislation was copied sometimes did not recognise the words and copied them out wrongly.[38]

It may be that the legislative draftsmen, both ancient and modern, found themselves using somewhat archaic language because they tended to stick to forms of expression which had been used before successfully. It was easier and safer to stick to a tried and tested formula than to devise new language which might turn out to have hidden traps which could not have been anticipated. And, if the result was to produce a legislative text which was distinctively formal, then they may not have regarded that as wholly undesirable. After all, legislation *is* the most solemn and formal of steps and there may be advantages in signalling by the very formality of the language that this is not just the equivalent of the rules of your local hockey club: this is what Parliament is laying down and it must be obeyed.

Even where the draftsman selects a simple form of words, Parliament may feel that something more formal and dignified is appropriate. So, as originally drafted, what became s 14 of the Criminal Justice (Scotland) Act 1980[39] was designed, not only to introduce a new safeguard for accused persons, but to simplify the language of the existing safeguards. The clause therefore provided that, if someone was kept in custody and his trial was not begun within 110 days, 'no proceeding shall be competent against him in respect of that offence'. At the Committee Stage in the House of Lords Lord Fraser of Tullybelton conceded that these words seemed to be perfectly adequate, but in his view they were 'colourless and rather uninspiring'. The ancient constitutional right of prisoners 'should be enshrined in words of some dignity and with some imposing ring about them'.[40] At the Report Stage, Lord Mackay of Clashfern, the Lord Advocate, moved an amendment deleting the draftsman's words and replacing them all through the clause with the grandiloquent words 'he shall be for ever free from all question or process for that offence'.[41]

As Lord Fraser perceived, formal language has a definite role to play in conveying an impression of authority. The language of the Prayer Book affords many examples, such as

[37] For a brief account of the different styles, see MH Crawford, *Roman Statutes* (London, Institute of Classics, University of London, 1996) vol 1, 16–19.

[38] See, for instance, the *Lex Irnitana* ch 91, Tablet XB lines 3 and 18 where the engraver stumbles over the formula *'siremps lex ius causaque esto . . .'.* The most accessible version of the text for people in this country remains J González, 'The *Lex Irnitana*: A New Flavian Municipal Law' (1986) 76 *Journal of Roman Studies* 147. See the commentary at 235 and 236.

[39] Cap 62 amending s 101 of the Criminal Procedure (Scotland) Act 1975 (Cap 21). The equivalent provision is now to be found in s 65 of the Criminal Procedure (Scotland) Act 1995 (Cap 46).

[40] 5 February 1980, *Official Report House of Lords*, vol 404, cols 1181–85. Lord Ross of Marnock referred (at col 1184) to an instance where words attributed to Pepys had been preserved when consolidating legislation on naval discipline.

[41] 26 February 1980, *Official Report House of Lords*, vol 405, col 1267. Though advanced on aesthetic grounds, the amendments were to have not inconsiderable practical repercussions. See *Gardner v Lees* 1996 JC 83, a decision whose far-reaching effects had to be neutralised by s 73(3) of the Criminal Procedure and Investigations Act 1996 (Cap 25).

the injunction in the Marriage Service: 'If any man can show any just cause, why they may not lawfully be joined together, let him now speak, or else hereafter for ever hold his peace.' The third person imperative and the use of 'hereafter' help to stress just how critical a moment it is for all concerned – as anyone who has ever attended a wedding well knows. At a more mundane level, in the days when schools were run on a system of strict discipline and drastic punishments, the apparent authority of the rules which were being thus enforced was enhanced by using formal language specifically designed to make them seem much more like Acts of Parliament than something dreamt up by the masters and mistresses. It is at least possible that a more informal style of legislative drafting may, in the long run, diminish the sense of authority which Acts of Parliament are intended to convey.

C Missing Words

Since draftsmen are told to use everyday language, you might expect to find that the words used in the statute book would now be in all respects similar to our everyday written language. Yet that is not the case, as a moment's reflection shows.

In the first half of this century in Kiel University in Schleswig-Holstein there lived and worked one of the great characters of Roman Law studies, Gerhard Beseler. The grandson of Georg Beseler, the renowned Germanist, he was a man of fiery temperament and formidable intellect, who delighted in nothing so much as writing violent criticisms of his fellow scholars. Not surprisingly, his scathing attacks frightened his contemporaries and they are said to have retaliated by making sure that he was never promoted to be a proper Professor. Let the junior staff here remember this awful example when next they are tempted to add another pejorative adjective to one of their articles. He has been dead for more than 50 years and his work has long gone out of fashion. Men much less talented than he now safely deride him.

I mention Beseler, however, not only because I have a very soft spot for him, but because his main scholarly endeavour related to the study of language. He was concerned to identify which texts in the Digest had been altered by the people who compiled it in the sixth century. His idea was that the lawyers of the earlier classical period of Roman Law were masters not only of impeccable logic but of the purest Latin style. Beseler considered that there were certain words which the classical lawyers would not actually have used and so, if you came across them in a text, that text must have been changed later by lawyers of an inferior kind. Unfortunately his method was faulty because no Roman lawyer ever actually thought so logically or wrote such pure Latin as Beseler himself.[42] He set too high a standard. Nonetheless, even though he went too far, there was more than a germ of a good idea at the heart of at least some of his work.

At first sight what he does is surprising and it is all the more surprising since he was much too grand to deign to explain his thinking – to a large extent you are left to work it out for yourself. So, for instance – and here we come to the point – he condemns all the passages in the Digest which contain legal statements using the Latin words meaning 'perhaps'. According to Beseler, none of them were written by a classical jurist.[43] Although he does not spell out his reason for saying this, it must be because statements with the word 'perhaps' are imprecise

---

[42] Professor Daube once remarked to me, only half in jest, that Beseler had written purer Latin than anyone since Julius Caesar.
[43] G Beseler, *Beiträge zur Kritik der römischen Rechtsquellen* (Tubingen, Mohr, 1913) vol 3, 83–90.

and statements of law written by great Roman lawyers should not be imprecise. I do not pause to investigate whether he was correct in what he said about the jurists, but we can see that his basic idea was correct when we note that none of the Latin words for 'perhaps' are found in the texts of ancient Roman statutes which have come down to us. This is because Roman legislation laid down enactments which were meant to be clear and which therefore had no room for the kind of doubts which the word 'perhaps' would introduce.

Better confirmation still of Beseler's thinking is to be found in our own statute book. A computer search of the pilot Statute Law Database[44] confirms that the word 'perhaps' does not occur even once in all the statutes currently in force. Again, this is not because draftsmen have any dislike of the word 'perhaps' – no doubt they use it all the time in the office and at home when speaking to their husbands and children. They do not use it, however, when they are about their serious business of drafting Acts of Parliament. Parliament always says things like 'this Act will come into force on a date appointed by the Secretary of State', and never says 'this Act will perhaps come into force on a date appointed by the Secretary of State'. In the world of statutes there is no room for 'perhaps'.

Indeed, only in very limited circumstances does Parliament envisage that its commands may be obeyed in a somewhat relaxed manner. This occurs when it prescribes a formality but the exact form may vary according to the circumstances. So, for instance, in Scotland a prosecutor who wishes to refer to an accused's previous convictions 'shall cause to be served on the accused . . . a notice in the form set out in an Act of Adjournal or as nearly as may be in such form'.[45] For the most part, however, precision is desirable, as another example makes clear. Ancient Roman Law texts containing legal statements with the Latin word for 'almost' tend to be regarded as having been altered by the sixth-century compilers of the Digest.[46] The reasoning is similar: 'almost' is not a word which you expect to find in the very best statements of legal principle. Certainly the word is not found anywhere in the surviving fragments of Roman statutes. Again the reason must be that it is a word which, by its very nature, introduces a degree of imprecision which is undesirable in a piece of legislation since legislation is meant to delimit rights and duties exactly.

It would be pleasant to think that judges today were so skilled at formulating legal rules that they never used 'almost', but in truth even the great Lord Reid himself in *The Wagon Mound No 2* said, when speaking of nuisance, that 'fault of some kind is *almost* always necessary'.[47] Long ago I wrote somewhat critically of that slightly slippery formulation which leaves the position rather unclear.[48] Times change. Surprising to relate, nowadays as a judge who has to try to frame statements in a considerable hurry, I am only too happy to comfort myself with the thought that even Lord Reid could not always state the law in a comprehensive fashion.

---

[44] I am grateful to James Shaw, Solicitor in the (Secretary of State's) Solicitor's Office, Edinburgh, for carrying out searches on my behalf and to my Assistant, Gordon Lamont, for arranging this.

[45] Criminal Procedure (Scotland) Act 1995, s 69(2); Act of Adjournal (Criminal Procedures Rules) 1996, Rule 8.3 and Form 8.3.

[46] A Guarneri Citati, 'Indice delle parole e frasi ritenute interpolate nel Corpus iuris' (1923) 33 *Belletino dell'istituto di diritto romano* 79, 118 sv *paene*. Beseler attacks quite a number of the texts where *paene* occurs: eg, D.9.2.41 pr., Ulpian 41 *ad Sabinum*, in 'Einzelne Stellen' (1922) 43 *Zeitschrift der Savigny Stiftung für Rechstgeschichte (Romanistische Abteilung)* ('ZSS') 535, 541; D.10.2.55, Ulpian 2 *ad edictum*, in 'Einzelne Stellen' (1926) 46 ZSS 267, 272; D.40.7.29 pr., Pomponius 18 *ad Auintum Mucium*, in 'Et (atque) ideo, et (atque) idcirco, ideoque, idcircoque', (1925) 45 ZAA 456, 478. It is not necessary for present purposes to examine how far Beseler's approach to these texts was actually correct.

[47] *The Wagon Mound No 2* [1967] 1 AC 617, 639 E–F.

[48] A Rodger, 'Report of the Scottish Law Commission on Antenatal Injury' (1974) *Juridical Review* 83, 89.

So far as statutes are concerned, the computer search confirms that 'almost' is not one of the draftsmen's words. In fact examples of 'almost' can be found, but there are only two. The first is in the preamble to the Cestui Que Vie Act 1666 which records that, when tenants for life go abroad and the reversioners are required to prove that they have died, 'it is almost impossible for them to discover the same'. Here the usage is entirely appropriate since the words are not in the enactment itself and are merely used to describe the mischief behind the Act, viz the difficulties which reversioners had encountered. The only other place where the word occurs is in a schedule to the Taxation of Chargeable Gains Act 1992[49] which refers to a company having 'assets consisting entirely, or almost entirely, of shares comprised in the issued share capital of' a particular principal company. The use of 'almost' in this passage can be criticised, because it seems difficult to know what is meant by assets consisting 'almost entirely' of certain shares. What is the relevant percentage? Presumably 99 per cent would pass, but what about 90 or 88 per cent? There is no obvious answer. Even so, we may forgive or, in my case at least, welcome one slip in a statute book covering hundreds of years, especially since the 'slip' may well have been made because of the instructions given to the draftsman.

The elementary point is that, however much the draftsman strives to make the language of the statute book more popular, it will never be quite the same as ordinary language because statutes are designed to operate in a particular way and their language is chosen accordingly. When the Statute Law Database becomes generally available and the texts can be searched by computer, we may well be able to gain new insights into the language used and so into the way in which the draftsmen give effect to Parliament's intention.

D The Structure of Statutes

In 1981 someone using a metal detector in the north of Spain found bronze plates on which were engraved large parts of a statute dating from the second half of the first century AD. The statute set out the constitution for the town of Irni which stood near there in ancient times. The local statute was a pattern used for many similar communities and so its structure can be regarded as giving us a good example of the kind of structure which similar statutes of the period would have had. Its complexity would have challenged the most formidable of modern draftsmen. For instance chapter 91, on various matters relating to the legal procedures to be sued in the courts, comprises two complementary sentences which are 34 lines long and contain no less than 341 words. They constitute a magnificent linguistic structure, so complex that a despairing modern editor has felt forced to adopt various devices to try to make it comprehensible to today's readers.[50] Despite the difficulties, however, the structure is coherent and the whole thing makes perfect sense. The draftsman's language is certainly not simple, however, and it takes a lot of concentration to follow what the provision says. It would not have won an award from the Plain Latin Society. Nor, one suspects, would the draftsman have cared. He was not trying to write more simply, but somehow failing and producing this magnificent structure instead. That is like saying that Henry James tried to write short simple sentences, but somehow ended up with the splendid periods which we all know.

---

[49] Paragraph 1(7)(b)(ii) of sch 7A.
[50] F Lamberti, *'Tabulae Irnitanae' Municipalità e 'Ius Romanorum'* (Napoli, Eugenio Jovene, 1993) 363, fn 166.

So, we are dealing with a phenomenon which is found in both Roman and British statutes and which cannot simply be accidental.

We shall almost certainly misunderstand things if we assume that draftsmen, whether Roman or British, write as they do, either because they know no better or because they deliberately set out to be pompous and obscure for the sake of it. As we noted when discussing preambles, a draftsman who wishes to go into solemn and dignified mode has ways of doing so. That is not his usual aim, however. So, if, for instance, we think of the long Roman sentence, it seems to me that their structure must be explained in some other way. Perhaps the most likely explanation is that there was some convention which required that all of a legislative provision, including the necessary qualifications, should be contained within a single sentence so that there could be no doubt about its precise scope. In other words, if you read each of the sentences, you learned from it all that you needed to know about the provision, including the various qualifications.

Equally, much of what is taken to be undue complexity in the drafting of our modern statutes stems from a somewhat similar desire that someone who reads a sentence in a statute – supposing that he can made head or tail of it – should, so far as possible, read not only the proposition but the qualifications of the proposition. That is certainly the model which was followed in older British statutes where often each section was preceded by a separate enacting provision. Nowadays the subject matter of legislation is often too complex to allow all the necessary information to be contained within a single sentence. The spirit of the original approach is reflected, however, in the idea that the whole of a discrete topic is covered within a section. In other words a section should 'have a unity of purpose and a central theme'.[51] The section may indeed contain only one sentence, but often it is divided up into subsections, each made up of one legislative sentence. Even in this looser model, however, within any section or subsection the drafting can be complicated. The complications are not just, however, the whim of the draftsman but are dictated by the material. They will be designed perhaps to ensure that similar cases are treated together, or to insert the necessary qualifications to what would otherwise be too general a proposition or else to close loopholes, preferably before, but sometimes in the case of an amending statute after, they have been spotted by astute companies or individuals and their sharp-eyed legal advisers.

E Loopholes

Elaborate drafting for the purpose of closing off loopholes is often criticised. It is suggested that, if statutes were written in more general terms, we would not need this kind of complicated drafting and could simply leave it to the courts to interpret the statutes according to the spirit rather than the letter. Two distinguished Scottish judges, Lord Emslie and Lord Wheatley, gave evidence to this general effect to the Renton Committee on the Preparation of Legislation which reported in 1975.[52] I am by no means persuaded. Again, perhaps it is my awareness of the kind of drafting which is to be found in Roman legislative texts[53]

---

[51] Thornton (n 6) 78.

[52] *The Preparation of Legislation*, Report of a Committee appointed by the Lord President of the Council, Chairman: Sir David Renton (Cmnd 6053, 1975) 29.

[53] There is a splendidly and obsessively complete list in the *senatusconsultum* of 19 AD dealing with performances on the stage or in the arena by members of the upper classes. The text was discovered in 1978 and can be studied conveniently in B Levick, 'The *Senatus Consultum* from Larinum' (1983) 83 *Journal of Roman Studies* 97,98. The Senate rules (lines 7–9) that no-one is to bring on to the stage 'a senator's son, daughter, grandson,

which makes me feel that those who favour general wording allied with purposive construction as the way forward may be underestimating the difficulties.

Many years ago Professor David Daube, the greatest living scholar of Roman Law, wrote a famous article in which he was able to uncover from the pages of the Digest and of the Code various rackets used by dishonest dealers and the owners of runaway slaves to get round the legislation enacted to stamp out the problem caused by their activities.[54] For instance, when the statute forbade the sale of a runaway slave, instead of selling the slave to someone, they got round the ban by entering into a transaction by which they made the person a 'gift' of the slave on the understanding that he would make a 'gift' of money in return. When that device was outlawed, they devised another – and so on. There was a struggle to and fro between the legislators and those who were determined to get round the legislation and, for all the skill of the Roman jurists, who undoubtedly understood what was going on, it seems to have been felt impossible simply to deal with the point by saying that the slave-dealers were trying to defeat the spirit of the legislation. The statute recently discovered in Spain, which I referred to earlier, provides another example of the need which was felt to legislate to counter schemes to get round the plain terms of the legislation. Chapter 84 of the statute imposes a limit of 1000 sesterces on the sum for which a plaintiff could sue in the local courts. If the case was for a larger amount, it had to be brought elsewhere – which might obviously be less convenient. Plaintiffs must have thought of a way round such local limits. If a plaintiff wanted to sue, say, for 1800, then he would raise two actions, each for 900 and each therefore coming within the local limit. The legislature had to insert a provision saying that you could not divide up claims in this way in order to defeat the limit on the jurisdiction of the local court.[55] Similarly, a measure prescribing the kinds of business which could be brought before the court in vacation required to be carefully drafted to prevent people smuggling in other kinds of business.[56]

These examples suggest to me that, thank goodness, human ingenuity is to be found at all times and at all places, even if it is quite often deployed for purposes which are not wholly admirable. I rather think that, just as in Rome, we shall find that what is criticised as somewhat heavy-handed drafting may indeed be required to outwit those who are sharp enough to spot the weaknesses in statutory wording.[57] Even if Parliament stated the principles behind the legislation in more general terms, the courts might not always be able to interpret those principles so clearly as to determine with precision and consistency which cases should be held to fall within and which fall outside its scope. We would be faced with the same kinds of very real problem as can occur at present when we have, say, to draw the line between tax avoidance and tax evasion. The fluctuations in the approach which the courts have adopted in the lines of cases before, and then after, *WT Ramsay Ltd v Inland Revenue Commissioners*[58] show just how problematical such decisions can be.

---

granddaughter, great-grandson, great-granddaughter, or any male whose father or grandfather, whether paternal or maternal, or brother, or any female whose husband or father or grandfather, whether paternal or maternal or brother, had ever possessed the right of sitting in the seats reserved for the knights . . .' (translation, page 99. I have omitted indications of reconstruction of the text.)

[54] D Daube, 'Slave Catching' (1952) 64 *Juridical Review* 17, reprinted in D Daube, *Collected Studies in Roman Law* (Frankfurt am Main, Klostermann, 1991) 501.

[55] Chapter 84, lines 3–4. See A Rodger, 'Jurisdictional Limits in the Lex Irnitana and the Lex de Gallia Cisalpina' (1996) 110 *Zeitschrift für Papyrologie und Epigraphik* 189.

[56] A Rodger, 'Postponed Business at Irni' (1996) 86 *Journal of Roman Studies* 61.

[57] ibid 73.

[58] *WT Ramsay Ltd v Inland Revenue Commissioners* [1982] AC 300.

F Offences

In his book on *Forms of Roman Legislation*,[59] Professor Daube draws attention to a phenomenon in ancient legislation relating to offences. Sometimes the legislator will say 'Any person who does X will be guilty of an offence. The penalty for the offence will be such and such', but at other times the legislator will simply say 'Any person who does X will be liable for a penalty of such and such'. When does the legislator use one form rather than the other? The recent Criminal Law (Consolidation) (Scotland) Act 1995[60] displays the phenomenon which Daube highlighted. In sections 2 and 4 we are told first that any step-parent who has sexual intercourse with his or her step-child shall in certain circumstances be guilty of an offence and then that a person who is guilty of an offence shall be liable to imprisonment. By contrast, section 7(1) of the same Act simply says that any person who procures any woman under 21 to have unlawful intercourse with any other person in any part of the world shall be liable on conviction to imprisonment for up to two years. Why does Parliament first say that the step-parent commits an offence and then specify the penalty for that offence in sections 2 and 4, but simply say that anyone who procures a woman under 21 for intercourse will be liable to imprisonment for up to two years in section 7? Why not say that the person who procures commits an offence and the penalty is up to two years in prison?

Daube's answer to his question was that the first form, which spelled out the conduct and said that it was an offence before going on to specify the penalty, was used when it would previously have been at best doubtful whether the conduct was criminal. So, in the example of intercourse with a step-child, there would previously have been some doubt about the legal position with respect to step-children as opposed to the parent's own children and now Parliament was making it clear: intercourse with a step-child is an offence and this is the penalty for that offence. The form is more emphatic. On the other hand the second form would be used when there would really be no doubt about the conduct being an offence and all that the legislator was doing was to prescribe the penalty. So the legislator would not say, 'Whoever commits murder shall be guilty of an offence' – that would be self-evident. All that was needed was to specify the penalty. In such cases the legislator would say 'Whoever commits murder shall be put to death'.

Following that line of argument, we should conclude that it was so obvious that anyone who procured a woman under 21 to have unlawful intercourse with any other person anywhere in the world was guilty of an offence that there was no reason to specify that – hence section 7(1) simply says that anyone who procures a woman for these purposes shall be liable to imprisonment. When you think about it, this seems slightly implausible. Could it really always have been obviously a crime in Scotland to procure a woman under 21 to have unlawful intercourse with someone in, say, Sweden? If so, why did Parliament leap in like this? What was the purpose of the legislation, since in Scotland any common law crime was punishable with imprisonment?

---

[59] D Daube, *Forms of Roman Legislation* (Oxford, Clarendon Press, 1956) 25–30. The thinking behind the book stems from Daube's familiarity with Old Testament form criticism. A useful summary of the approach is to be found in J Barton, *Reading the Old Testament*, 2nd edn (London, Darton, Longman & Todd, 1996) ch 3.

[60] Cap 39. Consolidation Acts are a wonderful playground for anyone who wishes to observe how individual styles of drafting may vary. The sections will often retain the imprint of the original draftsman, even though they have been combined and re-enacted several times.

The origin of the section is to be found in Section 2 of the Criminal Law Amendment Act 1885,[61] a statute which applied not only to Scotland but to England and Wales and Ireland too. If we look at section 2(1) of the 1885 Act, however, the form is quite different from the form of section 7(1) of the 1995 Act. As originally enacted, the provision used the first of the two forms identified by Daube. It said that any person who procures a woman under 21 to have unlawful carnal connexion, either within or without the Queen's dominions, with any other person shall be guilty of a misdemeanour or offence and shall be liable to imprisonment for up to two years. This form was chosen precisely because Parliament was making the conduct criminal for the first time. Somewhat surprisingly perhaps,[62] the form was changed when the Scottish legislation on sexual offences was first consolidated in the Sexual Offences (Scotland) Act 1976.[63] In England and Wales no such change was made[64] and the original form is reflected even now in section 23(1) of the Sexual Offences Act 1956[65] which says specifically that it is an offence for a person to procure a girl under 21 to have sexual intercourse in any part of the world with a third person. The penalty is specified in a schedule.[66]

It is clear therefore that, when originally enacted, the provision was in the first of the forms identified by Daube and it remains in that form for England and Wales but has slipped into the second form for Scotland. Why? What, if anything, are we to make of the difference?

It is possible that it is to be explained entirely by chance, by a whim of the Scottish draftsman to adopt one form and of the English draftsman to stick with the other. For my part, I doubt that. I rather think that the real reason lies in the different attitude of the two systems to criminal law. In their drafting the two draftsmen were reflecting that difference. In England many of the principal offences are statutory, eg assaults under the Offences against the Person Acts, theft under the Theft Act and rape under the Sexual Offences Act. In such a system it will not occur to a draftsman that there is anything odd about a section which specified that procuring of this kind is an offence. In Scotland, by contrast, all the main offences such as assaults, homicide, theft and rape are common law offences. The common law covers many types of conduct which would not be offences at common law in England and statutory offences tend to seem more unusual. I suspect therefore that, by the time the Scottish draftsman came to consolidate the 1885 Act offences in 1976, it did not strike him that conduct such as this kind of procuring was not an offence at common law before the 1885 Act. He must simply (and perhaps subconsciously) have assumed that such procuring was by its very nature obviously criminal and he therefore removed the part of the section which actually declared that it was an offence. Indeed, he did the same with all the other offences in the 1885 Act.

The draftsman's attitude seems to have been widely shared since, so far as I know, no-one has ever drawn attention to the point or sought to argue (however implausibly) that the repeal of the offence-creating provisions meant that the various types of conduct were no longer offences. On one occasion at least the writer of the leading textbook on Scottish criminal law must have noticed the problem. He adopted a bold solution. On finding that

[61] 48 & 49 Vict Cap 69.

[62] See n 59.

[63] Cap 67, s 1.

[64] In Ireland, s 2(1) of the 1885 Act remains in force, slightly amended by s 7 of the Criminal Law Amendment Act 1935 (No 6 of 1935).

[65] 4 & 5 Eliz 2 Cap 69.

[66] Schedule 2, as amended.

s 5 of the 1976 Act did not actually say that a person using lewd and libidinous practices towards a girl between 12 and 16 years of age commits an offence, he himself simply wrote in the words which the draftsman had omitted.[67] In this instance a study of the form of the legislation in the two jurisdictions helps to highlight the widely differing underlying attitudes of English and Scots Law to common law offences.

G Parliamentary Pressures

In practice, however, any differences in the legal systems of the United Kingdom are much less important for the form of legislation than Parliamentary and political pressures which are inherent in our procedures for legislation. These pressures will obviously be different from the kind of pressures which would be at work under the very different legislative procedures used by the Roman *comitia*[68] or, for that matter, under some of the modern Continental systems. The importance of such Parliamentary pressures has often been stressed,[69] but in this last part, I think it worthwhile to give some examples of how this comes about, if only because it is easy for those who have never been involved in the process to underestimate the significance of politics in this connection.

More than a century ago, the great Parliamentary Counsel, Sir Henry Thring, coined an aphorism which has ever since been quoted in the form, 'Bills are made to pass as razors are made to sell'.[70] Please note the combination of precision and almost total obscurity which marks it out as a statement which could only have been written by a Parliamentary draftsman of formidable skills. If I am allowed to attempt to interpret it, Thring's point, which is as true today as it was when he wrote it, is that any Bill must be drafted in such a way as to make sure that it passes through Parliament and obtains Royal Assent. That is the draftsman's principal task. No minister will thank him for preparing a Bill which is so splendidly drafted that it might win plaudits from the Plain English Society or the Hansard Society, if its form is such that it will not go through and so it never actually becomes law.

Very often the structure which is most convenient for the ultimate user of an Act is also the best structure for a Bill of parliament. In the case of many law reform measures, for instance, there is no reason why they should not be presented to Parliament in just the logical form which will be best for the user. But sometimes the most logical structure for the user of a statute may not be the one which is chosen when the Bill is presented to Parliament. Those who are surprised and disappointed by the fact that Bills are not always drafted as clearly and as logically as they would like tend to forget that, long before practitioners or judges get their hands on them, the provisions which they read in an Act are contained in a Bill and many Bills are quintessentially political documents. Even those Bills which are not purely political will often have at least some political element in them. Not surprisingly therefore the politics behind any Bill can play an important part in determining its shape and hence the shape of the resulting Act.

---

[67] GH Gordon, *The Criminal Law of Scotland*, 2nd edn (Edinburgh, W Green & Son, 1978) 903.

[68] See Crawford (n 37) vol 1, 9–14.

[69] For example, Thring (n 19) 4; Sir Courtney Ilbert, *Legislative Methods and Forms* (Oxford, Clarendon Press, 1901) 241–42.

[70] For the true form of the remark and for an explanation of its origin, see G Engle, '"Bills are Made to Pass as Razors are Made to Sell"; Practical Constraints in the Preparation of Legislation' (1983) *Statute Law Review* 7. Somewhat curiously, during the Lords Report Stage of the Human Rights Bill, Lord Lester gave a former Prime Minister of New Zealand, Sir Geoffrey Palmer, the credit for saying 'something rather wise' by remarking that 'Bills are made to pass': 29 January 1998, *Official Report House of Lords*, vol 585, col 420.

I can, for instance, think of one Bill during my time as Law Officer where at the very last moment before publication a whole lot of the clauses were swapped round on the instruction of the Minister concerned. A series of clauses which had originally occurred quite far into the Bill were put at the front and the ones which had originally come at the front were put towards the end. From a legal point of view it did not make the slightest difference in which order they came, but the change was made because the Minister thought that it would help the Bill through its Committee Stage in the Commons. More particularly, he knew that the Opposition desperately wanted to debate one particular group of clauses to which they had a powerful political objection. In the original version these clauses came first. There was a risk that the Opposition would take a long time on these clauses and that, if they then insisted on debating the later clauses even at reasonable length, the result might be that the Bill as a whole would take too long in Committee, with a consequential disruption to the Government's legislative programme as a whole. So, whether in consultation with the Whips I know not, the order was changed. The controversial clauses were now to be found much further on in the Bill and the Opposition therefore had an incentive to move more speedily through the earlier, relatively uncontroversial clauses in order to reach the bit which interested them. I doubt if, in this particular case, the change made much difference from the point of view of the ultimate user of the Act, but undoubtedly the change would still have been considered at least, even if there had been some consequential loss in coherence for the user of the statute. Logic and the convenience of the reader cannot always be the final determining factor for the ordering of clauses in a Bill.

It is often said that our Acts would be easier for users to understand if they contained a statement of principle. This was the subject of a debate in the House of Lords in January 1998 and on that occasion Lord Mackay of Drumadoon[71] appositely drew attention to the clear statement of principle contained in section 1 of the Church of Scotland Act 1921 which brought to an end generations of disputes about the position of the Established Church in Scotland.[72] The drafting of a more recent statute, the Arbitration Act 1996,[73] is much admired, not least because of the statement of general principles to be found in section 1. The lawyers who spoke in the debate in the House all seemed to favour such statements and indeed that is hardly surprising since almost everyone must at some time have felt that a statement of principle would have helped in interpreting an otherwise obscure provision. The debate in the Lords was most decorous, with not a hint of party politics. Yet one cannot help noticing that Lord Mackintosh of Haringey, who replied for the Government, was somewhat guarded in his remarks.[74] It seems likely that the material for his speech would have been carefully considered by his civil servants who would have advised caution.

There are two reasons why I suspect that clauses containing statements of principle will not come in to general use despite what are often thought to be their attractions.

The first reason is one which is openly discussed. You would often find it quite difficult to first identify, and then to encapsulate in a suitably brief form, the exact principle behind any particular piece of legislation. After all, the true principle may be one whose scope really only emerges from looking at the enactment as a whole, including all the qualifications which it contains.

---

[71]   21 January 1998, *Official Report House of Lords* vol 584, col 1587.
[72]   11 & 12 Geo 5 Cap 29.
[73]   Cap 23.
[74]   *Official Report House of Lords* (n 71) vol 584, cols 1595–1602.

The second reason is just as real, though perhaps less likely to be stated openly, and its importance will vary from time to time, depending on the size of the Government's majority in Parliament. At the time of writing we have a Government with a huge Commons majority and so they can probably get almost any legislation which they propose through the Commons. Neither Second Reading debates nor Committee Stage debates need hold any terror for them. Doubtless, ministers, and the draftsmen carrying out their instructions, could, if they wished, scatter clauses containing principles through all their Bills and win nothing but praise for doing so. Governments with massive majorities are unusual, however, and they will be even less common if any form of proportional representation is introduced. The last Government, for example, had a slim and ever-declining majority. Moreover, many members on its own benches were hostile to certain aspects of government policy and prepared to vote against it. For a government with a small majority, clauses containing statements of principle might well prove very tricky indeed.

The generally accepted rule is that a vote in favour of a Bill at Second Reading is a vote in favour of the principle of the Bill. Debates in Committee are then conducted against that background. If, however, one of the early clauses of a Bill contained a splendid encapsulation of the principle of the legislation, then a government with a small majority, which had safely, but perhaps with difficulty, negotiated the Second Reading, would find the whole principle of the Bill opened up for further debate as soon as the Committee came to consider the relevant clause, with the risk of losing a vote that the clause should stand part of the Bill.[75]

The European Communities (Amendment) Bill, the Maastricht Bill, which eventually received Royal Assent on 20 July 1993,[76] is an example of a Bill where a clause setting out the principle would have been dynamite. As drafted, the Bill contained nothing but rather technical clauses. Even so, the Government had enormous difficulty in securing its passage through the Commons. The Government's one strong card was, however, that in May 1992, before all the trouble broke out after the Danish Referendum vote, the House had given the Bill a Second Reading and so had accepted the principle of the legislation. During the Committee stage the Government had to face a series of amendments from the Opposition, all designed precisely to try to force votes on some underlying principle which was not to be found on the face of the Bill as drafted for the Government. Even with the Bill drafted as it was, the ingenuity of the Whips was taxed to maintain the Government's Commons majority. Just think how much more awkward their position would have been if the Bill had actually contained a clear statement, or worse still as a series of clear statements, of the principles underlying it. Many members, who were at best only lukewarm in their support for the Bill, could vote for it precisely because of its rather technical form. They might well have found it much more difficult to vote positively for some statement of the Maastricht principles which the Bill was designed to bring into force. In other words, there may be occasions when, in Parliamentary terms at least, clauses containing statements of principle could cause trouble for ministers promoting legislation. An undue emphasis on clarity could be dangerous to the health of a Bill. For that reason, I suspect that such clauses will not be inserted routinely into legislation.

We quite often come across sections in Acts which seem to be badly, or at least obscurely, drafted. Equally often, harsh words are said about the draftsmen. Here again the blame

---

[75] Sir Henry Thring seems to have seen an early clause encapsulating the principle of the Bill as an advantage precisely because it would allow Parliament to decide on the principle. See Thring (n 19) 5.
[76] European Communities (Amendment) Act 1993 (Cap 32).

may lie elsewhere. Problems of drafting are often caused by some amendment which the Government has decided to make in another part of the Bill at a late stage in its passage through Parliament, perhaps in deference to a point made by the Opposition or by its own back benchers. The change may require to be made very quickly and, in the rush, almost inevitably some consequential amendment to another provision is missed and so the problem arises. Even where some difficulty with the drafting is spotted in time to put it right, there may be good reasons why nothing is done to cure it. Again the reasons are likely to be political, to do with the need to get the particular Bill, and indeed other Bills, through Parliament.

The Maastricht Act is perhaps the best example. In it you will find sections which are not drafted in a very precise way – I hasten to add that they were not drafted by Parliamentary Counsel. They were drafted by Opposition members and, though skilfully drawn, their language is self-evidently not perfect, as was admitted on all sides. Parliamentary Counsel could have tidied them up in a trice, but they would have known better than to suggest that they should do so. Once the clauses were in the Bill, the Marshalled List of Amendments in the House of Lords was strewn with helpful proposals to improve their language. All these offers of help were courteously but firmly rejected by the Government. Why did the Government not tidy up these clauses and so make the resulting Act clearer for those who would have to apply the sections in the future? The answer, which was, of course, well known to everyone taking part in the debates, is that the Government's timetable for ratification of the Treaty could not have been met if the Bill had been amended, even in the very slightest way, in the House of Lords. Any amendment in the Lords would have meant sending the Bill back to the Commons for consideration of the amendment. If the Bill had been required to go back to the Commons, opponents of ratification would have had a further opportunity to delay it. Not only would this have risked holding back the ratification of the Maastricht Treaty, but it might have meant a delay in the start of the new session of Parliament the following October, with consequential effects on the legislative programme for that session. So, no amendments whatever were accepted in the Lords and the infelicities of language in the Act are the price which had to be paid for getting the Treaty of Maastricht ratified in time. It is to be hoped that the judges bear this in mind and do not rail at the draftsman if they ever have occasion to apply the section in question.

Much of what I have discussed here you may regard as trivial. If there is anything worth taking from my remarks, it is that in law a close study, not only of what judges and Parliament say, but of how they say it, is always important because it may help to reveal some of the background to the material which you are examining. I also hope that my remarks may do something at least to make you look more carefully at the form of statutes and so to appreciate the great skill which goes into their composition. All too often we tend to blame the draftsmen when something goes wrong and give them little or no credit for the remarkable intellectual endeavour behind the creation of the vast body of law which makes up the statute book. I shall doubtless be guilty of criticising them unfairly in the future, but today I am happy to make amends in advance by commending their work to your attention.

Finally, if my remarks do anything to make you like legislation a little more, or even to dislike it a little less, then perhaps the shade of Sir Otto Kahn-Freund will be content. In any event I am grateful to the Holdsworth Club for giving me this opportunity to put out a little propaganda for the study of ancient Roman Law under the guise of a discussion of modern legislation.

Part 3

Lawyers Advising Government

5

Legislation and Politics

STEPHEN LAWS

O NE OF THE situations where the worlds of law and politics invariably collide is in
the process of changing the law with legislation. Legislation – as a process rather
than as the product from that process – is essentially a political activity. Politics
and the democratic legitimacy they provide are both the motive and the justification for
legislating. The majority of legislation passed in the UK Parliament is for the purpose of
facilitating the implementation of the Government's policies, and to enable it to carry out
its political programme. Legislation forms a major part of the day-to-day work of practising politicians in government and in Parliament. The product of a political process necessarily retains political features deriving from its origins.

I THE POLITICAL ORIGINS OF LEGISLATION

Each year the Government has a programme of legislation for passage during the
Parliamentary Session; and top of the priorities for inclusion in that programme are Bills to
implement the governing party's election manifesto – or, under the current coalition government, the commitments in its coalition agreement. Time in Parliament for legislation is
strictly rationed by practicalities imposed by Parliamentary practice and procedure, and by
the calendar. Very rarely, if at all, do governments find that they have enough legislative
time for everything that they would like to do. Governments want to make the most efficient use of the opportunity they have earned by success at the ballot box to determine the
priorities for legislative change. The inevitable consequence is the allocation of the highest
priority to legislation that is needed for implementing the policies supported by the strong-
est political case.

Parliament's role includes being the main forum for the country's political debate. All
change attracts opposition; and, for reasons connected with the inherent values of the law
(which are discussed below), legal change attracts as much opposition as most, possibly
more. For a proposal for legislative change to be introduced as a Bill into Parliament, it has
to be politically desirable, and also important enough for the government to be willing to
put it, at least potentially, at the centre of the political stage. It must be worth paying the
price for its passage in terms of Parliamentary time and critical opposition. The management of a limited amount of Parliamentary time is important; but it is only one aspect of
the more complex business of ensuring that what the government does is relevant to the
national political agenda.

Surprisingly, the political priorities that govern the government's legislative programme are not always accepted as inevitable. There are frequent complaints, from lawyers and others, that not enough time is found for legislation on worthy, but politically neutral, topics. The Law Commission, for example, has frequently sought to encourage governments to find more time for implementing its recommendations for law reform. Nevertheless, it is usually the case that 'nice to have' legal change is possible only if it can be attached to a legal change that is necessary politically, and then only if its attachment, in parasitical form, does not distract either from the political objective of its host or from the government's political agenda more generally.

Furthermore, it is a paradoxical feature of the legislative process in the UK Parliament that the most troublesome legislation to get through – in terms of time and amendments – is often the 'nice to have' technical reform. Without a political wind behind it, or political commitment and political leadership to maintain its direction, such legislation can become ensnared in its own detail. If the main political objective of a piece of legislation is just to satisfy the demands of the special interests that are likely to be affected by it, the resulting Act is likely to be characterised by gratuitous complexity and to lack clear focus. The absence, in the case of any proposed legislation, of an ultimate policy objective with political importance means that it will have no protection from concessions to accommodate every reasonably plausible piece of lobbying. Law that has been produced to please everyone has a tendency to pointlessness, as the technical foundation for much law is the need to coerce those it does not please. Trying to please everyone can certainly lead to provisions that lack coherence and consistency, and to the abandonment of clarity. Legal change that lacks a political imperative is seldom easy to justify, when both the trouble of getting it through and the disruption that is the consequence of all change are taken into account. It is seldom likely to emerge from Parliament in a form that is significantly different enough from what it replaces to make it worthwhile.

II LEGISLATION AS AN INSTRUMENT OF POLITICAL CHANGE

Legislation is all about changing things. Sometimes, it is discussed as if it were an instrument of executive administration; but this notion represents a fallacy that fuels other misconceptions about the relationship between government and Parliament. Legislation is not a mechanism for governing. Governments do not need legislation to run things; and they do not run things with legislation.[1] Governments, generally speaking, need legislation only for the things they want to change.[2] Understanding the legislative process involves understanding how change is done and how it works, not only in the law, but also more generally. Effecting and managing change is a high priority for government, and it is an inherently political activity. Governments that do not want to change things do not need

---

[1] Perhaps, though, only a legislative drafter would worry about the ambiguous use of 'with' in the questions in the survey results set out in Table 6 on p 18 of the Report of the Commission on the consequences of Devolution for the House of Commons (the McKay Commission), http://tmc.independent.gov.uk/.

[2] Supply and appropriation legislation (which gives legislative endorsement to the government's annual spending plans) is perhaps an exception to this; but it does not form part of the government's legislative programme and follows a Parliamentary procedure that is very different from that for other legislation. Arguably, too, the annual renewal of income tax and the quinquennial renewal of the service discipline enactments (which are nearly always used as an opportunity to pass legislation that also makes real change in related areas) also provide further exceptions, which – though important – are quite limited.

legislation. But all governments want to make an impact, and that usually involves change, even if it is only (which it seldom is) changing things back to the way they were.

However, not all change requires legislation. Governments have extensive, existing statutory and non-statutory powers to bring about change. Crucially they have control of the allocation of financial resources. Legislation is often only an incidental or subordinate element of a wider project to implement change for the purpose of giving effect to policy. Nevertheless, the political case for or against a legal change, even if it is only incidental to a much bigger project for reform, will often concentrate on the arguments for or against the whole project. Even detailed arguments about the legal content of the proposed legislation will be framed in that context.

It is because the government's political priorities for change largely determine what legislation is introduced into Parliament that most UK legislation deals either with the relationships between different parts of the public sector or with relationships between government and its agencies, on the one hand, and the citizen or society in general, on the other. It is only relatively rarely that legislation intervenes in the areas of law that are of more day-to-day significance for lawyers spending their time on transactions or disputes that do not involve the public sector. Tinkering with the details of civil law is a relatively inefficient way of implementing public policy objectives.[3] Drawing inferences about legislation, or about the interaction of law and politics, from these rare cases will lead to erroneous conclusions.

III POLITICAL AND LEGAL ELEMENTS OF LEGISLATIVE EFFECTIVENESS

It is the regular presence of political factors in the content of the policy triggering legislative change that produces an inherent tension in legislation between the different disciplines of the law and of politics. These are tensions that play an important part in the work of the legislative drafters. It is the Parliamentary Counsel who draft all government Bills introduced into the UK Parliament. These are civil servants who are also qualified lawyers and specially trained in legislative drafting, and they are based in the Office of the Parliamentary Counsel, which is part of the Cabinet Office. They draft Bills on instructions prepared on behalf of ministers by other civil servants working in the department of the minister in charge of the Bill. It is that minister who will have been authorised by the Cabinet to prepare legislation for introduction as part of the Government's legislative programme.

As lawyers Parliamentary Counsel owe their professional responsibilities to their client, the Government and therefore to ministers. As civil servants they are subject to the Civil Service Code[4] and are expected to carry out their role with dedication and a commitment to the Civil Service and its core values: integrity, honesty, objectivity and impartiality. They are accountable to ministers and only through ministers to Parliament. In practice, they are given considerable freedom in the exercise of their professional expertise; but their duty is to apply that expertise in the interests of their client, the Government of the day; and they are subject to ministerial direction.

One aspect of the tension between law and politics in legislation is that what is politically essential may not always coincide with what is legally necessary. The ultimate objective of a proposal for legislation is always more or less political; and the mechanism for turning

---

[3] See Stephen Laws, 'Giving Effect to Policy in Legislation: How to Avoid Missing the Point' (2011) 32 *Statute Law Review* 1, 11.
[4] www.civilservice.gov.uk/wp-content/uploads/2011/09/civil-service-code-2010.pdf.

policy into law is certainly political. The case for or against legislation is made in a political context. Politics, however, often involves managing perceptions and expectations (including perceptions and expectations about the law), as well as facts. Law, by contrast, is concerned with what is actually the case and can stand up to legal analysis. Politically, as well as from the point of view of practical effectiveness, it may be very important that false assumptions are not made about the reasons for an enactment or its requirements; but, for the purposes of pure law, assumptions that can ultimately be falsified by legal reasoning are just irrelevant.

Another aspect of the tension results from the fact that one of the important functions of the legislative process is to de-politicise policy, or at least to create a perception that it has been de-politicised. The enactment of legislation is expected to have the effect that the new rules will command wider acceptance, adherence and respect as a result of having taken the form of law – even if they were politically controversial before and during the legislative process. This de-politicisation is important for making legislation effective. It is the political process that legitimises the conversion of a proposal into a law. However, once the conversion is complete, a line needs to be drawn under the process of transition; and the legal virtues of certainty and predictability, which in turn depend on clarity and stability, are expected to take over.

One interesting aspect of the de-politicisation of policy by enactment is the extent to which it can suggest that a drafting approach should be adopted that will put greater emphasis after enactment on the new rule, rather than on the change. Nevertheless, for practical purposes, the successful passage and implementation of a legal change require the legislative drafter, when drafting a Bill, to be at least as clear about the change as about what has resulted from it. It is essential that the communication of the practical changes in systems and conduct that will be required as a result of legislation is as clear as possible to those who need to act on them.

The process of converting policy from its political context into legal propositions having the desired policy-driven effect on day-to-day activities in the real world is an essential part of making legislation effective. However, an effect in the real world is not the inevitable result of the conversion of policy into law. The political approach wants to build a consensus for the continuing acceptance of new policy that goes beyond what can be achieved just by turning it into law, with any resulting de-politicisation. Furthermore, acceptance is also needed for the elements of policy that do not require legislation, as well as for those that do. The effectiveness of all policy will depend on the extent to which those affected by it co-operate with its implementation.[5]

Enactment may de-politicise the content of the law and give it a status requiring respect; but there will nearly always need to be additional political elements in the process of implementing a new law to bolster its likely effectiveness and produce behavioural change. New legislation to implement a policy is seldom simply abandoned to the judiciary on its enactment. The process of implementation is likely to involve, not only the completion of the legal implementation with subordinate legislation, but also further administrative decisions relating, for example, to appointments, new administrative and organisational arrangements, expenditure and the issue of guidance and other publicity. These decisions are all likely to have political elements.

---

[5] This assumption is made by governments and others with responsibilities for making legislation effective on the basis of experience and common sense. But see also Vilhelm Aubert, 'Some Social Functions of Legislation' (1966) *Acta Sociologica* 10, 98–120.

Of course, legislation should also be effective on its own, legal, terms. Legislative drafters generally operate on the basis that a legislative obligation should be accompanied by a sanction, or by other legal consequences or remedies.[6] From a purely technical point there can be, and is, no duty unless there is a sanction or remedy for its breach. Similarly, legislative drafters analyse instructions to provide new capacities or powers on the basis that conferring a new capacity or power can only make sense if there is an existing prohibition or restriction in need of disapplication.

However, a purely legal analysis of what makes law necessary and effective, though an essential part of the process, is not enough. Even with the mechanisms required to make legislation technically effective, legislative drafters must always be aware that it is respect for the law as such, rather than application of the sanction itself, which is the more usual explanation for compliance.[7] This is especially so if, as is often the case, the subject of a legal rule is in the public sector. There the political costs of conduct, even conduct subject only to civil financial redress, are higher if the conduct can be represented as 'illegal'. This may be different in non-public sector contexts, where it is likely to be more acceptable to make a commercial judgement whether to behave in a particular way or to accept the financial consequences of not doing so.

Furthermore, an express sanction or remedy can be relevant to the effectiveness of a law in different ways, apart from the inherent deterrent qualities that are required of it by legal analysis. The extent to which a sanction appears to be reasonable or arbitrary, for example, will also be significant. The greater part of the legislative audience for a sanction or remedy attached to a legislative obligation may well consist of those whose principal requirement of it is that it should provide reassurance that they will not be put at a disadvantage by complying. One thing a sanction or other remedy usually needs to do is to be fair to the naturally law-abiding – by not providing them with a grievance against those who are willing to risk breaking the rules.

So, the inclusion of a sanction or remedy in legislation is only the tip of the iceberg, so far as the coercive effect of law is concerned. Laws that are drafted with sanctions inserted purely for the purpose of satisfying the technical need for one are likely to be less effective than laws that acknowledge the need to use many different techniques to motivate the law-abiding to change their conduct in response to new laws. It is for this reason that clarity is so important in the drafting of laws. It is essential that they can be understood by those who wish to comply with them or to rely on them – or at least, who do not contest the need

---

[6] However, even this proposition is subject to the doctrine of Parliamentary sovereignty. So an exception is sometimes made in the case of 'constitutional legislation' where obligations are imposed which might, in theory, attract public law remedies but will not do so in practice because they deal, for example, with matters which are within the exclusive cognisance of Parliament or are subject to the principle enshrined in Art IX of the Bill of Rights 1688/89, protecting proceedings in Parliament from judicial proceedings (see Laws, 'Giving Effect to Policy in Legislation' (n 3) 15). An example of this can be found in s 19 of the Human Rights Act 1998, and also in cases where breach of a statutory duty gives rise to a reporting duty or other duty of transparency. Also, in a different way, supply and appropriation legislation again provides a special case. Ultimately, Parliament's legislative sovereignty is such that it should not be regarded as limited by the jurisdiction of the courts, nor (as the examples mentioned in this note demonstrate) must it be regarded as limited so as necessarily to invoke the jurisdiction of the courts where that is not the intended effect. To argue otherwise is to argue that the constitution and the separation of powers are outside the competence of Parliament.

[7] Even where a person's respect for the law is motivated by a desire to avoid the consequences of a breach, that person's conduct is self-regulated in the sense that in most cases it will be determined by their own assessment of what the law requires rather than a court's. See eg Aubert, 'Some Social Functions of Legislation' (n 5) and Harold G Grasmick and Donald E Green, 'Deterrence and the Morally Committed' (1981) 22 *The Sociological Quarterly* 1, 1–14 (which contains references to other relevant work on deterrence and compliance).

to do so. It is those people who are likely to form the largest part of those affected by a statutory provision. From a legal point of view, law is written with those who might break it in mind. Politically, law is written for those who are expected to abide by it. However, even the respect for the law of the law-abiding is confined to the law as they perceive it. It needs to be both clear and brought to their attention.

The likelihood that the law-abiding will change their conduct in response to a new law, and the extent to which that change will be willing or hesitant, is affected by a number of different factors, some legal and some political in nature. They include the complexity and certainty of the legislation, but they also include other things, such as the form and contents of any explanatory material or forms produced for the purposes of the legislation, the costs of compliance, the arrangements for administering and enforcing the law, the frequency with which the law is likely to be applied and by whom, its memorability and its consistency with what seems sensible – or has been made to seem sensible[8] – to those subject to it, and so on.

Engaging with the law-abiding involves political, as well as legal, factors in other ways that are not limited to new obligations. Often, legislation is intended to work by conferring new powers on statutory authorities. But those authorities have to be persuaded that it is worthwhile and desirable to exercise their new powers in the cases where it is intended that they should. This may mean that a power needs to be clearer or more specific – or otherwise framed in a different way – if, for example, it is intended to be exercised by a person in circumstances where that person might be reluctant to do so because of some perceived risk.[9] Here too, due account needs to be taken of perceptions of what the law does, as well as of what it actually does; and managing the perception, as well as the substance, is important and involves political considerations.

It is not always comfortable to have to accept this. Legislators, legislative drafters or other lawyers who complain that conduct is being determined by false assumptions about the law need to accept that one of the obligations of those who make law is to ensure that those subject to it make assumptions that are consistent with its intended effect. The text of the statute, and the logic of the law, should be the beginning of doing that; but it cannot be the end of it. 'I got it right, but was misunderstood' is seldom, if ever, a good excuse for the legislative drafter, or for any other lawyer.

Legislation works and is often intended to work through its 'chilling' effect on certain behaviours – not just for resolving disputes in the cases that come to court. Often, too, the effect is not confined, and is not intended to be confined, just to what crosses the line drawn by the legislation. In practice, legislation needs to be framed in the knowledge that

---

[8] An interesting aspect of the work done by Aubert, 'Some Social Functions of Legislation' (n 5) is the way in which it identifies, in the case in question, the very common tension or inconsistency in the political arguments for legislation, and for complying with it. They do often encompass both 'This is only formalising what for most people is already generally acceptable behaviour' and 'This will make a great improvement in the way things are done in practice.'

[9] Sometimes, legislation is criticised for making specific conduct criminal even though it can be prosecuted as an offence of more general application. Often, this can be explained as a legislative attempt to encourage prosecution authorities to give higher priority to the prosecution of the conduct in question, and to reduce the perceived risks of a prosecution (which are likely to be assessed as higher where the conduct has to be shown to fall within a more generalised prohibition). This, for example, may form part of the justification for ss 111–12 of the Protection of Freedoms Act 2012 on stalking. Similarly, the enhanced powers conferred in relation to anti-social behaviour by the Anti-Social Behaviour Act 2003 were justified partly on the basis that they provided added encouragement to local authorities to use existing powers which they had been reluctant to use. Powers conferred on regulators of certain business need to accommodate the risk that a regulator might see a power that is conferred to be exercised only rarely as involving a risk that its exercise will precipitate the sort of failure it is intended to prevent.

there is always a border zone short of that line into which many who are subject to the law will be reluctant to stray.[10] How many are likely to stray into the border zone and what the consequences will be if they do needs to be balanced against the likely consequences of moving the line, and inevitably also the border zone, further back. Neither legislators nor judges can escape responsibility if the effect of decisions they make with a potentially chilling effect is colder than they intended; and discussions about, for example, a compensation culture, or the adverse effects of excessive caution on health and safety matters, or about the risks to practical administration from the scope for the judicial review of political and administrative decisions should be conducted on that basis.

A contrast is sometimes drawn between the use of legislative regulation and the use of behavioural insight, or 'nudge', for giving effect to policy. The case is made that the latter is more effective and less intrusive than legal rules backed by sanctions and remedies. The preceding analysis of how legislation has effect in practice demonstrates that this is, at the same time, both true and false. It is often the nudging aspects of legal change that are the most effective; and behavioural insight very often needs to be applied in the preparation and implementation of legislation. Even legislation that specifically prohibits certain conduct is often intended principally to affect other conduct indirectly. So, for example, a ban on smoking in public places may have, as its principal, intended effect, the creation of a wider intolerance of smoking in other places, and a reduction in smoking in general.

In this way, legislation can be seen as no more than one of the tools in the nudger's tool box, rather than as a wholly different approach. In another sense too, legislation is not an alternative to nudging, because the powers to do the things that nudging requires may also sometimes need an element of cover in legislation.

On the other hand, the suggestion that nudging, when legal but without legislative cover, is somehow unconstitutional or contrary to the rule of law is misconceived. The notion that governments should exercise influence over their citizens by means of law, and law alone, is unsustainable. It would involve outlawing the exercise of political leadership, on the basis that it is a form of influence unsanctioned by Parliament. The influence that governments exercise over their citizens without the need for further legislative authority is fully legitimised by the process by which governments are elected in the first place, and also by the accountability of government ministers to Parliament.

IV LEGAL AND POLITICAL VALUES AFFECTING THE CONTENT OF LEGISLATION

Another element of the tension between law and politics in connection with legislation derives from the professional instincts of lawyers. These are based on the assumption that law is and needs to be predictable, stable and fixed. The training lawyers receive reinforces that assumption. This creates, in the legal mind, a presumption against change that is inconsistent with the usual perspective of politicians. They very often become involved in politics only because they think things can be changed and would be improved if they were.

For lawyers, it is natural to think that the best sort of change is the change which maintains continuity with what has gone before, involves the least possible disruption to existing systems and does not frustrate existing expectations. For many political policymakers, change can only be effective if it is manifest, radical and complete. Politicians and others

---

[10] There is a corresponding phenomenon in the case of the limits of a power (see n 9).

involved in policy formulation recognise that the sort of practical change they seek in the real world will usually be effective only if those subjected to it are made to realise that they cannot continue with their previous behaviour.[11]

The dynamics in the process of policy implementation through legislative change are incompatible with many of the underlying values of the law. Policymakers often want to take the risk of putting a ratchet on change to ensure its effectiveness. Lawyers whose perspective and training makes them naturally more cautious and risk-averse prefer to keep their options open, in case they have not thought of something. Paradoxically, they have this preference despite the lack of certainty that results from the flexibility of a reverse gear.

In this way, at a more detailed level, the perspective of the law also creates an instinctive preference in lawyers for the inputs to the legislative process to have characteristics that more closely resemble the characteristics that are necessary to make law of the outputs. It is obvious that law-making would be more straightforward if government policy were totally stripped of its political content before being enacted. That, though, is not possible, because most legislation is only passed because those who promote it wish it to achieve an objective that has been set for political purposes and promoted in the political arena. It will only succeed for that purpose if it is understood in that way.

Nevertheless, the legislative process does always involve an element of diluting the political content of the inputs to produce a legal output. This is essential because (quite apart from the de-politicising element of securing effectiveness[12]) it is necessary for the judiciary, with responsibility for construing and applying enacted law, to be insulated from political controversy and not drawn into any continuing process of political decision-making. This process of dilution is something that can sometimes leave politicians feeling that the legislation has missed the point:[13] that the Act they have fought a political battle to see passed has somehow suppressed the substance and the virtues of the policy objective it was passed to achieve. All this means that the distinction between the virtues of making pure law and the supposed lack of virtue in law as political rhetoric that 'makes a statement' or 'sends a message' is much less clear-cut than it is often thought to be. The need for some dilution should not tempt legislative drafters or other lawyers, who tend to like things clear-cut, into the dangerously false assumption that law is good and politics are necessarily bad.

The task of the legislative drafter usually involves responsibility for advising on how the process of dilution is carried out. In practice (but subject of course to political challenge and direction) the job of deciding how the legal and political factors should be balanced in the draft is also often delegated to them. The legislative drafter has many different audiences to satisfy. The need to satisfy both the legal and the political audiences produces a clear understanding that there is value in both approaches. Neither the political factors nor the legal factors can be totally subordinated to the other. The political objectives must be met – that is, after all, the whole point of the exercise; but they can only be met using the law. So the legislation must accommodate the values of the law. The difficulty for the legislative drafter is that the same document – the Bill or Act – has to be used for both purposes. On the one hand, it may be argued that everything remotely political is best excised from the legislation and put in other non-legal documents, where it would pose less risk to the

---

[11] See Aubert, 'Some Social Functions of Legislation' (n 5) n 8.
[12] See above.
[13] See Laws, 'Giving Effect to Policy in Legislation' (n 3).

proper legal operation of the Act.[14] On the other hand, if politics define the intended purpose and effect of a statute, there is a strong case for ensuring that those things are clear on its face and are given the same constitutional legitimacy as the law enacted to achieve them.

In this connection, it is also often necessary, for those involved in preparing legislation, to be conscious that the values of the law, with its presumption against change, can sometimes lead to territory already occupied by the political opponents of a proposed legislative change. The need to analyse whether policy objections are being presented in the guise of legal arguments, and vice versa, is a common feature of the legislative process – just as it is of other legal procedures, particularly those involving challenges to administrative or political decisions on procedural grounds. Arguments about process are often arguments for delay; and delay is often an effective and politically astute tactic for the opponents of change.

V STRIKING THE BALANCE BETWEEN THE DIFFERENT VALUES OF LAW AND POLITICS

So, legislative drafters have to do their job in the knowledge that politics cannot be eliminated from the legislative process, but need to be reconciled with things required of the legal output. Although ultimately the drafters are often left to strike the balance themselves, they can also often find themselves cast as the advocates for the need for legislation to be recognisable as law. Reconciling the two functions of striking the balance and being the advocate for one side of it is one of the more difficult parts of the job. It is particularly difficult because there are, by definition, no legal rules to mark the point at which the integrity of the legal system (and in particular the constitutional balance between the respective roles of elected politicians and judges) is called into question. A totally risk-averse approach to where the balance is struck is impossible without abrogating responsibility for deciding where it should be to others and, in that way, failing the legislative drafter's governmental client. On the other hand, drafters know that a single example of going too far could effect a permanent change in the constitutional balance, and not only because it is much easier to cross a line that has already been crossed once.

One way in which legislative drafters seek to strike the balance is by testing their drafts against certain identifiable values in the law. The doctrine of Parliamentary sovereignty, with the limited qualifications provided by the law of the European Union and the Human Rights Act 1998, provides legislative drafters and their policy-making clients with a clean sheet. Anything is possible, but some things are unwise from a legal point of view.

The identification of what is unwise from a legal point of view is sometimes said to depend on 'legal policy'. For the legislative drafter, that consists of a set of assumptions about what is best avoided when drafting a statute. Some of the former assumptions of legal policy have been subsumed into human rights legislation, in which they appear as more clearly defined and less flexible rules. What is left are things (some of which also overlap with convention rights) which need to be avoided because they would involve an increased risk that the effectiveness of a legislative provision will be diminished by the way it is interpreted in the courts. The assumptions have to be made for pragmatic reasons. Legislation has to communicate with the courts, amongst others; and no form of

---

[14] Something that can only be completely true if the courts do not take the extraneous documents into account when construing the Act.

communication can be effective if it ignores the assumptions and capabilities of those to whom it is addressed.

For some, no doubt, the assumptions may also have some higher value as components of the 'rule of law', and be seen as part of a system for the judicial regulation of politics. For others such a system has no place in our constitution and would represent no more than a political preference for the dominance of certain, possibly legal, values over democratically endorsed political values. This raises more questions, about the extent to which the rule of law is a legal or political principle, or both, than it is necessary or appropriate for a legislative drafter to answer, or than it is possible to discuss here.[15]

Less contentious perhaps would be the suggestion that these assumptions enable the drafter to identify when his work is straying into an area of uncertainty around the boundary between the proper constitutional roles of, respectively, the legislature and the courts.

In any event, whatever its value as morality, Lon Fuller's articulation of the eight routes[16] of failure for a legal system, as well as other works using similar functional tests for describing the rule of law,[17] provide a useful pragmatic guide to drafters on how to avoid producing legislation that cuts across the grain of the values of the law. As a guide, these works do not draw clear or uncrossable lines, but they do serve to identify the danger areas.

So, consistently with Fuller's first route of failure for a legal system, a warning bell rings for the drafter if a provision is directed at specific individuals or at a specific case or cases. There is a presumption in favour of drafting generalised propositions of wide application. Such propositions facilitate consistent (rather than ad hoc) decision-making and do not involve decisions that make arbitrary or unexplained distinctions between similar cases.

The legislative drafter has to be familiar with the rules of Parliamentary procedure that deal with 'hybridity' and, generally, has to seek to draft in a way that prevents them from being invoked. Those rules subject legislation that deals with legal persons otherwise than as members of a genuine class to Parliamentary procedures that are quasi-judicial in form. However, even when the hybridity rules are avoided, legislation that is tailored for particular cases or individuals is something legislative drafters know needs to be handled very carefully. If possible, it should be broadened and made general.

Similarly, law that cannot be known or is difficult to discover, perhaps because it is insufficiently publicised or unclear or obscure, also needs to be avoided if possible. That is covered by Fuller's second and third routes of failure for a legal system. The commencement of legislation is usually delayed for at least a couple of months, and one important reason for this is to allow time for those affected by it to be made aware of it and to adjust their behaviour. Where urgency makes a speedier commencement necessary, it is usual for government to make special arrangements for ensuring that notice of the legal change is given to those affected.

Difficult analytical issues arise around the question whether legislation is or is not properly to be regarded as retroactive. It is retroactive application that constitutes Fuller's fourth route of failure for a legal system. What legislative drafters know is that legislation should be formulated as clearly as possible to avoid suggestions of retroactivity, and that any retroactivity that is enacted has to have a clear and reasonable justification.

---

[15] For a discussion of the difficulties of treating 'the rule of law', in the 'thin' sense used here as capable of providing a legal inhibition on the legislative power, see eg Jeffrey Goldsworthy, *Parliamentary Sovereignty – Contemporary Debates* (Cambridge University Press, 2010) ch 3.

[16] Lon L Fuller, *The Morality of Law* (Yale University Press, 1964).

[17] Tom Bingham, *The Rule of Law* (Allen Lane, 2010).

Legislation needs to be consistent with existing systems and rules and must not contain unresolved contradictions that create unfairness for those seeking to discover the law. Fuller's fifth route of failure is contradictions in the law. It is mitigated in the case of UK legislation by the doctrine of implied repeal (which makes much legislative inconsistency theoretically impossible); but it is an encouragement to make implied repeals express wherever possible.

Fuller's sixth route of failure is the making of demands by the law that are beyond the powers of the subject. Legislative drafters know that legislation is more likely to work as intended if it does not seek to impose obligations that cannot be complied with. All the jurisprudence about strict liability offences illustrates the need for drafters to be clear about what is expected of those on whom obligations are imposed, and to have regard to the practicalities of compliance. Similarly, powers should not be conferred that cannot be exercised in practice in the prescribed manner or circumstances, or are subject to unreasonable constraints.

Fuller's seventh route of failure requires law to have an element of stability. Drafters know that legislation is likely to receive an unsympathetic construction if it confers very wide discretions and would empower the authorities with responsibility for implementing or administering the law to improvise their legal conclusions on a case-by-case basis, or to change the rules on a day-to-day basis. For related reasons, including concerns about the level of accountability and Parliamentary control for ministerial law-making and an aversion in administrative law to unfettered discretions, neither Parliament nor the judiciary look benevolently on 'Henry VIII clauses', allowing ministers power to modify primary legislation.[18]

Fuller's last route of failure for a legal system is where there is a divergence between the law and its application in practice. The process of preparing legislation can frequently throw up the temptation to elide the difficult or controversial elements of what is wanted, and to rely instead on an understanding with those who will administer the law that it will be applied in what is agreed to be a practical and sensible way. This is a point that occasionally arises in relation to the formulation of criminal offences in the light of the existence of a prosecutorial discretion.

Legislative drafters know that it is unwise to succumb to this temptation to leave it to practice to fill gaps in a legislative scheme. There are many good reasons for this. Not the least of these is the fact that an understanding about what will happen in practice is likely to be a lot more temporary than the legislation to which it relates. In addition, there is often a relatively high risk that there will be successful challenges to understandings about practice that are not expressly contemplated by the legislation. In the same way, legislative drafters also know that they should avoid the creation of a rule that is perfect in theory but will turn out, in practice, to be incapable of implementation because of its complexity. If the officials charged with operating a rule of that sort find it unworkable and apply a more practical and simpler (if less perfect) rule instead, then it is their rule that will matter in practice; and so theirs is the rule that should be enacted.

So best practice, when determining the legal effect to be secured by legislation is to assume that those subject to the law are entitled to rely on its terms for regulating their conduct. Non-legislative approaches may be helpful in promoting a better understanding

[18] See eg the Mansion House Speech of Lord Judge LCJ on 13 July 2010, www.judiciary.gov.uk/Resources/JCO/Documents/Speeches/lcj-speech-for-lm-dinner-13072010.pdf and the role and the various reports on government Bills of the Delegated Powers and Regulatory Reform Select Committee of the House of Lords, www.parliament.uk/business/committees/committees-a-z/lords-select/delegated-powers-and-regulatory-reform-committee/role/.

of legislation by the law-abiding. Governments will often want to supplement what a law says with explanations of how it will be applied in practice. However, it is important that the giving of these explanations is not allowed to become a less formal way of modifying the law itself. There should be no contradiction between the guidance and the law, and no ambiguity about the legal effect of clarification provided under an Act. This is something drafters often have to manage where, for example, a statutory duty to give guidance is being imposed. Mandatory guidance is a contradiction in terms.

VI VALUES APPLIED TO LEGAL CHANGE THAT DOES NOT ORIGINATE IN LEGISLATION

The eight routes of failure are a useful and effective way of testing whether a statute satisfies the legal values that drafters expect to influence the judiciary when they have to consider legislation. It is surprising, therefore, that they are often not satisfied by legal change initiated by the judiciary themselves in the form of modifications of the common law. The underlying legal value of predictability, in particular, which is comprised in most of the tests in the eight routes of failure, is necessarily abandoned when the judiciary involve themselves in legal change; but so too are other aspects of the assumptions used by drafters.

Legal change initiated by the judiciary will usually be made by reference to the facts of an individual case. Often, the usually cautious approach to change which is adopted by the judiciary and required by the values of the law (as well as by the way the doctrine of stare decisis works) will ensure that any new rule that emerges from a case has a limited application and is likely to be capable of being distinguished by reference to its particular facts. No general rule emerges immediately and uncertainty is produced by the need for the new rule to be worked up as a result of subsequent litigation.

Legal change originating in court decisions is not given the same publicity as legislative change. Often, it is difficult to unpick from a number of judgments. In addition, judgments implementing legal change tend not to be constructed to produce a clear distinction between what is new and what is not. Even allowing for all the difficulties there may sometimes be in finding an up-to-date legislative text, the law in judicial precedents is certainly less accessible than statute to those outside the legal profession, and arguably less accessible to those within it as well.

Legal change initiated by the judiciary is, in its nature, retroactive. It proceeds on the assumption that it is only revealing what the law has always been, despite previous possible indications to the contrary. To the extent that judicial legal change can retroactively impose liabilities on legal persons,[19] it can have the same effect as imposing impossible obligations and producing a divergence between the rules that are applied in practice and the rules that were thought to be in force at the time.

---

[19] The effectively retroactive adoption by the courts of a rule allowing recovery by taxpayers of tax paid under a mistake of law has resulted in a series of further cases, and legislative provisions, about how far the legislative authorities are precluded from retroactively curing, with legislation, the sometimes potentially very expensive, financial consequences of old cases which were thought to have been disposed of in accordance with the law as it was understood at the time. See eg *Marks & Spencer Plc v Customs and Excise Commissioners* (C-309/06) [2008] STC 1408; *Deutsche Morgan Grenfell Group Plc v Inland Revenue Commissioners* [2006] UKHL 49; *Fleming (t/a Bodycraft) v Customs and Excise Commissioners* [2008] UKHL 2; See also Jack Beatson, 'Common Law, Statute Law & Constitutional Law' [2006] 27 *Statute Law Review* 1, 5–11.

There is an inherent risk to the stability of the law at the prospect that judges may be persuaded to change the law in the course of litigation. Judicially initiated legal change can also leave the law in an inherently contradictory state. Certainly, contradictory or at least parallel but different descriptions of the same common law rule can often be found in different judicial authorities for it.

So, paradoxically, the mechanisms available for non-statutory legal change have a tendency to contradict the values of the law to which importance is attached in the course of legislative change. Of course, the judiciary are well aware of the potential difficulties of developing the common law independently of legislation in a creative way; and they take them into account, both when contemplating modifications of the common law[20] and also when contemplating changing the law indirectly, by means of more extensive use of any existing jurisdiction judicially to review the contents of statutory provisions or even just to change an earlier statutory interpretation of a statute.[21] There are self-imposed inhibitions by the judiciary on any sort of wide-ranging, non-legislative legal change. Nevertheless, it is possible to infer that these self-imposed inhibitions derive principally from concerns about constitutional and democratic legitimacy, and from an awareness by the judiciary that they lack the resources for policy-making that are available to government. There is a case, however, for attaching more importance, in this connection, to the relevance and value of the different decision-making methodologies of the law and of politics.

VII DIFFERENCES BETWEEN LEGAL AND POLITICAL DECISION-MAKING ABOUT LEGAL CHANGE

Certainly, politics and the law approach the task of decision-making about change and policy in radically different ways. So change that is undertaken for political purposes tends to be undertaken to fulfil a vision of the future. Any legal change that is associated with a policy formulated with a political vision in mind can be properly understood only in the context of the political vision and policy with which it is associated.

Change for political purposes is intended to have an effect that will make things better – from the point of view of a particular political conception of what better might be. The political approach to improvement will begin with an idea about what an improvement for the public collectively would involve and then move on to the question whether the collective benefit is justifiable in the light of any disadvantages for individuals.

The question whether, if a change has the desired impact, it will or will not improve things may be controversial, and so may the questions whether it will actually have that impact or (if it does) will be worthwhile in the light of the disadvantages. Nevertheless, the political case for change and the assessment of what it should be are always both essentially forward-looking. They involve estimating the likely future effects of a proposed change, even though the future is not predictable with logical or mathematical certainty. A similar assessment is also required for the risks of doing nothing. This means there is always likely to be an element of risk in proceeding with a political proposal, but also a risk in not proceeding with it. The political approach requires the risks to be assessed and managed. As already mentioned, those risks are likely to include the risks of ratchetting a proposed

---

[20] See eg the annual lecture to ALBA by Lord Dyson MR, 'Where the Common Law Fears to Tread' www.judiciary.gov.uk/Resources/JCO/Documents/Speeches/mr-speech-where-common-law-fears-to-tread-06112012.pdf.

[21] eg *R v Governor of Brockhill Prison, ex p Evans (No 2)* [2001] 2 AC 19.

change; and those risks need to be assessed against the risks to effectiveness of leaving room for existing practices to continue or to be revived.

It is the elements of unpredictability and risk in the implementation of a political policy (and also, usually, in all the other options, including doing nothing) that create a need for political leadership. It is needed not only to get support for the enactment and implementation of a policy proposal, but also to make sure the proposed changes stick and are effective when they are in place. Leadership involves persuading people of the value of the objective to be achieved and also justifying the risks involved in achieving it. It also involves accepting responsibility for taking those risks.

This, as well as constitutional or legal considerations, is why governments proposing new policy and legislation seek to build support for their proposals through public consultation. It is why the political process needs to be open and transparent and why the political case for change concentrates on the collective benefits of a proposal.

Policymakers, in their forward-looking, political approach to decision-making, also seek to predict the future using social research and other evidence about what is happening in practice and about what relevant public opinion says on the subject. The need for 'evidence-based' policy is often a mantra within government. There is no doubt that it is an essential discipline, even if the evidence will always need to be supplemented by judgements based on a political philosophy or other political starting place. It is a political premise that is usually needed both to help define what would constitute an improvement and to inform any judgements, based on the evidence, between a proposal's advantages and disadvantages.

Evidence supplemented by judgement is used in the consideration of how a proposed policy will affect relevant perceptions (as well as in the assessment of its likely impact in practical terms). For example, will those perceptions go with the grain of the policy objective or produce an undesirable 'chilling' effect on conduct that needs to be encouraged? One reason why governments are often willing to make concessions on the details of a Bill as it passes through Parliament is because they are seen as likely to enhance the acceptability of the policy when it comes to be implemented, and may change or clarify perceptions about its relevance or intended effect. The loss of some content or the addition or removal of some flexibility may be worthwhile if what emerges is more acceptable and better understood in practice.

All these factors ensure that political decision-making on change needs to be strategic and integrated. It needs to fit in with the other policy priorities of the government and with its normal business. But it also needs to be responsive to criticism and flexible if a spirit of compromise will produce a better outcome without loss of essential effectiveness. The machinery of government is available and is used to reconcile the conflicts that arise from these different needs.

Political policy-making involves decision-making on polycentric issues.[22] Numerous competing interests need to be balanced or reconciled where the value of each depends on the decisions made on the others. All the different interests are likely to be represented in the political process. One issue, which is both polycentric and strategic, affects almost all political decision-making. That is the impact of change on the use of public resources, including not only public money but also manpower and organisational capacity. Again, the machinery of government is used to help resolve any conflicts that arise and sets the financial constraints that apply to all solutions devised by government.

---

[22] See Laws, 'Giving Effect to Policy in Legislation' (n 3) 9–16.

The approach of the law to change is entirely different. Many of the aspects of political decision-making mentioned above are absent from legal decision-making, or would be thought, in the United Kingdom, to be inappropriate for use for that purpose. This is apparent from an examination of legal change initiated by the judiciary. But it is also sometimes apparent in the way the law responds to statutory change undertaken for political purposes.

Legal change begins with a presumption that things should remain the same and predictable unless there is a clear reason for changing them. In this sense it is backward-looking. It looks for a mischief: for something that has gone wrong and needs to be put right. It does not, in general, require research or evidence about the extent of the mischief. It certainly does not use research or evidence to determine how effective any proposed remedy will be, or whether it will have unintended effects, either in practical terms or on perceptions. The remedy is devised exclusively by inference from a logical analysis of the mischief. The wider risks of doing nothing are generally not regarded as relevant, only the immediate disadvantages of leaving the mischief unremedied.

This, it is true, is how departments are asked to analyse their legislative intentions when instructing legislative drafters.[23] What is important about that, however, is that it is a discipline for putting policy into a legal context, not a substitute, and certainly not an improvement, on the methodology that produces the policy in the first place. For legislation, the legal reasoning of the drafting instructions exists in the context of a policy that has been produced by prior political decision-making, which provides the direction and context for the legal decision-making.

Because legal decision-making is backward-looking, rather than forward-looking, it requires greater levels of certainty and lower levels of risk than political decision-making. The legal approach to risk tends to be to seek to eliminate it, rather than to assess and manage it. Any assumption that legal methods are superior for policy-making purposes, because they involve greater precision ignores the fundamental differences between the two processes. Sometimes, the legal view of political decision-making seems to be that it should adopt the legal approach, but is in practice sloppier. What might appear to be sloppiness, however, is the natural consequence of operating in a less controlled environment, involving much more that is uncertain and unpredictable.

Another point of difference is that the evidence used for the existence of a legal mischief in judicial decision-making will typically involve a very small sample – perhaps one case – and the sample will be unrepresentative, because it will be confined to those affected by the law who have chosen to litigate. Even where a political change is prompted by an identified existing mischief, efforts will be made to seek evidence of its wider impact. Moreover, from a political point of view, what constitutes a mischief in the law for which a remedy is needed is something that has given rise to a political demand for a remedy; and the nature of the demand and the reasons for it are what defines the mischief and helps to determine the nature of the remedy.

One inevitable consequence of the different approaches that have already been described is that priority in legal decision-making is very likely to be given to the interests of those involved in an individual case, rather than to the wider, collective interests, which are the priority for political decision-making. In this respect, legal decision-making and judicial

---

[23] See OPC, 'Working with Parliamentary Counsel' www.gov.uk/government/uploads/system/uploads/attachment_data/file/62668/WWPC_6_Dec_2011.pdf, p 31ff.

law-making are more likely to run up against the risks of extracting a rule from an instinctive response to particular facts[24] and to the cliché that hard cases make bad law. Conventional wisdom also holds – the evidence is rather slim – that this proverb is further borne out by examples of legislation that has passed at speed in response to high profile individual cases. The usual suspects – normally rounded up when it comes to finding examples of bad law in statutes – include the dangerous dogs legislation and the safeguarding legislation that was passed in response to the Soham murders.

Similarly, a legal approach to pre-legislative consultation treats consultation as a matter of fairness involving a right to be heard, similar to what would be needed if legislation were a judicial process.[25] The political approach to consultation, on the other hand, is that it is a tool of change management. It may produce evidence that will improve decision-making and it is likely to make the final outcome more acceptable. But from a political point of view, consultation may be counterproductive if it relates to matters that will not be changed. Any failure to meet the expectations of those who are consulted is a political, not a fairness problem.

In any event, the effectiveness of change often depends on maintaining the necessary pace of change. In politics there is always a balance between the advantages of being comprehensive and the disadvantages of delay. Once there is a commitment to a proposed change, it is necessary to escape as quickly as possible from the blight which is created by the proposal and is likely to last until the change is complete. These factors seem to have no significant place in legal decision-making.

The legal approach to change is neither strategic nor integrated. Judicial decision-making techniques are often ill-suited to polycentric issues,[26] particularly where those issues engage interests that are not directly represented in the proceedings in question. Legal change as a result of a judicial decision rarely, if ever, treats its impact on public resources as relevant, despite the crucial political importance of that consideration. In addition, the legal approach to change will often concentrate on the technical impact of new rules and not on their effect on perceptions. The process of legal reasoning and change lacks the transparency of the political process.

One of the most obvious differences between the political approach to legal change and the judiciary's approach to it is the absence of any room for leadership in the latter. In order to retain public respect for the law and their own impartiality, judges rightly refrain from entering the public arena to advocate the principles on which they make their decisions, to consult about them or to build support for them. They do not set out the policy objectives they are seeking to achieve or accept public responsibility for the risks which their decisions involve. They rightly believe that leadership is for politicians. This particular aspect of the difference between the approaches of the law and politics to decision-making highlights a matter of serious concern. Aspects of legal change, such as the development and implementation of rules protecting human rights and, equally controversially, the extent to which the courts should review administrative decision-making have been delegated to the judiciary – or, some may say, have been arrogated to themselves by the courts. Whatever the merits of any argument about the extent to which there has been a delegation or any independent rule

---

[24] See eg Sir Richard Buxton, 'How the Common Law Gets Made: *Hedley Byrne* and Other Cautionary Tales' (2009) 125 *Law Quarterly Review* 60–78, especially at 60–61, 73–78.

[25] See the way in which consultation requirements were considered *in Buckinghamshire v Secretary of State for Transport* [2013] EWHC 481.

[26] Lon L Fuller, 'The Forms and Limits of Adjudication' (1978) *Harvard Law Review* 355.

of law argument for these developments (which are not for this chapter), it is clear that the effect has been to create a leadership vacuum in relation to these matters. This vacuum is particularly significant so far as perceptions of how these matters are handled by the courts may depart from reality. Politicians are relieved of the responsibility to provide leadership on these issues and they are also exempted from accountability for the outcomes produced by the decisions of the courts; and judges are functionally prevented from using the techniques of leadership to provide it themselves.

VIII CONCLUSIONS

The process of legal change through legislation involves both politics and law. The process involves balancing political and legal factors that affect both the legislative process and the content and implementation of legislation. An examination of how these balances are struck reveals that politics and law involve divergent approaches to legal effectiveness, are influenced by different values, necessitate different approaches to the same values and require the use of different decision-making techniques.

All of this has implications for the proper demarcation between the constitutional roles of the executive and Parliament, on the one hand, and of the courts, on the other. These implications also need to be taken into account when assessing the extent to which the courts should involve themselves in legal change, or in maintaining or developing a jurisdiction to review the content of legislation. They are also relevant to judicial challenges to processes associated with legislative change and administrative decision-making.

The examination of the different approaches of politics and of the law to change casts doubt on whether the courts, using the legal approach, are qualified to determine where the demarcation between law and politics should be. The courts are tied to the legal approach. By contrast, decisions within government and Parliament can and do adopt the political approach, while at the same time accommodating the values of the law – sometimes more effectively than the courts themselves. The question where the demarcation between the legal and the political approach should be is a political question. It needs to be answered using the methods of political decision-making, particularly in areas where leadership is important. It would not be wise to leave it to be answered, by default, by the courts.

6

Whitehall, Transparency, and the Law

DAVID SEYMOUR

THE HOME OFFICE is a large organisation with a budget of around £11 billion and 32,712 staff in 2011–12. It has a wide range of responsibilities and generates a lot of legal work. From 2000 to 2012, I led a team of 50 lawyers in the Home Office HQ and was a member of its Executive Management Board. We did not do all the legal work ourselves. Parliamentary Counsel draft our legislation on instructions from us. The Treasury Solicitor conducts our litigation – again on instructions from us. We use the private sector for much, but not all, of our procurement work. We use the Bar. And, of course, the Attorney General is the Government's Chief Legal Adviser and we consult him on issues of difficulty or sensitivity. My job was to provide Ministers with legal advice in relation to policy, individual decisions, legislation, test cases and the consequences of judgments which have policy or legislative implications and to ensure that across the whole spectrum of our business the Home Secretary receives the legal advice she needs from whatever source.

When I started my career in Whitehall in 1976, I was told by my first boss that I should not discuss my work with anyone and should only do so if the person I was talking to 'needed to know'. The 'need to know' principle dominated. That generation of Whitehall mandarins had served in the Second World War where 'careless talk costs lives' and that experience must have contributed to the prevailing culture at the time – namely that you did not talk about or disclose what you did in government. But over the last 35 years the over-riding principle – now universally accepted – has become that people have a right to know everything about what the Government is doing unless there is some very good reason why they should not know. The burden of proof, so to speak, has dramatically flipped in a relatively short space of time.

This was perhaps the single most significant development during my career and has led to a profound culture change in Whitehall. It is a welcome development but it does now present us with a serious set of legal challenges which I shall come on to. But first, how did this change to greater openness come about? There were many factors (not all of them to do with the law) but I shall mention just a few.

First, judicial review developed and in particular the requirement to articulate reasons for decisions in a way and on a scale which had not happened before.

Then there were specific Acts of Parliament (eg the repeal and replacement of the Official Secrets Act; the Freedom of Information Act; and the Data Protection Act which makes us all data subjects with a right to make data subject to access requests to public bodies which hold information on us – a useful right if you are thinking of suing that body).

Thirdly, increasingly rigid and tough disclosure obligations (rightly so) were imposed in criminal trials.

Fourthly, of course, the European Convention on Human Rights (ECHR) (even before it was implemented in UK law through the Human Rights Act) led to the UK putting telephone intercept on a statutory footing and also to it establishing a bespoke and formal system of appeal for non-UK nationals who were being deported on grounds of national security. More generally the Convention requires that, when departing from the rights set out there, the arrangements have to be 'in accordance with the law' and therefore more often than not discussed and approved by Parliament – not achieved by the exercise of some residual discretion or dispensation on the part of the Secretary of State.

Next, the Intelligence and Security Agencies were for the first time put on a statutory footing with formal functions and accountabilities spelt out.

Sixthly, there is a growing trend towards pre-legislative scrutiny, and we have seen the growth of robust Select Committees which have led to greater openness and explanation of government policy.

Next, of course, the growth of government itself combined with technological advances means that there is simply more official information around – much of it in the public domain – and if you know some of it, you tend to want or need more of it, or all of it, whether out of curiosity, for academic research or to challenge a government policy or decision.

Eighthly, there are many other non-legal factors which have contributed to greater transparency, eg instant and 24-hour news which means that politicians are now interviewed by the media and publicly account for their actions and decisions with greater frequency and on a much greater scale than in the past.

Finally, and perhaps most significantly, case law has made government actions both inside and outside the UK justiciable and subject to challenge in a way that was unthinkable only a short time ago and this has been at a time when there has been increased armed conflict overseas. This has led to challenging disclosure issues. When I first joined the Home Office I was shown an official file and taught how to initial it and how it should be processed. What we knew, say, about a deportee, an asylum seeker or a prisoner was on that paper file and that was the extent of our knowledge. Now relevant information is electronically stored on computers and hard drives in vast quantities (both here and abroad) – and it is sometimes quite difficult to ascertain what we do know – to unearth the 'the known unknowns' let alone the 'unknown unknowns' in terms of disclosing information which is relevant and treated as being in Her Majesty's Government's possession. And more information comes on stream all the time, making disclosure a demanding and ongoing task in the litigation process.

In addition to greater transparency, there has been a huge increase in the amount of litigation involving government, often, as we have seen, in areas which had previously not been the subject of challenge. Several thousand judicial reviews are brought against the Home Office every year. Many turn on their own facts. But a significant number raise important issues of public, human rights and EU law. So our operations provide fertile ground for test cases. In addition, the Government has to formulate its policy and run its operations against the background of jurisprudence (whether created in Strasbourg, Luxembourg or London) which, like the universe, is expanding all the time and sometimes in unpredictable ways. This is a real challenge because you don't always know what policy or decision is going to be challenged – what you do know is that by the time the issue

reaches the Supreme Court or Strasbourg, the jurisprudence (or the assumptions and factual basis on which the original decision was made) may well have moved on.

Most private individuals and businesses never get involved in litigation. If they do they
normally want to win the case in a way which serves their own immediate interests. Rarely
would they be concerned about the wider implications of the judgment. But government
business means that it has to fight a large number of test cases. Very often the issue is not
whether we have won or lost but rather what the case means for the Government's wider
programme and aims. So an analysis about how many cases the Government has won or
lost is not really the issue and is rarely informative – you can win badly and lose well. So
when the Home Office has an important case it needs to have a strategy and look at the
implications for the Government as a whole. The advice given rarely consists of 'yes you
can do this' or 'no you can't'. It is more a question of exploring a menu of options, assessing the possible outcomes, providing a risk assessment, anticipating how a case might be
lost and providing advice on contingency arrangements in the event that there is an unfa-
vourable outcome. So the clarity of the final judgment is particularly important because,
whether the Home Office has won or lost, it can then plan for the future with confidence.

These two issues – greater transparency (which we all welcome) and the scale, breadth
and increasingly complex nature of government litigation – raise a real challenge for government particularly in those cases where litigation is in the security or defence field and
involves large amounts of intelligence material. How can you have an open, fair and transparent trial (whether civil or criminal) and also protect sensitive material which cannot be
placed in the public domain? Traditionally these issues have been addressed by a range of
measures – legislating for closed proceedings in limited areas (eg the Special Immigration
Appeal Commission); by making public interest immunity certificates and leaving it to the
trial judge to decide whether the balance of public interest requires disclosure or non-
disclosure; by 'gisting' the sensitive material where appropriate; or, in exceptional cases, by
dropping a prosecution or withdrawing a control order or terrorism prevention and investigation measure (TPIM) if the disclosure of material would damage national security.
However, these measures are not sufficient in cases where the only way to achieve a fair
result is for sensitive information to be before the court. You can always drop a prosecution, but if you are a defendant in a civil damages claim you cannot unilaterally bring that
case to an end. In those circumstances if that material has to be protected you either have
to settle or submit to judgment.

There have been recent developments in this area. First, two Supreme Court decisions in
July 2011 addressed this issue and provided further clarity. In *Al Rawi v Security Service
(Liberty intervening)* the Supreme Court held, broadly speaking, that it was not possible to
have a closed material procedure in a civil trial for damages without statutory provision.[1]
The Government lost that case, having argued the contrary, but it is an example of how,
even if the decision goes against the Government, if it clarifies an issue in a helpful way
then progress is to be made. In *Tariq v Home Office (Justice intervening)*, the Supreme
Court held that the closed material procedure in the Employment Tribunal (which is set
up under statute) is compatible with the UK's obligations under both the ECHR and the
Treaty on the European Union.[2] Secondly, the Government consulted on the issue following the Justice and Security Green Paper[3] and introduced the Justice and Security Bill to

[1] *Al Rawi v Security Service (Liberty intervening)* [2011] UKSC 34, [2012] 1 AC 531, SC.
[2] *Tariq v Home Office (Justice intervening)* [2011] UKSC 35, [2012] 1 AC 452, SC.
[3] Department of Justice, *Justice and Security – Green Paper* (Cm 8194, 2012).

Parliament in May 2012. The Act, which received Royal Assent in April 2013, broadly speaking provides a power for the Courts to order closed material proceedings in civil proceedings.

This is not the only issue that currently concerns the Home Office. There are other issues on the counter-terrorism front and issues relating to serious organised crime, immigration, deportation, asylum, public disorder, policing, extradition, compliance with EU obligations, issues with inquiries and a range of procurement challenges. The Home Office has also been working on a wide range of legislation – in addition to the Justice and Security Act 2013 already mentioned, the Crime and Courts Act 2013 introduces a National Crime Agency, the Police (Complaints and Conduct) Act 2012 gives new investigative powers to the Independent Police Complaints Commission, and the department is working on a draft Anti-Social Behaviour Bill. But the specific issue I have raised in this chapter is particularly challenging. It will involve public discussion and consultation and I hope it will lead to a degree of consensus on the best way forward in this difficult area.

7

The Role of International Lawyers in Government

SIR MICHAEL WOOD

THIS CONTRIBUTION FOCUSES on some aspects of the role of lawyers in the field of foreign affairs.[1] I am no longer a government lawyer, having left the Foreign and Commonwealth Office (FCO) at the end of February 2006. I was the FCO Legal Adviser for just over six years before that. I had hoped for five or six years of peace, and what came was Kosovo, 9/11 and Afghanistan, and the invasion of Iraq, plus one or two other interventions elsewhere.

When I first joined the FCO, back in 1970, Whitehall seemed a rather divided place. Each department had its own culture and there seemed to be some distrust of other departments. This even applied to the lawyers. For example, the Home Office had very good domestic lawyers. The Foreign Office lawyers were mainly international lawyers, and in the eyes of the Home Office did not really understand true law. We tended to interpret statutes as though they were treaties. The Home Office would run rings round us on domestic legal arguments. Things have changed radically over the years. Whitehall is now necessarily much more collegial than before, including – perhaps especially – among the lawyers. Public international law is mainstreamed in many government departments, though I would still like to think that the FCO is a centre of excellence on this within government. This is one among many reasons why the FCO legal advisers are, and should remain, a separate cadre, not directly part of the general Government Legal Service but within the FCO and members of the Diplomatic Service.[2]

---

[1] Much has been written on Foreign Ministry legal advisers, including those in the FCO. See M Wood, 'Legal Advisers' in R Wolfrum (ed), *Max Planck Encyclopedia of Public International Law*, with bibliography http://opil. ouplaw.com/home/EPIL. For recent writings see, eg, MP Scharf, PR Williams, *Shaping Foreign Policy in Times of Crises: The Role of International Law and the State Department Legal Adviser* (Cambridge, Cambridge University Press, 2010); D Bethlehem, 'The Secret Life of International Law' (2012) 1 *Cambridge Journal of International and Comparative Law* 23; S Bouthuis, 'The Role of a Legal Adviser to Government' (2012) 61 *International and Comparative Law Quarterly* 939.

[2] On the different ways of organising advice on international law within government, see Wood ibid. For a useful database, see Council of Europe, 'Database on the Office of the Legal Adviser of the Ministry of Foreign Affairs' (18 March 2013) CAHDI (2013) Inf.3, also available online at www.coe.int/t/dlapil/cahdi/office_legal_affairs.asp.

I PRIVATE PRACTICE VERSUS FCO LEGAL ADVISER

I now spend some of my time practising as a barrister, almost always for governments, no longer just the British Government. It is interesting to compare the experience of being a Foreign Ministry lawyer with that of being an international lawyer in private practice, part of what is sometimes misleadingly called the 'international bar'.[3] They are very different jobs, needing somewhat different skills. A former FCO Legal Adviser has written:

> [T]he main role of the Governmental legal adviser is to 'make' his Government comply with international law. One must of course put the word 'make' in mental inverted commas. It would be a rare case indeed if a Governmental legal adviser were in a position to compel the Government he serves to act in one way or another. But it cannot by the same token be the limit of the function of even someone whose role is that of 'adviser' simply to ascertain what the law is, to explain it to the best of his ability to his client, and leave it at that. Of course, when it comes to action the final decision may not be his. It is a truism to say that the question whether or not to comply with what international law requires is always a question of policy. But even the meanest definition of the role of the international law adviser in government cannot treat that policy question as if it were an entirely neutral one. It must be assumed to be a necessary part of the role that the international law adviser should be expected to use his gifts of exposition and persuasion to bring those with whom the power of decision lies to use this power to the right result.[4]

A government public international law adviser may well regard, and be expected by his or her client (the Government) to regard support for the international legal system as an important part of his or her functions. Given the specificities of that system (for example, the absence, generally speaking, of any court or tribunal with compulsory jurisdiction), this may be so to an even greater degree than a lawyer in private practice, or an in-house lawyer for a corporation, or indeed a government lawyer acting in the field of domestic law. It remains, however, the case that all lawyers, including all government lawyers, have a duty to the law going beyond a duty merely to advise on what the law is.

In a Foreign Ministry you often have to deal with big issues, and you are given perhaps five minutes to come up with advice – in fact that's quite a lot of time. I remember when I was very new in the office, James Callaghan was the Foreign Secretary, and I was the only lawyer in at lunchtime. (I never made that mistake again.) I was summoned to his grand office, and he said, 'Turkey's invaded Cyprus. There's obligation to consult under the Treaty of Guarantee with Greece and with Turkey. If I telephone them separately, will that be consultation?' So I said, 'Well, I'll have to look at the Treaty of Guarantee.' He replied, 'Fine. You can sit over there', and threw me a copy of the Treaty. The volume was several hundred pages long. I quickly decided that the only thing to do was to give a clear answer, if possible the answer he wanted. He obviously wanted to be able to say to Parliament that he had fulfilled this obligation to consult, and I thought that was indeed the right answer: separate telephone calls would suffice. I hoped I was right.

I recall, by way of complete contrast, the first thing I did in private practice. It was a matter of little importance. I was asked by an embassy about some point of law relating to a

---

[3] E Sthoeger, M Wood, 'The International Bar' in C Romano, K Alter, Y Shany (eds), *The Oxford Handbook of International Adjudication* (Oxford, Oxford University Press, 2013).

[4] FD Berman, 'The Role of the International Lawyer in the Making of Foreign Policy' in C Wickremasinghe (ed), *The International Lawyer as Practitioner* (London, British Institute of International and Comparative Law, 2000) 3–17.

diplomatic mission. I read the papers, and thought, 'This is hopeless.' Back in the FCO, I would just have said, 'No, you can't do it.' But as a barrister in private practice, when giving advice you are normally expected to write a long opinion, saying, 'I have been asked about the following problem' setting it out in detail, then you set out relevant legal provisions and authorities, and spend two, three or more pages analysing them before concluding that the answer is no, and then you charge for it.

Now, I think it is obvious from what I said that in the FCO one's advice is often quite superficial, necessarily superficial because there is no time. So you have to give advice almost instinctively, and with little or no explanation. You often just say 'yes' or 'no'. That is not how it is in private practice. Much of a barrister's practice, at least in the field of public international law, will concern litigation. That is not the case for most FCO lawyers, even with the great increase in litigation of concern to the FCO over recent years.

Another major difference is that, within government, law and policy are very closely linked and handled together; this is certainly so in foreign affairs, but I think the same is true of the rest of government. Much of the time when you are sitting around in meetings you are actually advising on policy, and certainly contributing directly to policy advice; policy with perhaps a high legal content, but still policy. Ministers and officials often want your views on policy; they may sometimes even want the lawyers to decide a matter because they cannot make up their minds. That is particularly true, I would say, at the lower levels within the FCO. For example, the Protocol Division of the FCO deals with privileges and immunities, on which they are the experts; but when in doubt they really want to be told what the policy should be, they want to be told what to do, not just what the law is. That is fine when it is run of the mill stuff. But it is different when they ask you whether a former head of state has immunity for acts done while he was head of state. If you give the wrong answer it has consequences.

Having said that, it is of course very important to know in your own mind what law is and what policy is – indeed, that is essential. Even if you are being asked for policy advice, or giving it, you have to know that, at the end of the day, that is not really your job. Your job is the law, and the higher up in the office you are operating, the more likely it is that you will be dealing purely with the law, setting out the legal options and leaving the policy to others.

Another very important difference between working in government and in private practice is that as a FCO Legal Adviser you have a single client, and that client is the Foreign Secretary/British Government. Your client may well already have taken a position on the law. You might look at the law and know that it is highly controversial among international lawyers. For example, in relation to the use of force there is a dispute as to whether a state can engage in 'anticipatory self-defence' where you defend yourself if somebody is about to attack you or must wait for the attack to be set in train before using force in self-defence. Well, you may have your own views on that, but the British Government has its views, which have been established over the years, through practice, and at the highest level. You cannot just turn up and say, 'Well, that's wrong. I think that there's no such thing as "anticipatory self-defence".' You have to follow the party line. If you are going to try to persuade the Government to depart from that, you will need to argue very thoroughly as to why the Government should change its traditional position on the law.

The other thing, of course, is that governments on the whole have to be consistent in their view of international law, because what they say is the law becomes, to a degree, part of state practice, and can be held against them. That leads to caution. You become quite good at not answering questions (in public anyway), and trying to avoid expressing a view as to what is the law. You can, for example, say that you are acting in accordance with law, without actually saying what it is. One of the reasons for doing that is that, in the field of international law, you may not want to commit your government more than you have to. Nevertheless, the *British Yearbook of International Law* currently has some 300 to 500 pages every year of United Kingdom materials on international law.[5] It is, in principle, good for governments to ensure that their practice is published. It ensures that it is taken into account in the development of international law; though of course what you do or say on one occasion can come back to haunt you.

Of course, a government can always change its mind, and more than once. One of the big changes the Government made in recent years was to decide that it was no longer going to recognise foreign governments, but only states. This happened following Samuel Doe's coup in Liberia in 1980. We had just told ministers that the UK Government would have to recognise the new government, and I think that they did; but the new government promptly started shooting people on the beach. Our Government said, 'This doesn't look good.' We pointed out that, fortunately, recognition of a government does not mean blessing it. It is just an acknowledgement that the government exists. But our Government said, 'No, we've got to stop recognising governments.' Of course, for practical reasons they still have to decide which persons are the government and which are not. That seemed very convenient in 1980. It did not apparently seem so convenient in 2011. As I read the press, the British Government reverted to the recognition of governments in the context of the overthrowing of the Gaddafi Government in Libya. On 27 July 2011 they explicitly said that they recognised the National Transitional Council of Libya as the sole governmental authority in Libya. The British Arab Commercial Bank Plc, which held the assets of the Libyan Embassy in London, had received parallel instructions from the Gaddafi Government and the National Transitional Council as to how they were to deal with those assets. They applied to the High Court for instructions. Mr Justice Blair held that the Foreign Secretary's certificate precluded any argument in British courts that the Gaddafi regime could give directions as to dealings with Libya's governmental assets. The Government thus clearly departed from their policy of not recognising governments.[6] If you asked them, I suspect they would say that it was an exceptional case.

II ADVISING ON INTERNATIONAL LITIGATION

I'll now say a word about some practical aspects of advising a particular government in a court case. The government in question was the Government of Kosovo, in relation to the advisory proceedings initiated by Serbia, on 8 October 2008 at the International Court of Justice, over Kosovo's Declaration of Independence.[7] First of all, how do you become involved as their lawyer? Someone obviously suggests your name to them. Then you have to form a team. Kosovo obviously could not afford to pay a great deal, so we formed a very lean team, three foreign lawyers and an assistant (together with two excellent Kosovar

[5] *The British Yearbook of International Law*, Oxford University Press. The section 'United Kingdom Materials on International Law' has appeared in each volume since 1978.

[6] *British Arab Commercial Bank Plc v National Transitional Council of the State of Libya* [2011] EWHC 2274 (Comm), 26 August 2011.

[7] *Accordance with International Law of the Unilateral Declaration of Independence in Respect of Kosovo, Advisory Opinion, ICJ Reports 2010*, p 403.

lawyers). That is, on the whole, a good thing: international litigation tends to produce teams that are far too large.

The next thing is that you have really got to set off on the right course. Decisions taken in the first few days of a case may be crucial. In the Kosovo case, I went to see the Pristina authorities within a couple of days, and said,

> We've got to write to the Court immediately, and demand that they allow you to take part on an equal footing with Serbia, even though the whole question might be whether or not you're a State, and in principle only States can take part. We should say that it will be contrary to natural law if they don't let you take part, so if they decide you can't take part they shouldn't hear the case.

The Kosovo authorities immediately agreed to such a letter,[8] and it seemed to have the right effect, for a couple of days later the Court made an order inviting Kosovo (or rather 'the authors of the unilateral declaration of independence') to take part.[9]

Next, it is very important to have clear lines of instruction from the client. In the case of Kosovo there was a coalition government, the President was from Rugova's party, the Prime Minister from the party of the former Kosovo Liberation Army (*UÇK*). There was talk of setting up some sort of a commission to oversee the case. So the first thing I did when I met the Kosovar leadership was to say, 'I've got to take instructions from one person, who should be the Foreign Minister.' That was swiftly agreed. In the event everone worked very well together on the case, and there was no difficulty in securing clear instructions.

Lastly, relations with the media need to be carefully handled. This is, in my view, best not done directly by the lawyers. Again, the Kosovar authorities were very sensible. The Kosovar media were very responsible too, as soon as I told them that I couldn't tell them anything they stopped asking. That wouldn't happen here.

III LEGAL ADVICE ON THE USE OF FORCE

If you compare being a practitioner in the field of international law in government with being an academic, the one big difference I would say is that in government you do not really have the luxury of saying 'on the one hand, on the other hand', and giving no steer. In this connection I shall say a word about legal advice and the use of force. At the end of the day, you need to say whether the invasion of Iraq is lawful or unlawful. But I shall not go into that as it is a matter before the Chilcot Inquiry.[10] Instead, I shall mention four practical points that government lawyers advising on the use of force are aware of but which are not often discussed.[11]

---

[8] Letter from the Minister of Foreign Affairs of the Republic of Kosovo, HE Mr Skender Hyseni, to the Registrar of the International Court of Justice, 15 October 2008, *Kosovo in the International Court of Justice/Kosova në Gjykatën Ndërkombëtare të Drejtësisë*, Ministry of Foreign Affairs of the Republic of Kosovo (2010), pp 17–20.

[9] For the Court's Order, see *Accordance with International Law of the Unilateral Declaration of Independence by the Provisional Institutions of Self-Government of Kosovo, Order of 17 October 2008, ICJ Reports 2008*, p 409. Paragraph 4 of the Order read: '*Decides* further that, taking account of the fact that the unilateral declaration of independence by the Provisional Institutions of Self-Government of Kosovo of 17 February 2008 is the subject of the question submitted to the Court for an advisory opinion, the authors of the above declaration are considered likely to be able to furnish information on the question; and *decides* therefore to invite them to make written contributions to the Court within the above time-limits'.

[10] The Inquiry's website contains a wealth of material shedding light on the relationship between legal advice and foreign policy: see www.iraqinquiry.org.uk/.

[11] See, more generally, M Wood, 'The Law on the Use of Force: Current Challenges' (2007) 11 *Singapore Year Book of International Law* 1–14.

First, it is important to distinguish between the international law rules on the use of force and rules of constitutional law determining when a government may deploy the state's armed forces or otherwise become involved in a conflict situation. For many states, though not for the United Kingdom, the crucial legal issues in this field often arise in the context of constitutional law rather than public international law as such. To the extent that it is considered, international law seems to play only an indirect or even a secondary role. Thus, for Germany and for Japan, the key issues are the limits on the use of force set out in their constitutions, which may or may not correspond to international law, as well as the role of the legislature in authorising the deployment of armed forces outside the national territory. For Ireland, Switzerland, and some other states, a key issue will be the conformity of any action (such as allowing over-flight or refueling) with constitutional or other commitments to neutrality. Even in the United States, domestic 'war powers' issues – the respective roles of the Commander-in-Chief and the Congress – loom large. Occasionally I would have bilateral discussions with other Foreign Ministry Legal Advisers to compare views on the rules of public international law on the use of force, only to find the conversation dominated by constitutional concerns.

Of course, domestic law concerns are by no means absent in the UK. What should the role of the courts be in relation to the use of force? In the *Campaign for Nuclear Disarmament v Prime Minister* case in late 2002, prior to the invasion of Iraq in March 2003, the Divisional Court was asked to interpret Security Council Resolution 1441 (2002) and the UN Charter, but declined to do so, for good reason.[12] What should the role of Parliament be? The Blair and Brown Governments engaged in a wide consultation on this and other constitutional issues. They eventually seemed to decide against legislation, but to be planning to proceed by way of a Parliamentary resolution that would introduce a presumption that Parliament would be consulted before the UK went to war (as did indeed happen before the invasion of Iraq in 2003). This idea, which raises some difficult legal and policy issues, continues to surface from time to time.

A second general point is this. It is important to bear in mind that the legal issues arise not only when a state uses force itself, but also when it aids or assists another state to use force. In the words of Article 16 of the International Law Commission's 2001 Articles on State Responsibility, 'A State which aids or assists another State in the commission of an internationally wrongful act . . . is internationally responsible for doing so'.[13] The Commission's Commentary to this Article gives the following example: 'The obligation not to use force may also be breached by an assisting State through permitting the use of its territory by another State to carry out an armed attack against a third State'. Given the fact of American air bases on United Kingdom territory (in the United Kingdom itself, but also in British overseas territories, in particular the Sovereign Base Areas of Akrotiri and Dhekelia in Cyprus, and Diego Garcia in the British Indian Ocean Territory) this is an issue that must presumably arise with some frequency. An example from the past is the use of United Kingdom territory by the US air force to carry out the bombing raids on Tripoli and Benghazi in 1986.

---

[12] *Campaign for Nuclear Disarmament v Prime Minister* [2002] EWHC 2777 (Admin) (17 December 2002).

[13] For doing so if (a) it does so with knowledge; and (b) the act would be unlawful if done by it. See J Crawford, *The International Law Commission's Articles on State Responsibility: Introduction, Text and Commentaries* (Cambridge, Cambridge University Press, 2002); J Crawford, *State Responsibility. The General Part* (Cambridge, Cambridge University Press, 2013), pp 399–412.

A third general point is how strong the legal basis has to be before a state embarks upon the use of armed force – or assists another state to use force. This can be a crucial issue. It is an issue that is not often discussed, but it was raised squarely in the Attorney General's secret Iraq advice of 7 March 2003, now published.[14] The Attorney General said:

27. [...] I remain of the opinion that the safest legal course would be to secure the adoption of a further [Security Council] resolution to authorise the use of force. [...]

28. Nevertheless, [...] I accept that a reasonable case can be made out that [Security Council] resolution 1441 is capable in principle of reviving the authorisation in 678 without a further resolution. [...]

30. In reaching my conclusions, I have taken account of the fact that on a number of previous occasions, including in relation to Operation Desert Fox in December 1998 [that was an intensive bombing operation in and around Baghdad, that lasted just a few days] and Kosovo in 1999, UK forces have participated in military action on the basis of advice from my predecessors that the legality of the action under international law was no more than **reasonably arguable**. But a 'reasonable case' does not mean that if the matter ever came before a court I would be confident that the court would agree with this view.

How strong a legal basis is required before a state resorts to armed force is, in my view, ultimately a policy question rather than one for government lawyers. But lawyers can and should advise on the risks of acting on the basis of a 'reasonable', or 'arguable' or 'reasonably arguable' case, for example the risk of domestic and international proceedings, including criminal proceedings. What is the relevance, if any, of the Kampala definition of the crime of aggression? Article 8 bis, paragraph 1 reads:

1. For the purpose of this Statute, 'crime of aggression' means the planning, preparation, initiation or execution, by a person in a position effectively to exercise control over or to direct the political or military action of a State, of an act of aggression which, by its character, gravity and scale, constitutes a manifest violation of the Charter of the United Nations.[15]

It is important to be clear that the definition of the crime of aggression for the purposes of the Rome Statute is not intended to have any effect on the *ius ad bellum*. This is clear from Article 10 of the Rome Statute,[16] and was repeated in an 'understanding' adopted at the Kampala Conference.[17]

A fourth general point is also little discussed: the issue of proof of the relevant facts. At least after the event, a state which has used armed force may be required to demonstrate that the facts as known to it prior to the use of force were such as to justify, as a matter of international law, the resort to force under the circumstances.[18] This can raise difficult issues where proof relies on intelligence.[19]

---

[14] (2006) 77 *British Year Book of International Law* 819.

[15] Article 8 *bis* of the Statute of the International Criminal Court (the Rome Statute), added by the 2010 Review Conference of the ICC held in Kampala (emphasis added).

[16] 'Nothing in this Part shall be interpreted as limiting or prejudicing in any way existing or developing rules of international law for purposes other than this Statute.'

[17] RC/Res 6, Annex III, Understanding No 4.

[18] As Sir Frank Berman has explained, '[...] only the State itself can assess the threat it faces and how to respond. This is, however, emphatically not to say that the State's own assessment is, as it were, final and binding; nor is it to say that, just because it is self-defence, it somehow escapes the possibility of objective judgement after the event [...]': F Berman, 'The UN Charter and the Use of Force' (2006) 10 *Singapore Year Book of International Law* 9, 14.

[19] The same difficulty may arise when a state seeks to persuade the Security Council to act. These issues have been addressed in S Chesterman, 'Shared Secrets: Intelligence and Collective Security' (Lowy Institute Paper No 10, Lowy Institute for International Policy, 2006).

IV CONCLUSION

The task of those who advise on matters of public international law is not always straight-forward, given the nature of international law and the delicate relationship between law and policy in international relations. In addition, they are often seen as having special responsibilities to the legal system in which they practice. As Kofi Annan, when still United Nations Secretary General, put it, 'Legal advisers of States and international organizations, as well as practitioners in the field of international law, are among those individuals most committed to promoting respect for international law.'[20]

---

[20] United Nations Office of Legal Affairs (ed), *Collection of Essays by Legal Advisers of States, Legal Advisers of International Organizations and Practitioners in the Field of International Law* (New York, United Nations, 1999), Preface ix. See also ch 8 in this volume by Matthew Windsor.

8

Government Legal Advisers through the Ethics Looking Glass

MATTHEW WINDSOR

I INTRODUCTION

R EPRESENTATIONS OF THE government legal adviser abound in the political and popular imagination: the Machiavellian counsellor in the shadow of the elected official; the hired gun who meekly accedes to executive policy proposals; or the conscience of the administration, tasked with 'speaking law to power'.[1] A cultural touchstone for the examination of the role and responsibilities of government legal advisers was the infamous release of the so-called torture memos in the United States.[2] The attempt to justify legally the enhanced interrogation of terrorist suspects was defended by some as 'standard lawyerly fare',[3] while condemned in certain quarters as loophole lawyering.[4] Others regarded the torture memos as evidencing institutional pathologies with respect to executive branch legal interpretation and decision-making.[5] Despite the chorus of academic critique, there was a remarkably muted reaction from the relevant professional ethics body. The lawyers who authored the memos were criticised for failing to provide a candid and objective analysis. But they were not subject to disciplinary action because there was no unambiguous obligation or standard by which their conduct could be assessed.[6] The torture memos controversy is a microcosm of the challenges faced by government legal advisers in providing candid and objective advice. In highly charged political environments, the risk of legal advisers oscillating

---

[1] D Kennedy, 'Speaking Law to Power: International Law and Foreign Policy' (2005) 23(1) *Wisconsin International Law Journal* 173.

[2] See F Johns, 'The Torture Memos' in F Johns, R Joyce and S Pahuja (eds), *Events: The Force of International Law* (London, Routledge, 2011); D Luban, 'The Torture Lawyers of Washington' in D Luban, *Legal Ethics and Human Dignity* (Cambridge, Cambridge University Press, 2009); P Sands, *Torture Team: Deception, Cruelty and the Compromise of Law* (London, Allen Lane, 2008).

[3] E Posner and A Vermeule, 'A "Torture" Memo and its Tortuous Critics' *Wall Street Journal* (6 July 2004) A22.

[4] J Waldron, 'The Rule of International Law' in J Waldron, *Torture, Terror, and Trade-Offs: Philosophy for the White House* (Oxford, Oxford University Press, 2010); J Goldsmith, *The Terror Presidency: Law and Judgment Inside the Bush Administration* (New York, WW Norton, 2009) 144–51.

[5] See B Ackerman, *The Decline and Fall of the American Republic* (Cambridge, Belknap Press of Harvard University Press, 2010); T Morrison, 'Constitutional Alarmism' (2011) 124 *Harvard Law Review* 1448; B Ackerman, 'Lost Inside The Beltway: A Reply to Professor Morrison' (2011) 124 *Harvard Law Review Forum* 13; D Fontana, 'Executive Branch Legalisms' (2012) 124 *Harvard Law Review Forum* 21.

[6] Memorandum from David Margolis, Associate Deputy Attorney General, US Department of Justice, to the Attorney General (5 Jan 2010). See D Cole, 'The Sacrificial Yoo: Accounting for Torture in the OPR Report' (2010) 4 *Journal of National Security Law and Policy* 455.

between acting as *consigliere* and conscience in their interactions with government officials is evident.

This chapter argues that the theoretical legal ethics scholarly tradition fails to pay sufficient attention to the distinct roles and responsibilities of government legal advisers. In Part II, the leading approaches to theoretical legal ethics are discussed. The conventional approach asks whether the 'standard conception' of the lawyer's role – a partisan advocate, who is neutral about the morality of her client's aims and unaccountable for them – can be justified.[7] It focuses on the role-differentiated morality of the lawyer based on the dictates of adversarial advocacy (the 'adversary system excuse').[8] In Part III, the applicability of the 'standard conception' to the roles and responsibilities of government legal advisers is considered. The distinctiveness of government representation gives rise to professional obligations that are not adequately captured by the principles of partisanship, neutrality and non-accountability. While the 'adversary system excuse' is of some relevance to the legal adviser's conduct with respect to adjudication, it is unresponsive to a wide variety of advisory settings. Accordingly, a new conceptual framework is required for evaluation and critique.

II THEORETICAL LEGAL ETHICS

A Introduction

The law of lawyering can be conceived of in a number of ways. The legal profession is governed by the generally applicable principles of agency, tort, contract, evidence, procedure, criminal and constitutional law.[9] However, scholarly approaches encompassing the theoretical, regulatory and sociological dimensions of professional responsibility have developed alongside black letter doctrine.[10] Theoretical legal ethics initially emerged as a distinct field of inquiry in the late 1970s in the United States, as a strand of applied moral philosophy. Applied moral philosophy examines how abstract ethical norms may be 'applied to, require modification in, or even be irrelevant or harmful to practical real-life moral issues'.[11] Early (and now canonical) scholarship in the theoretical legal ethics field was motivated by the 'apparent dissonance between impartial morality and the one-sided partisanship of the lawyer's role'.[12] The focus was on reasons that might be given to justify a lawyer's actions, as against a demand for justification by those whose interests are affected.[13] The reasons that were frequently given appealed to deontological ethics, consequentialism and virtue ethics as justificatory traditions.[14]

---

[7] GJ Postema, 'Moral Responsibility in Professional Ethics' (1980) 55 *New York University Law Review* 63, 73; WH Simon, 'The Ideology of Advocacy: Procedural Justice and Professional Ethics' (1978) *Wisconsin Law Review* 30, 36–37.

[8] D Luban, 'The Adversary System Excuse' in Luban (n 2) 19.

[9] WB Wendel, *Lawyers and Fidelity to Law* (Princeton, Princeton University Press, 2010) 19.

[10] See D Nicolson and J Webb, *Professional Legal Ethics: Critical Interrogations* (Oxford, Oxford University Press, 1999); R Abel, *English Lawyers between Market and State: The Politics of Professionalism* (Oxford, Oxford University Press, 2003); A Boon and J Levin, *The Ethics and Conduct of Lawyers in England and Wales*, 2nd edn (Oxford, Hart Publishing, 2008).

[11] Nicolson and Webb (n 10) 5.

[12] D Luban, 'Misplaced Fidelity' (2012) 90 *Texas Law Review* 673, 673. See Postema, (n 7); R Wasserstrom, 'Lawyers as Professionals: Some Moral Issues' (1975) 5 *Human Rights* 1; C Fried, 'The Lawyer as Friend: The Moral Foundations of the Lawyer-Client Relation' (1976) 85 *Yale Law Journal* 1060.

[13] Wendel (n 9) 19.

[14] Nicolson and Webb (n 10) 10–34.

In recent years, there has been a 'jurisprudential turn' in theoretical legal ethics.[15] Attention has shifted from what is appropriate for lawyers to value in order to lead an ethical life to the role that lawyers play in a democratic system of government.[16] Political, rather than moral, philosophy is deployed to explore the metes and bounds of acceptable lawyerly conduct. Bradley Wendel has argued that theoretical legal ethics made a 'conceptual wrong turn' by using 'the toolkit of ordinary ethics to address the problems of lawyers, who are better analogised to political officials than to ordinary moral agents'.[17] He advanced a theory of legal ethics grounded on the function of law as a basis for cooperative activity in the 'circumstances of politics',[18] notwithstanding persistent disagreement about morality.

The ambition of the theoretical legal ethics tradition, premised on the notion that ought implies can, is both to influence individual action and help shape public policy with respect to professional regulation.[19] It seeks to provoke professional introspection by focusing on 'what kind of lawyers we want to be, or what we are as persons that lawyering actualises or destroys'.[20] Theoretical legal ethics scholarship has been criticised for operating at a remove from practical realities,[21] and for presuming to have 'mechanical and immediately regulative implications for ethical life'.[22] Raymond Geuss rejected the application of casuistic ethical approaches to politics as follows:[23]

> Politics is more like the exercise of a craft or art, than like traditional conceptions of what happens when a theory is applied. It requires the deployment of skills and forms of judgment that cannot be imparted by simple speech, that cannot be reliably codified or routinised, and that do not come automatically with the mastery of certain theories.

Given that rival legal ethics theories tend to give competing accounts of the ethical foundations of the lawyer's role, there can be a problem of disagreement at the point when such theories are translated into action.[24] However, it is unsurprising that different normative visions of the lawyer's role exist within the philosophical community, not to mention amongst government officials and the professional bar.[25] Because the lawyer's exercise of professional judgement always contains within it an operative theory of the role of lawyers in society, the contribution of theoretical legal ethics is to bring such conceptions to the surface and subject them to critical appraisal.[26]

The remainder of this section details the cluster of concepts that have generated scholarly debate in theoretical legal ethics: role morality; the 'standard conception' of the

---

[15] K Kruse, 'The Jurisprudential Turn in Legal Ethics' (2011) 53 *Arizona Law Review* 493.

[16] A Woolley, 'If Philosophical Legal Ethics is the Answer, What is the Question?' (2010) 60(4) *University of Toronto Law Journal* 983, 987.

[17] Wendel (n 9) 7–8.

[18] J Waldron, *Law and Disagreement* (New York, Oxford University Press, 1999) 86.

[19] A Woolley, 'The Problem of Disagreement in Legal Ethics Theory' (2013) 26(1) *Canadian Journal of Law and Jurisprudence* 181, 183.

[20] A Essau, 'Teaching Professional Responsibility in Law School' (1988) 11 *Dalhousie Law Journal* 403, 417.

[21] See M Freedman, 'A Critique of Philosophising about Lawyers' Ethics' (2012) 25(1) *Georgetown Journal of Legal Ethics* 91; MBE Smith, 'Should Lawyers Listen to Philosophers about Legal Ethics?' (1990) 9(1) *Law and Philosophy* 67.

[22] D Markovits, *A Modern Legal Ethics: Adversary Advocacy in a Democratic Age* (Princeton, Princeton University Press, 2008) 18.

[23] R Geuss, *Philosophy and Real Politics* (Princeton, Princeton University Press, 2005) 15.

[24] Woolley (n 19) 83.

[25] S Koniak, 'The Law between the Bar and the State' (1992) 70 *North Carolina Law Review* 1389.

[26] K Kruse, 'Professional Role and Professional Judgment: Theory and Practice in Legal Ethics' (2011) 9(2) *University of St Thomas Law Journal* 250, 251.

lawyer's role, comprising the principles of partisanship, neutrality and non-accountability; and the 'adversary system excuse' used to justify the 'standard conception'.

B Role Morality

A fundamental issue underlying professional ethics is the existence and permissible extent of role-differentiated morality.[27] Is it desirable that occupying a professional role provides an institutional excuse for what would otherwise be wrongdoing according to the dictates of ordinary morality?[28] In relation to lawyers, role-differentiated morality is said to permit, and promote, the performance of actions on behalf of clients that would be regarded as immoral if performed by non-lawyers.[29] The potential schism between ordinary and role-differentiated morality gives rise to a central question in theoretical legal ethics: 'can a good lawyer be a good person?'[30]

Roles have been defined as 'constellations of institutionally specified rights and duties organised around an institutionally specified social function'.[31] The complexity of modern society makes it difficult to conceive of a freestanding morality apart from the contexts in which people act and the roles they occupy.[32] Indeed, a 'moral division of labour' may facilitate the achievement of valuable social functions.[33] Accordingly, actors occupying institutional roles are frequently required to act on 'restricted reasons for action' rather than 'all-things-considered evaluations about the goodness or the rightness of their actions'.[34]

The requirement to act on 'restricted reasons for action' recalls Joseph Raz's theory of practical reasoning, which distinguishes between first-order moral reasons for or against beliefs and actions, and second-order reasons, which foreclose engagement in first-order moral reasoning.[35] Raz's theory illustrates that there may be second-order reasons to follow role obligations, to the exclusion of otherwise applicable first-order moral reasons. In relation to the legal system, first-order moral reasons may justify particular institutional arrangements. However, participating in such institutions might require excluding the consideration of such reasons. On this logic, ethical justification for lawyers is 'not case-by-case, but systemic and institutional in nature'.[36]

In professional contexts where ordinary moral reasons justify institutions, but those institutions generate distinct obligations,[37] proponents of role-differentiated morality claim that professional conduct is to be governed by the institutional rules rather than

---

[27] D Luban, *Lawyers and Justice: An Ethical Study* (Princeton, Princeton University Press, 1988) 104–47; A Applbaum, *Ethics for Adversaries: The Morality of Roles in Public and Professional Life* (Princeton, Princeton University Press, 1999) 76–109.

[28] Wendel (n 9) 7.

[29] Boon and Levin (n 10) 191.

[30] Fried (n 12) 1060.

[31] M Hardimon, 'Role Obligations' (1994) 91(7) *Journal of Philosophy* 333, 334–35.

[32] Markovits (n 22) 163.

[33] V Held, 'The Division of Moral Labour and the Role of the Lawyer' in D Luban (ed), *The Good Lawyer: Lawyers' Roles and Lawyers' Ethics* (New Jersey, Rowman & Allanheld, 1983) 60.

[34] Applbaum (n 27) 5.

[35] J Raz, 'Authority, Law and Morality' in J Raz, *Ethics in the Public Domain: Essays in the Morality of Law and Politics* (Oxford, Oxford University Press, 1995) 210.

[36] Wendel (n 9) 7.

[37] T Dare, *The Counsel of Rogues? A Defence of the Standard Conception of the Lawyer's Role* (Farnham, Ashgate, 2009) 57.

ordinary morality. By redescribing their actions in role terms, role occupants aspire to judgement of their actions pursuant to role-specific rather than orthodox moral criteria.[38] This generation of distinct role obligations in the lawyering context arguably gives rise to a 'simplified moral world; often it is an amoral one; and more than occasionally, perhaps, an overtly immoral one'.[39]

The maintenance of a 'hermetically sealed professional personality' proves hard to sustain.[40] Although redescribing actors and actions in role terms purports to avoid their moral evaluation, act and actor descriptions persist.[41] Bernard Williams argued that if there is to be a second-order justification of professional conduct when acting in role, that conduct 'should be able to exist coherently with the consciousness of [its] justification, not just in one society but in one head'.[42] On this view, lawyers should not identify so strongly with their professional role that personal morality and responsibility is excluded. Indeed, role identification has been described as a 'strategy for evading one's freedom and, consequently, one's responsibility for who one is and what one does'.[43] Because roles purport to change the 'morally apt description of actions',[44] Arthur Applbaum argues that rigorous analysis of professional roles must insist on practice positivism: 'the idea that the rules of practices, roles, and institutions do not have any necessary moral content – they simply are what they are, not what they morally ought to be'.[45]

C The Standard Conception

The 'standard conception' of the lawyer's role in theoretical legal ethics comprises two principles that guide the action of lawyers (partisanship and neutrality), and a third principle that informs the normative evaluation of their conduct (non-accountability).[46] Although the three principles that constitute the 'standard conception' are 'heuristic constructions',[47] they are reflected in numerous regulatory instruments and represent the beliefs of many lawyers about the relationship between law and morality.[48]

i Partisanship

The principle of partisanship requires the lawyer to advance exclusively the interests of her client within the bounds of the law,[49] maximising the likelihood that the client will prevail.[50] The interests of affected third parties or the public interest must not modify

---

[38] Markovits (n 22) 157–62.
[39] Wasserstrom (n 12) 2.
[40] Postema (n 7) 64.
[41] Applbaum (n 27) 76–109.
[42] B Williams, 'Professional Morality and its Dispositions' in B Williams, *Making Sense of Humanity: And Other Philosophical Papers* (Cambridge, Cambridge University Press, 1995) 195.
[43] Postema (n 7) 74–79.
[44] Applbaum (n 27) 9.
[45] ibid.
[46] Postema (n 7) 73; Simon (n 7) 32.
[47] Simon (n 7) 32.
[48] Wendel (n 9) 30.
[49] ibid 6.
[50] ML Schwartz, 'The Professionalism and Accountability of Lawyers' (1978) 66 *California Law Review* 669, 673.

this 'aggressive and single-minded pursuit',[51] unless such modifications are in the client's interests. As Lord Brougham observed:[52]

> An advocate, in the discharge of his duty, knows but one person in all the world, and that person is his client. To save that client by all means and expedients, and at all hazards and costs to other persons, and amongst them, to himself, is his first and only duty; and in performing the duty, he must not regard the alarm, the torments, the destruction which he may bring upon others.

The principle of partisanship is reflected in professional codes of conduct in many jurisdictions and is protected by rules prohibiting conflicts of interest and other breaches of fiduciary duty.[53] The Code of Conduct of the Bar of England and Wales provides that lawyers have a duty to 'promote and protect fearlessly and by all proper and lawful means' their client's best interests.[54] Likewise, the American Bar Association's Model Rules of Professional Conduct stipulate that a lawyer should 'zealously assert the client's position under the rules of the adversary system'.[55]

Partisan representation finds its clearest justification where criminal defence advocates are tasked with protecting their clients' rights against state coercion.[56] However, a commitment to partisanship also permeates civil litigation and non-adversarial contexts. Lawyers commonly act as though the principle of partisanship characterises their relationship with clients generally, even when the 'representations do not involve the courtroom'.[57] Stephen Pepper argued that partisan representation is morally permissible if it enhances client autonomy,[58] a perspective that has been criticised for conflating the morality of a given action with the morality of autonomous choice.[59]

The advancement of client interests within the bounds of the law begs the question whether client interests transcend strict legal entitlement. Lawyers have the power and incentive to manipulate the bounds of the law that are intended as a source of constraint.[60] Indeed, many lawyers seek to advance client objectives 'full stop'.[61] In contrast, Wendel argues that lawyers should only act to protect their clients' legal entitlements. Because a lawyer's role is 'defined and bounded' by such entitlements, acting on another basis would exceed their power.[62] For Wendel, lawyers must regard the law from the Hartian 'internal point of view',[63] rather than as an 'inconvenient obstacle to be planned around'.[64] This requires lawyers to interpret the law with fidelity and advise clients on the basis of reasons internal to the law.

---

[51] Postema (n 7) 73.

[52] Lord Brougham, in Dare (n 37) 9.

[53] Wendel (n 9) 38; Markovits (n 22) 4.

[54] Bar Standards Board, *Code of Conduct of the Bar of England and Wales* (2004) [303(a)].

[55] American Bar Association, *Model Rules of Professional Conduct* (2012) [2].

[56] M Freedman, 'Professional Responsibility of the Criminal Defense Lawyer: The Three Hardest Questions' (1966) 64 *Michigan Law Review* 1469; D Kershaw and R Moorhead, 'Consequential Responsibility for Client Wrongs: Lehman Brothers and the Regulation of the Legal Profession' (2013) 76(1) *Modern Law Review* 26, 45.

[57] Luban (n 27) 57.

[58] SL Pepper, 'The Lawyer's Amoral Ethical Role: A Defense, A Problem, and Some Possibilities' (1986) *American Bar Foundation Research Journal* 613, 634.

[59] D Luban, 'The Lysistratian Prerogative: A Reply to Stephen Pepper' (1986) *American Bar Foundation Research Journal* 637, 638–40.

[60] D Wilkins, 'Legal Realism for Lawyers' (1990) 104 *Harvard Law Review* 469, 497.

[61] Wendel (n 9) 31.

[62] ibid 52.

[63] ibid 61; HLA Hart, *The Concept of Law* (Oxford, Oxford University Press, 1961) 112.

[64] ibid 3.

ii Neutrality

The principle of neutrality provides that lawyers should not exercise moral judgement over their client's cause or actions taken to advance it, provided that both are lawful.[65] It prohibits lawyers from picking and choosing between clients and prevents clients from being denied representation because certain lawyers regard their cause as morally objectionable. Such withholding of representation would usurp the function of judge and jury,[66] and give rise to an 'oligarchy of lawyers'.[67] A key manifestation of neutrality in the United Kingdom is the cab rank rule, which requires barristers to accept briefs in the order they are received, rather than selecting clients on moral grounds.[68]

William Simon rejected the principle of neutrality on the basis that lawyers should take actions that promote justice in the circumstances of the case.[69] Simon's conception of justice refers to the congruence between morality and the outcome of a legal proceeding.[70] Thus, he urged lawyers to act directly on moral values, with scant concern for the client's legal entitlements. In a similar vein, David Luban called for 'moral activism' on the part of lawyers, involving counselling clients concerning the 'rightness or wrongness of [their] projects'.[71]

Direct appeals to justice by lawyers, in contravention of the neutrality principle, have been challenged on political legitimacy grounds. Lawyerly conduct that aims directly at justice or other moral values undermines the ability of the legal system to supersede disagreement about those values in the 'circumstances of politics'.[72] Neutral representation has been defended on the basis that it makes 'stability, coexistence and cooperation possible in a pluralistic society'.[73]

iii Non-Accountability

When acting as a partisan and neutral advocate on the client's behalf, the 'standard conception' considers that a lawyer should not be held morally or legally accountable for their professional conduct. Of the three principles that comprise the 'standard conception', it is non-accountability that most clearly demonstrates that the lawyer's role obligations are not to be evaluated in ordinary moral terms.[74] The principle of non-accountability reflects the requisite deference of lawyers to their clients in a principal-agent relationship. If a lawyer is bound to act for a client, 'no reasonable man could think the less of any counsel because of his association with such a client'.[75]

Critics of the 'standard conception' have argued that lawyers' moral faculties are engaged in their professional role in a way that is difficult to reconcile with the principle of non-accountability.[76] Wendel considered that the dissonance between ordinary moral agency

---

[65] Luban (n 12) 673.
[66] Luban (n 27) 10.
[67] Wasserstrom (n 12) 6.
[68] Boon and Levin (n 10) 14. For recent criticism, see J Flood and M Hviid, 'The Cab Rank Rule: Its Meaning and Purpose in the New Legal Services Market' (2013) University of Westminster School of Law Research Paper No 13-01.
[69] WH Simon, *The Practice of Justice: A Theory of Lawyer's Ethics* (Cambridge, Harvard University Press, 1998) 138.
[70] Wendel (n 9) 45.
[71] Luban (n 27) 173.
[72] Waldron (n 18) 86.
[73] Wendel (n 9) 10.
[74] Wendel (n 9) 29–30; Dare (n 37) 10.
[75] *Rondel v Worsley* [1969] 1 AC 191, 227.
[76] Wasserstrom (n 12) 14.

and the demands of acting in a public role should be frankly acknowledged.[77] The problem of 'dirty hands' arises where actions that are politically justified may nonetheless be morally disagreeable.[78] The lawyer's 'moral remainder' acknowledges their perspective as an ordinary moral agent, despite adherence to their professional obligations when acting in a representative capacity.[79] Moral remainders may assist the lawyer in discerning options for clients that avoid conflicts between legal entitlement and ordinary moral obligation.[80] Alternative modes of atonement include working against legal injustice in areas that do not affect client representation,[81] or opting out entirely in cases of conflict between ordinary morality and professional obligation.[82] Notwithstanding his discussion of dirty hands and moral remainders, Wendel recognised that the principle of non-accountability facilitates the perception that 'as long as lawyers play by the rules of the game . . . the moral implications of their practice can safely be ignored'.[83]

D The Adversary System Excuse

If the three principles that comprise the 'standard conception' are the rules, the adversarial system is the game that purports to justify a distinct role morality. In the adversarial system, lawyers act as the champion of their client, safe in the knowledge that a judge will evaluate the competing claims in an impartial manner. The adversarial presentation of conflicting evidence and theories of the case, through a 'wholehearted dialectic of assertion and refutation',[84] has been defended as an effective method to test facts and arrive at the truth.[85] The adversarial system and the equality of arms have been supported by proponents of political liberalism as a means of protecting individual rights against state encroachment.[86] Extending the 'rules of the game' analogy, Tim Dare asserted:[87]

> In an umpired contest, it is the umpire's job to spot fouls, to interpret and apply rules and to decide who has won. Players may abrogate responsibility for ensuring compliance with the rules to the umpire, pursuing any advantage the umpire will allow.

However, the players may not completely abrogate responsibility to the judicial umpire in the adversarial paradigm. The extremities of zealous partisanship are tempered by a countervailing duty of candour to the court in many jurisdictions, which obliges lawyers to assist the court in administering justice.[88] This duty of candour typically involves an

---

[77] Wendel (n 9) 159.

[78] See D Thompson, *Political Ethics and Public Office* (Cambridge, Harvard University Press, 1987); T Nagel, 'Ruthlessness in Public Life' in S Hampshire et al (eds), *Public and Private Morality* (Cambridge, Cambridge University Press, 1978); M Walzer, 'Political Action and the Problem of Dirty Hands' (1973) 2 *Philosophy and Public Affairs* 160.

[79] B Williams, 'Politics and Moral Character' in B Williams, *Moral Luck: Philosophical Papers 1973–1980* (New York, Cambridge University Press, 1981) 63.

[80] Wendel (n 9) 173.

[81] Dare (n 37) 149–50.

[82] Applbaum (n 27) 67.

[83] Wendel (n 9) 31.

[84] Luban (n 27) 69.

[85] Boon and Levin (n 10) 18; NW Spaulding, 'The Rule of Law in Action: A Defense of Adversary System Values' (2008) 93 *Cornell Law Review* 1377.

[86] M Freedman, *Lawyers' Ethics in an Adversary System* (Indianapolis, Bobbs-Merrill, 1975).

[87] Dare (n 37) 7.

[88] TW Giegerich, 'The Lawyer's Moral Paradox' (1979) 28(6) *Duke Law Journal* 1335; C Andrews, 'Ethics Limits on Civil Litigation Advocacy: A Historical Perspective' (2012) 63(2) *Case Western Reserve Law Review* 381.

obligation not to mislead the court deliberately, which requires controlling legal authorities to be disclosed, including directly adverse controlling precedent.[89] In theory, the lawyer's duties as officer of the court counterbalance her partisan posture.[90] In practice, given that good faith arguments for a modification of existing law are permitted, the duty of candour does little to fetter lawyerly pursuit of client ends.[91]

Notwithstanding the duty of candour to the court, the 'adversary system excuse' deployed to justify 'standard conception' conduct has been vigorously debated. Luban reviewed the consequentialist and non-consequentialist arguments for the adversary system. Consequentialist arguments suggest that it is the best way of ascertaining the truth, defending litigants' legal rights and safeguarding against excesses by establishing checks and balances.[92] Non-consequentialist arguments include that the lawyer-client relationship in an adversarial paradigm is intrinsically valuable, that the system is required to honour human dignity, and that any change would disrupt the social fabric.[93] Luban concluded that the largely pragmatic considerations that justify the adversary system are not capable of excusing lawyerly conduct required by the 'standard conception'.[94]

Daniel Markovits examined the institution of adversarial advocacy from the lawyer's point of view and also found it wanting. He provocatively suggested that lawyers who practise 'in the shadow of the structural division of labour between lawyer and judge' are professionally obliged to lie and cheat.[95] He claimed that these professional vices are not the result of excessive partisanship but are necessitated by the 'genetic structure of adversary advocacy'.[96] However, an ethical interest in integrity leads lawyers to resist characterisation of their conduct in terms of the professional vices. For Markovits, the 'adversary system excuse' cannot vindicate the ethical appeal of the profession from the lawyer's point of view because the division of labour arguments underlying it appeal only to aggregate or collective interests.[97] Instead, he argued that role-based redescription helps recast the professional vices in terms of fidelity and assists lawyers in preserving their integrity. Through a process of self–effacement, the good lawyer assists people to state their claims in an 'undistorted yet effective fashion', in a way that 'engages the authoritative institutions of government'.[98] Unlike Wendel's coupling of fidelity to law and political legitimacy, Markovits connected fidelity to clients with the legitimacy of adjudication.[99] According to Markovits, the appeal of fidelity to clients becomes stronger as the lawyer's activities move closer to addressing 'state-imposed resolutions of their clients' legal claims – because this is when the legitimacy of such resolutions is most insistently in need of a defence'.[100]

---

[89] American Bar Association (n 55) r 3.1.
[90] ER Gaetke, 'Lawyers as Officers of the Court' (1989) 42 *Vanderbilt Law Review* 39; JA Cohen, 'Lawyer Role, Agency Law and the Characterisation "Officer of the Court"' (2000) 48 *Buffalo Law Review* 349.
[91] Markovits (n 22) 46, 53.
[92] Luban (n 27) 67.
[93] ibid 67–68.
[94] ibid 93.
[95] Markovits (n 22) 25.
[96] ibid 26.
[97] D Markovits, 'Legal Ethics from the Lawyer's Point of View' (2003) 15 *Yale Journal of Law and the Humanities* 209. See B Williams, 'A Critique of Utilitarianism' in JJC Smart and B Williams (eds), *Utilitarianism: For and Against* (London, Cambridge University Press, 1973); BC Zipursky, 'Integrity and the Incongruities of Justice' (2010) 119 *Yale Law Journal* 1948.
[98] Markovits (n 22) 5.
[99] ibid 177.
[100] ibid 172.

E Beyond the Adversarial System

Theoretical legal ethics has been habitually preoccupied with adversarial advocacy, demonstrated by the way the 'adversary system excuse' is said to justify the 'standard conception' of the lawyer's role. A welcome feature of recent theoretical legal ethics scholarship is a heightened sensitivity to the range of institutional contexts in which lawyers represent and advise clients. A 'monolithic lawyer's attitude' that is invariable among different practice settings has been questioned,[101] and the need for professional regulation tailored to specific lawyering contexts has been recognised.[102] The tendency to over-generalise from the adversarial advocacy paradigm to contexts where clients are represented in non-litigated matters should be resisted. For Wendel, adversarial litigation is a special case where lawyers are permitted to assert their clients' arguable legal entitlements and leave it to other institutional actors, including opposing counsel and trial and appellate courts, to evaluate whether their position is plausible.[103] In other practice contexts, an 'aggressive tendentious advocacy mindset' may be inappropriate.[104]

In advisory contexts, there are often no analogous institutional actors to ensure that the lawyer's legal interpretation is correct. Where the lawyer's interpretive judgement is unlikely to be challenged by another party or tested for adequacy by a court, the lawyer acts as a 'private lawgiver to the client'.[105] Luban argues that lawyers who advise clients must offer independent and candid advice about what the law requires 'even if the news frustrates or infuriates the client',[106] and must not 'deflect their own interpretive responsibility on to hypothetical others'.[107] Interpretation from the 'internal point of view' requires advisers to guide and evaluate conduct in accordance with the law, which is regarded as obligation-imposing rather than sanction-threatening.[108]

III THE GOVERNMENT LEGAL ADVISER

To what extent does the conceptual structure of theoretical legal ethics – role morality, the 'standard conception' and the 'adversary system excuse' – accommodate the roles and responsibilities of the legal adviser to government? The attempt to analyse the role of the legal adviser by recourse to the 'standard conception' exposes a minefield of dis-analogies. The complex nature of government representation gives rise to professional responsibilities that are not resolved with reference to partisanship, neutrality and non-accountability as an evaluative frame. The extension of this conceptual inapplicability beyond government legal advice to encompass some other organisational contexts is readily conceded. While the 'adversary system excuse' and the countervailing duty of candour shed some light on the legal adviser's involvement in litigation, the need to provide a justificatory account for the adviser's other professional commitments is evident. Put shortly, a different game requires different rules.

---

[101] Wendel (n 9) 82; Luban (n 27) 57.
[102] Wilkins (n 60) 470; American Bar Association (n 55) [2].
[103] Wendel (n 9) 66.
[104] ibid 80.
[105] ibid 189.
[106] D Luban, 'A Different Nightmare and a Different Dream' in Luban (n 2) 154.
[107] ibid 132.
[108] Hart (n 63) 112; S Shapiro, 'What is the Internal Point of View?' (2006) 75 *Fordham Law Review* 1157.

A The Standard Conception and Government Lawyers

The 'standard conception' is not an appropriate conceptual framework for the roles and responsibilities of government legal advisers.[109] While considerable scholarly effort has been expended in generically exploring the ethical obligations of lawyers, little attention has been directed at delineating and defending the distinct responsibilities of those who represent the government outside the criminal prosecution context. What happens when the 'lawyer-statesman' is not an aspirational ideal but a vocational reality?[110] The failure of theoretical legal ethics to address this question led one commentator to describe government lawyers as 'the orphan[s] of legal ethics'.[111] Although the equality of arms principle would suggest that government lawyers should consider themselves subject to the same ethical dictates as their counterparts in private practice, the key tenets of the 'standard conception' are 'woefully undertheorised' in relation to government lawyers.[112]

i Partisanship

The principle of partisanship cannot characterise the conduct of client representation by government lawyers. From the standpoint of the legitimacy of adjudication, this is because the government is 'not an ordinary disputant who confronts the authority of the state . . . but is, rather, itself in authority'.[113] On this view, government lawyers should seek to promote justice rather than assisting the government in 'pursuing its idiosyncratic ends as effectively as it can'.[114] This non-partisan standard is illuminated most clearly with reference to the heightened professional obligations applicable to the criminal prosecutor. Because they carry significant responsibilities in ensuring the fairness of the criminal justice system, prosecutors must act impartially and not seek to obtain a conviction by all means.[115] They must form their own views of the merits of cases, revealing a distinctive commitment to truth and fairness that 'elaborate[s] a role whose genetic structure departs from the structure of adversary advocacy'.[116] Rather than representing an ordinary client before a neutral tribunal, the prosecutor represents one arm of the state before another.[117] Arguments have been made that the standard applicable to criminal prosecutors should also pertain to government lawyers in civil proceedings.[118]

The applicability of partisanship to the government lawyer is further undermined, given the existence of competing loyalties that bedevil their professional practice. Unlike the

---

[109] AA Guerrero, 'Lawyers, Context, and Legitimacy: A New Theory of Legal Ethics' (2012) 25(1) *Georgetown Journal of Legal Ethics* 107.

[110] A Kronman, *The Lost Lawyer: Failing Ideals of the Legal Profession* (Cambridge, Belknap Press of Harvard University Press, 1993).

[111] AC Hutchinson, '"In the Public Interest": The Responsibilities and Rights of Government Lawyers' (2008) 46 *Osgoode Hall Law Journal* 106.

[112] WB Wendel, 'Government Lawyers, Democracy and the Rule of Law' (2009) 77 *Fordham Law Review* 1333, 1334.

[113] Markovits (n 22) 173.

[114] ibid 173; CJ Lanctot, 'The Duty of Zealous Advocacy and the Ethics of the Federal Government Lawyer: The Three Hardest Questions' (1991) 64 *Southern California Law Review* 951, 955; SK Berenson, 'The Duty Defined: Specific Obligations that Follow from Civil Government Lawyers' General Duty to Serve the Public Interest' (2003) 42(1) *Brandeis Law Journal* 13, 17–31.

[115] R Carne (ed), *Professional Ethics* (Oxford, Oxford University Press, 2010) 12.

[116] Markovits (n 22) 86–87.

[117] ibid 87; *Berger v United States* 295 US 78, 88 (1935).

[118] BA Green, 'Must Government Lawyers "Seek Justice" in Civil Litigation?' (2000) 9 *Widener Journal of Public Law* 235.

'cardboard clients' that abound in theoretical legal ethics – 'one dimensional figures who are only concerned with maximising their legal and financial interests'[119] – the government client has other concerns that shape the objectives it brings to legal representation. Neil Walker has described the antinomies faced by the Law Officers in the United Kingdom as follows: [120]

> Every constitutional order faces an exacting challenge to articulate a role for the law officers which reconciles their attachment to a particular government and its political objectives with their commitment to a broader set of values associated with the integrity of the legal and political order.

Government lawyers have an obligation to give impartial and objective advice, not least because it is a fundamental obligation of government that it should act in accordance with law.[121] Jeremy Waldron rejected the applicability of partisanship to government lawyers, on the basis that government must be constrained by law so that citizens can enjoy freedom under the law:[122]

> [T]he responsibilities of a lawyer advising the government are different from the responsibilities of a lawyer advising the private citizen or the individual businessman. The lawyer's job in private practice is certainly not to counsel law-breaking, but the lawyer may legitimately look for loopholes or ways of avoiding the impact of regulation and restraint on the freedom of his or her client. In government service, however, things are different. There, the lawyer's job is to hold the government to its responsibility under the Rule of Law. Government lawyers should not be in the business of looking for pockets of unregulated discretion or loopholes in such regulations as do exist. They should not be advising their political bosses that they are entitled to avoid the impact of legal constraint where it is ambiguous or unclear.

The principle of partisanship is premised on the 'antiquated assumption' that the paradigmatic lawyer-client relationship is between an individual client and a lawyer.[123] The results are homogeneous theoretical frameworks and codes of conduct that fail to account adequately for organisational clients, including governments, corporations and other institutions.[124] For example, the sole concession to the existence of organisational clients by the American Bar Association is a rule that provides that a lawyer retained by an organisation 'represents the organisation acting through its duly authorised constituents'.[125] However, major issues such as the challenge of determining the hydra-like organisation's objectives, ascertaining who speaks for the organisation and how to address divergent constituencies within it remain under-explored by such a formulation.[126]

---

[119] K Kruse, 'Beyond Cardboard Clients in Legal Ethics' (2010) 23 *Georgetown Journal of Legal Ethics* 103, 104.

[120] N Walker, 'The Antinomies of the Law Officers' in M Sunkin and S Payne (eds), *The Nature of the Crown: A Legal and Political Analysis* (Oxford, Clarendon Press, 1999) 135. See also NW Spaulding, 'Professional Independence in the Office of the Attorney-General' (2008) 60 *Stanford Law Review* 1931; KA Kyriakides, 'The Advisory Functions of the Attorney-General' (2003) 1(1) *Hertfordshire Law Journal* 173; JLJ Edwards, *The Attorney-General, Politics and the Public Interest* (London, Sweet & Maxwell, 1984) 391.

[121] F Berman, 'The Role of the International Lawyer in the Making of Foreign Policy' in C Wickremasinghe (ed), *The International Lawyer as Practitioner* (London, British Institute of International and Comparative Law, 2000) 5; AM Dodek, 'Lawyering at the Intersection of Public Law and Legal Ethics: Government Lawyers as Custodians of the Rule of Law' (2010) 33(1) *Dalhousie Law Journal* 1.

[122] Waldron (n 4) 323–24.

[123] KA Carpenter and E Wald, 'Litigating for Groups' (2013) 81 *Fordham Law Review* 3085.

[124] LJ Fox and SR Martyn, *The Ethics of Representing Organisations: Legal Fictions for Clients* (Oxford, Oxford University Press, 2009); SH Kim, 'The Ethics of In-House Practice' in L Levin and L Mather (eds), *Lawyers in Practice: Ethical Decision Making in Context* (Chicago, University of Chicago Press, 2012).

[125] American Bar Association (n 55) r 1.13(a).

[126] WH Simon, 'Whom (or What) Does the Organisation's Lawyer Represent: An Anatomy of Intraclient Conflict' (2003) 91 *California Law Review* 57.

Difficulties with client identification that pervade government and organisational settings more generally render partisanship an inappropriate principle to guide the action of government legal advisers.[127] For example, a collection of interviews with former Legal Advisers in the United States Department of State revealed a wide divergence of views regarding the identity of the client.[128] Answers included the instructing government department, the State Department, the Secretary of State, the President,[129] the Senate, the 'entire body of the public' and the 'public interest'.[130] One former Adviser acknowledged that client identity was an 'extremely difficult question to answer and one that Legal Advisers should lose sleep over'.[131] Sir Frank Berman, a former Legal Adviser at the Foreign and Commonwealth Office in the United Kingdom, agreed that this was a difficult question but concluded that the Legal Adviser 'ultimately serves the country at large'.[132] The conception of the lawyer as 'hired gun' for their client must be tempered by the recognition that government legal advisers may also be required to act as custodians or 'high priests' of fundamental legal values.[133] The principle of partisanship, as framed by the 'standard conception' of the lawyer's role, fails to account for these Janus-faced professional realities.

ii Neutrality

The principle of neutrality has little explanatory purchase on the conduct of salaried or in-house lawyers, such as government legal advisers, given that client selection and the prospect of denial of representation are not relevant considerations.[134] In the United Kingdom, civil servants are required to act according to the merits of the case and serve governments of different political parties equally well.[135] Ministers are required to uphold this political impartiality by not asking civil servants to act in any way that would conflict with the Civil Service Code or the Constitutional Reform and Governance Act 2010: [136]

> [Their] total dependence for support on apolitical civil servants means that they cannot secretly abuse their power without the knowledge of those who owe them no political allegiance and they cannot take decisions without the discipline of face to face discussions with them.

---

[127] See W Josephson and R Pearce, 'To Whom Does the Government Lawyer Owe the Duty of Loyalty when Clients are in Conflict?' (1986) 29 *Howard Law Journal* 539; J Rosenthal, 'Who is the Client of the Government Lawyer?' in P Salkin (ed), *Ethical Standards in the Public Sector*, 2nd edn (New York, American Bar Association, 2010); GP Miller, 'Government Lawyers' Ethics in a System of Checks and Balances' (1987) 54 *University of Chicago Law Review* 1293; K Clark, 'Government Lawyers and Confidentiality Norms' (2007) 85 *Washington University Law Review* 1033, 1049–72; GC Hazard Jr, 'Conflicts of Interest in Representation of Public Agencies in Civil Matters' (2000) 9 *Widener Journal of Public Law* 211.

[128] MP Scharf and PR Williams, *Shaping Foreign Policy in Times of Crisis: The Role of International Law and the State Department Legal Adviser* (Cambridge, Cambridge University Press, 2010) 151.

[129] G Blum, 'The Role of the Client: The President's Role in Government Lawyering' (2009) 32 *Boston College International and Comparative Law Review* 275; D Luban, '"That the Laws be Faithfully Executed": The Perils of the Government Legal Adviser' (2012) 38 *Ohio Northern University Law Review* 1043.

[130] SK Berenson, 'Public Lawyers, Private Values: Can, Should and Will Government Lawyers Serve the Public Interest?' (2000) 41 *Boston College Law Review* 789.

[131] Scharf and Williams (n 128) 153.

[132] ibid 173.

[133] Walker (n 120) 158.

[134] Guerrero (n 109) 121; JR Macey and GP Miller, 'Reflections on Professional Responsibility in a Regulatory State' (1995) 63 *George Washington Law Review* 1105.

[135] *Civil Service Code* (2010) [3].

[136] Sir Brian Cubbon before the Treasury and Civil Service Committee (5th Report of 1993–94, HC 27, vol III, Appendix 31, para 8) in C Turpin and A Tomkins, *British Government and the Constitution*, 7th edn (Cambridge, Cambridge University Press, 2011) 445.

The neutrality-dictated need for advisers to retain a detachment from client projects is challenged by the realities of institutional structure in the context of government legal advice. Such structural issues have a bearing on whether the legal adviser operates in a culture of independence or one of 'reticence, complaisance and complicity'.[137] In Whitehall, government legal work is largely undertaken within a departmental structure, in which functions and powers are allocated among a number of legally co-ordinate authorities.[138] Distinctions can also be drawn between appointment processes in presidential and parliamentary systems. While in-house lawyers are frequently political appointments in the United States based on loyalty to the President's agenda,[139] permanent civil service appointments are the norm in the United Kingdom.[140] The latter arrangement has been challenged by the appointment of special advisers who assist ministers from a 'standpoint that is more politically committed and politically aware' than would be available from the civil service,[141] and who are tasked with 'supplement[ing] or counter[ing] the conventional wisdom of the departments'.[142]

Like the principle of neutrality, the application of legal advice privilege turns on the need for independence and separation between a lawyer and a client's projects. Accordingly, a consideration of the application of legal advice privilege to in-house lawyers is illuminating. Legal advice privilege covers communications made in confidence between lawyers and their clients for the purpose of giving or obtaining legal advice, even where litigation is not contemplated.[143] The generally accepted rationale for the privilege is the public interest in the administration of justice in enabling persons to obtain appropriate legal advice and assistance,[144] and the recognition that effective and accurate legal advice requires absolute candour between lawyer and client.[145] Indeed, a party's decisions about whether to obtain legal advice about a contemplated act may be influenced by the existence of rules protecting the confidentiality of communications with legal advisers.[146]

In the United Kingdom and the United States, legal advice provided by government lawyers attracts legal advice privilege and is protected from disclosure.[147] Lord Denning endorsed the application of privilege to in-house and government lawyers as follows:[148]

> They are regarded by the law as in every respect in the same position as those who practise on their own account. The only difference is that they act for one client only, and not for several clients. They must uphold the same standards of honour and of etiquette. They are subject to the

---

[137] TM Franck, 'An Outsider Looks at the Foreign Office Culture' (2005) 23 *Wisconsin International Law Journal* 4, 5.

[138] T Daintith and A Page, *The Executive in the Constitution: Structure, Autonomy and Internal Control* (Oxford, Oxford University Press, 1999) 323.

[139] Wendel (n 112) 1334–35.

[140] G Drewry, 'Lawyers in the UK Civil Service' (1981) 59(1) *Public Administration* 15.

[141] Cabinet Office, *Code of Conduct for Special Advisers* (2010) [2].

[142] Turpin and Tomkins (n 136) 448; A Blick, *People Who Live in the Dark: The History of the Special Adviser in British Politics* (London, Politico's, 2004); R Klein and J Lewis, 'Advice and Dissent in British Government: The Case of the Special Advisers' (1977) 6 *Policy and Politics* 1.

[143] *Three Rivers District Council v Governor and Company of the Bank of England (No 6)* [2005] 1 AC 610 [50]; *R (Prudential) v Special Commissioner of Income Tax* [2013] UKSC 1 [19].

[144] *Upjohn Corporation v US* 499 US 383 (1981).

[145] *R v Derby Magistrates Court ex p B* [1996] 1 AC 487, 510; B Thanki (ed), *The Law of Privilege* (Oxford, Oxford University Press, 2011) xiii; Kershaw and Moorhead (n 56) 53–54.

[146] S Shavell, 'Legal Advice About Contemplated Acts: The Decision to Obtain Advice, its Social Desirability and Protection of Confidentiality' (1988) 17 *Journal of Legal Studies* 13.

[147] United Kingdom Cabinet Office, *The Cabinet Manual* (2011) [6.19]; *Upjohn Corporation* (n 144); *US v Anderson* 34 FRD 518 (Dist Colo 1963); MG Leslie, 'Government Officials as Attorneys and Clients: Why Privilege the Privileged' (2002) 77 *Indiana Law Journal* 469, 481.

[148] *Alfred Crompton Amusement Machines Ltd v Customs & Excise Comrs (No 2)* [1972] 2 QB 102, 129.

same duties to their client and to the court. They must respect the same confidences. They and their client have the same privileges.

In Australia, legal advice privilege applies between the government and its legal advisers, provided that the professional relationship between them 'secures to the advice an independent character notwithstanding the employment'.[149] The High Court of Australia has upheld the privilege on public interest grounds:[150]

> The wisdom of the centuries is that the existence of the privilege encourages resort to those skilled in the law and that this makes a better legal system. Government officers need that encouragement, albeit, perhaps, for reasons different to those which might be expected to motivate the citizen.

Issues of independence and competing loyalties were at the forefront of a recent Australian case regarding whether privilege applied to legal advice given by the Department of Foreign Affairs and Trade (DFAT).[151] The advice given by DFAT was not regarded as sufficiently independent because the work had been done in an office that had 'mixed responsibilities for legal work and policy work, by persons who may or may not be admitted to practice and who, at least in some instances, must switch from policy work to legal work'.[152] The decision also concluded that advice would not be characterised as legal for the purposes of privilege 'if it strays so far into considerations and interests that are not referring or relating to the law . . . for example, work predicated on commercial or political grounds'.[153]

In European Union law, the requirement of independence has been used to deny the application of privilege to advice given by in-house lawyers.[154] Privilege can only be claimed for communications with advisers who are not bound to the client by an employment relationship. Advocate-General Kokott explained this position as follows:[155]

> Both their considerably greater economic dependence and their much stronger identification with the client – their employer – militate against the proposition that employed in-house lawyers should enjoy the protection afforded by legal professional privilege in respect of internal company or group communications.

In a recent decision, the Court of Justice of the European Union used this line of authority on privilege and in-house lawyers to bar in-house lawyers from representing their clients before the Court.[156] This decision was made on independence grounds, on the basis that an entity represented by a salaried lawyer essentially represents itself. Although the constituent treaty continues to permit Member States to represent themselves,[157] concerns about the independence of in-house counsel obtain equally to government lawyers:[158]

---

[149] *Waterford v Commonwealth* (1987) 163 CLR 54, 62.
[150] ibid 62; *Attorney-General (NT) v Kearney* (1985) 158 CLR 500, 511.
[151] *Philip Morris Ltd v Prime Minister* [2011] AATA 556.
[152] ibid [185].
[153] ibid [156].
[154] *AM&S Europe Ltd v Commission* [1983] 1 QB 878; *Akzo Nobel Ltd and Akcros Chemicals Ltd v European Commission* [2010] ECR I-8301. See E Skonicki, 'Building a Wall Where a Fence Will Do: A Critique of the European Union's Denial of Attorney-Client Privilege to In-House Counsel' (2008) 21 *Georgetown Journal of Legal Ethics* 1045.
[155] *Akzo Nobel Ltd* (n 154).
[156] *Prezes Urzedu Komunikacji Elektronicznej and Republic of Poland v Commission* [2012] ECR Joined Cases C-422/11 P and C-423/11.
[157] Art 19, Statute of the CJEU.
[158] JN Stefanelli, 'Expanding *Akzo Nobel*: In-House Counsel, Government Lawyers and Independence' (2013) 62(2) *International and Comparative Law Quarterly* 485, 488.

Like in-house counsel, government lawyers are salaried employees for one employer only. They are valued for their specialised knowledge, their familiarity with the internal workings of their employer-client and they often possess confidential knowledge of their employer-client's business activities. They would therefore arguably feel similar pressures to those of in-house counsel, which may in turn affect their ability to offer independent legal advice.

The relationship between legal advice privilege and independence sheds light on the difficulties for in-house legal advisers in remaining neutral in a departmental government paradigm.[159] The coming together of lawyers and policy-makers within departments can mean that lawyers find their 'independence of mind being eroded by more intimate involvement in, and hence commitment to, the political purposes of the department'.[160] While calls for independence might function to 'disguise dissatisfaction with an administration's political goals [in the] language of professional misconduct',[161] without independence, the privilege rules might function as a smokescreen for conspiracy. A worrying corollary might be a shift from interpretation from the 'internal point of view' to the crafting of compliance mechanisms in order to evade legal control.[162]

iii Non-Accountability

If partisanship and neutrality are unable to guide the action of government lawyers, it is not clear why non-accountability should inform the normative evaluation of their conduct. Yet a principle of non-accountability appears to be operative in relation to government legal advisers, albeit for different reasons than those provided by the 'standard conception'. The tendency to think of government decisions as the product of a single, rationally calculating brain has been described as the 'anthropomorphic fallacy in policy analysis'.[163] However, a central issue in political ethics is the problem of 'many hands', and the associated difficulties of identifying who is morally responsible for political outcomes.[164]

Despite the concentration of legal expertise within particular departments, final decision-making authority typically resides with an elected official. In judicial review proceedings, a court will consider the minister as the person who is ultimately responsible for ensuring that a particular decision is made reasonably, fairly and according to law.[165] Ministers are under an overarching duty to comply with the law, to uphold the administration of justice and to protect the integrity of public life.[166] Henry Hart and Albert Sacks observed:[167]

> [T]he power and the ultimate responsibility of decision in these situations belong to the official whom the lawyer advises. The lawyer acts essentially in a staff capacity, and has always to remember this.

---

[159] P Jenoff, 'Going Native: Incentive, Identity and the Inherent Ethical Problem of In-House Counsel' (2012) 114(2) *West Virginia Law Review* 20; Suzanne Le Mire, 'Testing Times: In-House Counsel and Independence' (2011) 14 *Legal Ethics* 23.

[160] Daintith and Page (n 138) 345.

[161] Spaulding (n 120) 1934–35.

[162] Daintith and Page (n 138) 345.

[163] A Chayes, *International Crises and the Role of Law: The Cuban Missile Crisis* (Oxford, Oxford University Press, 1974) 4.

[164] Thompson (n 78) 40.

[165] United Kingdom Cabinet Office, *The Cabinet Manual* (2011) [6.13].

[166] ibid [3.46].

[167] HM Hart Jr and AM Sacks, *The Legal Process: Basic Problems in the Making and Application of Law* (Cambridge, Cambridge University Press, 1994) 1047.

Regardless of whether disputed legal questions are 'channelled unilaterally from a single department or involve interdepartmental conflicts of jurisdiction or interpretations of the law',[168] in the United Kingdom, the Attorney-General represents the ultimate advisory authority on matters of constitutional and international law.[169] By advising, the Attorney-General takes an issue out of the framework of intra-departmental relations between legal advisers and ministers and potentially into the sphere of inter-ministerial consideration.[170] However, the fact that the Law Officers have or have not advised, and the content of their advice, may not be disclosed outside government without their authority.[171] The implication of this constitutional convention is that, despite being ministers with advisory functions, the Law Officers are also not responsible in a parliamentary or public sense for the advice they give.[172] While there has been support for the 'imposition of an impregnable moat around Law Officers' opinions',[173] talk of an absolute prohibition against disclosure is inaccurate:[174]

> Expressed in realistic terms, the rule enables consideration of political advantage or embarrass-
> ment to the government to govern the decision whether to reveal what advice the Law Officers
> have given a Ministerial colleague or the government as a whole.

The emergence of freedom of information legislation, underpinned by principles of public authority accountability, has reshaped the governance terrain by turning a spotlight on executive legal interpretation. Immanuel Kant considered that 'all actions affecting the rights of other human beings are wrong if their maxim is not compatible with their being made public'.[175] Framed positively, the availability or public promulgation of government information provides 'greater incentive to ensure [that it is] factually right, neutral, comprehensive and well-judged'.[176] However, the prospect of disclosure heightens hermeneutic sensitivity and means that advice might be written in a way that 'anticipates scrutiny from outside the circle of decision makers to whom it has been tendered. In such a case, it could lose its character of candid guidance offered in confidence'.[177] More detrimentally still, there is the risk that actions will be shrouded in complete secrecy, and not reduced to writing, to avoid judicial review and compelled statutory disclosure.[178]

The diffusion of advice and ultimate decision-making is a quintessential feature of modern bureaucracy.[179] Legal advisers can frequently fall back on a 'causal excuse', where a

---

[168] Edwards (n 120) 181; M Palmer, 'The Law Officers and Departmental Lawyers' (2011) *New Zealand Law Journal* 333.

[169] ibid 181.

[170] Daintith and Page (n 138) 301.

[171] United Kingdom Cabinet Office, *Ministerial Code* (2010) [2.12]; United Kingdom Cabinet Office, *The Cabinet Manual* (2011) [6.9].

[172] Daintith and Page (n 138) 311.

[173] ibid 210.

[174] Edwards (n 120) 225. See *HM Treasury v Information Commissioner and Evan Owen* [2009] EWHC 1811 [7].

[175] I Kant, 'Perpetual Peace: A Philosophical Sketch' in HS Reiss (ed), *Kant's Political Writings*, 2nd edn (Cambridge, Cambridge University Press, 1991) 126. See also D Luban, 'The Publicity Principle' in RE Goodin (ed), *The Theory of Institutional Design* (Cambridge, Cambridge University Press, 1998) 154.

[176] M Shroff, 'The Worldly Task' in C Geiringer and DR Knight (eds), *Seeing the World Whole: Essays in Honour of Sir Kenneth Keith* (Wellington, Victoria University Press, 2008) 267.

[177] House of Lords Select Committee on the Constitution, Fifteenth Report of Session 2005/6, HL Paper 236-I, 29, in M Weller, *Iraq and the Use of Force in International Law* (Oxford, Oxford University Press, 2010) 253.

[178] D Pozen, 'Deep Secrecy' (2010) 62(2) *Stanford Law Review* 257.

[179] D Rhode, 'Ethical Perspectives in Legal Practice' (1985) 37 *Stanford Law Review* 589, 631. Sir Francis Floud discussed the 'wise, experienced, and tactful legal adviser' who exercises influence 'over the whole range of policy of a Department without having any executive power': 'The Sphere of the Specialist in Public Administration' (1923) 1 *Public Administration* 117.

subsequent act by another official controls whether their action has any effect and bears the entire responsibility for any harmful consequence.[180] As the satirist Tom Lehrer quipped, 'Once the rockets go up, who cares where they come down. It's not my department'.[181] The decisional division of labour in bureaucracy carries the risk of the cabining of moral attention, such that no actor sees themselves as responsible for overall policy outcomes.[182] Such cabining exacerbates the potential for 'complicity with cruelty induced by passive faith in authority and the bracketing of personal responsibility under an explanation of just following the rules'.[183] The risk of tunnel vision for legal advisers, in restricting their attention to legal questions rather than polycentric political or policy ones, is that they may be unlikely to dwell on the underlying substantive conduct of their client, a confrontation that it is hoped would activate their independent sense of moral responsibility. As Philip Allott observed, government legal advisers have: 'A unique public responsibility – the uniqueness being a reflection of the esoteric and hermetic character of law, national and international, and of the special role of law in public decision-making, national and international'.[184]

B Government Lawyers and Adversarial Adjudication

Notwithstanding their behavioural divergence from 'standard conception' conduct, are the 'adversary system excuse' and a countervailing duty of candour to the court operative for government lawyers before national (and international) courts? The visibility of government legal advisers in adjudication has increased with the growth of judicial review as a tool for the control of administrative action,[185] not to mention other non-judicial accountability mechanisms.[186] The scope of the law relevant to policy decisions has been profoundly modified by the increasing penetration of international legal obligations into the domestic sphere.[187]

When government legal advisers are involved in adversarial advocacy, they are not called upon to offer their views on the range of legal outcomes or the best interpretation of the law, but rather to endorse the actions taken by their government. This accords with Sir Michael Quinlan's discussion of ethics in the public service:[188]

> One may think a particular policy concept to be a square circle, and indeed within the confidence of Whitehall one may argue fervently to that effect, but once the decision is taken, it is a matter

[180]   Thompson (n 78) 52.

[181]   T Lehrer, in D Howarth, *Law as Engineering: Thinking About What Lawyers Do* (London, Edward Elgar, 2013) 115.

[182]   H Arendt, *Eichmann in Jerusalem: A Report on the Banality of Evil* (London, Penguin, 2006) 289; Z Bauman, *Modernity and the Holocaust* (New York, Cornell University Press, 1989) 199.

[183]   M Koskenniemi, 'Faith, Identity and the Killing of the Innocent: International Lawyers and Nuclear Weapons' in M Koskenniemi, *The Politics of International Law* (Oxford, Hart Publishing, 2011) 216; S Milgram, *Obedience to Authority: An Experimental View* (New York, Harper & Row, 1974).

[184]   P Allott, 'The International Lawyer in Government Service: Ontology and Deontology' (2005) 23(1) *Wisconsin International Law Journal* 13, 16.

[185]   C Harlow and R Rawlings, *Law and Administration*, 3rd edn (Cambridge University Press, Cambridge, 2009) 734; Treasury Solicitor's Office, *The Judge Over Your Shoulder*, 4th edn (London, Treasury Solicitor's Office, 2006).

[186]   M Elliott, 'Ombudsmen, Tribunals, Inquiries: Re-Fashioning Accountability Beyond the Courts' in N Bamforth and P Leyland (eds), *Accountability in the 21st Century Constitution* (Oxford, Oxford University Press, 2013).

[187]   D Dyzenhaus, M Hunt and M Taggart, 'The Principle of Legality in Administrative Law: Internationalisation as Constitutionalisation' (2001) 1 *Oxford University Commonwealth Law Journal* 5.

[188]   M Quinlan, 'Ethics in the Public Service' (1993) 6 *Governance* 538, 542.

not just of duty but of professional pride to help make the very best square circle that effort and imagination can contrive.

There are obvious structural asymmetries that exist between the state and the individual in adversarial settings. Given their size and resources, and by virtue of being repeat players, government litigants are often unfairly advantaged over individuals.[189] Left unchecked, there would be a tendency for the dynamics of adversarial litigation to 'constantly drive the executive into purely negative argument in the courtroom'.[190] To mitigate asymmetries and offset excessive adversarialism, the government is regarded as a 'model litigant' in many jurisdictions, with a heightened duty of candour to the court.[191] As the United Kingdom Cabinet Manual states:[192]

> The duty of candour weighs particularly heavily on ministers and civil servants, as they will have the information showing the basis for the decision under review and because they are representatives of the public interest, and it cannot be in the public interest for the Court to be presented with an incomplete or inaccurate account of the facts.

The Treasury Solicitor's Office recently issued *Guidance on Discharging the Duty of Candour and Disclosure in Judicial Review Proceedings*,[193] in the aftermath of the *Binyam Mohamed* litigation.[194] In language reminiscent of the ethical standards applicable to criminal prosecutors, government agencies were reminded that their 'objective must not be to win the litigation at all costs but to assist the court in reaching the correct result and thereby to improve standards in public administration'.[195] In responding to applications for judicial review, public authorities are subject to a 'very high duty of candour' and must 'set out fully and fairly all matters that are relevant to the decision that is under challenge'.[196]

The dynamics of adversarial litigation and the duty of disclosure, and the uncertainties inherent in predictive judicial reasoning, are the conditions in which the adviser must give precautionary advice. Lord Bingham observed that 'many a bright twinkle in a minister's eye must fade in the light of adverse advice given by departmental lawyers'.[197] In the context of foreign ministry legal advisers, Sir Daniel Bethlehem discussed the challenge of giving precautionary advice as follows:[198]

> As a foreign ministry legal adviser, you must advise on what the law is today. But you should also advise on the uncertainties and the risks that may be associated with your advice, because the law may be unclear. You ought to advise on the consequences of your advice turning out to be wrong. You ought to advise on the potential for the evolution of the legal principle in question away from

---

[189]   C Cameron and M Taylor-Sands, '"Playing Fair": Governments as Litigants' (2007) 26 *Civil Justice Quarterly* 497, 503.

[190]   Daintith and Page (n 138) 342.

[191]   *Sebel Products Ltd v Commissioners of Customs and Excise* [1949] 1 Ch 409, 413; *SCI Operations Pty Ltd v Commonwealth of Australia* (1996) 139 ALR 595, 613; *Solicitor-General v Miss Alice* [2007] 2 NZLR 783 (HC), [48]; *McMoran Oil & Gas Co v Federal Energy Regulatory Commission* 962 F 2d 45 (1992).

[192]   United Kingdom Cabinet Office, *The Cabinet Manual* (2011) [6.15].

[193]   Treasury Solicitor's Office, *Guidance on Discharging the Duty of Candour and Disclosure in Judicial Review Proceedings* (2010).

[194]   *R (Binyam Mohamed) v Secretary of State for Foreign and Commonwealth Affairs* [2010] EWCA Civ 65; Turpin and Tomkins (n 136), 105–07.

[195]   Treasury Solicitor's Office (n 194) 1.

[196]   ibid 2.

[197]   T Bingham, 'Governments and Judges: Friends or Enemies?' in T Bingham, *Lives of the Law: Selected Essays and Speeches 2000-2010* (Oxford, Oxford University Press, 2011) 150.

[198]   D Bethlehem, 'The Secret Life of International Law' (2012) 1(1) *Cambridge Journal of International and Comparative Law* 23, 33.

your interpretation if the matter came before a court, and this against the background of a significant increase in litigation against government. So if you are a responsible and sensible legal adviser, an element of your advice will be precautionary: 'Secretary of State, there is a significant risk that if you act in this way and if it goes to Court, you may be found to be in breach with all the risks, political, reputational and other that this may bring'.

One of the purposes of the Human Rights Act 1998 was to allow the United Kingdom to develop its own take on the rights contained in the European Convention on Human Rights and not need to follow Strasbourg slavishly.[199] However, the United Kingdom is bound by the European Convention as interpreted by the European Court of Human Rights as a matter of international law. The adviser thus stands before a British court with two possible courses of argument. Either she argues that the contested action is valid under the European Convention as interpreted by Strasbourg or she argues that the Human Rights Act permits an alternative reading.

When lawyering across multiple orders, the correct advisory posture towards an indeterminately evolving international law norm does not permit easy answers. Bethlehem referred to the legal definition of torture as an example of the indeterminate evolution of a 'bright-line' legal principle.[200] In *Ireland v UK*,[201] the European Court of Human Rights held that conduct such as hooding, sleep deprivation and other forms of ill treatment associated with interrogation amounted to inhuman or degrading treatment, but not torture. Almost 30 years later, in *A v Secretary of State for the Home Department*, the House of Lords indicated that the same conduct would now be described as torture.[202]

The uncertainties that attend the giving of precautionary advice have led some advisers to take strategic procedural decisions outside the courtroom, in order to preserve the substantive status quo. In relation to challenges to corporal punishment in schools before the European Commission of Human Rights, the United Kingdom frequently deployed the 'friendly settlement' mechanism to pay off disgruntled parents and avoid a merits hearing on a politically sensitive point.[203] The use of such procedural mechanisms rather than risking losing on the merits falls outside the remit of adversarial adjudication, but nonetheless had a distinct bearing on the ebb and flow of doctrinal development.

Significantly, the 'adversary system excuse' used to justify the 'standard conception' in theoretical legal ethics is unresponsive to a wide variety of government advisory settings outside the courtroom. Practice contexts aimed primarily at policy implementation, as opposed to dispute resolution, typically adopt a non-adversarial conception of professional ethics.[204] In contexts such as policy development and legislative drafting,[205] there is no

---

[199] See R Clayton QC, 'Smoke and Mirrors: The Human Rights Act and the Impact of Strasbourg Case Law' (2012) *Public Law* 639; E Bates, 'British Sovereignty and the European Court of Human Rights' (2012) 128 *Law Quarterly Review* 382; B Dickson, 'The Record of the House of Lords in Strasbourg' (2012) 128 *Law Quarterly Review* 354.

[200] ibid 27–28.

[201] *Ireland v UK* [1976] ECtHR 5310/71.

[202] *A v Secretary of State for the Home Department* [2005] UKHL 71.

[203] D Feldman, *Civil Liberties and Human Rights in England and Wales*, 2nd edn (Oxford, Oxford University Press, 2002) 256; H Keller, M Forowicz and L Engi, *Friendly Settlements Before the European Court of Human Rights: Theory and Practice* (Oxford, Oxford University Press, 2010).

[204] M Damaska, *The Faces of Justice and State Authority: A Comparative Approach to the Legal Process* (New Haven, Yale University Press, 1986) 142–44, 174–77.

[205] See R Hazell, 'Who is the Guardian of Legal Values in the Legislative Process: Parliament or the Executive?' [2004] *Public Law* 495; G Hawke, 'Lawyers in the Policy Process' in C Geiringer and DR Knight (eds), *Seeing the World Whole: Essays in Honour of Sir Kenneth Keith* (Wellington, Victoria University Press, 2008) 298.

functional equivalent to a duty of candour to the court, which offsets the extremities of 'standard conception' conduct in adjudication contexts. This should not be taken to suggest that there is no adversarial dynamic at work in the inter-departmental advisory context. Although a hierarchically organised government legal service might produce systematic legal advice that is less likely to bend to departmental policy imperatives,[206] the allegiance of legal advisers to the legal service rather than their client administrators with different policy requirements would 'muffle the argument and deprive it of the vigour which now clearly characterises inter-departmental legal discussion'.[207] Terence Daintith and Alan Page pose the following question: 'Would it not be a little odd if the adversary procedures on which our system has relied to form both its common law and its legislation found no echo in the arrangements for developing legal opinion within the executive?'[208]

That said, the interplay between the 'adversary system excuse' and an overarching duty of candour to the court that provides the justificatory framework for the 'standard conception' in theoretical legal ethics cannot be deployed to evaluate much government legal advisory conduct.

IV CONCLUSION

Notwithstanding a growing interest in the relationship between government legal advice and professional responsibility, theoretical legal ethics has remained intent on defending or critiquing a 'standard conception' of the lawyer's role that does not engage with the distinct roles and responsibilities of legal advisers to government. This chapter has argued that the 'standard conception' lacks descriptive and analytical utility with respect to government legal advisers. The insufficiency of the 'standard conception' as a conceptual framework is not of mere theoretical concern:[209]

> This under-specification of the different roles of lawyers . . . result in an account of legal ethics that often gets the wrong answer, which lacks the resources to get beyond the defence of simple platitudes, and which generally fails to give detailed and well-motivated guidance in what all acknowledge are the 'hard cases' that lawyers face.

Unless the 'standard conception' is altered to take account of the professional and disciplinary realities of government legal service, situational ethics fuelled by politics and pragmatism is inevitable. Given that such an approach is unpalatable, it is a critical task for theoretical legal ethics to recast the 'standard conception' so it is fit for purpose in evaluating the role and responsibility of government legal advisers in the contemporary political landscape.

---

[206] AH Dennis, 'The Official Lawyer's Place in the Constitution' (1925) 46 *Law Quarterly Review* 378, 383.
[207] Daintith and Page (n 138) 347.
[208] ibid 347.
[209] Guerrero (n 109) 117.

Part 4

Politics and Legal Change

9

Law Reform in a Political Environment: The Work of the Law Commissions

ELIZABETH COOKE AND HECTOR MACQUEEN*

I ELIZABETH COOKE'S ADDRESS

THANK YOU VERY much for giving me the opportunity to speak this afternoon. It is very good to be here at home with my academic colleagues. When I looked at the title of this session I did wonder: 'do I fit here'? As a Law Commissioner, I hear from a distance the stress and excitement of turning politics into law. But that is not what we do. So what I would like to speak about is the rather ambivalent relationship of independence and dependence that the Law Commissions have with government and with politics, and to talk about the implications of that relationship for the way in which our recommendations are turned into law.

The Law Commissions for England and Wales and for Scotland were created by the Law Commissions Act 1965. The Law Commission for Northern Ireland was created just a few years ago.[1] Our founding statute requires us to keep the law under review and to recommend reform to government.

Behind that statute was a 1960s dream of a law reform body unconstrained by politics. You can share that dream if you have a look at *Law Reform Now*,[2] the book written by Gerald Gardiner and Andrew Martin in 1963, with a collection of chapters setting out the elements of the law that so desperately needed reform at that date, largely due to their age. The idea was that a Law Commission would have the time, the resources and the intellectual freedom to get rid of that dead wood. There were no votes in that task. The idea was that the Commissions were needed precisely because they were not to turn politics into law, but to do a task that for which a government department might well not have the time or the resources because it was constrained by a political agenda.

---

* These addresses were originally given under the title 'Turning Politics into Law' at a plenary session of the Annual Conference of the Society of Legal Scholars in Cambridge in September 2011. In writing up these addresses in March 2013, we have retained references to time as it stood when the address was given in 2011, but have updated matters in the footnotes where relevant. So, for example, when we spoke in 2011 the project on the Electronic Communications Code had just begun, but at the time of writing the project has just been completed.

[1] Established in 2007 following the recommendations of the Criminal Justice Review Group. the Northern Ireland Law Commission is established under the Justice (Northern Ireland) Act 2002 (as amended by the Northern Ireland Act 1998 (Devolution of Policing and Justice Functions) Order 2010).

[2] G Gardiner and A Martin, *Law Reform Now* (London, Victor Gollancz, 1963).

What happened to the 1960s dream? In 1987, Richard Oerton wrote a book called *Lament for the Law Commission*.[3] Richard was what we now call a team lawyer, working alongside commissioners and research assistants, with a voice in the development of policy. For Richard, the dream turned into a nightmare; he experienced deep frustration when valuable law reform projects were abandoned because they had no tie in with the political agenda or with government willingness to enact reform. His book is bitter and salutary and is required reading, I think, for anyone considering working for the Commission. I was very familiar with it before I applied for the job. I had a hunch, which I believe is correct, that things were not as bad as the picture he painted.

The reality is that law reform and politics are inevitably neighbours; they are perhaps uneasy neighbours, but they have to get on. Two practical points come to mind. One is that we are never wholly remote from items of political interest. Certainly we could not contemplate examining the death penalty or abortion. But we have considered divorce, cohabitation, rented homes, sale of goods, homicide – these are all issues on which the man on the street has a view and may cast a vote.

The other point is that at the end of every completed Law Commission project sits the goblin of implementation. The Law Commission is not a government department, and cannot take its own projects or its own Bills forward into law. We have the privilege of working with Parliamentary Counsel and producing draft Bills alongside our Reports. But do they become law? They have two routes. One is that the Government may adopt them. At that point the Bill ceases to be our baby. It becomes a government Bill. It will be sent to Parliamentary Counsel again and will be amended, possibly just for updating, possibly for more fundamental change but it is not ours anymore. And then it is taken forward by a Bill team; this is a very labour-intensive process. The other route is by becoming a Private Members Bill. You will be aware that Private Members may, literally, by the luck of the draw, get the right to introduce a Bill. It is not unknown for a successful Private Member, who has come near the top of the ballot, to pick up an unimplemented Law Commission Bill and take it through – as did Greg Knight MP earlier this year. The result was the snappily titled 'Estates of Deceased Persons Forfeiture of Law and Succession Act 2011' implementing a short Bill that we produced in 2005. In watching that happen I was struck by the aleatoric nature of the process. There were many points at which that Bill could have fallen – not through its own merits or demerits but because somebody else might have spoken a bit too long on another topic. It was not dissimilar, in terms of discomfort, to the process of watching sausages being made.

So implementation depends on either the chancy fortunes of a Private Member or on the willingness of government to invest time and resources in one of our Bills. It was expected by our founders that our recommendations would in the normal course of events be regarded, in the words of the authors of *1066 and All That*,[4] as a Good Thing, and would of course be taken swiftly into law. But the reality is that although the rate of implementation is not directly proportional to political interest there is a correlation. Consider the Land Registration Act 2002. For some people (not for me) this is not the sexiest of topics, but it rode into Parliament on swift steeds two days before the Report was published; might this have had something to do with the fact that it was seen to promise cheaper conveyancing (for which there might be votes)?

---

[3] RT Oerton, *A Lament for the Law Commission*, (Chichester, Countrywise Press, 1987).
[4] WC Sellar and RJ Yeatman, *1066 and All That*, (London, Methuen Publishing, 1930).

Very recently we have seen two major new developments. One is the introduction of the Special Public Bill procedure for uncontroversial Law Commission Bills. Two Bills have gone through so far. One is the Perpetuities and Accumulations Act 2009 and the other is Third Parties (Rights Against Insurers) Act 2010. The procedure is initiated by the introduction of a bill in the House of Lords. It is a Government Bill, managed by a Government Bill team, but the magic of the procedure – and the reason why it opens a door into Parliament that might otherwise be closed – is that Second Reading takes place in Committee and in a Committee Room. It does not take time on the floor of the House. However, it is not a fast-track procedure. Second Reading takes as long as it would otherwise take; scrutiny in Second Reading Committee may even be more rigorous because the calm and rather intellectual atmosphere of a House of Lords Committee Room lends itself to expert probing of technical issues. The Bill must be a Law Commission Bill; but it is unlikely to be unamended from its original form. The perpetuities Bill was a case in point, since it was 10–years-old by the time of its introduction and needed considerable updating.[5] It is not known how far the process of updating and adjustment can go before a Bill ceases to be a Law Commission Bill and so ceases to be eligible for the procedure. But certainly a Bill going through this procedure cannot be a vehicle for a piece of non-Law Commission policy, and it must be 'uncontroversial' – an undefined term. What does that mean? Does it mean that the Bill must be so boring that noone cares? Clearly not, perpetuities arouse passions. Does it mean there can be no amendments? Apparently not.[6] What is clear is that it must not be politically controversial. Support and opposition must not fall on party lines. So the new procedure is not a way to turn politics into law.

The other recent development is for England and Wales only. It is the new Protocol signed in 2010[7] regulating the relationship between government and the Commission in the adoption, execution and completion of our projects, and it is intended to put an end to the problem of unimplemented reports sitting on the shelf. It states that when the Commission takes on a project, there must be a government department expressing a serious intention to carry forward law reform in that area. At first blush that is music to the ears of the law reformer; but it is modern music which does not take the listener quite where he expected to go, because the corollary of that statement is that we *cannot* take on a project in which the relevant department is not able to express a commitment to reform.

A year ago we consulted on our Eleventh Programme of law reform, which has just begun.[8] Many of you made suggestions. Most of those suggestions could not be taken forward. They were all good but most fell at the first fence because they were not ones in which a department had an interest.

Many of you will be gestating law reform babies. If you wish to use a Law Commission midwife for those babies, it is worth thinking now, two years in advance, of the next consultation and how you are going to get a government department interested. That is something we should work on together. The Law Commission for England and Wales has never had a wholly free hand in setting its agenda because we have always had to have our programme approved by the Lord Chancellor. But certainly the Protocol changes things. We

---

[5] Law Commission, *The Rules Against Perpetuities and Excessive Accumulations* (Law Com No 251, 1998).

[6] As I write up this paper in March 2013, two further Acts have been passed by means of the procedure, of which the latest was the Trusts (Capital and Income) Act 2013. Two amendments were put forward in Second Reading Committee, both were voted upon and both were defeated.

[7] http://lawcommission.justice.gov.uk/publications/940.htm.

[8] http://lawcommission.justice.gov.uk/docs/lc330_eleventh_programme.pdf.

retain and jealously guard the right to say 'no' to projects even if government wants us to do them. But the Protocol curtails our freedom to say 'yes' to suitable projects that we want to do, if government and the relevant department will not express an interest.

One of the effects that that will inevitably have is on the size and scale of our projects. In the past we have done very successful work on what we might call investment law reform; long term projects which take time to produce profound recommendations, which may well be implemented not immediately but later when there is time – the perpetuities work was a good example. But it is very hard to imagine a government department expressing interest and support in that sort of long term project. I and my team have just completed a report on Easements, Covenants and Profits à Prendre, again very close to my heart.[9] Work on that began in 2003, under my predecessor Stuart Bridge. It is very hard to imagine a project like that being taken on now.

So the new and closer link with government and its own reform priorities carries obvious risks for independent law reform. It does however open the door to new co-operation. We are starting the first batch of new projects under the Eleventh Programme; the experience of doing so in a context where a government department is interested and to some extent committed – not necessarily to our policy, but certainly to reform – is new and refreshing.

Three particular examples spring to mind. One is our project on Adult Social Care.[10] It was not negotiated under the new Protocol, but it is the sort of project that the Protocol most readily facilitates. We worked on the legal organisation of the topic and reported in May 2011, while at the same time the Commission on Funding of Care and Support ('the Dilnot Commission') was looking at the truly central and political question of funding. That meant that instead of riding the lonely bicycle of aspiration we were riding a tandem, with a government department waiting to pick up both pieces of work, produce a Bill and take it through.[11] It meant we had to tread a very careful line, and you can look at the first few pages of our Report to see how we define what we could consider and what we could not.

The second example is a new project on the Electronic Communications Code – otherwise known as schedule 2 to the Telecommunications Act 1984. It is the legal means of getting electronic communications apparatus on to land in order to maintain and complete the networks on which we depend so closely for so many forms of communication. In 1984, of course, the internet barely existed and there were no mobile telephones; the original Code was designed for landline telephones and adapted by amendment in 2003 for the modern range of telecommunications providers. Its drafting has been criticised from the High Court bench,[12] and a fresh start is needed. But the interests involved – those of landowners and of telecommunications operators – are in some ways opposed. The Department for Culture, Media and Sport asked us to take on the project precisely because they needed an *independent* consultation; and because we offer independence and expertise they are funding a project.[13]

---

[9]   Law Commission, *Easements, Covenants and Profits à Prendre* (Law Com No 327, 2011).

[10]   As I write in 2013, this project is completed: Law Commission, *Adult Social Care* Law Com No 326, 2011).

[11]   The Department of Health published the draft Care and Support Bill for pre-legislative scrutiny in July 2012. The Joint Committee on the Draft Care and Support Bill issued a report which recommended changes to the draft Bill and the next stage will be the introduction of the revised Bill into Parliament in autumn 2013. The Social Services and Well-being (Wales) Bill was introduced into the National Assembly for Wales in January 2013.

[12]   *Geo Networks Ltd v The Bridgewater Canal Company Ltd* [2010] EWHC 548 (Ch), [2010] 1 WLR 2576 [7] (Lewison J).

[13]   See now Law Commission, *Electronic Communications Code* (Law Com No 336, 2013).

The third example of corporate endeavour takes us back to the Parliamentary process. One of the costly aspects of a Bill is the work required of the Bill team that takes it through Parliament. The next candidate for the special procedure is the Trusts (Capital and Income) Bill, appended to our 2009 Report *Capital and Income Trusts Classification and Apportionment*,[14] affectionately known as 'Citcat'. Work is going on quietly behind the scenes to get ready for introduction – it is much more work than I thought it would be. The Bill team is composed not of several Ministry lawyers and policy officials, as would formerly have been the case, but one Ministry official and the Law Commission project team. That would have been beyond the imagination of our founders but it is a very efficient way of using the team's expertise.

We do not 'turn politics into law' at the Law Commission. But we do have an ambivalent relationship with politics and the politicians. That relationship has been facilitated through the new Parliamentary procedure, and redefined by the protocol which brings us a little closer to politics, makes our dependence on the political process a little more explicit, bringing risks and bringing potential.

The Law Commissions need you as our academic partners and we are immensely grateful for all you do, some of you very generously work with us directly by talking to us when we are doing projects. Many of you provide the research upon which we draw, many of you propose new projects. We are very grateful for that work and we bring these developments to your attention in order to give you a better idea of our relationship with the political process of what we can't do and what we can do. Thank you.

II HECTOR MACQUEEN'S ADDRESS

Thank you, Lizzie, for that very helpful conspectus. I certainly learned one or two things that I wasn't quite aware of before. When we come to the Scottish Law Commission, much of what Lizzie has been talking about applies but not the Protocol with which she finished, unless we are working together on joint projects.[15] However, things are moving on in Scotland as well.

I should however first stress that whilst the Scottish Parliament and the Scottish Government are, as it were, our main customers from the point of view of translating what we propose into legislation, we too are part of the UK structure (at least for the moment), and the Westminster Parliament's doings are of considerable interest to us. One of the things on which we at the Scottish Law Commission work is those parts of Scots law which under the devolution settlement remain reserved to the exclusive legislative competence of Westminster. That is actually a complete nightmare of a dividing line. One can draw very crude overall pictures, to the effect that Scots private law is devolved, while 'single market' commercial, consumer and employment law are reserved. But what is the difference between Scots private law, for example contract, the area in which I am much involved at the moment, and commercial law? One of the examples we have run into recently was a Report on what we call Unincorporated Associations – clubs and so on.[16] We realised only

---

[14] Law Commission, *Capital and Income Trusts Classification and Apportionment* (Law Com No 315, 2009).

[15] An example is the Advice to the Department of Business, Innovation and Skills on Unfair Terms in Consumer Contracts, commissioned by the Department and published in March 2013. This is expected to be implemented in the so-called 'Consumer Bill of Rights'.

[16] Scottish Law Commission, *Report on Unincorporated Associations* (Scot Law Com No 217, 2009). All the Commission's publications are available at www.scotlawcom.gov.uk/publications/.

quite late that, although this is very much a classic area of Scots private law quite distinct in content from its English counterpart, it is a reserved area under the Scotland Act 1998 and so can only be implemented at Westminster.[17] The present law is very unsatisfactory – if the members of such associations realised the liability risks they run as a result, they would if sensible immediately disband themselves. But such organisations are of considerable significance, I think it is fair to say, for a wide variety of activities in the third or voluntary sector and, of course, by implication, for the 'Big Society' idea so dear to the heart of the Prime Minister. I am afraid we have made slightly shameless use of that idea in promoting the implementation of the draft Bill attached to our Report in the Westminster Parliament through the Special Public Bill procedure that Lizzie described in her remarks. Somewhere in the pipeline, probably after the Bills that Lizzie was talking about, will be a Bill applying entirely to Scotland. That will most likely be our Unincorporated Associations Report Bill where we are currently trying to persuade the Advocate General for Scotland and the Scotland Office that no controversy is likely to derail our Bill on this matter. So, having used politics in the sense of attaching our project to the Big Society agenda, we are now trying to say that actually it is not really political at all.[18]

The basic point is that Law Commissions exist to reform the law through legislation. In Scotland, however, we are not necessarily as tied to the Law Commissions' success being entirely measured in the actual legislation emerging from it because we can see that our material has impact on the courts, sometimes explicitly by reference in judicial decisions. From time to time, a law reform project has explicitly concluded that development is best left to the courts. Law Commission reports are quite frequently referred to in the Scottish courts as part of the background material to help in the understanding of legislation resulting from those Reports. The key really is the achievement of law reform, and the process is not necessarily entirely by means of legislation.

Be that as it may, a law reform body which makes proposals for law reform, which then lie unimplemented by the legislature, is, I think, probably rightly to be described as a failing law reform body. So in Scotland we have noticed with interest the Law Commissions Act of 2009 and we have been in quite significant discussions for some years now with the Scottish Government about achieving better implementation rates for our proposals that fall within the legislative competence of the Scottish Parliament. We are in the relatively fortunate position, possibly, that the SNP Government has an absolute majority in a Scottish Parliament allowing it to pursue its policies with an expectation of success that it did not have in its 2007–11 incarnation as a minority government. I cannot stress enough how remarkable the present situation is: the electoral system for the Scottish Parliament was designed to produce coalition governments, the politics of which make the achievement of any legislation necessarily more complex, whether or not its content is political in the

---

[17]   Scotland Act 1998 sch 5 Head C1.

[18]   In the event the public consultation by the Scotland Office on the subject in 2012 extended beyond unincorporated associations to include another more recent Report by the Scottish Law Commission on the prosecution of dissolved partnerships (Scottish Law Commission, *The Criminal Liability of Partnerships* (Scot Law Com No 224, 2011)). The consultation showed a small number of unresolved issues of detail with unincorporated associations, but none with prosecuting dissolved partnerships, see: www.gov.uk/government/consultations/reforming-the-law-on-scottish-unincorporated-associations-and-criminal-liability-of-scottish-partnerships. As a result, the Partnerships (Prosecution) (Scotland) Bill was laid before the Westminster Parliament on 1 December 2012, the first purely Scottish Bill to be brought forward in this way. The Bill made unamended progress towards the statute book and received the Royal Assent on 25 April 2013: see: http://services.parliament.uk/bills/2012-13/partnershipsprosecutionscotland.html.

sense of dividing parties from each other. The SNP Government has achieved its present pre-eminence, it is generally thought amongst other key factors, on the basis that it was managerially competent in its first term of office, keeping Scotland ticking over in general through their four years in power in a way that had not been so apparent with their coalition predecessors from 1999 to 2007. The SNP is now extremely keen to play on this perception, not least for what it might in due course entail in the coming debates on the possibility of Scottish independence. Further, not only does it have the obvious advantage of its overall majority, it also has a five rather than a four-year term. The normal Scottish Parliament term is four years, but for various reasons to do with the fixing of the date of the next UK General Election in 2015, we are going to have a Scottish Parliament running until May 2016. So the SNP Government has been given an opportunity, unparalleled in the admittedly very short history of Scottish devolution, to really achieve things, to do things that it thinks it wants to do.

What has emerged in the process since May 2011, apart of course from the pursuit of the SNP's primary goal of Scottish independence, is that it wants to do law reform. Law reform, that is, not in the general sense that any legislation reforms the law in some way, but in the very specific Law Commissions sense that Lizzie has described, ie non-political, but the sort of stuff that will help to shape Scottish civil society and enable, as one of my fellow Commissioners put it, the plumbing of the legal system to be kept in good order.[19]

This law reform objective has been carried forward in discussion with us although what this means so far is that the relevant civil servants turn up for meetings, we talk a lot about what is possible, and they then walk away and deliberate further on what can be done. The Scottish Parliament is involved as well, since the creation of a specific procedure akin to that at Westminster may be needed, and that would involve one of the Parliament's committees assuming a new responsibility. We are still currently awaiting an outcome, although we do have some idea of where our projects (and, indeed, more recent unimplemented Reports) stand in the current legislative queue. Although there is no annual Queen's Speech in the Scottish Parliament, the First Minister announces every September what the legislative programme for the coming year is going to be, and there is an ongoing (and regularly revised) list inside the Scottish Government associated with that. In addition, legislation not passed during the year does not thereby fall. It will only do so if it is not passed at the end of the five-year period now underway. So Bills can run for quite a long time, although that should also remind us of one of Lizzie's points which applies as much in the Scottish as in the UK context, Bills are resource-intensive in the Civil Service.

In sum, what we have in Scotland at the moment is a law reform element in the programme for the five-year period of this present Scottish Parliament under its majority SNP Government. The content of what it is looking for in that law reform package is more or less precisely what Lizzie was describing as coming under the special procedure at Westminster: Bills that are essentially politically non-controversial, while also likely to attract significant extra-Parliamentary support (eg from the legal profession or the business sector), and that can accordingly be time-managed very clearly, with a schedule set down in advance that is likely to be kept.[20] This will not be a 'fast track', any more than the Westminster procedure is,

---

[19] See text accompanying n 21 below.
[20] Candidates in our current projects include Scottish Law Commission, *Report on Execution in Counterpart* (Scot Law Com No 231, April 2013) and Scottish Law Commission, *Report on Judicial Factors* (Scot Law Com No 233, August 2013).

as Lizzie explained; but it should allow for better implementation rates of Law Commission Reports than have been previously achieved.[21]

The plumbing metaphor already mentioned for law reform actually appears in the opening paragraph of our Report on Land Registration published in 2011.[22] That Report has been very successful and we are going to have a Land Registration Bill very shortly.[23] One of the things that I learned more or less straightaway when I came on to the Commission in September 2009 was the vital necessity in one's law reform projects and proposals to think about and articulate what good this would do for Scottish society, particularly in relation to economic activity. Talk of land registration as part of the country's legal plumbing played into this as well as the SNP Government's self-image of managerial competence. So Law Commission Reports can, to adapt Sir Henry Thring's famous dictum that Bills are designed to pass as razors are to sell,[24] be written to catch the prevailing wind in government.

I came into the Commission with the notion of doing a review of contract law pre-eminent in my thinking; but that that would happen was not a given. It was a gamble, if you like, that I took when I accepted the appointment because what I had to do first was to share in the formulation of our Eighth Programme of Law Reform.[25] Lizzie has described exactly how that process works. The Scottish Law Commission is free to propose, but government disposes and it has the power to refuse our proposals.[26] This is not yet a matter of our doing only what government has said it is interested in implementing (ie what Lizzie has described for our English colleagues as arising through the 2010 Protocol). But in proposing a review of general contract law I had first to give my colleagues some explanation of why that was a good idea when I couldn't in all fairness point to popular outcry and rebellions across the country, demand from the legal profession, or even perhaps to particular problems in the courts or decisions that were going manifestly wrong in either law or policy terms. But the idea which ultimately appealed to the Scottish Government in accepting the contract law proposal was that a health check would be useful. Contract law is of importance to a thriving economy, as the legal basis upon which it will operate. There was merit therefore in having a look at the law of contract to see whether there are rules or factors in the Scots law – and this was perhaps a bit of play to an SNP Government – that were pushing business people, when otherwise they were operating in a Scottish context, to choose another legal system as their contract's governing law. One mentioned English law in particular in this context, of course, to get the SNP Justice Secretary's hackles rising. But

---

[21] The Scottish Parliament decided on 28 May 2013 to accept recommendations for changes to its Standing Orders to allow Commission Bills where the need for reform is widely agreed, but no major or contentious political or financial issues arise, to be referred to the Subordinate Legislation Committee, which is accordingly to be re-named the Committee the Delegated Powers and Law Reform Committee. See the Official Report for 28 May 2013 (www.scottish.parliament.uk/parliamentarybusiness/28862.aspx?r=8173&mode=pdf), cols 20374–79.

[22] Scottish Law Commission, *Report on Land Registration* (Scot Law Com No 222, 2010).

[23] See now the Land Registration etc (Scotland) Act 2012.

[24] Found quoted in Lord Rodger of Earlsferry, *The Form and Language of Legislation* (Holdsworth Club, University of Birmingham, 1998) 17, reprinted in this volume, ch 4 above, p 65. Lord Rodger's observations on the preparation and progress of legislation, written mostly from the perspective gained as a Scottish Law Officer, frequently chime with my own as a Law Commissioner. See also on the parallel experience within the recodification project of the Louisiana Law Institute, S Herman, 'Civil Recodification in an Anglophone Mixed Jurisdiction: A Bricoleur's Playbook' (2012) 58 *Loyala Law Review* 487–558.

[25] Scot Law Com No 220, 2010.

[26] Government may, and often has done so, refer issues to the Scottish Law Commission for review – see eg the criminal law reference following the World's End murders trial in 2007 and resulting in three reports on Crown appeals, double jeopardy, and similar factual evidence between 2009 and 2012. The Commission may refuse the reference but does not generally do so. The Reports on Crown appeals and double jeopardy have both been implemented in legislation.

there were other points. The context in which the proposal was framed in the programme was to look at the law in a European and modernising context. That is in fact the primary purpose of the project, but it was rather important to set it out for the Government in a way that would attract its interest and, in the end, its support, albeit without any commitment to legislate on whatever might emerge.[27] Support was forthcoming and we are now embarked upon the project. It will form part of the law reform programme already mentioned,

The one other thing that I would like to mention in this is just to clarify one or two elements in procedure. One is consultation. Both Commissions do a lot of consultation in formulating the discussion paper or consultation paper that is the first public manifestation of a law reform project, and obviously the paper itself then stimulates further responses which are taken into account at the Report and draft Bill stage. What we are increasingly finding is that it is actually vital, not just to put out your discussion or consultation paper, receive your comments back, and then proceed thereafter without thought of further consultation. We have to do more consultation because quite often what comes out of the initial round of responses to a paper is actually contradictory or perhaps unclear in certain respects; or there is silence from potential consultees whom you would wish to have heard. So we are engaging in more active consultation of our own initiative at all stages of our projects.

But one of the aspects of the law reform programme under discussion at the moment in Scotland is the question of whether the Scottish Government will take over the proposals and draft Bills that we have made. Should the Government then engage in a further process of consultation? They have always done that up until now, so that there is a potential for duplication. My wife is a civil servant and has engaged in consultations on Law Commission proposals, and what she says to me (and I can well believe it) is that the Scottish Government finds things that the Scottish Law Commission never uncovered in its consultation. So a contradiction sometimes emerges between the two processes: possibly because the two bodies are reaching different audiences, or perhaps because consultees are more alert when the Scottish Government is consulting since they realise that action is now quite likely. Now part of the law reform package of ascertaining whether Law Commission Bills are indeed uncontroversial, unlikely to attract significant opposition on their way through the Parliamentary process, and indeed widely supported by relevant stakeholders, is this process of consultation. What I suspect is going to happen is that the Law Commissions are going to be engaging in yet more consultation than is already the case as part of the process of trying to find out what the support for and opposition to particular proposals may be. The success we had with the Land Registration project mentioned earlier was because the Commissioner in charge worked with the stakeholder constituency – the conveyancers, the Land Registry people themselves, the civil servants who are backing all that – and took them with him all the way in the development of the proposals that eventually appeared in the report.[28] So the end result was an extremely short government consultation in the summer of 2011 which was extremely uncontroversial because everyone was already on board.

I think this is the way forward for the Law Commission, in this new world where government actually wants to be seen to be implementing these reports. Why otherwise would

---

[27] Eighth Programme of Law Reform, paras 2.16–2.21.
[28] We have tried to follow this example in the project on execution in counterpart as well as publishing a draft Bill on the Commission website and inviting (and receiving) comment. We also shared later drafts privately with interested practitioners.

you fund a Law Commission? And perhaps the final point to make is the overall context of this is cuts in government expenditure.

We are seeing huge cuts in government expenditure and not only in the Civil Service. The Scottish Law Commission itself is facing up to a very deep cut over the next two or three years. It is trying to make the best use of the resources that remain available. What that is doing at the moment, I think, is drawing the Law Commission and Government closer together. The interesting question, indeed the political question, which arises from this, is that is it going to be a good thing in the end? Is this going to compromise the independence which has been the hallmark of what the Law Commission has done up until this time?

Thank you.

III QUESTIONS

(**Q1**) This is really directed to the Law Commissioners. I am wondering if you have become aware of any directed lobby activity in the consultation process? Obviously that is possible, obviously it is not wrong per se and obviously it is potentially – well it would raise some questions. So are you aware of it happening and if you are, or if you are not, what is your opinion upon it?

(**A1**) (Elizabeth Cooke (EJC)) I am just wondering what lobbying means. People do talk to us; we do a very longitudinal consultation process so we talk to people as much as we can before we publish a consultation paper. Then, when we have got responses we talk to people again after that because, as Hector says, there may be contradictory responses and indeed lack of consensus.

There is lobbying in the sense that sometimes an organisation responds and then lots of individuals write in to express their agreement; that is one reason why it is very important that consultation responses are weighed and not counted – it is not a voting process, nor is it a statistically significant representation of public opinion.

(Hector MacQueen (HMacQ)) The only other comment I would like to make is when you are in the process of formulating your programme you are particularly open to lobby groups and I was fascinated by that when I arrived in a Commission already in the middle of the process of formulating that programme.

(**Q2**) A question about the relationship between the Law Commission and the courts – the judiciary. Not so much in the sense of providing material to help with statutory interpretation when reports are implemented, but when they either have not been implemented or are yet to be. Particularly in the Supreme Court in the House of Lords in areas under Professor Cooke's expertise (although I don't want to put her on the spot), there has been a dispute amongst their Lordships and Justices over whether it is appropriate to pre-empt an area that has been considered by the Law Commission. And then equally the Government, and sometimes the Law Commission, has given a reason for not recommending reform or pressing ahead with reform, the courts have got on with it and seem to be dealing with it. Sometimes because it has been 10 years since the Law Commission reported. So do Law Commissioners view their reports as being material for the judges as well as Parliament and what do judges make of Law Commission reports that haven't been implemented?

(A2) (HMacQ) Yes, perhaps I should start. One of the key points about Scotland and the Scottish legal system is that it is a very small community and everybody knows everybody else. And yes, you can be writing bits that are aimed as much at the courts as at the legislators. The judges are consultees, of course, but quite often it is an informal sort of thing. What you are looking to do is to provide what one of my Edinburgh University colleagues once described as 'pabulum' for the courts.[29] I had to look the word 'pabulum' up – it is basically foodstuff. Perhaps more specifically it is fodder for the Bar arguing before the court, drawing counsel's attention to various ways of approaching or structuring the existing material. There was a bit in our recent discussion paper on Interpretation of Contract where I tried to draw the threads of a whole string of unreported cases together in a way I knew practitioners would love. There were seven bullet points, each with authority attached to it, most of it unreported.[30] This has been picked up, not least in the lower courts.[31] The rest of it, I am afraid, less so.[32] But the statement of what I think the current law is, in that listed form, was quite deliberately intended to get into circulation, as it were, a reasonably authoritative statement of what the position is at the moment.

(EJC) That is another difference between Scotland and England: we are not supposed to use Latin! I agree that there is a judgement call sometimes to be made as to whether we should recommend legislation on a point or should recommend that the courts should take a particular approach. The problem with taking the latter option is that it depends upon the right case getting to the right level of the court system in order to produce an authoritative precedent. So it is quite a difficult one. We did take that approach in our report on illegality.[33] We are aware that we are indeed producing fodder for the courts, but fodder that they can choose whether or not to eat.

(Q3) This is directed to the Law Commissioners. You didn't really touch on this, but it is essential to what you do, which is when you say you look into the present law, and you make proposals, for the preferable direction for the law, indicating that there is a choice. I want to press you on how you make the choice. I know Roy Goode and I, and perhaps some others here, are involved in the American Law Institute. Although the American Law Institute is known for restating the law, quite often what we do in the Institute is actually try to find what the better solution to an area of law is. The question I want to press you on is that when the Americans are looking across their 51 jurisdictions, the 50 states and the federal jurisdiction, for what might be the best rule, these are really the only catchment areas. There is no serious attempt to look outside to the rest of the common law world, and certainly not to European Union jurisdictions. That might be embedded somewhere in the reporters' notes, an interesting sideline about what other people do, but it is not really the meat of the comparative study. Now in your work, obviously the rhetoric would be in some quarters when you are looking for the best rule, you should also be looking at, say, your partner's law and European Union law. But to what degree do you actually do that?

(A3) (HMacQ) Well I think I can answer that fairly confidently, quite extensively. Contract law is specifically a review in the light of the Draft Common Frame of Reference

---

[29] WA Wilson, 'Knowing the Law and Other Things' (1982) *Juridical Review* 259, 260.
[30] Discussion Paper No 147 on Interpretation of Contract (2011) para 5.13.
[31] See eg *Scotia Homes (South) Ltd v McLean*, Kirkcaldy Sheriff Court, 30 November 2012, accessible at www.scotcourts.gov.uk/opinions/A216_10_.html.
[32] This has been apparent in the diverse consultation responses.
[33] Law Commission, *The Illegality Defence* (Law Com No 320, 2010).

on the basis that that is an attempt to state best rules of contract law for the European Union. Now you may agree or disagree. That is part of the discussions that we are having, that we explicitly used that as our point of departure and we have observed where our law differs from it. We also of course take close account of English law. We have to because that is our nearest neighbour and obviously our largest comparator. In trust law we are looking at the moment at all the trust law jurisdictions, including not only England but also the Channel Islands and places altogether outside Europe, to see what ideas they have that we could usefully deploy. This is because a justification for the Trust project is that the Scottish financial sector, a very significant economic player, is very interested in further developing Scotland as a trusts jurisdiction. There are limits to this, obviously, because Scotland does not have the power to vary the taxation rules relevant to trusts. But the SNP Government is of course lobbying like anything for more such powers. In land registration we looked at the German system in particular. We looked at others but the German system was the one that particularly took the eye. So we do use comparative law a great deal in the Scottish Law Commission because again it inevitably follows from being a small legal system. We have to look outside for our ideas.

(EJC) I would like to answer the question on two levels. One is a question about sources; a Law Commission project would be sadly lacking if it didn't take proper account of the relevant comparative materials. Scotland is a civil law jurisdiction and therefore, particularly in areas like land law and family law, more akin to the European systems. Those are areas where English lawyers would more naturally look to the common law world than to the European world. My colleagues doing commercial and contract law would look to Europe.

So the quick answer to what you are saying is, of course we do as much comparative law as we can in the context of time and resources. We will be publishing a report on intestacy in December 2011 where we have done a lot of work on 'conduit theory' (which is about wicked stepmothers) – an area developed particularly in the USA but not so far looked at very much by English lawyers.[34]

The deeper question, to which I do not know the answer, is how we decide what to recommend. We can recommend what people want; we can recommend what works; but how do we decide the big issues of principle? To take a really practical and workmanlike group of projects: we have just started work on the Electronic Communications Code, and we are going to be working on Rights to Light; both of those raise deep questions about the relationship between my land and other people's rights, to which there is no one right answer. But there is a big issue there that has to be answered in order to decide what the law is going to be, and I do not think there is any one answer to how we decide that. If we were politicians we might find that our answer was dictated by our politics, but we are not.

(HMacQ) Just one further thought on this. From the Government's point of view, the Law Commission is a useful sounding board for alternative possibilities and in the end the Law Commission may have to decide between them. In this, you have to persuade your four fellow Commissioners to take the line that you personally think is indeed the right answer. They have all got to sign up to it. So there may well be compromise concealed within the bland assurances of the report that this is the way to go forward. But actually the key point is that you have canvassed the different issues as far as you can. That is apparently what the

---

[34] Law Commission, *Intestacy and Family Provision Claims on Death* (Law Com No 331, 2011) see also E Cooke, 'Wives, Widows and Wicked Step-Mothers: A Brief Examination of Spousal Entitlement on Intestacy' [2009] *Child and Family Law Quarterly* 423.

civil servants particularly appreciate in our papers and reports. It also helps them to decide whether this is, in my language, a law reform Bill, in Lizzie's language a Protocol Bill, or is it something that is going to have to run the political gamut. The example that is current in Scotland is a Succession Bill where we have the question of legal rights for spouses, cohabitants and children that cannot be willed away by a testator. Can you disinherit the children? Should you be allowed to do so, and if so, to what extent? We have come up with a specific set of proposals. I understand that a lot of people disagree with it. In the end there is no escape from that question; it is a social and political question. That Bill will not go into the law reform process I have tried to describe; but it is obviously a Bill that should be there. The law of succession, especially intestate succession, is in desperate need of modernisation for modern social conditions but it is going to be up to the politicians, using our thinking, one hopes, as a basis for decision-making in a rational fashion, to come up with the final answer.

(**Q4**) Mine is a question about audience, and to some extent looks to both groups of persons on stage. For my part I am quite sad that there will be in some sense a limit under the new Protocol. A number of major reforms of criminal law have happened because for instance the draft criminal code at the end of the 1980s was picked up by the courts. I am not entirely sure that I believe that legislation is the only way for the Law Commission to make a serious impact.

   (EJC) So far as the English Law Commission is concerned, perhaps a very important reason for having academic Law Commissioners is that we are more conscious of the wider audience than perhaps practitioners are. 'Facing the Future' was the Law Commission's report on divorce reform.[35] It hasn't been implemented (or rather it has, but the statute hasn't been brought into force)[36] but we are still teaching it. It is still absolutely essential to thinking on grounds for divorce on how things should be. Law reform is a bigger process than the enactment of statutes; statutory implementation is often the best way forward, but if that fails the work is not wasted.

   (HMacQ) The only thing I would add is that the way I have described it recently to friends, partly because I had experience in such bodies before I became a Commissioner, is that the Scottish Law Commission has a capacity to act as a think tank about law in Scotland, and what it says can have a wide influence on a whole variety of different ways on what happens in the legal system thereafter. So as I think I said in my presentation, legislation isn't everything, although it is the most important.

(**Q5**) The Government has introduced a regulatory reform regime which is designed, I think, to reduce regulation and has in fact succeeded in creating a massive bureaucracy which is designed to make it even harder to get ratification of an international convention than it is to put a camel through the eye of a needle. I am just wondering whether the Law Commission has some dispensation from this process which generally speaking requires not only that there has to be a good number of people supporting the project or even, as in the case of the Convention I am thinking of, almost the whole of the industry affected, but there has also got to be an economic impact assessment. There has got to be a quantitative assessment which shows exactly what benefits will ensue, what the costs will be and so on. The whole process is a nightmare. One would like to think that since you work on the

---

[35] Law Commission, *Facing the Future: A Discussion Paper on the Ground for Divorce* (Law Com No 170, 1988).
[36] Family Law Act 1996, Part II.

English Law Commission on the basis of references from relevant departments, that actually you won't have to go through those hoops. But I wonder whether that is the case?

(A5) (EJC) No. There is no dispensation. We do not yet know what effect that will have. We do indeed produce impact assessments with our reports, and we have constructive relationships with departmental economists. The impact assessment is crucial to implementation decisions; but the science or art of impact assessment is still evolving, particularly in areas that are extremely difficult to quantify.

Perhaps I might tell a short story about the reduction of regulation. Not long ago the House of Lords thought it would be a good idea if the Land Registry required joint purchasers of property to make a declaration of trust to say whether they were joint tenants or tenants under common law.[37] The difference is crucial, and it is important that joint owners choose which form of ownership to adopt – particularly in view of the difficulties which arise if they separate having left this question unresolved. It is also part of a solicitor's duty to advise on the point. In response to what the House of Lords said, the Land Registry set up a Working Party of which I was an academic member. We agreed that although it was not part of the Land Registry's function to require joint purchasers to set their house in order, we would recommend a new procedure that would make the declaration of trust a compulsory precondition to registration. Sadly, that recommendation could not be implemented because it was regarded as an increase in regulation. I have written at more length about this elsewhere;[38] as I understand it, the Land Registry has introduced a new form on which declarations of trust can be recorded, but without any compulsion and therefore without, in my view, the benefits to individuals that the Working Party's recommendation would have effected.

(HMacQ) I found the writing of an impact assessment, or attempt at an impact assessment, an intellectual challenge which I quite enjoyed but it was in the discussion paper and it was asking people to tell me things.[39] We have now got all the consultation stuff back and nobody has answered the questions about impact assessment, so we are no further forward. I have had one experience of impact assessment jointly with the English Commission[40] and it was great fun doing the sums.[41]

---

[37] *Stack v Dowden* [2007] UKHL 17, [2007] 2 AC 432.

[38] Elizabeth Cooke, 'In the Wake of Stack v Dowden: The Tale of TR1' [2011] *Family Law* 1142.

[39] Discussion Paper No 147 on Interpretation of Contract, paras 1.16–1.21.

[40] See the Joint Reports on Consumer Insurance Law: Pre-Contract Disclosure and Misrepresentation (Law Com No 319, Scot Law Com No 219, 2009), Part 11, and Consumer Redress for Misleading and Aggressive Practices (Law Com No 332, Scot Law Com No 226, 2012), Part 11.

[41] The Scottish Law Commission is now required to provide a Business and Regulatory Impact Assessment (a BRIA) with its Reports. The first of these appeared online alongside our *Report on Prescription in Moveables* (Scot Law Com No 228, 2012) at www.scotlawcom.gov.uk/index.php/download_file/view/1000/138/. Another accompanied our *Report on Execution in Counterpart* (above, n 20).

10

Parliament Act 1911 in its Historical Context

PHILIP NORTON

THE PARLIAMENT ACT 1911 could be seen as the consequence of a long campaign for reform. The House of Lords was a subject of debate for much of the nineteenth century. The existence of a House of prelates and hereditary peers gave rise to criticism at a time of the widening of the franchise. The fact that it was a Tory-dominated House exacerbated the criticism, not least during periods of Liberal government. However, the campaign for change was neither the trigger for the decision to introduce a Bill to limit the powers of the House, nor responsible for its outcome.

The trigger for the introduction of the Parliament Bill in 1910 was the rejection of the budget by the House of Lords the previous year. It was, though, a different issue that determined the shape of the debate as well as the eventual outcome. The enactment of a measure to restrict the veto power of the second chamber is attributable to the issue that dominated British politics at the time – Irish home rule.[1]

I PRESSURE FOR REFORM

The House of Lords was a powerful body in the nineteenth century, initially as much as for who was in it as for the House exercising its powers as one chamber of a bicameral legislature. Many peers exercised political power more through their control of seats in the House of Commons than through attending and voting in the House of Lords. Politics at the time was characterised by Ostrogorski as 'the pet hobby of a select group, the sport of an aristocracy'.[2] The Reform Act 1832 served to lessen the grip of the aristocracy on the House of Commons, but it left the formal powers of the House of Lords unaffected. On the issue of supply, the Commons had already asserted and achieved primacy over the Lords. Its position as the originator of proposals for taxation was affirmed by Henry IV in 1407 and was reasserted after the Restoration (not just of the Monarch but of the House of Lords) in 1660. After the Restoration, the Commons also began to deny the right of the Lords to amend money Bills. However, in all other respects, the two Houses remained co-equal in law-making. The House of Lords could amend or reject non-money Bills and while it may not be able to amend money Bills, its right to reject them remained intact.

---

[1] This particular thesis draws heavily on my History of Parliament Annual Lecture 2011, published as Philip Norton, 'Resisting the Inevitable? The Parliament Act 1911' (2012) *Parliamentary History* 31 (3) 444–59.

[2] Moisei Ostrogorski, *Democracy and the Organisation of Political Parties* (New York, Anchor Books/Doubleday, 1964, first pub 1902) 15.

The extension of the franchise not only weakened the grip of peers on the membership of the House of Commons, but also served to undermine the claim of the House of Lords to be a moral equal to the elected House. This was especially so in the latter half of the century following the enactment of the Reform Act 1867 and the Representation of the People Act 1884, the passage of the latter ensuring that a majority (just) of working men had the vote. The implications were recognised by some peers during the passage of the 1867 Bill, most notably the Earl of Shaftesbury. I have variously quoted his contribution before.[3] His prophetic words merit repetition:

> When we come to look at the House in which I have now the honour to address your Lordships, I ask how it will be affected by this great democratic change? So long as the other House of Parliament was elected upon a restricted principle, I can understand that it would submit to a check from a House such as this. But in the presence of this great democratic power and the advance of this great democratic wave . . . it passes my comprehension to understand how an hereditary House like this can hold its own. It might be possible for this House, in one instance, to withstand a measure if it were violent, unjust, and coercive; but I do not believe that the repetition of such an offence would be permitted. It would be said, 'The people must govern, and not a set of hereditary peers never chosen by the people'.[4]

The House, however, took a different view and was prepared to, and did, amend and reject Bills passed by the House chosen by the people. Tory peers led by the Marquess of Salisbury took the view that, although the Commons may be *chosen* by the people, it did not necessarily *speak* for the people, at least on particular issues.[5] Salisbury developed the referendal theory. This came into play if the Government had no clear mandate for a particular policy and the House of Lords believed that the Commons was not truly representing the views of the people. Salisbury conceded that such an event would be exceptional. In most cases, he argued, the people took little interest in matters discussed in Parliament and in such cases there was no distinction between the prerogatives of the two Houses. But there were a small number of cases in which the nation must be called upon to give its council and determine the policy of the Government. 'It may be', he declared,

> that the House of Commons in determining the opinion of the nation is wrong; and if there are grounds for entertaining that belief, it is always open to this House, and indeed it is the duty of this House to insist that the nation shall be consulted, and that one House without the support of the nation shall not be allowed to domineer over the other.[6]

In such an exceptional circumstance, the House of Lords was entitled to reject a Bill until such time as the people had the opportunity to pass judgement on it.

His acknowledgement of the need to have the opinion of the nation, and not simply the people, was subsequently to be developed into a second hurdle to the Commons simply being able to get its way. For the view of the nation to be clear, the people of each part of the United Kingdom needed to be in agreement, and that applied especially to what Lord

---

[3] Philip Norton, *The Commons in Perspective* (Oxford, Martin Robertson, 1981) 16; Norton, 'Resisting the Inevitable?' (n 1) 447.

[4] Hansard, *Parl Debs*, 3rd ser, vol 188, cols 1925–6: 23 July 1867.

[5] See Corinne Comstock Weston, 'Salisbury and the Lords, 1868-1895' (1982) *Historical Journal* 25, reproduced in Clyve Jones and David Lewis Jones (eds), *Peers, Politics and Power: The House of Lords, 1603-1911* (London, The Hambledon Press, 1986) 461–88.

[6] Hansard, *Parl Debs*, 3rd ser, vol 197, col 84: 17 June 1869.

Rosebery as Prime Minister was to refer to as 'the predominant member of the partnership of the three kingdoms', namely England.[7]

The referendal theory created a situation that was clearly partial to the dominant party in the House of Lords. Since the time of Pitt the Younger, there had been a Tory majority in the House. The result of the theory was that, as Liberal MP Sir Charles Dilke objected in 1881, 'the claim of Lord Salisbury to force us to "consult the country" is a claim for annual Parliaments when we are in office and septennial Parliaments when they are in office.'[8] The theory created the justification for refusing to pass Liberal measures, culminating in 1893 with the rejection of the Home Rule Bill. The ensuing general election saw the return of a Conservative government and in Tory eyes the result vindicated the work of the Lords. To Liberals, the referendal theory was an affront to Shaftesbury's 'great democratic wave' and the rejection of Liberal measures confirmed them in the view that reform was necessary. Lord Morley coined the phrase 'mend or end'. The policy of 'mending or ending' became part of the 1891 Newcastle Programme and, following the rejection of the Home Rule Bill, the Liberal Conference in 1894 voted in favour of abolishing the Lords' power of veto.

Although the referendal theory was a means of enabling the Conservatives to block Liberal measures – Salisbury and his allies failing to distinguish between the national will and Conservative preferences, indeed seeing the party as the expression of the national will[9] – there was also an ultimate danger for its proponents. If a measure was referred to the people and they supported it, then the theory required the Lords to accept the will of the people. Salisbury accepted that consequence in expounding the theory during debate on the Irish Church Bill. The disestablishment of the Irish church had been the dominant issue in the general election of November 1868. Given the result of the election, it could not now, on the logic of Salisbury's argument, be blocked by the Lords, even though most Tory peers wanted to vote it down. Salisbury was among 36 Conservative peers to vote with the Liberals to ensure that the Bill received a Second Reading.[10]

A Liberal government was returned with a substantial majority in the general election of 1906. The Conservative majority in the House of Lords was deployed in order to amend or force the abandonment of a number of Bills, such as the Education Bill and the Plural Voting Bill. The stance prompted the Prime Minister, Sir Henry Campbell-Bannerman, to introduce a motion stating

> That, in order to give effect to the will of the people as expressed by their elected representatives, it is necessary that the power of the other House to alter or reject Bills passed by this House should be so restricted by law as to secure that within the limits of a single Parliament the final decision of the Commons shall prevail.[11]

Campbell-Bannerman argued that both parties were agreed that the will of the people should prevail:

---

[7] Quoted in Comstock Weston, 'Salisbury and the Lords, 1868-1895' (n 5) 483.

[8] Cited in Norton, *The Commons in Perspective* (n 3) 22.

[9] See the comments of GH LeMay, *The Victorian Constitution: Conventions, Usages and Contingencies* (London, Duckworth, 1979) 144. Salisbury's successor, Arthur Balfour, in 1906 declared that it was the duty of everyone to ensure that the party 'should still control, whether in power or whether in opposition, the destinies of this great Empire'. Quoted in Robert Blake, *The Conservative Party from Peel to Churchill* (London, Eyre & Spottiswoode, 1970) 190.

[10] Comstock Weston, 'Salisbury and the Lords, 1868-1895' (n 5) 473.

[11] Hansard, *Commons Debates*, 4th ser, vol 176, col 909: 24 June 1907.

How, then, is that will of the people to be got at and ascertained unless you take the view of the elective House as expressing it? The supremacy of the people in legislation implies, in this country at any rate, the authority of the Commons.[12]

The Conservative leader, Arthur Balfour, pursued the distinction drawn by his uncle, the Marquess of Salisbury, in claiming that the motion made clear the intention 'not to carry out the will of the people, but the will of the House of Commons of the moment'.[13] The Government got its way and the motion was passed by 432 votes to 147.

In his speech, Balfour did query why a motion was being pursued rather than a Bill.[14] It was a pertinent question. The Government appeared intent on making a point, while being reluctant to pursue it through a measure that would be highly contentious and time-consuming. Crucially, such a measure had not been placed before the electors in 1906 and so would have triggered an election. Calling an election specifically on the issue may not have been prudent. The Conservatives were initially adroit in their response to the Government's programme. The Lords made changes to Bills that were not especially popular in the country, while not preventing the passage of measures such as the Trades Disputes Act, the Old Age Pensions Bill and the Eight Hours Bill, which favoured the working class and which, if rejected, could have triggered a peers-versus-people conflict.[15] The measures that were opposed were supported by particular interests, but open to the claim that they lacked the wholehearted consent of the people as a whole. A Licensing Bill failed to get through the Lords in 1908, but it was largely unlamented. As time passed, the Government's reluctance to call an election grew rather than diminished, as economic problems became more prominent and the Government's popularity decreased. It was thus keen to limit the power of the House of Lords, but without feeling able to take steps to achieve that through formal restraint.

This may have remained the situation for the lifetime of a full seven-year Parliament and possibly beyond had it not been for an unexpected and dramatic action on the part of the House of Lords and that was the rejection of the 1909 budget. 'A more stupendous act of foolishness', declared Lord Marchamley, 'never was perpetrated by any House of Parliament'.[16]

II THE TRIGGER FOR REFORM

The budget introduced by the Chancellor of the Exchequer, Lloyd George, in 1909 was radical but not so extreme as to be expected to fall foul of the Second Chamber. The Government needed to raise substantial sums to meet a deficit and to fund their social and defence programmes, not least old age pensions and reinforcing the navy. It introduced a super-tax, a car and petrol tax, land valuation, and four new land taxes. There were increases in income tax, death duties, and alcohol, beer and tobacco duties. The budget attracted vocal and vehement opposition from the City, landowners and brewers, even from some Liberal MPs. The opposition, though, was not particularly well organised or designed to carry popular support. Dukes were especially prominent in decrying its

---

[12] Hansard, *Commons Debates*, 4th ser, vol 176, col 911: 24 June 1907.
[13] Hansard, *Commons Debates*, 4th ser, vol 176, col 937: 24 June 1907.
[14] Hansard, *Commons Debates*, 4th ser, vol 176, col 940: 24 June 1907.
[15] See Neil Blewett, *The Peers, the Parties and the People: The General Elections of 1910* (London, Macmillan, 1972) 61.
[16] Hansard, *Lords Debates*, 5th ser, vol 8, col 723: 23 May 1911.

provisions, doing so in terms that left them open to being mocked by government supporters.

Despite the attacks on the budget, there was no expectation initially that the Finance Bill would not be passed by both Houses. Passage of the Bill through the Commons was tortuous but, as Rowland records,

> Neither Lansdowne nor Balfour seems to have felt, at this time, that the Upper House should reject the measure and on July 16th, at the annual dinner of the Conservative and Constitutional Associations, Lansdowne declared that the House of Lords would 'do its duty' (i.e. accept the Budget) but not 'without wincing'.[17]

However, as opposition became more intense, the prospect of the Lords rejecting the budget began to gain currency. Land valuation was especially anathema to the landed interests, while the brewers were opposed to the new licensing duties, seeing the budget as a way of reintroducing provisions of the failed Licensing Bill. For Tories, and many in the City, it was a Socialist measure and some Tory peers took the view that if the House of Lords did not resist the Bill, then there was little point in the House.

Balfour eventually came round to supporting the view that the Lords should reject the Bill, essentially as a means of keeping his party united.[18] It was a major miscalculation – not the first he was to make in response to the political situation – and one that appears to have been borne of over-confidence. As Neil Blewett observed, 'The mood of the Lords was not unimportant. Success had bred recklessness.'[19] The tactics employed up to that point had proved successful and the view of party leaders was that the budget was sufficiently unpopular to deliver the likelihood of the Liberals losing the election or at least having their large 1906 majority massively reduced. They also believed that the election would be confined to the merits of the budget rather than the actions of the Lords in rejecting a measure approved by the elected House.

The budget was not only contentious but detailed. Lloyd George took over four hours to deliver it and at one point Balfour suggested an adjournment so that the Chancellor could rest his throat. The extensive debate in Committee reflected Tory opposition, but may also have not been unwelcome to the Government. Realising that the Bill may not make it through the Lords, thus resulting in an election, there was merit in not rushing proceedings and so delaying an election, ideally into the New Year, when it could be fought on a new electoral register (thought to favour the Liberals).[20] The Tories also saw merit in delay, believing that come 1910 the Government would be more unpopular and also taking the view that *they* would benefit from a new register.[21] The Bill cleared the Commons on 4 November.

The Lords spent six days debating the Second Reading in November. The Tory leader, the Marquess of Lansdowne, moved an amendment 'That this House is not justified in giving its consent to the Bill until it has been submitted to the judgment of the country.' The Tories attacked the contents of the Bill – covering the principal provisions, rather than concentrating on one – and justified the rights of the House to reject it. Lansdowne developed the referendal principle embodied in his amendment. The Bill, he declared,

[17]   Peter Rowland, *The Last Liberal Government* (New York, The Macmillan Company, 1968) 222.
[18]   Max Egremont, *Balfour: A Life of Arthur James Balfour* (London, Collins, 1980) 219.
[19]   Blewett, *The Peers, the Parties and the People* (n 15) 79.
[20]   Rowland, *The Last Liberal Government* (n 17) 228.
[21]   Blewett, *The Peers, the Parties and the People* (n 15) 97.

has never been before the people of this country. It needs the concurrence of the House of Lords. The House of Lords should not, in our opinion, undertake the responsibility of giving that concurrence until it has become aware that the people of this country desire that this Bill should become law.[22]

The Lord Chancellor, Lord Loreburn, developed the point made by Dilkes in 1881, arguing that unelected peers would be able to hold the House of Commons, and the Government of the day, in the hollow of its hand:

If the House of Commons should displease your Lordships, however recently they may have come from the country, you will be able to remit them again to the torture of the poll. If the Government displease you, all you have to do is wait for the psychological moment, when some gust of dissatisfaction in regard to their conduct, some momentary displeasure, may be visible in the constituencies, and put an end to them if they happen to be of an opinion hostile to your own. No wise man would desire that this House should possess such authority as that, and no man of spirit will submit to it.[23]

Tory peers laid into the provisions – if it was accepted, Lord Willoughby de Broke declared,

we shall have both Houses of Parliament definitely committed to a policy of Socialism, and nothing else but Socialism; and there will be a perfectly legitimate and natural demand for the abolition of the House of Lords both by its former friends and by its enemies.[24]

The opposition of the dominant party in the House left little doubt as to the outcome. In closing the debate, the Lord Privy Seal, the Earl of Crewe, anticipating defeat, declared that, after the action taken by the Lords, 'we must . . . set ourselves to obtain guarantees . . . guarantees which will prevent that indiscriminate destruction of our legislation of which your work to-night is the climax and the crown.'[25] Despite such warnings, Lansdowne's amendment was carried by 350 votes to 75. Seventeen Dukes voted for the amendment and none against it.

The rejection of the Bill necessitated a general election – the Government could not continue without obtaining supply. On 2 December, the House of Commons passed, by 349 votes to 134, a motion declaring that the action of the House of Lords 'was a breach of the Constitution and a usurpation of the rights of the Commons'.[26] The following day Parliament was prorogued. It was dissolved on 10 January. The election took place over several days, the first polling taking place on 15 January and the last (Orkney & Shetland) on 8 and 9 February.[27] The Conservatives gained 105 seats, leaving the Liberals with 274 seats to the Conservatives' 273, and dependent on the votes of Irish Nationalists in the House. With the support of all Nationalist and Labour MPs, the Government had a majority of 124 over the Conservatives.

The result was sufficient to demonstrate support for Lloyd George's budget. Under Salisbury's referendal theory, there was little scope for the Lords to resist it and the Bill was given a Second Reading, without a division, on 28 April. As Lansdowne conceded:

Last year we withheld our concurrence from this Bill solely with the object of obtaining a reference of it to the constituencies, and now that the constituencies, through the mouths of their

[22] Hansard, *Lords Debates*, 5th ser, vol 4, col 731: 22 November 1909.
[23] Hansard, *Lords Debates*, 5th ser, vol 4, col 755: 22 November 1909.
[24] Hansard, *Lords Debates*, 5th ser, vol 4, col 777: 22 November 1909.
[25] Hansard, *Lords Debates*, 5th ser, vol 4, col 1342: 30 November 1909.
[26] Hansard, *Commons Debates*, 5th ser, vol 13, cols 546–81: 2 December 1909.
[27] *The Times Guide to the House of Commons 1910*, The Times, 1910 B-2.

representatives in the House of Commons, have expressed themselves favourably to the Bill, we are, I conceive, as honourable men bound by the pledges we have given in and out of this House to acquiesce in the passage of the Bill through all its stages to-night.[28]

That, however, was not the end of the controversy. The Government was determined now to address the issue of the House of Lords. Two weeks before the Lords passed the Finance Bill, Prime Minister Herbert Asquith introduced a Parliament Bill to give effect to the resolutions approved by the Commons in 1907.

III CAUSE OF THE OUTCOME

The events leading up to the passage of the Parliament Bill can be briefly sketched before addressing the reasons for the outcome. The Parliament Bill provided that a money bill (as certified by the Speaker) was to be passed unamended within one month by the Lords, otherwise Royal Assent would be sought without the Lords' concurrence. For non-money Bills, there was an effective delaying power of at least two years. If the Lords rejected such a Bill in three successive sessions, then, upon its third rejection by the Lords, it was to be presented for Royal Assent. The only proviso was that there was to be a period of two years between being first introduced in the Commons and being passed for the third time by the Commons.

The Bill was introduced in the Commons, but the unexpected death of the King, Edward VII, on 6 May, created a new political situation. In deference to the wishes of the new sovereign, and believing it was in line with the popular mood, the Government convened a constitutional conference to see if agreement could be reached between the parties. It met 21 times in the period from June to November 1910. It failed to reach agreement and the Government called a second election, ostensibly on the issue of the Parliament Bill. The result of the election was not greatly different to that of January – 'The second election merely confirmed the new order'[29] – but it meant that there was a majority in the House of Commons to ensure passage of the Bill.

The Bill was reintroduced in the new Parliament without any changes. It was given a Second Reading in the Commons by 368 votes to 243. The Government resorted to the use of the guillotine to ensure it was not unduly delayed. After 10 days in committee, and four on report, it was given a Third Reading on 15 May by 362 votes to 241. The Bill was sent up to the Lords largely as it had been introduced, the Government having accepted very few amendments.

In the Lords, the Bill was given a Second Reading without a division, but in committee it was effectively gutted and rewritten. As rewritten, it effectively embodied the referendal principle, without the need for the intervention of the Lords, in respect of constitutional measures. Under its provisions, any measure establishing home rule for any part of the United Kingdom, or affecting the Protestant succession, or which, in the view of a joint committee, 'raises an issue of great gravity upon which the judgement of the country has not been sufficiently ascertained' would not receive Royal Assent unless approved by the electors. The Bill was given an unopposed Third Reading on 20 July.

---

[28] Hansard, *Lords Debates*, 5th ser, vol 5, col 780: 28 April 1910.
[29] Blewett, *The Peers, the Parties and the People* (n 15) 388.

On the same day as the Bill left the Lords, Asquith wrote to Balfour to inform him that the King had previously given a pledge that he would be prepared to use his prerogative to create a sufficient number of peers to ensure the passage of the Bill.[30] This was the Government's trump card. The pledge had been extracted from a reluctant monarch shortly after the failure of the constitutional conference, but was kept secret until the outcome of the Lords' position on the Bill was known. Revelation of the King's pledge transformed the situation, the Conservative leadership accepting that the Bill as passed by the Commons should now be accepted. When the Commons rejected the Lords' amendments, Balfour advised Tory peers to support Lord Lansdowne in the decision not to insist on their amendments.[31] The Bill returned to the Lords on 10 August. For the Government, Lord Morley made clear that, if the Bill was defeated, the King would 'assent to the creation of peers sufficient in numbers to guard against any possible combination of the different parties in opposition, by which the Parliament Bill might again be exposed a second time to defeat'.[32] This foreclosed any possibility of preventing the passage of the Bill. Although many Tory peers remained 'ditchers' – prepared to die in the last ditch in opposition to the Bill – others became 'hedgers', prepared to let the Bill through. Despite Balfour's letter, his leadership on the subject had proved weak[33] and the result was uncertain. On a sweltering hot day, the House debated the motion not to insist on the key Lords' amendments.[34] As *The Times* recorded, 'At 20 to 11, the question was put that the House do not insist, and without delay, Lord Lansdowne leading, many members of the Opposition rose and left the House in perfect order.'[35] Most Tory peers absented themselves, but that was not sufficient to ensure that the motion was carried. To ensure passage, it required some Tory votes. It was passed by 131 votes to 114. The majority included 13 Lords Spiritual and 37 Tories (the so-called 'Judas peers').[36] The Parliament Bill made it to the statute book.

However, when we look at the debate that took place over the future of the House of Lords, we can see that it embodied two distinct arguments. One was between the Conservatives and the Liberals. The other was within the ranks of the Government.

The Conservatives were vehemently opposed to the Government's proposals to limit the powers of the House of Lords. However, they were keen to stress that they were not against reform. For them, reform was a matter of composition. Salisbury had been an ardent advocate of such reform. He introduced two Bills, one to provide for the creation of life peers and the other to discontinue issuing writs to those peers who did not normally take their seats. Both Bills cleared the Lords, but not the Commons. 'The Commons . . . feared the creation of what would have been a much stronger Second Chamber and the Bills were withdrawn'.[37]

---

[30]   *The Times*, 22 July 1911.

[31]   Letter from Balfour to Lord Newton, dated 25 July 1911, published in *The Times*, 26 July 1911.

[32]   Hansard, *Lords Debates*, 5th ser, vol 9, col 1000: 10 August 1910. There were reported to be more than 500 names of potential nominees on a list held by the Chief Whip. *The Times*, 17 July 1911.

[33]   See, eg, David Dutton, *Austen Chamberlain: Gentleman in Politics* (Bolton, Ross Anderson Publications, 1985) 86–90.

[34]   On the debate, see David Gilmour, *Curzon* (London, Papermac, 1995) 391–93.

[35]   *The Times*, 11 August 1911.

[36]   See Corinne Comstock Weston and Patricia Kelvin, 'The "Judas Group" and the Parliament Bill of 1911' (1984) *English Historical Review* 99, 551–63. See also Peter Dorey and Alexandra Kelso, *House of Lords Reform Since 1911* (Basingstoke, Palgrave Macmillan, 2011) 25–33.

[37]   Conservative Political Centre, *The House of Lords: A Survey of its History and Powers* (London, Conservative Political Centre, 1947) 20.

Tory peers returned to the issue following the return of the Liberal Government in 1906. Lord Newton introduced a Bill in 1907 to achieve similar goals to those of Salisbury's Bills. His Bill provided for the creation of life peers and a reduction in the number of hereditary peers, restricting the latter to certain categories of peers (those of first creation, those who had held high office or served in the Commons, and a number elected by their fellow peers). Tories pursued this particular line, contending that although they opposed the Parliament Bill, they favoured reform. It was, in effect, a parallel debate to that being pursued by the Government over the powers of the House. However, Tory votes alone were not sufficient to ensure the enactment of the Bill and, failing to persuade the Government of the merits of the measure, it never made it to the statute book. The House also established a select committee to consider the issue, but its report was never debated.[38]

However, the peers persisted. At the end of the 1910 Parliament, Lord Rosebery, the former Liberal Prime Minister and now a cross-bencher, achieved passage of a motion declaring that in future the House of Lords should consist of Lords of Parliament chosen by the whole body of hereditary peers from amongst themselves, plus those sitting by virtue of office and qualifications, and those 'chosen from outside'.[39] Six days later, in a two-day debate, Lord Lansdowne widened the proposal to encompass composition and process. He achieved approval for motions asserting that the House should be reconstituted in line with recent motions passed by it, differences between the Houses on non-money Bills should be resolved by a joint sitting, and that matters of great gravity which had not been adequately submitted to the judgement of the people should be decided by the people by referendum.[40]

For ministers, the problem with reforming the composition of the House was less one of merit, but rather one of expediency. Their focus was one of limiting the powers of the House, not retaining the existing powers in the hands of a different or reconstituted body of unelected members. They needed to address powers, not least, as we shall see, because of the need to carry the votes of Irish Nationalist MPs. For them, the attempt to focus on composition was an attempt to distract from what needed to be done. 'The Opposition plan', declared Morley in the debate on Lansdowne's motions, 'is really no plan at all. It is a mere school-boy sketch on a piece of paper.'[41] Asquith assailed the 'death-bed repentance' of the peers: 'The patricidal pick-axes are already at work', he declared, 'and constitutional jerry-builders are hurrying from every quarter with new plans.'[42]

The debate within the Government took place as to the most desirable means of limiting the powers of the Lords. Campbell-Bannerman had favoured limiting the veto power of the House, substituting the absolute veto with a delaying power, or suspensory veto. Under a plan drawn up the Clerk of the House of Commons, Sir Courtney Ilbert, disagreement between the Houses would lead to a conference of a number of MPs and peers. If agreement could not be reached, the Bill could be re-introduced six months later. If again agreement could not be reached, the process could be repeated, but with a failure to agree leading to the Bill becoming law without the assent of the Lords. However, Campbell-Bannerman's successor, Asquith, had sympathy with a proposal, the Ripon plan, under

---

[38] The report is reproduced in Sydney D Bailey (ed), *The Future of the House of the Lords* (London, Hansard Society, 1954) 140–47.

[39] Hansard, *Lords Debates*, 5th ser, vol 6, cols 714–58: 17 November 1910.

[40] See Hansard, *Lords Debates*, 5th ser, vol 6, cols 924–1012: 24 November 1910.

[41] Hansard, *Lords Debates*, 5th ser, vol 6, col 999: 24 November 1910.

[42] Blewett, *The Peers, the Parties and the People* (n 15) 176.

which, in the event of a failure to agree between the two Houses, a conference would be convened, comprising all MPs and 100 peers, and the vote of the conference would determine the fate of the measure. The 100 peers would comprise 20 members of the Government with the rest chosen by the House. The suspensory veto was the more radical option, enabling any government secure in a majority in the Commons to gets its way, whereas the Ripon plan would necessitate a substantial government majority in the Commons to ensure the passage of a Bill over the objection of the Lords.[43]

The Ripon plan had found favour with members of Campbell-Bannerman's Cabinet, but the Prime Minister had managed to persuade his colleagues to support his approach[44] and this was embodied in the motions agreed in 1907 and formed the basis of the Parliament Bill. The Ripon plan was nonetheless not dead. It was resurrected at the constitutional conference. The Conservatives were keen to push for a constitutional Bill twice rejected by the Lords to be referred to the people for determination, in effect, maintaining Salisbury's referendal theory. The Liberal members were more drawn to the Ripon plan. They had some sympathy with the Conservative demands, but pursued the proposal for a joint conference of the two Houses. The suspensory veto, generally referred to as the C-B plan, found little support. However, the two sides failed to reach agreement and the conference ended without resolution. The Government thus fell back on the Parliament Bill as it stood.

The reason for the collapse of the constitutional conference and the eventual outcome of the controversy – the limitation of the veto power of the Lords – was not to be found in a principled stance on the relationship of the two chambers. There was clearly a case for asserting that the elected House should be able to get its way – that had underpinned the debate since the passage of the Reform Acts. However, what explained the stance taken on Lords' reform in 1910 and 1911 was the position of participants on a particular issue of public policy – Irish home rule. That had bedevilled political debate since Gladstone had embarked on a policy of home rule. It is difficult to overstate the impact of the issue on political debate and opinion in the last decades of the nineteenth century and the first two decades of the twentieth century. Until 1922, as Robert Blake observed, 'the Irish question obsessed English Parliamentary life to an extent seldom equalled – and never surpassed – by any political issue before or since.'[45]

The Liberals were supporters of home rule, but Asquith and a number of his colleagues were not particularly sympathetic and the issue had not been prominent in the 1906 election. However, it was at the heart of the debate after 1909. The Liberals needed Irish Nationalist support to get the Finance Bill through following the January 1910 election. Irish Nationalist support was contingent on a commitment to achieving home rule. As George Dangerfield put it, 'the Irish party as good as held Mr Asquith's IOU'.[46] Conservatives were vehemently opposed.

Although the January election had been held ostensibly on the issue of the budget (though in practice various other issues were also prominent), that was superseded by debate on home rule. That underpinned the stance taken on the issue of the Parliament Bill. Irish Nationalists saw the House of Lords as an impediment to achieving home rule. So long as the House had a veto and Tory majority, it stood between them and their cher-

---

[43] Neither proposal was original. See Joseph Jaconelli, 'The Parliament Bill 1910-11: The Mechanics of Constitutional Protection' (1991) *Parliamentary History* 10, 288–89.

[44] Chris Ballinger, *The House of Lords 1911-2011* (Oxford, Hart Publishing, 2012) 17–18.

[45] Robert Blake, *The Unknown Prime Minister* (London, Eyre & Spottiswoode, 1955) 120–21.

[46] George Dangerfield, *The Strange Death of Liberal England* (London, MacGibbon & Kee, 1966) 42.

ished goal. For Conservatives and Liberal Unionists, the House of Lords was an essential protector of the existing constitution and especially the union.

The Government's plans for reform of the Upper House have thus to be seen through the prism of Irish home rule. Home rule was not an issue hidden from view. Lansdowne, during debate on the Second Reading of the Finance Bill in April 1910, made clear what he saw as the motivation for the Parliament Bill:

> It seems to me absolutely clear and established beyond possibility of doubt that what carried the day and enabled you to take your Irish allies with you into the Lobby was the statement made by the Prime Minister a very few days ago, 'the unmistakable declaration' – as it has been called – of the Prime Minister. Now I do not believe there is any reason for supposing that the Irish are in favour of a Single Chamber, or that they owe any particular grudge to the House of Lords. But, in their view, these Resolutions for the abolition of the Veto of the House of Lords spell Home Rule for Ireland.[47]

During the December election, Balfour promised a referendum on tariff reform – in the event another miscalculation, as it failed to have any discernible electoral impact – but the focus was essentially on the constitutional issue precipitating the election. As the *Times Guide* to the general election recorded:

> The contest was carried out with the utmost keenness, and although Tariff Reform, Imperial defence, the land question, the Osborne judgment, and other subjects of importance were discussed, the attention of the electors was concentrated mainly on the alternative policies with regard to the Constitutional issue – the Parliament Bill, which was understood to be intended to facilitate Home Rule for Ireland, and the reforms suggested by Lord Lansdowne and Lord Rosebery, with the Referendum as an essential feature.[48]

The motivation for the Bill was the focus of Conservative attacks throughout the Bill's passage in 1911. As *The Times* reported of one speech, 'Mr J. T. Middlemore, M.P., addressing his constituents on the Parliament Bill, said that he preferred calling the Bill the "Redmond Bill", because it was the outcome of negotiations with that gentleman and the Government.'[49] It was a common refrain throughout the debate on the Bill. Among the amendments moved in the Commons, for example, was one by JB Lonsdale to exclude from the operation of the Bill 'any Bill to establish a separate Parliament and Executive for Ireland.' This, as *The Times* observed, 'raises one of the most important issues in connexion with the Bill'.[50] For the Conservatives, it was the most important. The avowed object of the Bill, wrote Lord Deerhurst, was 'the passing of a measure to give Home Rule to Ireland'.[51]

The Conservative opposition to home rule explained both the failure of the constitutional conference and the willingness of the Tory leadership to let the Parliament Bill pass.

The constitutional conference had come close to reaching agreement. The Conservatives did not have a problem with restricting the Lords' powers over Bills that were exclusively money Bills. However, in respect of non-money Bills, they wanted to distinguish ordinary legislation from 'organic', or constitutional, legislation. In respect of the former, there was agreement that resolving differences through a joint committee – in other words, the Ripon plan – was an appropriate mechanism, though the composition of the committee proved

---

[47] Hansard, *Lords Debates*, 5th ser, vol 5, col 787: 28 April 1910.
[48] *The Times Guide to the House of Commons 1911*, The Times, 1910 9.
[49] *The Times*, 20 July 1911. John Redmond was the leader of the Irish Nationalist MPs.
[50] *The Times*, 22 April 1911.
[51] Letter, *The Times*, 8 August 1911.

contentious. As for the latter, the principal focus of the proposal was seen as any measure for home rule and, as such, it proved unacceptable to the Government. There were various attempts to break the deadlock. Lloyd George, perhaps as a harbinger of things to come, produced a document advocating a coalition government. Asquith suggested that if the Lords rejected the next Home Rule Bill, there should be an immediate general election.

The position was well summarised in a note of the proceedings by Sir R Findlay drawn from Balfour's statement at a meeting to discuss progress (or lack of it):

> On 16th October the Conference broke off on the difficulty of Home Rule. A. J. B. proposed that if a Home Rule Bill was twice rejected it should go to a plebiscite. Lloyd George, while admitting the reasonableness of this, said it was impossible for the Government to assent to this.
>
> The Conference met again last Tuesday. Government proposes compromises.
>
> One was that a General Election should intervene on the next occasion on which a H. R. Bill, having passed the H. of C., was rejected in the H. of L., but only on this occasion, and that H. Rule Bills if introduced afterwards should be treated like ordinary Bills.[52]

The Conservatives were opposed to an election on only one occasion: they wanted the proposal to apply to all subsequent Bills dealing with home rule. Asquith indicated he would have no objection to treating measures dealing with the Crown and the Protestant succession as in a separate category, but not to extend it to other measures, including home rule.

The conference failed to reach agreement on the proportion of peers who would be part of any joint committee to resolve differences on ordinary legislation, but, as Harold Nicolson recorded, it was home rule that was fundamental to the failure.[53] It overshadowed the negotiations. As Rowland observed, there were three factors shaping Balfour's behaviour:

> opposition to home rule per se; a reluctance to abandon the position which he had taken up on Ireland in 1886 and maintained ever since, and finally a determination not to betray the trust placed in him by the Unionist Party.[54]

There was ultimately no meeting of minds. As Asquith wrote to the King, 'The proposed exclusion from the new machinery for settling deadlocks of Home Rule and other so-called organic changes was exhaustively discussed. The result showed an apparently irreconcilable divergence of views.'[55]

Austen Chamberlain was of the view that agreement could have been reached on the proportion of peers in a joint committee to resolve conflicts.[56] Had there not been the 'irreconcilable divergence of views' on home rule, the Ripon plan was likely to have been the agreed means of dealing with disputes between the two Houses.

Conservative opposition to home rule not only resulted in the collapse of the constitutional conference, it also shaped the willingness of the leadership to accept, or at least not to oppose, the Parliament Bill once the King's pledge had been made public. There was an obvious reason to accept the Bill rather than allow the House to be swamped by several hundred new peers. However, there was also an overriding tactical consideration. This was exemplified by a letter written to *The Times* by the great constitutional lawyer and Unionist, AV Dicey. Unionists, he declared, must follow their leaders in whatever tactic the leader-

---

[52] Reproduced in Sir Austen Chamberlain, *Politics From Inside* (London, Cassell and Company, 1936) 296.

[53] Harold Nicolson, *King George the Fifth: His Life and Reign* (London, Constable, 1952) 133.

[54] Rowland, *The Last Liberal Government* (n 17) 318. Balfour's stance on Ireland also appears to have put paid to Lloyd George's proposal for a coalition. Egremont, *Balfour* (n 18) 228–29.

[55] Quoted in Rowland, *The Last Liberal Government* (n 17) 324.

[56] Chamberlain, *Politics from Inside* (n 52) 297.

ship 'hold to be best adapted for the defeat of agitation in favour of Home Rule'.[57] It was also spelled out in a subsequent letter by Bonar Law. He recognised that at least under the provisions of the Parliament Bill, the House of Lords retained a power of delay. 'It might or might not be wise to use this power', he wrote, 'but if I am right in thinking that the House of Lords would have the means of compelling an election before Home Rule became law, that surely is a power which ought not to be lightly abandoned.'[58] If new peers were created on such a scale as to provide the Government with a majority that would mean the provisions would count for little, since the House would be unlikely to reject a home rule Bill. There was thus clearly merit, under this argument, for letting the Bill pass and retaining the existing membership than see the Bill passed after the creation of several hundred new peers.

The remarkable thing about the debate surrounding the Parliament Bill was how little the relationship between the two chambers – or the fundamental role of the second chamber – was discussed in terms of enduring constitutional principles. There was little interest in the role of the second chamber as such, other than in respect of the immediate political issue of home rule. It was not so much a peers-versus-people debate as a home rule-versus-the union debate, with the House of Lords viewed primarily from the perspective of which side of the argument one took.

The need to achieve home rule not only determined the need to limit the power of the House of Lords, it also led to other aspects being left unresolved. This was especially the case in respect of the composition of the House. As we have seen, Conservatives pursued the issue, but the Government was intent instead on achieving a limitation on the powers of the House. There was no time to generate and embody in legislation an agreed change to the membership of the House. Lansdowne introduced a reform Bill early in 1911, but the Government regarded it as falling short of what needed to be done. 'The Cabinet declined to enter into "talks about talks" on reform before the Parliament Bill had been secured.'[59] The issue was left hanging in the preamble to the Act, stating that 'it is intended to substitute for the House of Lords as it presently exists a Second Chamber constituted on a popular instead of a hereditary basis', but noting that 'such substitution cannot be immediately brought into operation'. It went on to record that any such measure would need to define the powers of the new second chamber. As Roy Jenkins observed,

> The suggestion that a reconstituted Upper House might be invested with greater powers than those which the bill would leave the House of Lords was a little sinister, but it was all so vague as not to cause great radical agitation.[60]

The statute book thus acquired a major piece of constitutional legislation, the significance of the legislation far outlasting the issue that caused it to be enacted in the form that it was. The Government in 1912 introduced a Government of Ireland Bill and that was, as anticipated, rejected by the House of Lords. The situation in Ireland rapidly deteriorated, leading to armed conflict and the Conservative Party, under Bonar Law, 'straining the constitution to the uttermost limits',[61] coming close to endorsing armed rebellion by Ulster Unionists. The delay provided time for the Conservatives to mobilise support for the cause of Ulster.[62]

[57] Letter in *The Times*, 21 July 1911.
[58] Letter in *The Times*, 26 July 1911.
[59] Ballinger, *The House of Lords 1911-2011* (n 44) 30.
[60] Roy Jenkins, *Mr Balfour's Poodle* (London, Heinemann, 1954) 136.
[61] Blake, *The Conservative Party from Peel to Churchill* (n 9) 191.
[62] See Andrew Adonis, *Making Aristocracy Work* (Oxford, Clarendon Press, 1993) 159.

We cannot know how events would have unfolded had the Ripon plan been implemented or, perhaps more importantly, had the Lords insisted on their amendments to the Parliament Bill, resulting in hundreds of new peers being created, sufficient in number not only to carry the Parliament Bill but also a Home Rule Bill.

IV LESSONS FOR THE FUTURE

The enactment of the Parliament Act was distinctive both for what triggered its introduction and what determined the form it took. Neither condition has existed since that time. The campaign for reform of the second chamber has been an enduring feature of British politics, albeit varying over time in its political saliency.[63] However, there has been no specific trigger in terms of actions by the House of Lords, nor a burning political issue that has shaped debate when reform has been attempted.

The Parliament Act thus has to be seen in a distinctive historical context. The debate in 1911 was underpinned and shaped by views on an issue other than the role of the second chamber in the political system. The issue of the second chamber, as such, failed to rouse popular interest. This was variously acknowledged during debate on the Parliament Bill. Tory leader Viscount Middleton stressed the lack of popular agitation.

> Why, the whole of London almost were in Palace Yard in 1832. Is anybody outside moved by the introduction of this Bill? Has any one of your Lords received from the parts of the country in which you reside demands that you should vote for 'the Bill, the whole Bill, and nothing but the Bill', which was the case in 1832? I go to as many public meetings as most men, and I have never yet on an election platform been asked a single question on this Bill. . . .[64]

As George Dangerfield wrote of the December election campaign, 'The country was indifferent, and politicians were hard put to it to stir up its lethargy.'[65] The outcome of the vote in the Lords letting the Bill through also failed to stir the nation. Roy Jenkins noted that 'there were few repetitions of either the fury of the die-hards or the extreme relief of the King. The general public remained as unexcited as it had been throughout the long struggle'.[66] Mr JT Middlemore MP, when he was addressing his constituents, declared that 'If the Lords ran away from their carefully-considered amendments, they would sink beneath the contempt of the nation, probably never to rise again'.[67] It proved to be more a case of indifference.

Subsequent debate has revolved around the powers (Parliament Act 1949) and composition (Life Peerages Act 1959, Peerages Act 1963, Parliament (No 2) Bill 1968, House of Lords Act 1999, House of Lords Reform Bill 2012) of the second chamber. The conditions that existed in 1911 have been absent.

The Parliament Act 1949 was enacted in anticipation of what the House of Lords may do rather than as a response to a particular and politically unacceptable action on its part. The Parliament (No 2) Bill was introduced because of the Labour Party's objections to a Tory-

---

[63] See Ballinger, *The House of Lords 1911-2011* (n 44) and Dorey and Kelso, *House of Lords Reform Since 1911* (n 36).

[64] Hansard, *Lords Debates*, 5th ser, vol 8, col 709: 23 May 1911.

[65] Dangerfield, *The Strange Death of Liberal England* (n 46) 45.

[66] Jenkins, *Mr Balfour's Poodle* (n 60) 267.

[67] *The Times*, 20 July 1911.

dominated hereditary House.[68] The Labour Government was in effect the equivalent of the nineteenth century Liberal governments, conscious that when there was a Tory government the House of Lords was not a threat, but when it was in office the House was a potential impediment to achieving its legislation. On this occasion, not only was the Government not able to rouse notable public support for its Bill, it could not even rouse sufficient support on its own benches.[69]

The House of Lords Act 1999 was another attempt by a Labour government to achieve change, focusing, as in 1969, on the hereditary rather than the unelected nature of the House. The lesson it learned from the failure to enact the 1969 Bill was procedural rather than political. Unlike in 1969, it introduced a short, in essence a one-clause, Bill and achieved its passage. The unelected nature of the House was hived off and left to a Royal Commission (the Wakeham Commission) to make recommendations for change.[70] Though broadly accepting its recommendations for a partly-elected House, the Labour Government, despite various efforts, failed to enact any measure of further reform. There were White Papers but no Bill introduced, although a draft Bill was published.[71]

The House of Lords Reform Bill of 2012 was the product of a unique situation – a formal coalition agreement – with a measure of reform agreed with little discussion.[72] There is a case to be made that its failure was a product of wider political considerations – Conservative attitudes towards the coalition – but the principal motivation for opposition was that of the role of the second chamber in the political system. It was very much a debate that was lacking in 1911.

---

[68] See Janet Morgan, *The House of Lords and the Labour Government 1964-1970* (Oxford, Clarendon Press, 1975) 208–20.

[69] It withdrew the Bill after it failed to mobilise 100 of its own MPs to carry a closure motion. See Philip Norton, *Dissension in the House of Commons 1945-74* (London, Macmillan, 1975) 353–54.

[70] Royal Commission on Reform of the House of Lords, *A House for the Future* (London, The Stationery Office, 2000) Cm 4534.

[71] See Dorey and Kelso, *House of Lords Reform Since 1911* (n 36) ch 6 and Philip Norton, 'The House of Lords' in Bill Jones and Philip Norton (eds), *Politics UK*, 8th edn (London, Pearson, 2013) 359–60.

[72] See David Laws, *22 Days in May* (London, Biteback Publishing, 2010) 97.

11

The Parliament Act 1949

CHRIS BALLINGER

> The expression 'unconstitutional' has, as applied to a law, at least three different meanings varying according to the nature of the constitution with reference to which it is used. . . . The expression, as applied to an English Act of Parliament, means simply that the Act in question, as, for instance, the Irish Church Act, 1869, is, in the opinion of the speaker, opposed to the spirit of the English constitution; it cannot mean that the Act is either a breach of law or is void.
>
> AV Dicey, 1915[1]

FOR ALL THE discussion by the House of Lords in their judgment in *R (Jackson) v Her Majesty's Attorney General*[2] of the historical and constitutional context in which the Parliament Act 1911 had been passed into law, there was no similar discussion of the circumstances surrounding the Parliament Act 1949. Indeed, the later Act warranted hardly any mention at all. That is, perhaps, fair enough: the case turned not on the language and circumstances of the 1949 Act, nor on the validity of the 1911 Act, but on whether the 1911 Act could be amended under its own procedures. However, in overlooking the 1949 Act, their Lordships missed the opportunity to test the political and constitutional understanding in which an amendment to the Parliament Act 1911 had been deemed permissible. Lord Bingham noted in *Jackson* that the validity of the Parliament Act 1949 had been accepted by governments of varying political persuasion in the years since its enactment; yet he did not note the views of those who supported and opposed the 1949 Act during the years in which it was passing through Parliament, who overwhelmingly accepted the validity amending the 1911 Act under its own procedures, even if they disliked the consequences.

The Parliament Act 1911 had contained three principal provisions: it incorporated into law the convention that the Lords could not delay financial provisions; it replaced the absolute veto of the House of Lords over primary legislation which had originated in the House of Commons (except for measures extending the life of a Parliament) with a suspensory veto of approximately two years; and it reduced the maximum length of a Parliament from seven years to five. The first provision has not since needed to be enforced.[3]

---

[1] AV Dicey, *Introduction to the Study of the Law of the Constitution*, 8th edn (London, Macmillan, 1915) 516 (Note VII of the Appendix: 'The Meaning of an "Unconstitutional" Law').

[2] *R (Jackson) v Her Majesty's Attorney General* [2005] UKHL 56, [2006] 1 AC 262 (HL).

[3] Jaconelli terms this a rare example of a constitutional convention being enshrined in statute: J Jaconelli, 'The Parliament Bill 1910–1911: The Mechanics of Constitutional Protection' (1991) 10 *Parliamentary History* 277, 280. JW Lowther, Speaker of the House of Commons during the 'constitutional crisis' of 1909–11, wrote in his memoirs

The third provision was uncontroversial.[4] The second provision was relied upon twice later in that Parliament, and then not again for over 30 years.[5]

For an Act that was destined to generate such controversy, the Parliament Act 1949 itself had seemed very simple. Excepting the technical Title Clause, it was a one-clause bill which sought slightly to amend the words of a similar clause of an existing Act. It replaced the suspensory veto under section 2(1) of the Parliament Act 1911 with a requirement that to overcome the Lords' veto the Commons must pass a bill in two successive sessions (rather than three) and that one year (rather than two) must have elapsed from the date of the bill's second reading in the House of Commons in the first of these sessions before it is sent to the Lords for the final time.

The purpose of the 1911 Act had been very clear: to limit the capacity of the unelected, Conservative-dominated, House of Lords to impede the legislative programme of a government which possessed a majority in the House of Commons. The 1949 Act had exactly the same objective; its main difference over its predecessor was a changed view as to the reasonableness of the amount of impediment that the Lords should be permitted to impose. An assessment of the 1911 Act showed that it left the House of Lords with 'almost all the effective power it had exercised before 1909'.[6] The advocates of the 1949 Act argued, in effect, that the purpose of their legislation was to leave the Lords with the power it rightfully possessed before 1947.[7]

I THE POLITICAL AND CONSTITUTIONAL CONTEXT

Commenting on the House of Lords at the time of the passage of the Parliament Act 1911, Lord Bingham noted that:

> Save for a relatively small number of archbishops, bishops, lords of appeal in ordinary and former lords of appeal in ordinary, the membership of the House of Lords in 1911 was wholly hereditary. The great majority of the members had either succeeded, or been appointed, to hereditary peerages. They were predominantly holders of Conservative opinions. Thus it was possible for the majority in the Lords to block the legislative programme of a government with which it disagreed.[8]

that the Finance Bill of 1909 would not have qualified as a 'money bill' under cl 1, s 2 of the Parliament Act 1911, 'for it contained a number of provisions which were not within the definition of that clause and section' (Lord Ullswater, *A Speaker's Commentaries* (London, E Arnold & Co, 2 vols, 1925) ii 103 (quoted by Vernon Bogdanor, written evidence to the Joint Committee on Conventions (2006, HL 265-II, HC 1212-II). On the Parliament Act 1911 generally, see also: Andrew Adonis, *Making Aristocracy Work* (Oxford, Clarendon Press, 1993); Chris Ballinger, 'Hedging and Ditching: The Parliament Act 1911' (2011) 30 *Parliamentary History* 19; Corrine Comstock Weston, 'The Liberal Leadership and the Lords' Veto, 1907–1910' (1968) 11 *Historical Journal* 508.

[4] Parliament had experimented with three-, five- and seven-year Parliaments. When 100 years later, Parliament again legislated for the length of a Parliament, it settled on five years as the length of a Parliament, though stating that five years should be presumed as the fixed duration between general elections, rather than simply an upper limit (Fixed-term Parliaments Act 2011, s 1(3)).

[5] The 1911 Act was used to pass two constitutional reforms – the Welsh Church Act 1914 (which disestablished the Church in Wales), and the Government of Ireland Act 1914 (which set up Home Rule in Ireland) – after which no measures were passed subject to the Lords' new suspensory veto until the Parliament Bill 1947 was conceived.

[6] Adonis (n 3) 159.

[7] Prior to the general election, Mr Attlee had outlined a 'four-year plan', and sought a period of four years of unfettered legislative time in which to enact this. He later told the House of Commons that the veto limitation proposal represented, in the Government's view, 'the minimum requirements to meet the needs of present conditions' (HC Deb 10 November 1947, vol 444, col 37).

[8] *Jackson v Her Majesty's Attorney General* [2005] UKHL 56 [10] (Lord Bingham).

The bases of membership of the Lords were unchanged by 1945, and the political balance between membership of Commons and Lords was even more imbalanced in the period 1945–47, when the second Parliament Act was being drafted, than it had been during the Liberal governments of 1906–11. Indeed, the proportion of the House of Lords who were affiliated to the Government was much lower under Attlee than under Asquith: in 1945 there were just 16 Labour peers in a House of 789.[9] 'In the House of Lords', wrote Lord Addison, Leader of the Government in the Lords, 'the Labour Benches are, as it were, but a tiny atoll in the vast ocean of Tory reaction.'[10]

The concern within the Labour Government was that this imbalance in numbers in the upper House would translate into obstruction to its radical post-war agenda. In its manifesto, it issued a clear threat against the upper House – 'we give clear notice that we will not tolerate obstruction of the people's will by the House of Lords'.[11] The leader of the Conservatives in the Lords, Lord Cranborne,[12] stated at the beginning of the 1945 Parliament that 'Whatever our personal views . . . it would be constitutionally wrong when the country has so recently expressed its view, for this House to oppose proposals which have been definitely put before the electorate' (the 'Salisbury–Addison' doctrine); nonetheless the Cabinet focused not on what would happen when the general election was 'recent', but in the second half of the Parliament, at the point at which the Lords' suspensory veto could delay an issue to beyond the next general election. Lord Addison, Leader of the Government in the upper House, trusted Cranborne's judgement that his colleagues had accepted their role as a revising chamber, which could not hold sway over questions of policy; but admitted that there were few years since 1911 in which these peers would have wished to defy a government.[13] There remained, both in Cabinet and in the wider Parliamentary Labour Party, a lingering worry that the House of Lords might, after three years, come out of its slumbers to use its powers under the Parliament Act 1911 to, in Lord Addison's own phrase, 'play old Harry with the Government's programme'.[14] The Government's reaction to this lingering worry was to prepare to limit the Lords' veto even further and within 18 months of the general election, the Cabinet was giving serious attention to reform proposals.[15]

[9] Asquith's liberals could count on the support of around 80 peers, or 13% of the House.

[10] See G Dymond and H Deadman 'House of Lords Library Note: The Salisbury Doctrine', June 2006. As Prime Minister, Ramsay Macdonald had recommended the creation of 11 Labour (hereditary) peers; others who were formerly Liberal MPs or peers had joined the Labour benches in the Lords. There remained, however, very few Labour peers with which to carry the Government's business in the House, and increasing difficulties in attempts to recruit more.

[11] Labour Party, 'Let Us Face the Future: A Declaration of Labour Policy for the Consideration of the Nation' (1945) in FWS Craig, *British General Election Manifestos 1900–1974* (London, Macmillan, 1975) 125.

[12] Lord Cranborne was an active member of the House of Lords from 1941. He succeeded his father to become the fifth Marquess of Salisbury on 4 April 1947 and continued as leader of the Conservative peers in the House of Lords.

[13] CP (46) 382. Cabinet: Amendment to the Parliament Act. Memorandum by the Secretary of State for Dominion Affairs and Leader of the House of Lords [Viscount Addison], 15 October 1946.

[14] These were Lord Addison's own words, used by him in a conversation with Lord Cranborne, leader of the Conservative peers in the House of Lords: Hatfield House Papers, 5M/Box F, Minute by Lord Cranborne, February 1947.

[15] CM (46) 90th Conclusions, Minute 1. The Cabinet considered two papers by ministers, and decided to postpone action on amending the Parliament Act until the 1947–48 Session. CP (46) 276, Amendment of the Parliament Act: Memorandum by the Lord Chancellor (Viscount Jowitt), 11 October 1946. CP (46) 382 (n 13).

II WHAT LED THE GOVERNMENT TO ACT?

The immediate spur to action in October 1947 was constitutional. The Government wished to keep open the opportunity to pass the Parliament Bill under the procedures of the Parliament Act 1911 if necessary. The options for legislation, outlined to Cabinet a year beforehand, now needed to be acted upon if they were to be guaranteed to become law in time for the next general election, due in 1950, building into the legislative timetable for a Parliament Bill time for a delay of the minimum suspensory veto period of at least two years under section 2(1) of the Parliament Act 1911. The appropriateness of the Parliament Act 1911's procedures as a vehicle for amending those same procedures was, therefore, an explicit driver of the timing and scope of the Parliament Bill.

The secondary reasons for the Government introducing its veto limitation bill in October 1947 were political. Whereas the House of Lords certainly had not acted so as to trigger the Government to invoke its manifesto threat – indeed, the Prime Minister acknowledged to his colleagues that 'the House of Lords had not rejected any Government Bill and had in fact passed a number of important socialisation measures'[16] and accepted that the Lords were unlikely to use the suspensory veto they retained under the Parliament Act – Ministers were unwilling to work on the assumption that peers would certainly not oppose the Government in the later stages of the Parliament. This risk was persuasive in encouraging the Cabinet to act before the Government was perceived as being weakened in the country (whilst 1947 had been a politically difficult year, the Government had lost no by-election since the 1945 general election). 'I think it good tactics', the Prime Minister told his leading minister in the House of Lords, the day after the Cabinet had made its decision 'to make the necessary reform before any trouble between the Houses has arisen.'[17]

Of the policies planned for the later years of the Parliament, the nationalisation of the iron and steel industries was especially vulnerable to obstruction from the House of Lords. Differences of opinion within the Labour Party on the merits of iron and steel nationalisation, present even before the 1945 election, persisted, in the Parliamentary Party and within the Cabinet itself. The Government needed to pass its measures through Parliament, and overcame any delay imposed under the Parliament Act 1911, before the next general election, which was due in 1950. The longer that the priority given to other measures early in the parliament, and the internal politics of the Labour Party disagreeing on iron and steel, delayed the introduction of the legislation, the greater the probability that the Conservatives in the House of Lords could use the Parliament Act 1911 to delay the reform long enough for it to expire at the general election. There were also technical difficulties in legislating for the socialisation of the iron and steel industries: of the remaining nationalisations, the gas industry was the easier for the Government to control because of the organisation of the iron and steel industry (which was dominated by large companies, for whom the production of metals was usually only a small part of their operation, so nationalisation meant depriving companies, and their shareholders, of some of their activity rather than nationalising whole companies).

---

[16] CM (47) 80th Conclusions, Minute 1, 14 October 1947 (Confidential Annex).

[17] The National Archives PREM 8/1059. Prime Minister to Lord Addison (who was on official business in Ceylon, as Secretary of State for the Dominions). Prime Minister's Personal Telegram T406/47, 15 October 1947. In the Second Reading debate in the House of Commons the following month, Attlee commented on this point that: 'We do not wait today for a disease to break out, but try to cure it in advance.' (HC Deb 11 November 1947, vol 444, col 310.)

Moreover, the Conservative Party had consistently opposed the nationalisation of the iron and steel industries. Whereas other nationalisations – for example, the railways, gas, and electricity – merely formalised de facto state monopolies, and the Conservatives had expected the nationalisation of coal, 'steel lay at the heart of British industry and its nationalisation was to be a decisive step towards state ownership of the means of production, the realisation of Clause 4 of the Constitution of the Labour Party.'[18]

If the Government's difficulties continued, and if the Government became less popular over time in the country, the probability that the Conservative Opposition in the Lords might seek to exploit these weaknesses, by delaying a future Iron and Steel Bill to beyond the next general election, increased. A reduction in the Lords' period of delay would prevent such action by the upper House. Even if the risk of delay to the nationalisation proposals was not likely, internal party politics promoted a move on the Lords' veto: 'a decision to proceed with legislation amending the Parliament Act would offset the disappointment which would be felt by many Government supporters at the decision to postpone the Iron and Steel Bill until a later Session of this Parliament.'[19] For these reasons, the Government decided on 14 October 1947 to introduce the Parliament Bill without delay. The King's Speech of 21 October 1947 announced that 'Legislation will be introduced to amend the Parliament Act 1911',[20] and the Parliament Bill was presented just 10 days later, containing a retrospective provision that would guarantee the subsequent passage of any Iron and Steel Bill.[21] Internal Labour Party politics on the merits of extending their programme of nationalisation to the iron and steel industry, perhaps even more than the risk of Conservative Party action in the Lords, drove the Cabinet to introduce the Parliament Bill early in the 1947–48 Session.[22]

The Cabinet did consider the possibility of bringing forward fuller House of Lords reform (as opposed to veto limitation), not least because Lord Addision, who had been discussing reform proposals since 1943 with the fourth Marquess of Salisbury and his son Lord Cranborne, kept reform on the Cabinet's agenda. However, the view of the Cabinet just before the start of the 1947–48 Session was that the time was not right for introducing reform-proper, and that in any case it preferred that the impetus for developing reform proposals should lie with the Opposition rather than with the Government, even though proposals developed in this way were highly unlikely to find favour with Labour backbenchers.[23] Notwithstanding the enthusiasm on the part of Lord Addison for pursuing reform, the Cabinet as a whole was unwilling to risk its firm resolve to secure a reduction in the Lords' suspensory veto being derailed by opening the potentially uncontainable and unending questions of wholesale reform. Addison was overseas on government business and missed the crucial Cabinet meeting of 14 October 1947; but had he been present he would have been unlikely to have overcome the resolve of the Prime Minister, who had been a long-term opponent of Addison's reforming instinct. The Cabinet's position was

[18] Sir Harold S Kent, *In on the Act: Memoirs of a Lawmaker* (London, Macmillan, 1979) 199.

[19] CM (47) 80th Conclusions, Minute 1, 14 October 1947 (Confidential Annex).

[20] HL Deb 21 October 1947, vol 152, col 3.

[21] Kent (n 18) 200 states: 'The Government never admitted that the purpose of the Parliament Bill was to prevent the House of Lords defeating the Iron and Steel Bill, but no one doubted this.' However, it is clear from the discussions within Cabinet, and by Officials, about the Parliament Bill that its retroactivity was explicitly designed to ensure that the Iron and Steel Bill could come into law under the amended Parliament Act procedures.

[22] On the passage of the Iron and Steel Bill through the Commons, see AH Hanson and H Victor Wiseman, *Parliament at Work: A Casebook of Parliamentary Procedure* (London, Stevens & Stevens, 1962) 121–80; GW Ross, *The Nationalization of Steel* (London, Macgibbon & Kee, 1965) 60–119, details the politics of the Bill.

[23] CM (47) 83rd Conclusions, Minute 3, 30 October 1947.

clear: further veto limitation was required, was non-negotiable, and would be pursued at the quickest pace possible – with the presumption that the application of the Parliament Act 1911 would be required to bring it into law.

III THE PARLIAMENT BILL ITSELF

The Parliament Bill 1947[24] was very short and simple. It contained the following provisions. First of all, it sought to amend section 2 of the Parliament Act 1911, changing the requirements for the House of Commons to pass a Bill once in each of three successive sessions, to once in each of two successive sessions; and to require that one year (rather than two years) must have elapsed between the Second Reading of a Bill in the Commons in the first of these sessions and its final enactment. Secondly, it sought to apply its own provisions retroactively, so that whenever the Parliament Bill 1947 reached the Statute Book, this reduced period of delay could be used to enact any relevant bill that had been introduced into the House of Commons at or after the start of the 1947–48 Session (except for the Parliament Bill itself). The Bill did not affect the 1911 Act's other two provisions, relating to Money Bills and the lifetime of a Parliament. The Prime Minister described it publicly as 'a very simple little amendment'.[25]

A Period of Delay

Alongside the proposals which were incorporated into the Parliament Bill (in effect, reducing the Lords' suspensory veto to 12 months' duration), Cabinet had considered more drastic cuts in that power, not least because a noticeable element within the Parliamentary Labour Party was braying for this. Cabinet had discussed three possible limits on the delaying power of the Lords: (i) the reduction of the delay under the Parliament Act to one year; (ii) that Bills passed by the House of Commons should become Law, even against the opposition of the Lords, within six months, or at the end of the Session, whichever was the longer; or (iii) that the Lords be required to pass by the end of the Session all Bills sent up by the Commons within a reasonable period.[26] The first proposition was preferred by the Cabinet; the other two, variants on the same theme as each other (that the Commons should have its business within the Session) would have rendered the House of Lords completely without teeth – something that ministers deemed not to be in the interests of government.

In supporting the proposal that a Bill, passed in two successive Sessions by the House of Commons, should become law notwithstanding the opposition of the House of Lords, ministers could have appeared even more radical by reducing the minimum delay from the proposal 12 months to nine, or even six, months. However, in practice, such a radical

---

[24] Commons Bill (8) and (1) 1948.

[25] HC Deb 11 November 1947, vol 444, col 310 (the second, and final, day of the House of Commons debate on the Second Reading of the Parliament Bill).

[26] CM (47) 81st Conclusions, 20 October 1947; also CM (47) 83rd Conclusions, Minute 3. The Machinery of Government's deliberations (MG (47) 2, 16 October 1947. Amendment of the Parliament Act, 1911: Memorandum by Officials) were presented to Cabinet on 20 October as CP (47) 292, Amendment of the Parliament Act, 1911: Memorandum by the Lord President of the Council.

gesture would have been just that: the constraints of the Parliamentary timetable meant that the de facto minimum period would be a delay of 12 months from the Bill's first Second Reading in the House of Commons, even if legislation allowed for less. It was, by 1947, clear that the Conservative Party had abandoned thoughts of revoking the 1911 Act, though in doing so had come to regard its suspensory veto as the minimum required to prevent the adoption of single chamber government. Nonetheless, for the Labour Government – not least, given the pressure from the backbenches for more drastic action – one year's delay by the House of Lords was an absolute maximum legislative position, not a starting point for negotiations. The content – and enactment – of the Parliament Bill were, therefore, non-negotiable.

In any case, because the Bill would, in in the firm view of ministers, become law two years after its first Second Reading in the House of Commons, the Government had little incentive to bow to pressure on the terms under which it was drafted. Agreed amendments could speed its passage; but the worst case scenario for the Government was to force through their Bill without amendment. Reducing the Lords' delay to one year was guaranteed to happen, so far as the Government was concerned, from the day on which the House of Commons gave the Bill a Second Reading.[27]

B Passage under the Parliament Act 1911

The discussion between ministers had been conducted in the firm belief that the period of suspensory veto in the Parliament Act 1911 could be reduced, even against the firm opposition of the House of Lords. Nonetheless, before proceeding with legislation, the Cabinet ensured that their protocol was fully scrutinised. Cabinet's Machinery of Government Sub-Committee concluded without qualification that:[28]

> If the Lords refused to accept the amending Bill, it would have to be passed under the existing provisions of the Parliament Act – i.e., within a period of not less than two years from the date of its original Second Reading in the Commons, it must have been passed by the Commons in three successive Sessions. It should be possible to comply with these conditions, and secure the Government's objective, provided that –
>
> (i)   the amending Bill was given its original Second Reading before the end of 1947;
> (ii) after the coming Session, a special short Session was held, during which the Bill was passed for the second time by the Commons and dealt with by the Lords;
> (iii) the amending Bill was so drawn as to enable the Parliament Act as amended by it to be applied to Bills which had already been introduced by the time that the amending Bill became law.
>
> <u>The Committee were assured that there were no legal or constitutional obstacles to the fulfilment of these conditions</u>. [Emphasis added.]

---

[27] Salisbury had accepted this point, and referred to it in several of his personal minutes, eg his minutes of 9 January 1948 and 16 January 1948: Hatfield House Papers 5M/Box F.

[28] Parliamentary Archives WHE/2/8. MG(47) 2nd Meeting, Cabinet: Committee on the Machinery of Government, 17 October 1947. Its members were Herbert Morrison MP (Lord President of the Council), Hugh Dalton MP (Chancellor of the Exchequer), and J Chuter Ede MP (Home Secretary). Also present were: Viscount Jowitt (Lord Chancellor), Sir Norman Brook (Cabinet Office), Mr AE Ellis (First Parliamentary Counsel), Mr A Johnston (Office of the Lord President of the Council). Its Secretary was Mr W Armstrong (Treasury).

Dicey's views were not debated by Cabinet or presented as impediments to the Parliament Bill 1947 by the officials from the Government and Parliament who advised the Government. In fact, Dicey's views on the constitutionality of law, and his views on the status of legislation passed by the Parliament Act 1911 procedure – 'that the Act in question, . . . is, in the opinion of the speaker, opposed to the spirit of the English constitution; it cannot mean that the Act is either a breach of law or is void' – are consistent with the view taken by the Government and its advisers in 1947.[29] By the time the Government announced the legislation in the King's Speech on 21 October 1947 it had fully made up its mind that 'This change could be made by a simple amending Bill',[30] and that such a procedure was not only possible, but lawful.

The timing of the introduction into Parliament of the Parliament Bill was, therefore, chosen specifically because the Government had in its mind that they might need to pass the Bill under the procedures laid down by the Parliament Act 1911.

C Passage through Parliament

Introducing the debate on the Second Reading of the Parliament Bill on 10 November 1947, Herbert Morrison MP noted that 'The fundamental step of depriving the House of Lords of their absolute veto was taken under the Parliament Act of 1911',[31] but that an unfairness remained that progressive governments risked trouble with the upper House, whereas Conservative governments did not. The main objections raised to the Bill at Second Reading in the House of Commons were twofold.[32] First of all, the Bill proposed a substantial alteration to the constitution without any preceding public discussion about the issue or attempt at seeking inter-party agreement. Multiple references were made to the lengthy constitutional amendment procedures required in other countries and a need to temper the swift process of amending the British constitution with a period of consultation. Secondly, substantial objections were made to the retrospective aspect of the Bill, by which the shorter period of delay would be applied to bills which began their passage in the House of Commons before this Bill had passed into law. This second ground for opposition to the Bill was felt especially strongly since the proposal was for a retrospective change to a constitutional provision – and the Government could cite no precedents for a retrospective constitutional change.[33] After a two-day debate, the Bill was given a Second Reading by 345 votes to 194.

At the Commons committee stage on 4 December, two amendments were put: one to delete the retrospective application of the Bill; the other to halve the proposed one-year minimum period of delay.[34] Both were defeated, and the Bill was reported without amend-

---

[29] Dicey (n 1). Dicey's views are notable, not least since he vehemently opposed the constitutionality of Home Rule for Ireland, which was one of the few measures passed under the 1911 Act.

[30] CM (47) 80th Conclusions, Minute 1, 14 October 1947 (Confidential Annex).

[31] HC Deb 10 November 1947, vol 444, col 36.

[32] See, eg, the speech of Mr Kenneth Pickthorn MP (Conservative, Cambridge University), HC Deb 10 November 1947, vol 444, cols 149–55.

[33] The Home Secretary (James Ede MP) in response to strongly-put claims by the senior Burgesses for Oxford and Cambridge (Sir Arthur Salter MP and Mr Kenneth Pickthorn MP) that there were no such precedents, stated at Committee Stage that: 'I have made no claim that there is any precedent.' HC Deb 4 December 1947, vol 445, col 608.

[34] The former was moved by James Reid MP (Scottish Unionist member for Glasgow Hillhead), a former Solicitor General for Scotland and Lord Advocate; the latter by John Parker MP (Labour member for Dagenham) who later became Father of the House and the longest-ever serving Labour MP.

ment. The Bill was given a Third Reading after 'a long discussion on this reading, which was principally of a political nature',[35] by 340 votes to 186.[36]

Dicey, though not cited at the Cabinet table, made brief appearances during the House of Commons debates on the Bill. However, he was not prayed in aid of arguments about the constitutional appropriateness of amending the Parliament Act under its own provisions, but rather was cited by both sides on a number of questions about the role of the second chamber and the nature of constitutional discussion. The Government had been upfront about its intentions: for instance, early in the Second Reading debate in the House of Commons, the Lord President of the Council, Herbert Morrison MP, had explicitly addressed the possibility of the Parliament Bill being passed under the Parliament Act's procedures: 'If the Bill is itself rejected by the House of Lords, it will have to be enacted under the existing provisions of the Parliament Act, 1911.'[37] Subsequent speakers openly, and without question, discussed the possibility that the Bill might not become law until 1949 because of these procedures. The suggestion that the Bill might be ultra vires was raised in the context of its retrospective application to other bills, but not the proposed route to the Statute Book of the Parliament Bill itself.[38]

By the time that the House of Lords had its Second Reading debate on the Bill, on 27 January 1948, the leader of the Conservative peers in the upper House, Lord Salisbury, had become excited by the question of whether to amend the Parliament Act under its own procedures was ultra vires, not least through receiving a letter from an American academic, Mr Gwyther Moore, who had argued just that point. Salisbury sent the argument to Viscount Simon, who had been a Liberal MP during the passage of the original Parliament Act, a lawyer, and later Lord Chancellor. He dismissed the argument out of hand, stating that the British constitution was fundamentally different from that of the United States, with which Mr Moore was familiar. He wrote to Salisbury:

> Our Parliament (King, Lords and Commons) can validly legislate anything, and the effect of the Parliament Act of 1911 is to say that (save for an exception specially mentioned) a bill which is carried by the Commons in the way there refined, may be presented for the Royal Assent, and become law, even if the Lords have consistently rejected it. . . . No English Constitutional lawyer, and no Court in this country would ever maintain the opposite view. Moreover, the exception (namely, this does not apply to a bill extending the life of the Commons beyond five years), is a further proof that in other cases the provision <u>does</u> apply.[39] (Emphasis in original.)

However, in the same letter Simon referred to the Parliament Act 1911 having delegated to the House of Commons the power to legislate, notwithstanding the obstruction of the

---

[35] Owen Clough, 'The Parliament Bill, 1947–48' (1948) XVII *The Table* 136, 148.

[36] HC Deb 10 December 1947, vol 445, cols 1089–90. RA Butler, for the Opposition, had sought – unsuccessfully – to amend the motion to delay the Third Reading for six months. The Third Reading debate lasted for less than a day.

[37] HC Deb 10 November 1947, vol 444, col 52.

[38] At Committee Stage, Kenneth Pickthorn MP (Conservative, Cambridge University) stated on the question of retrospectivity: 'none of our ancestors would have thought this Bill constitutional until, relatively speaking, the day before yesterday. I will go further. I believe that all our ancestors certainly down to the 18th century, and most of them during the 18th century would have taken it for granted that this Bill was ultra vires and had or would have been argued to have had no force.' HC Deb 4 December 1947, vol 445, col 602.

[39] Hatfield House Papers, 5M/Box F. Simon to Salisbury, 17 January 1948. Quoted in Chris Ballinger, *The House of Lords 1911–2011: A Century of Non-Reform* (Oxford, Hart Publishing, 2012) 59–60. Simon's view was that the 1911 Act was so clear and unambiguous that reference to the Preamble was unnecessary (*cf* the reasons outlined by Lord Bingham in *Jackson*).

House of Lords. There was much emphasis in subsequent academic discussion,[40] and in the discussion in the various judgments in *Jackson*, about whether the Parliament Act 1911 delegated authority to the House of Commons and Sovereign, or whether it created an alternative mechanism for the enactment of primary legislation. Simon's use of language in January 1948 seems to have drawn no distinction between the two: he wrote of the effect of delegating legislative power to the Commons in the same sweep as averring that the Parliament Act procedures could be used to amend itself. Simon seemed clear in his mind that whatever the language used to describe the change, the power of the House of Commons to overcome the Lords' veto was all-encompassing, and not qualified.

On the question of the constitutionality of the proposed amendment of the Parliament Act, Salisbury consulted not just Viscount Simon, but also a number of other constitutional experts, including all of those whom he considered the great lawyers within the House of Lords, who concluded unanimously that there was nothing that could be done, from a legal point of view, to prevent the amendment of the United Kingdom's uncodified and unentrenched constitution – including the Parliament Act itself – under the Parliament Act's procedures.[41] It was clear to Salisbury that a challenge to the legality of the measure could not be sustained.

On the second day of the Second Reading debate in the Lords, the Government indicated that, following representations from Lord Salisbury and Viscount Samuel, it was willing to engage in a conference of party leaders to discuss the issue of House of Lords reform. The Cabinet had been loath to engage the Opposition parties in the question of House of Lords reform (which was distinct from the proposals of veto limitation contained in the Parliament Bill). Viscount Samuel had been seeking such a conference for several months; but the Cabinet had concluded 'that the Bill amending the Parliament Act, 1911, should be passed into law before any negotiations were opened for the reform of the House of Lords'.[42] However, by early 1948 the Cabinet determined that it would avoid the risk of public disapprobation, and strengthen its hand, if it agreed to enter into discussions on reform.[43] However, the Cabinet was mindful of two factors that meant reform discussions might be against its interests: the difficulty of fashioning a consensus amongst Labour MPs for any particular reform proposal, let alone one which might come out of inter-party discussions, and the need to secure the Parliament Bill without it being delayed by being subsumed within a larger reform project. The Government therefore entered inter-party discussions on two conditions: that any agreement between party leaders would be *ad referendum* their Parliamentary parties; and that whatever the outcome of discussions the Opposition in the House of Lords would agree either to pass the Parliament Bill or definitely to reject it (thus enabling the Parliament Act procedures to begin). Having agreed to these two conditions, the representatives of the senior leadership of the Labour, Conservative, and Liberal parties met eight times between February and May 1948.

---

[40] eg HWR Wade, 'The Basis of Legal Sovereignty' (1955) 13 *Cambridge Law Journal* 172; also the discussion in the judgment of the Court of Appeal in *R (Jackson) v Attorney General* [2005] EWCA Civ 126, [2005] QB 579 (CA).

[41] Hatfield House Papers, 5M/Box G. Salisbury to EF Iwi (Solicitor), 18 February 1948. (cited in Ballinger (n 39) 59).

[42] CM (47) 87th Conclusions, Minute 3, 13 November 1947.

[43] CM (48) 9th Conclusions, Minute 1, 2 February 1948.

D The Party Leaders' Conference

The Party Leaders' Conference concluded in May 1948, having made little progress beyond the convergence of views expressed at its initial meeting: the discussions effected no real convergence between the views of the parties' key negotiators, let alone their Parliamentary parties.[44] The breakdown in negotiations was on an apparent small difference in powers – a dispute amounting to a difference of three months in the proposed suspensory veto of the House of Lords – but in fact there had never been any formal agreement about proposals for the composition of the upper House, not least since powers and composition were interdependent.[45] It was politically easier to break negotiations on the question of the specific proposed period of the Lords' delaying power; but the true cause of the lack of agreement was 'a fundamental difference of view regarding the purposes for which the period of delay should be granted and used';[46] as Salisbury put it, 'an unbridgeable gap between them which was not related merely to a difference of three months on the period of delay.'[47] The 1948 Party Leaders' Conference, like the constitutional conference called in 1910 during consideration of the previous Parliament Act, had achieved nothing except a few months' delay in the consideration of the veto limitation legislation, and the publication of an agreed statement. The Conference had made no contribution to advancing the likelihood of achieving Lords reform. The Second Reading of the Parliament Bill therefore resumed in the House of Lords on 8 June. Nonetheless, despite fears that the parties being no closer to agreement on reform peers might give the Bill a Second Reading and then amend and delay it in committee,[48] the Second Reading was in fact negatived at the end of two further days of debate.[49] The first of the Lords' rejections required under the Parliament Act had been secured.

E Special Session

Whilst the Bill was being drafted, ministers knew that its passage under the Parliament Act would require a special, short, session of Parliament to be convened. By mid-June 1948, following the end of the Party Leaders' Conference and the first rejection of the Parliament Bill by the House of Lords, the key decisions on the timing of the remaining stages of the Parliament Bill were being driven firmly by the need to ensure that its provisions could be ready in time to apply it to the Iron and Steel Bill.[50]

The Government needed to secure another rejection of the Bill by the House of Lords in each of two subsequent sessions; but time was against them to do this before a general election. The most likely option was to have a very short session of Parliament in the autumn

---

[44] Elsewhere, I show a high degree of convergence between the positions of party leaders expressed at the Conference's first preliminary, and those expressed in its *Agreed Statement* (Cmnd 7380, May 1948). See Ballinger n 39 65.

[45] As noted by Anthony Eden in the Sixth Meeting of the Party Leaders' Conference, 20 April 1948 (The National Archives CAB 130/47).

[46] CM (48) 28th Conclusions, Minute 5, 15 April 1948.

[47] The National Archives CAB 130/37. Party Leaders' Conference, Fifth Meeting, 18 March 1948.

[48] CM (48) 35th Conclusions, Minute 5, 3 June 1948.

[49] Contents, 81; Not-Contents, 177. HL Deb 9 June 1948, vol 156, cols 600–1.

[50] The National Archives. PREM 8/1059. *Amendment of the Parliament Act 1911*, WS Murrie to the Prime Minister, 12 June 1948.

of 1948, lasting about six weeks, to secure a further rejection of the Parliament Bill, followed by a very long session from October 1948 until the very end of 1949 during which both veto limitation and iron and steel nationalisation could reach the Statute Book. Ministers were unwilling to risk deferring the short session until 1949. However, they did seriously canvass the possibility of not manipulating the Parliamentary timetable, but instead having two normal sessions, during which the Government would have to carry a risk that both Bills might not be passed, or rejected, in good time to become law.[51] The Prime Minister was warned against convening a special session, on the grounds that 'the interpolation of a third session in the autumn of 1948 might possibly be criticised as not being in the spirit of the Parliament Act', whereas the latter option of two normal sessions 'exempts the Government from any possible criticism for manipulating the arrangements of the sessions.'[52] However, the fear of not securing both bills outweighed the risk of public and procedural criticism, and the Cabinet opted to manipulate the Parliamentary timetable to ensure that the Parliament Bill met the requirements of section 2 of the Parliament Act 1911. As the Prime Minister was advised: 'This remains the decisive point.'[53] The Government pressed on with its plan to have a special session designed to solely pass the Parliament Bill under the Parliament Act,[54] and the Bill was duly passed by the Commons, and rejected by the Lords, for a second time.

F Passing the Bill

In May 1949, Cabinet restated its resolve to seek the enactment of the Parliament Bill before the end of the calendar year, and the Bill would be reintroduced to the Commons in July, to make clear the Government's resolve to secure the Bill by the end of the calendar year, with a Second Reading to follow the summer recess.[55] That resolve was reinforced by the knowledge that it was necessary to enact the Parliament Bill by the end of the year in order to secure the Iron and Steel Bill in the present Parliament.[56] The Parliament Bill left the Commons for the final time with its original provisions unaltered. In debates in late 1948 and early 1949, attempts had been made to amend the Bill to introduce aspects of

---

[51] CP(48)147. Cabinet: Amendment of the Parliament Act 1911: Memorandum by the Lord President of the Council (Herbert Morrison MP), 11 June 1947.

[52] The National Archives (n 50).

[53] The Cabinet had made their decision to prefer a short session for the Autumn of 1948 at its meeting on 14 June (CM (48) 39th Conclusions, Minute 7). Sir Gilbert Campion, Clerk of the House of Commons, was later consulted by officials and did not advise against the short session; indeed, he indicated that any other course of action might increase the difficulty of the Speaker providing a certificate under s 2 of the Parliament Act: 'This still remains the decisive argument and Campion's advice does nothing to detract from its force.' The National Archives. PREM 8/1059 Laurence Helsby to the Prime Minister, 21 June 1948. Sir Henry Badeley, Clerk of the Parliaments, confirmed that the Cabinet's preferred course of action would not result in procedural difficulties in the House of Lords, though he advised of a risk of the Lords seeking to amend, rather than reject, the Bill during that short session (The National Archives. PREM 8/1059 Note for the Record: Parliament Bill, by WS Murrie, 21 June 1948).

[54] The King's Speech, opening the session, stated simply: 'I have summoned you to meet at this time in order that you may give further consideration to the Bill to amend the Parliament Act, 1911, on which there was disagreement between the two Houses last Session. It is not proposed to bring any other business before you in the present Session.' HL Deb 14 September 1948, vol 158, col 1.

[55] CM (49) 34th Conclusions, Minute 2, 12 May 1949. See also: CM (49) 47th Conclusions, Minute 1, 21 July 1949.

[56] The National Archives. PREM 8/1059. GR Downes (Principal Private Secretary to the Lord President of the Council) to LN Helsby (Principal Private Secretary to the Prime Minister), 20 July 1949.

reform – for example, to enable peeresses by succession to sit in the House of Lords – but these were not pushed. That was fortunate for the Government, which would otherwise have been forced to choose between opposing an extension of the heredity principle on the one hand, and opposing the extension of sex equality on the other hand. In any case, such amendments would have been out of order. As the Clerk of the Parliaments had noted in discussions with Lord Salisbury in 1947, since the scope of the Bill was limited to amending an existing piece of legislation relating to the Lords' powers, amendments relating to composition would have been out of order.[57] Parliament had not diverged from the proposals which had first been canvassed by ministers more than three years earlier.

There was some apprehension on the part of ministers that the Parliament Act's procedures might be difficult to operate, not because there was any doubt about the constitutionality of their applicability to the Parliament Bill, but rather because of the difficulties of being sure when the Speaker of the House of Commons would issue his certificate as required under section 2(3) of the Act.

Under section 2(1) of the Parliament Act 1911, if a bill was sent to the House of Lords at least one month before the end of a session, and had been rejected by the House of Lords in three successive sessions, then 'the Bill shall on its rejection be presented to His Majesty and become an Act of Parliament on the Royal Assent being signified thereto'. Yet it was not at all clear to officials what constituted 'rejection' of the Bill by the House of Lords.[58]

At the time, *Erskine May* observed:

> The third method of opposition is by challenging a vote on the motion for the second reading. It not infrequently occurs that, although no notice of opposition has been given in advance, objection to the measure transpires in the course of debate and the motion is opposed and may be negatived. Strictly, in theory, when this occurs the second reading is only negative for that particular day, but in practice it is usual to treat it as a rejection of the bill, which is thenceforward removed from the order paper. It could, however, be reinserted at the request of the Peer in charge of it.[59]

Officials warned ministers that, if the Speaker was unable to accept a simple negativing of a Second Reading motion as a rejection, then he could certify under section 2(2) of the Parliament Act that its procedures had been met. If that occurred, the Government would have to engage section 2(3) of the Act: 'a Bill shall be deemed to be rejected by the House of Lords if it is not passed by the House of Lords either without amendment or with such amendments only as may be agreed by both Houses.' Reliance on the later subsection would have delayed the enactment of the Parliament Bill until just before the end of the session, rather than having the Bill presented for Royal Assent straight away, and that would potentially have caused problems for the Iron and Steel Bill.[60]

Having considered the risks involved with proceeding, the Lord Chancellor's opinion was that 'the rejection of Bills in the technical sense had become obsolete before 1911' and that his view was that 'the Speaker would interpret the term used in the Parliament Act, 1911, in a non-technical sense.'[61] He thought that the Speaker would consider rejection in

[57] Hatfield House Papers, 5M/Box G, Sir Henry Badeley to Salisbury, 24 October 1947.
[58] A point raised in November 1949 by Sir Alan Ellis, First Parliamentary Counsel.
[59] Thomas Erskine May, *A treatise on the law, privileges, proceedings and usage of Parliament* 14th edn, Sir G Campion (ed), (London, Butterworths, 1946), 468.
[60] The National Archives. PREM 8/1059. Memorandum on the Parliament Bill, 10 November 1949.
[61] Parliamentary Archives WHE/2/8. Gen 396/1st Meeting. Parliament Bill. Meeting of Ministers held at 10, Downing Street, SW1, on Monday, 28th November 1949.

the context of contemporary Parliamentary practice, and was sure that '[t]he Opposition in the House of Lords certainly regarded what they were going to do as amounting to a rejection of the Bill.'[62] However, given the ambiguities involved under the 1911 Act's requirements, and the impact on the Government's programme if the Speaker took a different view from the Government, then the Speaker was approached in advance of the final Lords rejection of the Bill.[63] The Parliament Act, so assuredly relied upon by ministers, had proved at the end not to be a technically well-crafted piece of constitutional machinery.

But there was to be no last-minute impediment. The promise from the Conservative leadership that their peers would negative the Bill without a reasoned amendment or long debate held good. The Lords received the Bill for a third time in November 1949,[64] and, on 29 November, voted for a third time to negative the Second Reading motion – this time by 110 votes to 37.[65] The Speaker of the House of Commons issued his certificate under the terms of the Parliament Act 1911, and the Royal Assent was granted the following month.[66] The Iron and Steel Bill, the principal cause of the inclusion in the Parliament Bill of the retrospective provisions which had caused so much debate in Parliament, had received the Royal Assent three weeks earlier without recourse to either Parliament Act.

IV CONSEQUENCES

It is ironic that the immediate political driver for the introduction of the Parliament Bill 1947 – the forthcoming Iron and Steel Bill – did not, in the end, require either Parliament Act to pass into law, although it is more difficult to say for sure whether, had the Parliament Bill not existed, the Iron and Steel Bill and other legislation in the final years of the Attlee Government would have had such swift passages through Parliament. Certainly, the Government in 1947 thought they would have suffered greater impediments without the Parliament Bill.

The Parliament Act 1949, in addressing only the House of Lords' period of delay, left in place the overwhelming party imbalance which the Government cited as one of its reasons for promoting the Bill. It confirmed a preference within Labour for limiting the role of the upper House rather than rationalising its membership, a view which, for the most part, prevailed for another half a century. The 1949 Act also left in place the 1911 Act's procedural ambiguities which had caused ministers and officials so much concern, and it did nothing to bring within the ambit of the suspensory veto the Lords' powers over secondary legislation.[67] Many of the substantial powers which the Lords had retained in 1911 remained intact.

The one-year period of delay did, however, come to be accepted as the norm quite quickly,[68] and the first use of the combined Parliament Acts procedures was by a Conservative

---

[62] ibid.

[63] ibid.

[64] In order to comply with the Parliament Act 1911's procedures, the Commons could not send the Parliament Bill to the House of Lords for a third time earlier than 11 November 1949.

[65] HL Deb 29 November 1949, vol 165, col 1039.

[66] HC Deb 16 December 1949, vol 470, col 3056.

[67] Removing the Lords' veto on subordinate legislation was canvassed by the Lord Chancellor in 1946 (CP(46)376); but never came to the fore. It was generally thought that the political difficulties of the Lords challenging subordinate legislation made a legal remedy unnecessary. That decision had important implications: subordinate legislation became increasingly important; but the Lords' veto proved difficult to use in practise.

[68] Not least because of an acceptance that, with the subsequent spread of television viewing, public opinion could coalesce, and be expressed, much more quickly than at the start of the century.

Government (in passing the War Crimes Act 1991, which itself included a retrospective provision). Those involved in drafting the Parliament Bill in 1947, and in advising Cabinet, were resolutely of the view that the Parliament Act 1911 could be amended under its own procedures. That view was shared by the key opponents of the amendment Bill. Despite the academic debate on the issue that ensued, this view prevailed amongst successive governments over the decades that followed the passage of the 1949 Act. When the Royal Commission on Reform of the House of Lords considered the amendment of the Parliament Acts 50 years later, it both implicitly and explicitly accepted the prevailing view: it was advised that 'it is a weakness of the Parliament Acts that they can at present be amended by Parliament Act procedures'.[69] Indeed, the advisers to the Royal Commission did not assume, as the Law Lords did in *Jackson*, that the provision which prevented the lifetime of a Parliament being extended was itself exempt from amendment under Parliament Act procedures.[70] It was only outside Parliament that the existence of the 1949 Act became more controversial in the years that followed its enactment, and even there opinion was divided.

The reduced period of delay not only made it easier for governments to overcome the Lords' veto, but also made the upper House more wary of exercising its powers.[71] It is important to remember that the 1949 Act not only reduced the number of years of delay which the upper House could impose, but also reduced the time that the Commons and Lords needed to spend debating the measure before the Acts could be invoked, thus making it easier for a government to express a credible threat to invoke the Acts.

V CONCLUSION

The Parliament Bill 1947 was a simple one-clause Bill. Its purpose was limited in scope – to guarantee that a majority government in the House of Commons could be effective in four, rather than three, of its five years in office – though that general aim overlaid a specific difficulty for the Government in bringing forward legislation to nationalise the iron and steel industries. Its aim was to defuse concerns about short-term impediments to a government's legislative programme, rather than a desire to reform the House of Lords. Whereas the 1911 Act had evolved from House of Commons resolutions developed and debated during years of constitutional opposition, the 1949 Act was written privately and without open debate, to overcome fears of future obstruction. The implicit view of the Government in 1945 was that the Parliament Act of 1911 had created a primary legislature of Commons and Monarch, to which the alternative formulation of King, Lords, and Commons, should remain subordinate.

---

[69] The view was also implicitly accepted by Sir Christopher Jenkins, who wrote that to 'Exclude the Parliament Acts from amendment under their own procedures . . . should not be a technically difficult amendment.' Parliamentary Archives. WHE/1/2/27. Sir Christopher Jenkins to David Hill, 29 September 1999.

[70] The Secretariat, who had been advised by Sir Christopher Jenkins, advised that to exclude the Parliament Acts from amendment under their own procedures 'would also effectively entrench the Second Chamber's veto over extending the life of a Parliament beyond five years, which is a matter of some current concern (and the subject of one of the Lords amendments to the House of Lords Bill)'. Parliamentary Archives. WHE/1/2/27. RCRHL(99)44 'Possible Changes to the Parliament Acts', note by the Secretariat, 30 September 1999.

[71] The House of Lords Bill in Session 1998–99 was introduced in the Commons specifically in order to facilitate the application of the Parliament Acts, if required, and the Lords came to know that the Weatherill Amendment, which retained 92 hereditary peers as members of the House, would be lost if the Parliament Acts were to be invoked (see Ballinger (n 39) 173).

The framers of the 1949 Act sought no innovation at all. The 1911 Act had been transformative in constitutional theory, even though it sought to enforce a de facto political reality. The 1949 Act was avowedly unrevolutionary: its backers sought to update the constitutional position to align with their view of the democratic position, not to produce a constitutional innovation. Though the question of the constitutionality of amending the Parliament Act under its own procedures did not go unasked, no official, minister, or leading figure in the Opposition, considered that there might be any validity in the idea that the 1949 Act was unconstitutional. The constitutionality of the 1949 Act was a non-issue at the time. The fact that the key actors were, at the time, so certain about the constitutionality of the 1949 Act does not necessarily mean that they were correct to hold that view; but it is persuasive about the intention of those who were involved with the scrutiny of the proposals, a few of whom had been in government when the 1911 Act was passed. In any case, the new Act could not be questioned by the courts; indeed, the Prime Minister had been confidently advised in 1947 that 'the courts could not go behind his [the Speaker's] certificate', that the Bill had validly met the requirements of the Parliament Act.[72] Ironically, perhaps the greatest impact of the 1949 Act was the leverage it gave to lawyers to induce the courts into the unprecedented questioning of the validity of an Act of Parliament. What is certain is that this outcome was not in the minds of those who supported the Parliament Act of 1949.

---

[72] The National Archives. PREM 8/1059. Norman Brook to the Prime Minister, 27 October 1947.

12

The Realities of the Parliament Act 1911

DANIEL GREENBERG

I INTRODUCTION

THE OPERATION IN practice of the Parliament Act 1911[1] depends to a considerable extent on the exercise of functions by the Clerks – the authorities of the two Houses. An understanding of the way in which the Act works will be incomplete without an appreciation of the role that the House authorities play in administering the Act. This chapter aims to provide a brief sketch of the Clerks' role.

II TWO REASONS FOR CLERKS' INVOLVEMENT

From the outset, it may be helpful to divide the ways in which the authorities in each House become involved in the operation of the Parliament Act 1911 into two classes.

First, there are a number of statutory functions under the Act which are vested in the Speaker of the House of Commons. Given the typical background and nature of a Speaker, it is not to be expected that he or she will take decisions about complicated technical matters other than on the advice of the Clerks. The situation may fall short in theory of the kind of *Carltona*[2] delegation permitted to Ministers and civil servants in respect of other statutory functions, but the reality is that the same degree of reliance on advice is likely to manifest itself in practice.

Secondly, there are aspects of the procedures relating to the Parliament Act 1911 that arise off the face of the statute and concern either Parliamentary procedure under the Standing Orders of either House or questions of Parliamentary practice that have no formal underpinning. In relation to these matters, Members, including front-bench and back-bench Members and including government and opposition, habitually seek the advice of the Clerks. As against the very small number of formal rulings issued by the Speaker on matters of practice or procedure by way of Speaker's Statement, literally hundreds of less formal questions are asked and answered by the Clerks every week. Many of these will be dealt with at a very junior level within the Clerks' structure; and in relation to

---

[1] 1911 c 13; it is fashionable to refer to actions as being taken under 'the Parliament Acts 1911 and 1949', but since the 1949 Act is a wholly amending enactment it is more accurate simply to refer to the 1911 Act, and this chapter does so.

[2] The case of *Carltona v Commissioners of Works* [1943] 2 All ER 560 CA gave its name to the doctrine according to which ministerial functions are in general exercisable on their behalf by civil servants.

the vast majority, an informal word from a Clerk in either House will be the end of the matter for all practical purposes. Perhaps the most significant example of this kind of clerical involvement concerns the 'packaging' of amendments, which can be of crucial importance in relation to the operation of the Parliament Act 1911 and is discussed in more detail below.

Who are the Clerks?

This is not the place for a detailed description of the structure of the authorities in each House or the different roles and individuals within it. But a very brief sketch is necessary by way of background simply to make clear to what we refer when we talk about discussions and correspondence with 'the Clerks'. One of the reasons for not trying to be too specific about the precise structure is that it, and particularly the titles used within it, have tended to change quite frequently in recent years, in both Houses.

In essence, the authorities of each House are headed by a senior Clerk – the Clerk of the Parliaments in the House of Lords and the Clerk of the House in the Commons – who stands in relation to the Speaker of each House and its other officials in a position similar to that of the Permanent Secretary of a government department in relation to its senior Minister and other civil servants. In particular, the two senior Clerks represent a degree of continuity and corporate memory, and bring a degree of practical authority and sphere of influence that is at least as high as that of a departmental Permanent Secretary, possibly much higher: a 'decision' of the Clerk is unlikely to be referred to the Speaker unless the Clerk decides to refer it, and the Speaker in either House is likely to rely very heavily on advice tendered by the senior Clerk of that House, and depart from it only for very pressing political reasons. (Of course, the precise balance of power depends to a large degree on the respective personalities of the incumbents of the offices of Speaker and senior Clerk from time to time.)

Within each House the clerical structure forms a hierarchy and as a result of which relatively junior Clerks may find themselves answering more or less formal questions posed by politicians of any level of seniority, and their officials and advisers. Of particular significance for the purposes of this chapter is the fact that in each House there is a Public Bill Office, the senior Clerk of which may be the last court of appeal for all practical purposes on a range of procedural questions relating specifically to the passage of primary legislation. Again, questions may travel further up the chain if the senior Clerk refers them; and, again, the precise balance of power and degree of autonomy enjoyed by the senior Clerk in the Public Bill Office will depend on the personalities of the incumbents from time to time.

This background is designed to show that when discussing the involvement of the House authorities in the operation of the Parliament Act 1911, one may be referring to a wide range of different kinds of decision: from the extreme of a decision taken by the Speaker, whether or not under a statutory discretion, on the combined advice of the Commons Clerks, to the opposite extreme of a chance word spoken in a corridor, by a relatively junior Clerk with limited understanding of the wider political context and sensitivities, in response to an actually or apparently casual and informal inquiry.

III CLASSIFICATION OF MONEY BILLS

The first statutory function of the Commons Speaker under the Parliament Act 1911 relates to the classification of Money Bills.

Section 1(2) of the Act says:

> A Money Bill means a Public Bill which in the opinion of the Speaker of the House of Commons contains only provisions dealing with all or any of the following subjects, namely, the imposition, repeal, remission, alteration, or regulation of taxation; the imposition for the payment of debt or other financial purposes of charges on the Consolidated Fund, the National Loans Fund or on money provided by Parliament, or the variation or repeal of any such charges; supply; the appropriation, receipt, custody, issue or audit of accounts of public money; the raising or guarantee of any loan or the repayment thereof; or subordinate matters incidental to those subjects or any of them. In this subsection the expressions 'taxation,' 'public money,' and 'loan' respectively do not include any taxation, money, or loan raised by local authorities or bodies for local purposes.

It will be seen that this is a definition that raises a number of technical and complex issues, the application of which may be far from clear in any particular case.

The most obvious and regular area of difficulty are the words 'or subordinate matters incidental to those subjects or any of them', and the lore of the Public Bill Office in the Commons, as well as traditionally within the Office of the Parliamentary Counsel, is replete with wisdom and examples on the question of what is merely incidental for these purposes. Erskine May's *Parliamentary Practice*[3] records some precedents, but the discussion in *Parliamentary Practice* on this potentially very important issue is surprisingly brief; in any event, although precedents are relied on heavily in correspondence and pronouncements on Parliamentary procedure, there is no formal doctrine of *stare decisis*, nor is it generally too challenging to find distinguishing features of any case in which it is desired to depart from precedent for political or other reasons.

The practical significance of a Bill being certified as a Money Bill is potentially enormous. Technically, there is no reason why the Lords should not take a Money Bill through all its Parliamentary stages, and pass amendments to it. But the amendments will be nugatory unless the Commons choose to disapply the 1911 Act by a 'direction to the contrary' under section 1(1). The result is that a significant degree of technical scrutiny of a Money Bill by the Lords is generally thought to be futile, and the Lords rarely exert themselves very hard on a Money Bill as a result. In any event, the Lords have a statutory month to complete proceedings on a Money Bill (again, in the absence of a direction to the contrary by the Commons), which allows for little in the way of detailed scrutiny allowing for the usual intervals between stages.

In essence, therefore, certification of a Bill as a Money Bill amounts to removing it from effective scrutiny by the House of Lords. Put another way, the decision in relation to a Bill of size and complexity that might require a number of sitting days in Committee and on Report in the Lords, is the difference between taking a maximum of one month following the Bill's passage through the Commons on a Whipped Vote, and taking anything between two months and six, or even more, depending on complexity and controversy. It follows that the difference between certification and non-certification in the case of a Bill that leaves the Commons around or after the middle of a Session could well be the difference

---

[3] *Erskine May's Parliamentary Practice*, 24th edn (London, LexisNexis Butterworths, 2012) 797–98.

between the passage of the Bill being a certainty and extremely unlikely (depending on the likelihood of a deal being done to allow the Bill through in the 'wash-up' negotiations at the end of the Session).

So this decision can be of crucial legal, Parliamentary and political importance; and it is a decision taken by reference to some highly technical, not to say arcane, concepts, such as supply and appropriation, and will inevitably be driven largely by the advice of Clerks in the Commons drawing on the learning and corporate memory of the Public Bill Office. The fact that the Speaker is under a statutory duty to consult two other Members of Parliament before certifying a Bill under section 1[4] is not likely to make the decision any less technical or dependent on clerical advice, particularly since the Members are to be drawn not from front-line political circles but from the Chairmen's Panel.

Through the mechanism of Speaker's certification, the House of Commons effectively controls the operation of the Money Bill regime under the 1911 Act, and particularly its application to borderline or doubtful cases.

There are, however, aspects even of the section 1 Money Bill procedure which come under the control of the Lords authorities for practical purposes. In particular, section 1(1) of the Act provides as follows:

> If a Money Bill, having been passed by the House of Commons, and sent up to the House of Lords at least one month before the end of the session, is not passed by the House of Lords without amendment within one month after it is so sent up to that House, the Bill shall, unless the House of Commons direct to the contrary, be presented to His Majesty and become an Act of Parliament on the Royal Assent being signified, notwithstanding that the House of Lords have not consented to the Bill.

Taking the subsection in the round, and considering it from a purposive perspective, one might take the view that the provision provides a mechanism for presentation for Royal Assent without the cooperation of the House of Lords, and that the Act has no sensible application to cases where the Lords have considered a Money Bill and have passed it without amendment, even if they failed to do so within their allotted month.

In practice, however, presentation of Bills for Royal Assent is handled by the Clerk of the Parliaments in the Lords; and successive Clerks have taken the view that subsection 1(1) must be taken to apply even in a case where the Lords have passed a Bill, if they have passed it outside their statutory month.

One might think that it would be a nonsense to present a Bill for Royal Assent with an enactment formula disregarding the Lords and citing the Parliament Act in a case where the Lords had actually considered and passed the Bill; but the line has been taken that a Bill would have to be so presented where the Lords consider a Money Bill out of time, even if only by a matter of a day or two. In such cases the Lords authorities have required the Commons to arrange for a contrary direction under section 1(1) of the 1911 Act, on pain of having the Bill presented for Royal Assent under the Parliament Act.[5]

---

[4] Section 1(3) of the Parliament Act 1911.

[5] See, for example, on the Ministerial and Other Salaries Bill, HC Deb 5 November 1997, col 365: 'The President of the Council and Leader of the House of Commons (Mrs. Ann Taylor): . . . The motion is simple and straightforward. It directs that the provisions of section 1(1) of the Parliament Act 1911 should not apply to the Ministerial and Other Salaries Bill. The aim is to avoid any confusion that might otherwise arise because the House of Lords did not consider this money Bill within a month of receiving it. . . . The Bill was received by the House of Lords on 24 July, but the Lords rose on 31 July without considering it. The allotted month therefore expired during the parliamentary recess. The Lords considered the Bill and passed it on 16 October. This motion will provide that, as the House of Lords has consented to the Bill, it is presented for Royal Assent in the normal way. Mrs. Gillian

IV BILLS OTHER THAN MONEY BILLS

Although the Parliament Act operates most frequently in relation to the certification of Money Bills and the consequent restriction of Lords' proceedings on them, the public debate about the Parliament Act generally centres on its much rarer use in relation to other Bills.

Perhaps the most famous recent use of the Parliament Act for a non-Money Bill was in relation to the passage of the Hunting Act 2004, following which there was an unsuccessful challenge in the courts to the legitimacy and efficacy of the 1911 Act itself, based on the fact that the amendments to it made by the Parliament Act 1949 were themselves passed under the 1911 Act.

There have, however, been a number of other uses of the Parliament Act in recent years, including the War Crimes Act 1991, the European Parliamentary Elections Act 1999 and the Sexual Offences (Amendment) Act 2000. There have also been other occasions on which the shadow of the Parliament Act has strongly influenced political negotiations in relation to particular Bills.

Non-Money Bills are handled under section 2 of the Parliament Act 1911 and, as in relation to Money Bills under section 1, there are a number of points of the operation of section 2 that in practice depend upon the decisions of the House authorities.

V ROYAL ASSENT 'AT' END OF SESSION

It is interesting to note that section 2(1) of the 1911 Act is actually a nonsense on its own terms; and but for a helpful protocol between the authorities in the two Houses it would not be capable of working at all. The section provides that a Bill is to be presented to the sovereign for Royal Assent 'notwithstanding that the House of Lords have not consented to the Bill' provided that it is sent to the Lords twice in successive sessions and 'is rejected by the House of Lords in each of those sessions'. In order to prevent an obvious route of avoidance, section 2(3) provides that a Bill is deemed to be rejected if the Lords fail to pass it without amendment 'or with such amendments only as may be agreed to by both Houses'. It is not to be assumed that the Lords will necessarily be so obliging as to reject the second reading of a Bill, or otherwise take some positive move which amounts to rejecting the Bill. The Act therefore provides that at the end of the Second Session if the Lords have not passed the Bill they are treated as having rejected it.

The practical problem with that, of course, is that Royal Assent requires to be signified before the end of a Session. Technically, therefore, the deemed rejection under section 2(3) arises only when the Session closes and there is no further opportunity for the Lords to consider and consent to the Bill; but at that stage, the direction that the Bill 'be presented to her Majesty and become an Act of Parliament' can no longer be complied with; once the Session has ended, the Royal Assent can no longer be signified whether by the Lords Commissioners or under the Royal Assent Act 1967. One possible resolution of that would be to present the Bill for Royal Assent during the recess, and have Royal Assent signified at

Shephard (South-West Norfolk): The Conservative party supports the measure ... It has reappeared today because of a technicality in the House of Lords' handling of the matter, so it would be perverse in the extreme not to support today a measure which we supported in July.'

the beginning of the following Session. That would, however, as well as necessarily involving potentially significant delay, be a somewhat bizarre proceeding, particularly where the Session is the final Session of a Parliament.

To avoid this problem, the two sets of House authorities agreed decades ago that a short time before the end of the Session, if it becomes clear that the Lords are not intending to consider the Bill (for example because the Order Paper under the Future Business section shows no mention of the Bill in the remaining days), the Speaker would informally request the Lords authorities to return the Bill to the Commons authorities, for the Speaker to endorse on the Bill the certificate required by section 2(2) 'that the provisions of this section have been duly complied with'. That then in practice allows the Bill to be presented very shortly before the close of the Session for Royal Assent along with any other Bills awaiting Royal Assent, and for Royal Assent under section 2(1) to be signified at the close of the Session along with those other Bills.

This is of course a good example of cooperation in practice being able to rectify theoretical defects in legislation; but it is possibly not without its troubling features. In terms of accountability it is arguable that it would be preferable for people to admit that section 2(1) simply does not work, and to have it amended appropriately so that it does work.

VI SUGGESTED AMENDMENT PROCEDURE

Undoubtedly, the most controversial technical aspect of the Parliament Act 1911 is the 'suggested amendment' procedure provided for by section 2(4). The essence of the procedure is as follows.

The Parliament Act operates only to allow the Commons to force through a Bill which has been presented to the Lords in two successive Sessions in the same form. Clearly, it would not be appropriate to allow the Commons to add new material in the second Session that the Lords had not considered on the first occasion; otherwise, in effect, the most contentious aspects of a Bill could be deliberately reserved for the second Session and the Lords would, thereby, be given only one opportunity to consider and accept them and not the statutory two opportunities.

However, it is also clear that it would be extremely unhelpful if negotiations between the two Houses in relation to the passage of the Bill during the second Session could not be assisted by the possibility of amendments to give effect to political compromise. For this reason, the subsection allows the House of Commons to 'suggest any further amendments without inserting the amendments in the Bill'. Those amendments are to be considered by the House of Lords and 'if agreed to by that House, shall be treated as amendments made by the House of Lords and agreed to by the House of Commons'.[6] The subsection concludes that 'the exercise of this power by the House of Commons shall not affect the operation of this section in the event of the Bill being rejected by the House of Lords'.

One particular controversy in relation to section 2(4) concerns the situation where suggested amendments are accepted by the House of Lords in the process of a movement

---

[6] This is another occasion on which the Act slightly slips up, and whereas it generally tries to avoid telling either House what they must or must not consider, the Lords are placed under a statutory duty to consider the suggested amendments proposed by the House of Commons. In practice, however, unless those amendments are presented in some form of a motion by a member of the House of Lords, there is no mechanism in that House by which they can be considered.

towards compromise, but the compromise eventually fails and the Bill is rejected. What happens to the suggested amendments that have been accepted by the Lords at that point?

In terms of policy, there are arguments either way, and which is the most appropriate in relation to a particular Bill may depend on the precise circumstances of the case. For example, where the suggested amendments have simply been required to accommodate real-world changes in relation to the subject matter of the Bill, without which it cannot be made to work at all, it might be thought that the Parliament Acts are themselves frustrated if the amendments cannot be incorporated in the Bill as presented under the Parliament Act, and that the Lords' acceptance of the amendments amount to realism and acceptance that the Parliament Acts need to be allowed to operate effectively.

The opposite argument, which may be more apt in particular cases, is that where the House of Lords accepts suggested amendments because there is movement towards a political compromise, once that compromise breaks down then 'all bets are off', and the Lords are entitled to be assumed to have retreated from their original concessions.

The reality is simply that the precise intended effect of the final phrase of section 2(4) is obscure, and, in relation to the whole subsection, it is clear that this was intended to arise so infrequently, and was given such little consideration as being a mere technical possibility, that very little clear thought was given at the time of the passage of the 1911 Act as to how this might actually work. It has, however, been required to be operated on a number of occasions, most notably in relation to the Hunting Act 2004.

On balance, it is probably right that one should err on the side of caution and not 'hold against the Lords' any concessions made by them on suggested amendments during the passage of the Bill in their House, if negotiations then fail and the Bill is rejected wholesale by them.

It has also been asserted by some that the suggested amendment procedure is part only of the operation of the Parliament Act 1911 and that the amendments are not to be treated as having been passed between the two Houses in the ordinary way, other than for the purpose of the 1911 Act. The result is that it has seriously been asserted by some that if the suggested amendments are made but the Bill is then passed by the House of Lords so that it does not require to be presented under the Parliament Act at all, the suggested amendments fall and the Bill is presented for Royal Assent without them. By contrast, if the Bill is rejected by the House of Lords, it is argued that this is the situation for which section 2(4) provides, and the suggested amendments then do form part of the Bill as presented for Royal Assent. This result appears extremely perverse: in particular, it means that a compromise that is ultimately so successful that the Lords pass the Bill, is then frustrated by key aspects of that compromise being removed from the text on Royal Assent.

As a result of these confusions it would be highly beneficial if the final passage of section 2(4) were clarified, in particular so that a perverse construction of the final sentence could be finally disregarded.

In the meantime, however, the only way to avoid any possible application of this perverse doctrine would be to ensure that the House of Lords on agreeing to the suggested amendments under section 2(4) also tables its own amendments and passes them in the same terms, returning the Bill to the Commons with those amendments inserted, as a result of which these would be 'such amendments only as may be agreed to by both Houses', the House of Lords would not be deemed to have rejected the Bill, and the Bill could be presented for Royal Assent with the inclusion of those amendments in the normal way.

This is yet another illustration of aspects of the Parliament Act 1911 that presently depend upon the interpretation and application by the House authorities of the technicalities of the Act, which might better be made the subject of clearer legislation.

VII STALEMATE AND THE PACKAGING OF AMENDMENTS

One aspect of the practical operation of the Parliament Act, that depends crucially on the attitude of the House authorities, does not appear on the face of the Act at all, but relates to the non-statutory doctrine of 'two strikes and you're out' at the to and fro stage.

The 'double-insistence' rule provides that when stalemate is reached between the two Houses, a Bill is lost and simply falls away.[7] In the case of a Bill that has been sent by the Commons to the Lords twice and is now in its second Session, stalemate will also result in the automatic invocation of the Parliament Act. In political terms, therefore, the stakes in respect of avoiding stalemate in these circumstances may be particularly high. In particular, the Commons and Lords are each likely to want to show that it was the other House that 'killed' the Bill by intransigence, and will not want to have been the House that is seen to have caused the stalemate.

The operation of the stalemate rule depends on whether precisely the same amendments are being presented by one House to the other. There are two ways in which this can be avoided.

The first is by making very minor changes to the text of an amendment purely for the purposes of keeping the ball in the air, without the variation effecting any change of substance whatsoever. Although this has sometimes been questioned by individual Clerks, there is no recorded instance of the authorities of either House refusing to place an amendment on the Order Paper on the grounds that it is the same in substance as a previous amendment; the European Parliamentary Elections Bill 1997–98 which holds the record for passage between the Houses 11 times used this technique more than once, although the process ultimately resulted in stalemate and the Bill was lost.

The second technique for keeping negotiations alive is the packaging of amendments and suggesting substantive alternatives to the package as a whole, while continuing to insist on rejecting individual amendments within the package. The House authorities have voiced objections to this on more than one occasion, but again the technique was used successfully in relation to the Hunting Act 2004.

In relation to both these techniques the operation involves considerable discretion of the House authorities and is another illustration of the centrality of the Clerks in the application of Parliamentary procedure that directly affects the operation of the Parliament Act.

VIII IDENTICAL BILLS

A final point of potential controversy where the House authorities are involved in the operation of section 2 of the 1911 Act arises in respect of what amounts to 'identical' Bills.

The Parliament Act applies to non-Money Bills only if the Bill sent up in the second Session is 'identical' to the Bill sent up in the first Session, 'or contains only such alterations

---

[7] For detailed discussion of the practical operation of the stalemate rule, see *Craies on Legislation*, 10th edn (London, Sweet & Maxwell, 2012) 285–86.

as are certified by the Speaker of the House of Commons to be necessary owing to the time which has elapsed since the date of the former Bill'.

Theoretically, the phrase 'necessary owing to the time which has elapsed' could be construed fairly widely.

In practice, the authorities of the two Houses have agreed to treat it with circumspection and it is pretty much limited to the substitution of the appropriate year in the short title of the Bill.

However, this is, of course, a potentially useful mechanism for avoiding the controversy about the inclusion or non-inclusion of suggested amendments at a later stage. Where, for example, the amendments were required to reflect the fact that legislation to which the Bill refers has been amended in the interim, and the amendments require consequential alteration, it remains to be seen whether a Speaker would be advised, and would feel it appropriate, to certify the amendments as 'necessary owing to the time which has elapsed' since the date of the former Bill.

IX SPEAKER'S CERTIFICATES

Section 3 of the 1911 Act provides that 'any certificate of the Speaker of the House of Commons given under this Act shall be conclusive for all purposes, and shall not be questioned in any Court of Law'.

In one sense, it is surprising that this section was thought necessary or appropriate in 1911. One might surmise that it would simply have been assumed that Article 9 of the Bill of Rights would have prevented any interference by the courts, and that to express a proposition of this kind would create more doubt than it solved.

In particular, as a legislative proposition, it is, at least on its own terms, open to scrutiny by the courts; and one wonders whether an *Anisminic*-like method of circumvention might be adopted by the courts in an appropriate case. That would not, of course, have been possible had the proposition not been expressed on the face of the Act but had simply been left to the automatic operation of the Bill of Rights.

X CONCLUSION

In a number of ways the relationship between the House of Lords and the House of Commons has become significantly more strained in recent years. On a number of occasions, for example, the House of Lords has expressed the view that the House of Commons has relied upon assertions of financial privilege in relation to matters for which it was not entirely appropriate. And the removal of the hereditary peers has led some to suggest that the democratic legitimacy of the Lords is now much closer to that of the Commons than it was formally.

Lords reform is not presently on the immediate legislative agenda, but it tends to re-emerge from time to time and sooner or later, one imagines, it will be addressed to a greater or lesser extent. Although it was suggested at one point that a Bill reforming the House of Lords might leave the Parliament Act 1911 untouched, it seems extremely unlikely that reform could be made effective without considering all aspects of the relationship between the two Houses; and that therefore seems unlikely that it could be practicable to leave the

1911 Act untouched, particularly as so much of it is unworkable without a robust attitude on the part of the House authorities as described above.

Irrespective of wider Lords reform, it would certainly be highly beneficial for the 1911 Act to be revisited and re-crafted having regard to a thorough analysis of how the Act is intended to work in practice.

13

The Impact of the Parliament Acts 1911 and 1949 on a Government's Management of its Legislative Timetable, on Parliamentary Procedure and on Legislative Drafting

RHODRI WALTERS[1]

T HE PARLIAMENT ACTS 1911 and 1949 apply to two categories of Bills. The first is Money Bills. This category was created by the 1911 Act as one which contains only provisions relating to taxation, supply, appropriation or the raising or repayment of loans. The second category is any other public Bill – other than a Money Bill or a bill containing a provision to extend the maximum duration of Parliament beyond five years – and which originates in the House of Commons. The considerations which apply to these two kinds of Bill are very different.

I MONEY BILLS

The Parliament Act 1911 provides that any Bill certified by the Speaker as a Money Bill, unless passed by the Lords without amendment within one month of its receipt from the Commons, shall be presented for Royal Assent without the Lords' agreement – unless the House of Commons direct to the contrary.

It is perhaps worth dwelling on that last little phrase, 'unless the House of Commons direct to the contrary', because it admits to the possibility of the Lords amending Money Bills and of the Commons agreeing to those amendments. Indeed, there are examples in the 1920s and 1930s where the Lords amended Money Bills and the Commons accepted the amendments. On one occasion when the author was private secretary to the Leader of the House of Lords and Government Chief Whip in the late 1980s, Her Majesty's Treasury made contact with a view to moving amendments to a Money Bill in the Lords. Once political masters had been engaged, the Treasury was persuaded to drop the idea. As recently as 1995 the Lords held a committee stage on a Money Bill (the European Communities (Finance) Bill). However, the fact remains that the Money Bill provisions of

---

[1] This chapter is based on a paper delivered by the author in November 2011 at a seminar held by the University of Cambridge Centre for Public Law at the London offices of Clifford Chance to commemorate the centenary of the passing of the Parliament Act 1911.

the Parliament Acts have never been invoked in order to achieve Royal Assent. Even when a Money Bill through inadvertence or the arrival of a parliamentary recess had not been passed within the statutory month, the Bill passed under the normal procedures.

Provided that a Money Bill is drafted in such a way as to enable it to be certified by the Speaker, there are no particular procedural or timetable issues. Indeed, everything is accelerated. But one must never underestimate the burden that this places on parliamentary counsel in ensuring that, in drafting a potential Money Bill, the terms of the Parliament Act 1911 are observed. The Bill must deal exclusively with money as defined in the Act. Ultimately it is for the House of Commons authorities to advise Mr Speaker on whether or not to grant his certificate.

The expedition afforded by the Act to Money Bills does not, however, extend to other public Bills.

II OTHER PUBLIC BILLS

The Parliament Acts, having set out the arrangements for Money Bills, then provide for the 'restriction of the powers of the House of Lords as to bills other than Money Bills'. Any public Bill other than a Money Bill or a Bill extending the maximum duration of a Parliament beyond five years can be subject to these restrictions. Such a Bill, if passed by the Commons in identical form in two successive Sessions, and having been sent to the Lords at least one month before the end of each Session, and rejected by the Lords in each Session, shall be presented for Royal Assent without the consent of the Lords. A Bill shall be deemed to be rejected by the House of Lords if it is not passed by the Lords either without amendment or with such amendments only as may be agreed by both Houses. Indeed when the Parliament Acts are resorted to now it is usually because of an irreconcilable difference between the Houses over particular amendments rather than over the whole Bill. An exception was the War Crimes Bill which was rejected by the Lords at Second Reading in two successive Sessions: 1989–90 and 1990–91. Finally, one year must elapse between the date of Second Reading in the Commons in the first Session and the date of passing by the Commons in the second.

These provisions are the so-called suspensory veto. The one-year minimum interval prescribed and the one-month obligatory minimum period allowed to the Lords before the end of each Session for their debates, combine to give a total of 13 months, and the Lords' powers of delay are often described in those terms – that is to say, a year and a month. In fact, the period of delay depends very much on the handling decisions of the Government business managers on the one hand and the approach of the Bill's opponents – whether the official opposition or backbench members – on the other. Two recent examples illustrate the point.

The European Parliamentary Elections Bill failed in the Lords at the end of the 1997–98 Session because of a disagreement over the regional closed-list system. These amendments were insisted upon by the Lords during ping-pong. The Bill was re-introduced early in the 1998–99 Session and rejected at Second Reading in the Lords on 15 December 1998. This allowed the Bill to be certified by Mr Speaker and presented for Royal Assent in January 1999, when the statutory period of 12 months prescribed in the Parliament Acts 1911 and 1949 had lapsed. Thus, the official opposition had made its point without preventing the elections taking place on time the following June.

The history of the passage of the Sexual Offences Bill is an altogether different story. First introduced in the 1998–99 Session, the Bill received its Second Reading in the Commons on 25 January 1999. It was rejected at Second Reading by the Lords, by the dilatory motion procedure, on 13 April. It was reintroduced into the Commons in the following Session and sent to the Lords at the end of February 2000. It was given a Second Reading and committed to a committee of the whole House. Knowing that they needed to do nothing further, and knowing that opponents of the Bill were ready with their amendments, the Government business managers took no further action until 13 November 2000 when one day's disastrous committee stage took place. There were no further proceedings until the end of the Session later that month when Royal Assent was given under the Parliament Acts. So in the case of that Bill, the period of delay was one year and 10 months.

III IMPLICATIONS FOR THE LEGISLATIVE TIMETABLE AND HANDLING

The most important effect is that contentious Bills likely to run into trouble in the Lords must start in the Commons if it is thought that the Acts are to be used. Relatively few Bills can, in advance, be recognised as Parliament Acts material, but the general rule applies.

In 2004, business managers were faced with a particularly difficult choice. While their legislative programme was being prepared, there was a real possibility of a further Bill on Lords reform which, if it went ahead, was clearly a Commons starter. Then at shorter notice the Constitutional Reform Bill entered the lists and for business management reasons was started in the Lords. This was a decision which Sir Humphrey – had it been an episode of *Yes, Minister* – might have described as 'courageous'. In fact it proved very troublesome and, in the event, there was no Lords Reform Bill.

As a tool of business management the Parliament Acts are clunky. Administrations and ministers want their Bills through as quickly as possible. And many Bills have financial consequences – spending or saving – which are already factored in to the estimates. So when a Bill runs into heavy weather in the Lords, it comes as little comfort to the minister to know that as a last resort he can have his Bill possibly as late as the latter part of the next Session. The minister wants it instantly.

Once a Bill is passed by the Commons in the Second Session and sent to the Lords very little more needs to be done. As proceedings on the Sexual Offences Bill illustrate, a Second Reading and perhaps a day of committee for form's sake are all that is required. The opinion of the Lords in the Second Session – unless agreement is a possibility – is of no consequence to the Government.

To what extent can the Parliament Acts be used as an instrument of reconciliation between the Houses? Clearly in the exchanges between the Houses which precede its use there will be dialogue between government and opposition with a view to achieving agreement. These will, of course, be off the floor, informal and usually unrecorded for posterity. They represent a final attempt to avoid recourse to the Parliament Acts.

The Act of 1911 contains very limited provisions for further amendment of the Second Session bill. The first is that the Speaker may certify in the Second Session Bill any amendments necessary owing to the time which has elapsed since the date of the First Session Bill, or to represent any amendments made by the Lords in the preceding Session and agreed to by the Commons. The second is that in the text presented for Royal Assent the Speaker may certify any Lords amendments made in the second session and agreed to by the

Commons. Essentially, these provisions enable the Government to incorporate such Lords amendments as they may wish to approve.

Thirdly, there is provision for the Commons to propose further 'suggested amendments'. No Bill has ever received Royal Assent under the Parliament Acts including such amendments, though they have been suggested on three occasions. Most recently, a suggested amendment was proposed by the Commons to the Hunting Bill when it was sent up to the Lords in the Second Session, on 16 September 2004. The provision takes the form of a proviso to section 2(4) of the 1911 Act and reads:

> Provided that the House of Commons may, if they think fit, on the passage of such a Bill through the House in the second session, suggest any further amendments without inserting the amendments in the Bill, and any such suggested amendments shall be considered by the House of Lords, and, if agreed to by that House, shall be treated as amendments made by the House of Lords and agreed to by the House of Commons; but the exercise of this power by the House of Commons shall not affect the operation of this section in the event of the Bill being rejected by the House of Lords.

There are two points to be made here. First, the suggested amendments are not in the House Bill – the text of the Bill which is transmitted from one House to the other. They are the subject of separate resolutions. Secondly, although the provision states 'any such suggested amendments shall be considered by the House of Lords', the Acts are silent as to when they are to be considered, and do not require the House to come to a decision on them. The suggested amendment to the Hunting Bill would have delayed commencement of most of the Bill, and a motion to 'consider' the suggested amendment was moved formally after the motion for Second Reading, thus fulfilling the requirement of the Acts. But the motion to agree the suggested amendment was not decided until the second stage of ping-pong on 17 November 2004, the day before the end of the session. By then the Lords had rewritten the Bill and so the amendment was irrelevant and it was defeated.

What, then, is the point of suggested amendment procedure? Clearly it allows the Commons a further attempt at compromise in the second session. In the case of the Hunting Bill, the delay in commencement was meant to butter parsnips. But as a procedure it is deeply flawed. It is also rather pointless. If, say, suggested amendments have been arrived at after further discussions with a Bill's opponents, and if those amendments were likely to help carry the day in the Lords, why not simply table them as amendments in the Lords in the usual way and watch the Bill sail on to Royal Assent without recourse to the Acts? Perhaps the ultimate irony is that amendments which are meant to facilitate the passage of a Bill, if agreed, can only be included if the Bill is then rejected.

IV CONCLUSION

The provisions of the Parliament Acts, other than those on Money Bills, are perhaps best described as a framework within which an administration which is prepared to wait can get its bills to the Statute Book without Lords agreement, while retrieving from the debris of Lords consideration such amendments in either session as it may find convenient. They are not instruments of reconciliation, though the disciplines they impose can focus minds in that direction. The real significance of the Acts in terms of business management is as much psychological as it is practical. They state loud and clear which House is boss.

Part 5

Politics, the Constitution, and Beyond

14

International Law and Great Power Politics

MATTHEW PARISH

W HAT IS INTERNATIONAL law? My thesis is that it is incapable of being law in the conventional sense, because it is not enforced by an independent third party. From this it follows that international courts cannot adjudicate international legal disputes free from political considerations. Hence the qualities we associate with the rule of law are necessarily absent from international law, and the determination of international legal disputes owes more to the politics of international relations than the impartial application of legal principle. That is why we find international courts commonly delivering such unusual results which are often inconsistent with legal principle. The dynamics of Great Power politics means that despite the growth of international law in recent years, this essential frailty in the discipline is unlikely to change.

Law is a system of social rules that govern how people are obliged to interact with one-another. But that alone is not a sufficient definition of the law. Social rules may exist outside the context of law. Social rules may be mere norms (for example do not commit adultery; do not lie), which do not become crimes or legal wrongs save in specified circumstances. They may be rules of voluntary association: a club may require its members to behave in certain ways. Unlike law, those rules are not compulsory. One may walk away from those rules by departing the club. In principle one may also walk away from the law, by departing the country whose laws govern one's behaviour. This is possible at least to a degree, consistent with states' undertakings to extradite one another's suspects. But there is a sense in which the measures necessary to abandon one's legal obligations are altogether more dramatic than those required to abandon the sorts of voluntary social undertakings entailed by membership of a club or society, or association of oneself with a religious, ethnic, political or cultural group or class. Within a state, legal obligations are mandatory and are enforced by the state with legitimate violence.

I LAW AND THE IMPORTANCE OF COMPULSION

Rules are transformed into law by the existence of independent authorities that adjudicate and enforce those rules. Rules that are enforced purely through social disapproval or reputational stigma do not amount to law. We may look down upon a greedy and successful businessman who does nothing with his wealth to support his family or friends. We may consider his behaviour selfish and immoral. He may attract our censure. But there is no judicial authority that takes decisions condemning his conduct, penalising his wrongdoing or coercing him to change his ways. It is also imperative that the authority enforcing law is independent. If the local villagers form a lynch mob to persecute a notorious paedophile, that is not law. It is merely the baying of the pack. The wrongdoer's conduct may be criminal, but it is central to the concept of 'the rule of law' that criminal sanctions are imposed and their suitability adjudged by an impartial organ of the state rather than by one's fellow private citizens.

From these observations, the simplest analysis might lead us to conclude that international law is an oxymoron. This superficially controversial assertion follows from the most indisputable and elementary premises. Traditionally conceived, international law concerns the rules governing the relations between states. As a rule, international law imposes obligations upon states. The only area in which international law imposes obligations upon individuals rather than states is in the field of international criminal law; but even the defendants in such trials are often prosecuted for the things they have done in their capacity either as state actors or as representatives of quasi-state authorities in the course of a civil war.

States are sovereigns. By this we mean that the institutions of a state have exclusive authority over a territory.[1] The concept of sovereignty is not straightforward, because sometimes states may lose their authority (as in a civil war or insurrection) and states may come to exercise authority over territory traditionally associated with another state (as where Russia has come to exercise military control over its Georgian exclaves of South Ossetia and Abkhazia).[2] Nevertheless, some level of de facto or de jure exclusive control over a determinate geographical area is an important part of what it is to be a state. Another instance of the complexity of sovereignty comes from the internationalisation of authority represented by the growth of international law.

Nevertheless we can construct the following argument from the concept of sovereignty. International law asserts that states owe obligations; but if states are sovereign in their territories then they have exclusivity over the legal authority exercised in respect of that territory. Hence it cannot make sense to say those states themselves owe legal obligations. This is a simple corollary of the fact that where a state exercises exclusive authority in its territory, the only authority existing there is the state itself; and if the state is exercising authority over itself then the authority in question is obviously not independent. Therefore the definition of law previously posited – namely a set of rules enforced by an independent authority – cannot possibly be met. Accordingly, states cannot owe legal obligations. They can owe moral or customary obligations, and they can enter into informal agreements that even though are expressed to be binding are not really so. They can also owe obligations to themselves through their own internal legal procedures, over which they remain exclusive

---

[1] Sovereignty is no easy concept, and political scientists typically conceive it as having multiple dimensions of which exclusive control over territory is only one. See eg Stephen Krasner (ed), *Problematic Sovereignty: Contested Rules and Political Possibilities* (Columbia University Press, 2001). Nevertheless, it has been a theme of international relations at least since Hobbes that exclusivity of legitimate control over territory is one of the most fundamental preconditions for state sovereignty, and it is on this simplified assumption that this chapter will proceed.

[2] Although formally the enclaves within the Republic of Georgia of South Ossetia and Abkhazia have declared themselves to be independent states since 1990, their independence has never been recognised by the international community as a whole. Only a handful of countries recognised their independence, of which Russia, Venezuela and Nicaragua are the principal states. The Russian army maintains a significant presence in both territories and exercises significant de facto control over the external and many of the internal affairs of both regions. The former President of South Ossetia, Eduard Kokoity, was forced to step down in 2011 following political pressure orchestrated by Russia.

sovereigns. But none of these things are legal obligations in the strict sense; they are some-thing less, because they have no independent third-party enforcement procedures to be applied against them in the event that they fall short of the obligations they owe. Accordingly international law cannot exist. The subject we call international law is not a branch of law at all, and might better be described as international ethics or some such thing.

II THE FALLACY OF DEFINITION

One might harbour scepticism over this argument simply because it rests so heavily upon such a rigid definition of state sovereignty. Some of humanity's most egregious logical fal-lacies have commenced with definitions. If one starts, as Hegel did, by defining history as the progression of an intellectual dialectic, then some sort of utopian ideology such as fas-cism or communism seems almost inevitable. With the right definitions, any argument can adopt the alluring quality of a priori reasoning. Hence one might counter that we ought to be wary of any analysis that commences with a clear definition of terms. There is nothing innately wrong with defining the language we use, save that we must always recall that lan-guage does not acquire meaning through definition. It acquires meaning through the way it is used; definitions are created after the event of meaning, not before, in an attempt to clarify the sometimes messy boundaries of ordinary use. Those taking care with definitions are engaging in exercises of housekeeping rather than pursuing vigorous intellectual leaps.

Yet definitions can be illustrative, because they reveal the extent to which the use of lan-guage can slide over time. If definitions illustrate conventional usage, then arguments from definitions that lead to absurdity might illustrate the extent to which meaning has changed. International law is just such a phenomenon. International law was not created overnight. International law's tenets go as far back as Grotius at least[3] and possibly even to the *jus gentium*.[4] Yet the conventional precepts that we associate with law do not apply to interna-tional law. International lawyers talk of states as having legal obligations.[5] But when they use language of this kind, they mean something very different from what we mean when we say that Mr Jones has a legal obligation not to steal a loaf of bread from the grocery. When we talk about Mr Jones, we are not just registering our moral disapproval of his theft of loaves. We are not just saying that we will shun him for his acts, and we are not saying that we, or some vigilante group, will go over to his house and break his windows as retribution.

---

[3] Grotius's book *De Jure Belli ac Pacis* (1625) is generally regarded as one of the first treatises on international law in the early modern era, addressing both questions of what makes a war just (*jus ad bellum*) and what methods may properly be used in the waging of war (*jus in bello*). In the Aquinean tradition, it sets out the obligations upon states as a matter of natural law. Revealingly, the work says nothing about how these principles might be enforced against errant states.

[4] There might be a debate as to whether the *jus gentium* was really international law in the modern sense of the term. While the phrase was used in Roman law to refer to the 'law of nations', it consisted of a set of norms of conduct for non-Roman people across the Empire. Accordingly, it was not a law governing the conduct of states but rather a law governing the conduct of peoples in the Empire and hence at least in principle subject to a single (and ultimately central) authority. Ultimately, the *jus gentium* disintegrated as individual European nations devel-oped their own distinctive legal codes.

[5] Consider in particular the American legal scholar Louis Henkin's famous aphorism about international law, that "'almost all nations observe all principles of international law and almost all of their obligations almost all the time'" (from *How Nations Behave*, Columbia University Press, 1979). This appears more to be an expression of optimism than an empirical thesis. Henkin thought that moral and political considerations alone were sufficient for international law to have a causative influence upon states' conduct, and the sort of impartial enforcement mechanism considered in this paper to be unnecessary to international law's efficacy.

Rather we are saying that the police, an independent authority, may exercise the prerogative of investigating what he has done, and they will exercise legitimacy in doing so. The matter may be prosecuted, and Mr Jones may be convicted after due process. He may be punished, and his punishment will be enforced. Should he abscond, he will be pursued and imprisoned by the authorities. If necessary, he will be subject to violence to ensure his compliance with the procedure imposed upon him. It is important that the violence be executed without passion or discretion, for the law is impartial and unemotional and treats all persons equally (or at least it very much should do).

International law is not like this. If states are sovereign, then they cannot be subject to such measures executed by independent third parties. Sovereignty implies authority over the self. The existence of a genuinely impartial authority regulating the affairs of states must entail that they are not fully sovereign. Hence we hear scholars say that states are no longer sovereign in an era of international law.[6] It is argued that the proliferation of international courts and tribunals that exist to adjudicate claims that international law has been violated illustrates the demise of sovereignty as a concept in contemporary international relations. Sovereignty, it might be said, is a notion belonging to the nineteenth century in which the Great Powers occupied absolute dominion in their own territories and fought wars with and traded with other sovereigns. It was an era of European monarchies. The theoretical absolute power of monarchies over their dominions fitted well with the historical notion of state sovereignty. But this is a vision of international affairs no longer appropriate to the modern world. It may be argued that in the course of the twentieth century, international cooperation developed in such fundamental ways that states abdicated their sovereignty to a significant degree.[7]

III THE LEAGUE OF NATIONS AND BEYOND

Perhaps the first paradigmatic instance of this kind of abdication of state sovereignty was the League of Nations, an inter-war predecessor to the United Nations that aimed to preserve global stability through the creation of mechanisms of global governance. The League failed to prevent recurrence of world war but its successor, the United Nations Organization, became a major actor in the Cold War struggles between the United States and the Soviet Union. As the international community strengthened itself through proliferation of a wide variety of international organisations, so the sovereignty of states was undermined. While states would remain masters of their own destinies in the greater majority of activities they undertook within their territories, their conduct would become subject to regulation by international institutions.

A proliferation of international treaties and conventions created legal obligations upon states; and it was not expected that the sole method of enforcement of these obligations should be states enforcing those obligations against themselves. Instead, these legal standards would be applied by international institutions. The European Union is the most developed example of this model. Over the decades since the creation of the European Economic Community in 1957, a weight of international rules has been developed by European institutions and applied

---

[6] See eg Andreas Osiander, 'Sovereignty, International Relations, and the Westphalian Myth', (2001) 55(2) *International Organization*, 251–287.

[7] ibid. Osiander criticises the UN charter's declaration of respect for sovereignty for being regressive in the pursuit of the cooperative benefits arising from an international legal order.

by the Union's international courts in Luxembourg which issue binding decisions against EU Member States. This remarkable development has been replicated to a degree across the world by other international courts, particularly in the period since the end of the Cold War. Human rights courts, investment tribunals, the World Trade Organisation's (WTO) dispute system and UN human rights committees all adjudicate the lawfulness of states' conduct. Now there are laws (treaties), courts and jurisprudence. The actions of states are being judged before international tribunals pursuant to international legal rules. One might consider that international law has reached a period of renaissance.

Hence the narrative develops that sovereignty is in decline. Although states once had unilateral control over their affairs, this is no longer the case. In many instances they have voluntarily given a part of their sovereignty away, in the interests of promoting the higher goals of international cooperation. Partial abdication of sovereignty may be a short-term burden for a state, but it reflects a longer-term mutual advantage. The ideals promoted by international cooperation are more sustainable for all states if those states jointly engage in a mutual delegation of some sovereign authorities to international institutions. Within this space, international law may grow. Hence what has been termed the theory of 'liberal institutionalism' – the view that states will voluntarily abdicate sovereignty in the interests of the common good – has developed within international relations.[8] Some scholars have embraced this conclusion to its fullest logical degree. The constructivist political theorist Alexander Wendt sees sovereignty as the root of much evil, a socially constructed concept of unaccountable state indifference to the law that we are best off without.[9] In his view there is nothing necessary or inevitable about sovereignty. The dialogue of international relations can change in favour of more cooperative approaches, and this will give rise to the logical space for international law and global government. Wendt sees this trend as inexorable; he believes the confluence of powers in international institutions will eventually yield the creation of a world government.[10]

Hence the world is becoming a better place. Sovereignty is a reflection of anachronistic political brutalism, entailing as it does a lack of legal accountability for the most fundamental unit of organisation in the international sphere. Accountability is desirable to improve any organisation's governance. Sovereignty precludes legal accountability for states save for that of an eminently unreliable kind in which states regulate themselves. Self-policing is unrealistic because nobody can be expected to highlight their own wrongdoings as a matter of course and enforce rules against themselves when their most fundamental interests are at stake. Rule of law in the international sphere represents the boldest ideals of eliminating wrongdoing from the relationships between states. International treaties will hold states to the highest standards in both war and peace, and international courts will adjudicate compliance. In time, international law will ensure that wars of aggression become a thing of the past; trade barriers damaging to the global economy are eliminated; states will respect the civil rights of their own citizens and foreign investors alike; and the advantages of long-term cooperation are secured. The partial erosion of state sovereignty is a moderate price to pay for these advances in international law, a discipline that moves from oxymoron to superlative saviour of the modern era.

---

[8] For an overview see eg David Baldwin, *Neorealism and Neoliberalism: The Contemporary Debate* (New York, Columbia University Press, 1993).

[9] See eg Alexander Wendt, 'Anarchy is What States Make of it: The Social Construction of Power Politics', (1992) 46(2) *International Organization*, 391–425.

[10] 'Why a World State is Inevitable', (2003) 9(4) *European Journal of International Relations*.

Or so we would like to see things. The most significant bursts in the growth of international law have emerged from eras of global tragedy. Grotius wrote amidst the horrors of the Thirty Years War that tore continental Europe apart. The League of Nations was driven by US President Woodrow Wilson's aspirations for a peaceful world to emerge from the end of the First World War. Likewise, the United Nations emerged from the Second World War. Modern international criminal law grew from atrocious conflicts in Yugoslavia and Rwanda at the end of the twentieth century. The horrors of conflict played a significant role in the visions of scholars and politicians for the development of international law as a tool to prevent their recurrence. The aspiration of international law is that superficial self-interest of state entities, from time to time lead to armed conflict amidst the ever-precarious balances of geopolitical power, can be placed to one side in the interests of pursuing a more peaceful world.

IV INTERNATIONAL LAW AND THE PRISONERS' DILEMMA

This is the logical space occupied by international law, a force to ameliorate the destructive forces of Great Power politics. Without a legal structure to govern their interactions, sovereign states could descend all too easily into violent confrontation. With competing geopolitical interests, from time to time states may go to war in pursuit of these differing goals. Forever entrapped in a security dilemma should another sovereign acquire sufficient power to overrun them, states were bound not just to pursue policies aggrandising themselves but also policies beggaring their neighbours. The constant pressure to prevail over one's neighbours on relative terms, generated by a security dilemma, compelled states to pursue mutually destructive policies.[11] International law can overcome this prisoners' dilemma by creating a framework of legal rules governing acceptable state behaviour. Confidence in compliance with these international rules on the part of one's fellow states releases states from the security dilemma and ultimately obviates the need for war. States can achieve more through cooperation than conflict. That recurrent bête noire of history, armed conflict, can be overcome and history's vicious cycles can be broken. Such are the modernist aspirations for the growth of international law.

International law may not be perfect, so its advocates continue. The International Court of Justice, the United Nations' court for resolving international disputes between sovereigns, serves a useful purpose but only for those states who wish to avail themselves of it. Its so-called 'compulsory jurisdiction' is in fact optional.[12] If an aggrieved state wishes to withdraw, it will do so. Not every state has recognised the jurisdiction of the International Criminal Court (ICC).[13] Nevertheless, international law is developing, gradually, in a

---

[11] The concept of a 'security dilemma' is commonplace in international relations theory and can be traced at least as far back as John Herz, *Political Realism and Political Idealism* (1951). Realists in international relations see the security dilemma as the prevailing dynamic in states' relations with one- another. See in particular Kenneth Walz, *Theory of International Politics*, (New York, McGraw-Hill, 1979).

[12] Article 36 of the Statute of the International Court of Justice (ICJ) provides that the Court has jurisdiction in disputes between states either where a specific treaty so provides, or in matters where the states in question have made a declaration recognising the Court's jurisdiction. Those declarations may be subject to conditions, including limited periods of time. Accordingly, any state may simply cease to renew their declaration and the ICJ thereafter ceases to have compulsory jurisdiction over them.

[13] As of 31 May 2013, 122 states have both signed and ratified the Statute of the ICC, meaning that they recognise its jurisdiction and will enforce its arrest warrants. Amongst states that have not signed or ratified the Statute are three out of five permanent members of the UN Security Council: Russia, the USA and China. India has not

desirable direction. More countries than ever are joining the WTO.[14] There is a proliferation of international treaties.[15] Slowly but surely, the ICC is completing its first trials.[16]

V INDEPENDENT ENFORCEMENT?

No international organisation encompasses an independent agency to enforce court judgments. Where an international court issues a court judgment against a defendant, then as a rule the court has no independent capacity to enforce that judgment. It must rely upon sovereign states to apply such enforcement measures as they may consider appropriate within their own territories. This applies as much to the ICC, which relies upon states to extradite criminal defendants,[17] as it does to the International Centre for Settlement of Investment Disputes (ICSID), the World Bank-based investment tribunal,[18] which relies upon states to enforce its arbitration awards. In theory states are bound to enforce the decisions of the international courts and tribunals to which they are parties, by the terms of international treaties. But a treaty is only a multilateral contract between states; and contracts can be broken even by those who agree to their terms. Hence, while a country may have committed by treaty to observe the edicts of international justice, where they are unhappy with those edicts they may simply decline to do so. Alternatively, they may withdraw from the treaty in question.

International courts ostensibly exist over and above the legal systems of the countries that create them. International law is supposed to override domestic laws, such that a state cannot plead its domestic legislation in answer to a complaint that it stands in disregard of its international legal obligations.[19] International courts must enforce international law against their recalcitrant subjects, as must all courts in order to enjoy credibility. Just as the institutions of state must, in Weber's words, enjoy a monopoly over the legitimate use of force over the citizens of that state,[20] so the institutions of a global government must exercise a monopoly over the legitimate use of force over states. International courts must have at least the capacity to exert overwhelming force over the subject of their edicts; and it is clear that international courts have no such capacity. This affects their jurisprudence and the decisions they take. For if their judgments cannot be impartially enforced, then the

---

acceded to the ICC Statute either. The fact that at some of the world's most significant powers have not agreed to the terms of the ICC's Statute illustrates the thesis of this chapter, namely that the Great Powers have no incentive to agree to delegation of authority to a legal institution outside their control.

[14] As of 31 May 2013, the WTO has 159 members (including all five UN Security Council permanent members of the UN Security Council) and a further 25 observers. The largest economy outside the WTO is Iran.

[15] As of the end of 2005, over 46,000 international treaties had been registered with the United Nations. Of these, some 50% per cent had been registered since 1990. In 2009, a mean of approximately 100 treaties per month were being registered. See Matthew Parish, *Mirages of International Justice: The Elusive Pursuit of a Transnational Legal Order*, (London, Edward Elgar, 2011), page 54.

[16] The ICC's first trial (Thomas Lubanga Dyilo) finished in March 2013 with a conviction, now under appeal. Its second trial (Katanga-Chui) concluded in May 2013 with an acquittal, is, at the time of writing, also being appealed.

[17] The ICC has no independent enforcement authority. Article 89(1) of the ICC's Statute obliges the Court's mMember sStates to extradite suspects to the Court upon its request.

[18] Article 54 of the ICSID Convention obliges signatory states automatically to recognise and enforce ICSID arbitration awards.

[19] See eg *CME v Czech Republic*, Partial Award 13 September 2001, para 467; *Siemens v Argentina*, Award 6 February 2007, para 267; *Kardassopoulous v Georgia*, Decision on Jurisdiction, 6 July 2007, para 182.

[20] Max Weber, *Politics as a Vocation* (1919): a state 'upholds the claim to the monopoly of the legitimate use of physical force in the enforcement of its order'.

integrity of the process is lost. Fearful of appearing irrelevant or wasteful, a court may temper its decisions by the prospect of them being executed. Absent effective means of compulsion, a subject of a court decision might turn its sights against that court rather than succumbing to voluntary compliance. A society in which the individuals are more powerful than the legal system will never achieve the advantages of rule of law, for the legal system will not be able to act impartially, and this applies as much to a society of states as it does to a society of individuals. If such a legal system attempts to act impartially, then its decisions may be ignored. This applies as much to the society of states in the international legal order as it does to legal relations between individuals within the territory of a sovereign.

VI LAW, SCIENCE AND THE IMPORTANCE OF AUTHORITY

A legal system which does not contain a system of impartial enforcement is necessarily denuded, as a matter of principle, from that which renders it a genuine system of laws. For law is not a science. There are no logically correct answers to the question of proper construction of a statute or a treaty, or a set of rules of substance or procedure. All legal documents are merely the product of words, and words can be construed to mean anything. Quine taught us that there is no determinacy of meaning within any system of language.[21] There may be more or less plausible meanings for words within a linguistic matrix governing an area of discourse such as law; but an assessment of plausibility requires an element of judgment, and hence common sense, that the purveyor of international law cannot take for granted amidst international cultural diversity.

The element of judgment required to make a legal system work requires lawyers and judges to act in good faith, assuming that the legal system reflects some bedrock of morality or at the very least some commonly accepted general principles. The assumption of good faith is absent where incentives exist upon the legal system to make decisions in the interests of the Great Powers. These incentives derive from the fact that otherwise judicial decisions might be ignored by the powerful, or measures might be undertaken to interfere with the courts or with the way they make decisions. The absence of a sufficient power base to enforce international judicial edicts renders the system of international law prone to bias. It is inevitably unrobust. If courts can have no confidence that they are protected in the exercise of their role as impartial adjudicators, they will abandon that role and become political players in a broader morass. Hence, the good faith necessary for courts to give tolerably determinate answers in debates about the application of international law will evaporate.

This phenomenon is common in countries which lack strong rule of law traditions. In communist Eastern Europe, the power of the executive far overarched that of the judiciary. A judge who decided a case against the prevailing political wishes of the governing party could expect admonishment at best, or to lose his life or liberty at worst. Judges had neither effective tenure nor political insulation, because they were entirely reliant upon the whim of the executive for respect for the decisions they made. Judicial decisions would therefore bend to the will of the party in power. The legacy of this style of government, in which the

---

[21] Willard van Orman Quine's thesis is called the 'indeterminacy of translation'. For the most well-known statement of this argument see Willard V.O. Quine, *Word and Object* (Boston, MA, MIT Press, 1960).

lack of judicial independence and authority renders judicial decisions politically skewed, has survived the demise of communism and investing judges with the requisite sense of authority and independence has proven a daunting task.

Much the same considerations pertain in the development of international courts. The international judiciary is painfully aware of its own isolation in the international political system. Castigated by the United States' refusal to sign up to its Statute, the ICC is treading on eggshells. It must take the utmost care not to upset the USA or its allies in the decisions it makes to prosecute or convict.[22] International investment tribunals are the same: the United States has never lost a case,[23] just as in the Soviet Union the communist party seldom lost a case. If courts sit above the power relations of the political environments in which they operate, they have the prospect of operating fairly and impartially and in good faith. If they lack the capacity to operate above those power relations, because they have no independent capacity for overwhelming force, then they are forced into political compromises and they will construe international law to mean whatever they need it to mean in order to survive. International courts are ensnared in the balance of power between states, precisely because they are so much weaker than the subjects they purport to exercise jurisdiction over.

Hence international courts, imbued with these political frailties, do not operate as courts of law at all in the conventional sense. Instead those courts, and the international organisations that create the international legal rules they apply, are beholden to the favours of the most powerful states that create them and support them. They must also take heed of the objections and hostilities of powerful states that do not support them; for they remain politically delicate and must make every effort to avoid political attacks by powerful states. International courts remain inevitably politicised, because the impartial enforcement infrastructure characteristic of societies with high rule of law does not exist to support their ostensible majesty. International courts find themselves perpetually dancing upon political pinheads. Nor can we simply rely upon the cultural propensities of the judges who populate international tribunals to adjudicate impartially and in good faith.

Even if those judges who hail from societies traditionally associated with high traditions of rule of law, when immersed in the politically contested world of international law and international relations, their own self-interest in swaying with the political currents will soon outweigh their impartial cultural principles if they are to stand any chance of survival in so toxic an environment. In fact, the majority of international judges do not hail from such societies, because the majority of countries in the world do not harbour effective rule of law traditions. Those habits prevail only in a relatively small collection of mostly western societies. The values we wish to associate with rule of law do not attain even a plurality of conventional recognition amongst the community of states. Hence it is all the harder to expect those traditions to prevail in the far more politicised world of international relations where there are positive structural incentives for them not to do so.

---

[22] For an example of the ICC's reluctance to cross the United States' political interests, see Luis Moreno-Ocampo, *Letter Concerning the Situation in Iraq* (9 February 2006). Some 240 individuals and organisations had asked the ICC prosecutor to investigate the US–UK joint invasion of Iraq in April 2003. He refused.

[23] See for example the notorious case of *Loewen v United States*, ICSID Case No. ARB (AF)/98/3. A *North American Free Trade Agreement* NAFTA claim, the claimant complained that a Mississippi jury had awarded massive damages on the basis of a prejudicial trial against a foreign investor. The claimant was then precluded from appealing due to a procedural requirement to lodge a bond larger than the size of the damages in award in order to pursue an appeal. While the Tribunal was damning of the legal procedure adopted by the US Court, it declined to make a finding that the Court's procedure breached the treaty standard of fair treatment.

VII CAN WE EXPECT INTERNATIONAL LAW TO IMPROVE?

What is the value of a system of law without an independent mechanism for enforcement? Is international law politically nugatory, or might it be a project with some hope for improvement in the future? In the interim, is there some hortatory value in the system of international law? Might international law develop from a politically infected embryo to a genuine system of laws amidst a future global government? Might Wendt be right in seeing the further future deconstruction of domestic sovereignty and its replacement with a genuinely impartial system of international law, enforced by a global impartial military force much as the Federal Bureau of Investigation enforcing American federal laws amongst the country's several states? If this might happen, then under what conditions, and would it be desirable?

To untangle this thicket of possibilities, we might begin by looking back to the history of international law embodied in the writings of scholars such as Grotius and Kant.[24] There was a period during the early modern and Enlightenment eras during which international courts did not exist at all. A corpus of international law existed, but it was purely aspirational in nature – a code of good governance for states – rather something that anybody thought might be enforced against states or their agents. At this moment, international law was more a set of ethical mandates for statesmen than a legal system. Why then did it borrow the term 'law' at all? Throughout history it has been common for moral theorists to use the vocabulary of law to confer additional legitimacy upon the ideas they advance. The Bible used legal analogies to confer worldly compulsion upon what it characterised as divine mandates. Kant used an analogous tool: a moral philosopher who wrote about the 'moral law', he meant moral principles so fundamental that they derived from the nature of practical reasoning itself and therefore had the mandatory quality of legal prohibitions even without a method of material enforcement. Neither the Bible nor Kant were writing about law as it is conceived in the contemporary world. Without methods for the enforcement of legal obligations against states existing or even being contemplated at the time, scholars of international law in the early modern era were not writing about law, strictly conceived, either.

Even early instances of international legal adjudication were not law as such. The Jay Treaty of 1794, which provided for arbitration between England and the United States of certain disputes relating to the sovereignty of Canada outstanding from the American War of Independence, was not truly an instrument of legal adjudication within the relatively narrow confines we are considering here. The outcome of the Jay Treaty arbitration[25] was observed voluntarily between the parties, not because they stood in fear of some third party impartial enforcement mechanism, but because the issues at stake were less important than the desirability of avoiding war. International law has often been at its most successful as a form of diplomacy. Where some issue in international relations has achieved disproportionate importance in the public mind such that unilateral concession proves impossible; but where that issue is not objectively nearly so important as the public may consider it to be, international adjudication may play a valuable role. It defers the

---

[24] For Grotius's seminal work on international law, see (n 3) *De Jure Belli ac Pacis*, ibid; for Kant's principal work on the same subject, see Immanuel Kant, *Perpetual Peace* (1795).

[25] The Jay Treaty arbitration set the southern boundary of modern Canada and its determination persists to the present day.

contentious issue to some subsequent politically calmer moment, once the wheels of due process have turned.

The process of adjudication can formalise a division of spoils between the disputing parties, in the name of legal principle. It can also emphasise the priority of law over politics as a way of defusing popular outrage. This sort of international adjudication is not based upon legal principle but political pragmatism, using the language and tools of law to achieve a diplomatic solution at the expense of legal principle with a view to preventing bloodshed. This model is significantly more common than might be imagined amidst the annals of international law. A more recent instance of the same was the Taba arbitration, settling the boundary dispute between Israel and Egypt after the 1979 Camp David accords.[26] Decisions of the International Court of Justice also often have this quality, not requiring anyone actually to do anything.[27] They often reinforce the status quo in disputes where losing face is a greater peril than the concrete issues at stake.

In such cases we are not really engaging in law at all, because the judges or arbitrators involved are self-consciously engaged in defusive diplomacy. They will not permit themselves to be deflected from their primary task – of keeping the peace – in the interests of upholding legal principle. To do so would be obtuse, no matter how hard they cloak the language of their conclusions in the vocabulary of legal legitimacy. Where a legal process is being used for political ends, the politics of the dispute must prevail. To what extent should all exercises in international law be seen in this light? The question facing those who hope international law might grow into something more is approximately this: whether moral theory can develop into a pragmatic political tool, and from there into a genuine impartial coercive authority embodying the ideas of the rule of law that we admire amongst certain developed western states.

If that last step cannot be made, then international law remains a mere organ of diplomacy and never becomes a branch of law at all. All the intellectual abstractions, theorising, jurisprudence and institutions simply become a way of rendering more palatable the political realities of Great Power politics. The eventual outcome of confrontations between sovereigns will be those mandated by their relative power. The institutions of international law may legitimise those outcomes or render them more politically tolerable to domestic audiences. But that is the limit of the influence of international law without impartial enforcement. The significant quantity of intellectual debate the subject creates becomes merely a by-product of what, in the final analysis, must, like all diplomacy, be regarded as an intellectually dishonest affair: reconciling the interests of power politics by pretending that high principles are at work in forging muddy compromises or, where armed conflict has been decisive, securing the domination of the winners over the losers.

VIII THE PRISONERS' DILEMMA CANNOT BE RESOLVED

It is not obvious that international law can move in a more substantial direction that would lend it the qualities typical of a developed legal system. There is scant evidence to date of independent enforcement mechanisms being created to lend authority to the roles of international courts. International tribunals continue to rely upon Member States to enforce

---

[26] *Case concerning the location of boundary markers in Taba between Egypt and Israel*, Decision of 29 September 1988, Reports of International Arbitration Awards, XX, pp 1–118, United Nations, 2006.

[27] See Matthew Parish, *Mirages of International Justice*, (n 15) ibid, ch 3.

their decisions. The United Nations has no independent police or military force, and there is no indication of any steps being taken to create one. Its peacekeeping forces remain on loan from national armies and ultimately subject to national control in the event of a division of loyalties. Accordingly it is impossible to expect the United Nations to enforce the judgments of international courts, and there is no other independent authority ever likely to take on this role. In these circumstances, the growth of international law might be argued to be otiose. For all the increase in courts, legal textbooks, jurisprudence and international budgets funding international organisations, the institution of international law will remain perpetually unstable because it lacks that which Hobbes says the Leviathan must always possess: a monopoly on the use of force. Such a monopoly is not a sufficient condition of the impartiality inherent in the ideal of rule of law. But it is most certainly is necessary, and no concrete steps can be observed towards creating that Leviathan in the international sphere. Until we see such movement, Wendt's project will remain an evasive utopia.

Indeed, there are compelling reasons to suspect that international law will never develop this additional layer of sophistication. If it does, then it will not be the product of the forces that have shaped international law to date. Surely no powerful nation in its prime would ever voluntarily agree to the development of an impartial and independent enforcement mechanism. A powerful nation would have no interest in the creation of a mechanism stronger than itself that might turn against it and within which it would necessarily have a disproportionately small influence. It is better that a powerful nation keep all the guns for itself than irreversibly (for the system to have integrity it would have to be irreversible) vest them in an authority at least partially under the influence of other states. For a weaker nation, a purportedly impartial authority is at risk of capture by more powerful nations and legitimising the sort of domination that weaker nations routinely fear in any event. Creation of impartial institutions of physical force may make the predicament of weaker nations all the worse, in part because it may legitimise the use of superior force over them.

Nor is a grand bargain feasible between stronger and weaker nations. Quite apart from the transaction costs of achieving agreement between nearly 200 nations of varying sizes and levels of political and military power, the prospect that strong and weak nations jointly delegate power to genuine supra-national legal institutions that do genuine justice between them seems fanciful. It could only conceivably work if all nations were equally powerful or anticipated that they might become so. During the Cold War, when the globe was dominated by two powers of roughly equal size, the idea of international law as a mechanism for resolving their disputes remained wanting. The two superpowers preferred the prisoners' dilemma of perpetual struggle, because each of them felt that it might be on the cusp of dominating the other and each was fearful itself of being so dominated.

The wastage involved in Cold War military confrontation could not bring them to their senses. How much less likely is cooperation to create impartial enforcement mechanisms in a modern multi-polar world in which it is still harder for the various powers to judge one-another's strength, in which regional alliances complicate the patchwork of relative political power, and in which the relative economic and military fortunes of the different global political blocs are so hard to predict in even in the medium term? The creation of a permanent and genuine international legal order on a voluntary basis, by states agreeing between one-another to pool their military power into a common impartial judicial authority, also seems particularly unlikely given that the majority of the world's states harbour somewhat low rule of law traditions. Why would states agree to create something of which they have no experience and hence scant confidence?

Where a unitary legal and political authority has been established over a single territory, it is most rare that this has resulted from common agreement reached by competing sovereigns in times of peace. Sovereign states are too insecure amidst the global anarchy, and have too severe an information problem about the relative military and economic strengths (both now and in the future) of their competitors. They live in too acute a security dilemma to reach grand bargains of this kind. Instead, collective security arrangements, in which the power of coercion is delegated to a third party, generally come about solely as a result of one power conquering another. To assume that one country will conquer all others and thereby create global government seems unlikely in a world where nuclear weapons and the potential for mutually assured destruction are commonplace. Were it ever to occur, the global legal system created as a result would no doubt look very different from the mould of international law propagated today and would likely embrace legal colonialist models of the past in which a victorious power has imposed its legal traditions on the territories it has subjugated. In any event, the hope for a cooperative approach towards the gradual development of international law belies the meagre historical record of voluntary concentration of power in central institutions. International cooperation can grow in a modern globalised world of easy travel and instantaneous communications. But the internationalisation of a genuine legal system, entailing as it does the voluntary abdication of power in favour of a central external authority, seems far more remote a prospect.

IX IS INTERNATIONAL LAW DESIRABLE AT ALL?

Would the internationalisation of global legal power be a good thing, even if it could occur in principle? Would Alexander Wendt's ideal of global government really be the paradise a generous imagination might suggest? Quite possibly it would not be. One of the drivers of effective government is competition. It is hard to create competition in the public sphere, entailing as it does an element of monopoly. Even the prospect of periodic elections in developed democracies has only a limited effect upon the ever-expanding weight of seemingly irreversible government bureaucracy and legislation.[28] One form of competition that might improve government is between jurisdictions. If a country can operate with a low corporation tax rate or with a lower regulatory burden, businesses will migrate from higher-tax jurisdictions. This applies likewise to legal systems. Competition between effective systems of law may serve to improve their quality. If a system of global legal obligations is genuinely proliferated, the advantages of jurisdictional competition might be lost.

If the expansionist aspirations of international lawyers are destined to be dashed, then we should ask what future the discipline might have. Is international law entirely irrelevant, as some species of realist maintain, simply supervening upon states' affairs but having no causal impact upon them?[29] Is it a mere lumbering mastodon in the field of international relations with no discernible purpose? We have already seen that such a negative account is not entirely fair. Resolution of inter-state disputes under international law sometimes serves as a valuable diplomatic function, even if it is not an impartial legal process in the ordinary sense of the phrase. It also serves to structure the dialogue about the

---

[28] For some of the seminal econometric work in this field, see eg Sam Pelzman, 'The Growth of Government' (1980) 23 *Journal of Law & Economics* 209.

[29] See eg Jack Goldsmith and Eric Posner, *The Limits of International Law*, (Oxford, Oxford University Press, 2006)

moral obligations of states. Nevertheless we must be honest about the limits of international law, or we might burden it with expectations that it must inevitably fail. In the final analysis, international law is a moral framework, the breach of which may entail reputational consequences but not impartial judicial sanction, strictly conceived. What we must not do is slip into the comforting illusion that the decisions of international courts and tribunals represent the impartial application of legal principles. They cannot do so, because international courts are destined to lack the monopoly on authority that is a precondition for genuine legal impartiality.

As a general rule, international courts cannot achieve the goal their advocates hope for, because the relative poverty of their power within the international legal systems renders their operations subject to inevitable politicisation. International courts are but minor players in the game of Great Power politics, liable to be buffeted in the winds of political storms as those powers clash from time to time. They are far too insignificant alone to shape outcomes. At best they can shape an intellectual or political debate. They are not irrelevant; but they are not engaged in the practice of true law either, and it seems unlikely that they will ever develop into a genuinely impartial legal superstructure presiding over international relations. We must not ask too much of international law, for it cannot deliver. It is not the answer to all the world's international problems. At its best its achievements are modest: to help us think about how states should and should not behave, and to facilitate diplomacy in delicate situations.

At its worst, international law may lead to an intellectual hypocrisy: a belief that legal adjudication can solve perennial political problems of war and confrontation. Of this it is incapable; and should we hold too dear to the hypothesis that it can, we are in danger of overlooking the more effective weapons available in the armoury of the international community's foreign policy to shape outcomes. Above all, international law must not become an excuse for failures of military intervention or diplomacy. The International Criminal Tribunals for Yugoslavia and Rwanda were created amidst international community guilt for failure to save lives amidst atrocities. Those courts did not themselves save any lives, and we must not cling to the illusion that they heralded in some new international order that might do so. Finally, to think of international law by too strict an analogy with the high standards we in the West ascribe to domestic law, we may prove ourselves of guilty of falling into a fallacy of definition. The strengths of a robust system of domestic law cannot automatically be ascribed to the system of international law, and it remains far from clear that those strengths can ever become features of the global legal order.

15

Law and Democracy in a Human Rights Framework

PHILIP SALES

I INTRODUCTION

I N THIS CHAPTER I examine the relationship between democracy and the European Convention on Human Rights (ECHR). To what extent does the ECHR promote or reduce the scope for democracy and the resolution of disputes in society by democratic procedures? What forms of democracy does the ECHR promote or restrict? My thesis is that the ECHR has created the platform for an increasingly articulated and concrete balance between competing traditions in European political and legal philosophy. It provides for a practical juxtaposition of a liberal tradition of rights and freedoms with a tradition of democratic self-government.[1] The doctrine of the margin of appreciation is at the heart of the accommodation encapsulated in the case law of the European Court of Human Rights (ECtHR) between these traditions.

II THE TERRAIN OF DEMOCRACY AND HUMAN RIGHTS

Those competing traditions have developed in an uneasy tension, being reconciled in different ways in different European polities. The balance struck between them in different polities depends on the political culture, patterns of decision-making and distribution of powers in each case.[2] There is no a priori or natural template which must be taken to apply in every case. Nonetheless, at a level of some abstraction, since World War II there has been a strong congruence in the basic constitutional make-up of western European countries, specifically in their willingness to create space for both the liberal and the democratic traditions to have a vital role in structuring the public domain and in separating the public sphere from the private. These polities are aptly described as liberal democracies. The ECHR has operated as one driver towards the creation of a distinctive European liberal democratic model,[3] and as a cement to lock it in place.

---

[1] Chantal Mouffe, *The Return of the Political* (London, Verso, 1993), especially chs 7–9; Ramond Geuss, *History and Illusion in Politics* (Cambridge, Cambridge University Press, 2001), especially ch 3.

[2] Tim Koopmans, *Courts and Political Institutions: A Comparative View* (Cambridge, Cambridge University Press, 2003).

[3] Jan-Werner Müller, *Contesting Democracy: Political Ideas in Twentieth-Century Europe* (New Haven, Yale University Press, 2011) 5: '. . . we can make sense of the particular character of the democracies erected in Western

The European liberal democracies have grown out of the scarring experience of the wars of religion (and the consequent desire to separate the public and the private spheres),[4] the powerful development of the ideology of self-determination and democracy[5] and the battle against and experience of fascism and communism in the twentieth century. The Council of Europe, the parent organisation under whose auspices the ECHR was drafted, was established to create a common zone of liberal democratic states which could live at peace and support each other in the maintenance of their common values.[6] The ECHR has provided a code of common standards to be maintained. But it is drafted at a level of generality and includes obvious scope for unresolved conflicts between rights,[7] so that it was accepted that a practical mechanism would be required to determine the application of the ECHR in specific cases. That mechanism is judicial decision-making by the ECtHR.

By reason of the under-specification in the ECHR itself of human rights standards in concrete situations and the creation of the ECtHR to fill that gap, the ECtHR has generated what can best be regarded as a form of common law of European human rights by its case law. The Court has assumed a role as a major generator of public policy at the pan-European level, with an authority founded on the ECHR which reaches deep into resolution of practical disputes and social questions within the national legal systems of the states which are party to the ECHR. The limits within which the ECtHR feels able to articulate detailed practical standards of conduct for states to observe are given by its recognition of underlying principles of state sovereignty and democratic legitimacy and by self-created principles emerging from the Court's own case law.[8]

Europe after 1945 only if we understand that they were constructed with an eye both to the immediate fascist past and to the claims their Eastern rivals were making to embody true democracy. . . . Europeans created something new, a democracy that was highly constrained (mostly by unelected institutions, such as constitutional courts). The constitutionalist ethos that came with such democracies was positively hostile to ideals of unlimited popular sovereignty . . . European integration . . . was meant to place further constraints on nation-state democracies through unelected institutions.' Also see P Sales, 'Strasbourg Jurisprudence and the Human Rights Act' (2012) Public Law 253, 266–67.

    [4] Mouffe, *The Return of the Political* (n 1) and Annabel S Brett, 'The Development of the Idea of Citizens' Rights' in Quentin Skinner and Bo Stråth (eds), *States and Citizens* (Cambridge, Cambridge University Press, 2003) ch 7; see also the account given by Michael Oakeshott of the development of the modern European state in *On Human Conduct* (Oxford, Oxford University Press, 1975) essay III.

    [5] Jonathan Israel, *A Revolution of the Mind: Radical Enlightenment and the Intellectual Origins of Modern Democracy* (Princeton, NJ, Princeton University Press, 2010); John Dunne, *Setting the People Free: The Story of Democracy* (London, Atlantic Books, 2005).

    [6] See P Bobbitt, *The Shield of Achilles* (London, Penguin Books, 2002) ch 17 and 776–77; Susan Marks, *The Riddle of All Constitutions: International Law, Democracy and the Critique of Ideology* (Oxford, Oxford University Press, 2000) 34–36, commenting on the suggestion by Kant in his *Perpetual Peace* that one condition for stable international peace is that each state should have a republican constitution; A Moravcsik, 'The Origins of Human Rights Regimes: Democratic Delegation in Postwar Europe' (2000) *International Organisation* 54.2, 217–52, especially 243–46; AWB Simpson, *Human Rights and the End of Empire: Britain and the Genesis of the European Convention* (Oxford, Oxford University Press, 2001) 560–97, 605–06; Sales, 'Strasbourg Jurisprudence' (n 3) 266–67. The attempt to bolster constitutional arrangements in one state by spreading common constitutional forms to other states is a familiar impulse in history: see eg M Mazower, *Governing the World: The History of an Idea* (London, Allen Lane, 2012) 5–6, 49, 121–26, 188.

    [7] eg between Art 8, the right of respect for private life, and Art 10, the right of freedom of speech.

    [8] For an insightful theoretical analysis of the operation of a common law system, incorporating an element of reflexivity between general social standards and legal doctrine as both change over time, see MA Eisenberg, *The Nature of the Common Law* (Cambridge, MA, Harvard University Press,1988). Aspects of this model can usefully be adopted as a framework for understanding the processes of doctrinal formation by the ECtHR. I touch on this further below.

The Council of Europe has had considerable success, through the ECHR and the ECtHR, and acting alongside the European Union, in stabilising European polities on a liberal democratic model since World War II. The ECtHR has been successful in creating common European standards of public law, which operate as an important guide for and influence upon national legal systems.[9] The ECHR has also come to suffuse EU law by informing what are regarded as fundamental principles underlying the EU treaties; and its influence is getting stronger. Many provisions in the new EU Charter of Fundamental Rights are formulated explicitly by reference to Articles in the ECHR and are to be interpreted in conformity with them; and the EU is preparing to accede to the ECHR as an international organisation, so that it will be directly bound by its terms and subject to the jurisdiction of the ECtHR.

Over time there has been an exponential increase in recourse to the judicial and legal mechanisms available under the ECHR for resolution of disputes at the national level. The ECHR has been transformed – particularly with the spread of the right of individual petition (now a requirement for states acceding to the ECHR) and the routine resort to legal proceedings before the ECtHR – from a statement of values (a sort of liberal democratic creed[10]) to an effective legal underpinning for liberal democracy. By suffusing EU law, ECHR values have also colonised another powerful transnational legal regime with similar effect. Both the ECHR and the increasingly human rights oriented EU have reinforced and provided judicial underpinning for the practical liberal democratic compromise at the heart of European states.

It remains open to question how far this judicialisation of a particular balance between competing political and philosophical traditions may be a reflection of underlying strength of support for this form of polity among contracting states, or rather a reflection of fragility and a desire by certain elites to try to cement such a balance in place while support for it comes under pressure from democratic politics.[11] Ultimately, its stability will require some level of popular and elite support.[12] Such support has previously been strongly bolstered by memories of fascism, active opposition to communism and the material prosperity brought by the EU. But as those memories fade, and with the collapse of communism and a faltering in the EU project with the Eurozone crisis, it is less obvious that it can be maintained without more active engagement at the political level.[13]

Populist democratic politics and ideology always impose pressure on liberal constitutional rights and their application. Precisely because of the abstract formulation of such rights, they

---

[9] H Keller and A Stone Sweet (eds), *A Europe of Rights: The Impact of the ECHR on National Legal Systems* (Oxford, Oxford University Press, 2008).

[10] *cf* Lord Hoffmann, 'The Universality of Human Rights' (2009) 125 *Law Quarterly Review* 416.

[11] *cf* Ran Hirshl, *Towards Juristocracy: The Origins and Consequences of the New Constitutionalism* (Cambridge, MA, Harvard University Press, 2004); Moravcsik, 'The Origins of Human Rights Regimes' (n 6).

[12] *cf* Charles R Epp, *The Rights Revolution: Lawyers, Activists and Supreme Courts in Comparative Perspective* (Chicago, University of Chicago Press, 1998). In 2–5, Epp emphasises the importance for rights regimes of a broad support structure in civil society. See also Keith E Whittington, *Political Foundations of Judicial Supremacy: The Presidency, the Supreme Court and Constitutional Leadership in U.S. History* (Princeton, NJ, Princeton University Press, 2007), emphasising that judicial supremacy rests on political foundations: 'Constitutional maintenance is above all a political task. Constitutions cannot survive if they are too politically costly to maintain, and they cannot survive if they are too distant from normal political concerns' (26). Concern regarding whether there is adequate public support for the ECHR Convention rights as incorporated in the Human Rights Act 1998 infuses the recent report of the Commission on a Bill of Rights, *A UK Bill of Rights? The Choice Before Us*, published on 18 December 2012 (and the various supplementary notes appended by the members of the Commission).

[13] *cf* Müller, *Contesting Democracy* (n 3) 150.

leave considerable discretion to judges at the point of application.[14] Judicial action may therefore have to be legitimated to a large degree by appeal to technical expertise and standards of judgment derived from legal tradition and culture,[15] often in opposition to such democratic pressures. Below the level of the broad statement of rights in an instrument such as the ECHR or the US Constitution, the precise interpretation and articulation of the law follows processes akin to those employed by United Kingdom or US courts in the development of the common law. That is particularly true in the case of the ECHR, because of the absence of a principle of stare decisis[16] and the adoption of the 'living instrument' doctrine[17] rather than a strong notion of original intent such as has come to haunt American legal theory. The ECtHR (and domestic courts acting under the Human Rights Act 1998 to apply Convention rights) have considerable latitude to develop the law of European human rights at the level of legal doctrine.

By reason of the range of application of Convention rights and the standards they impose (which may in this respect be compared with, say, US constitutional rights), they cover far wider areas of public policy and demand more intrusive review of administrative and legislative action than the English common law courts were familiar or comfortable with before the passing of the Human Rights Act. The US Supreme Court, the ECtHR, the Court of Justice of the EU (CJEU) and domestic courts of judicial review (in particular, the United Kingdom's Supreme Court) are constitutional courts, which have a significant role in making or endorsing public policy. They cannot ignore issues of legitimation of their actions.[18] That is especially so because the scope of their power to make or intrude upon policy can bring their actions into acute conflict with democratic ideas of majoritarian rule, which tend to call such legitimation into question. Where the courts have to resolve disputes which may lie close to the heart of political debate and controversy, where the precise content and characterisation of human rights may themselves be part of the controversy, with strong views on both sides, an appeal to the technical expertise of the court in deploying human rights argumentation may provide only a comparatively weak basis to justify the exercise of judicial power.

It has been observed that when operating under these conditions the US Supreme Court tends to follow the election returns in its decision-making over the longer term,[19] demon-

---

[14] *cf* Tom D Campbell, *The Legal Theory of Ethical Positivism* (Aldershot, Dartmouth Publishing, 1996) 163, expressing wariness from a positivist's perspective of any system depending on very general or abstract rights, because their content is unjusticiable by positivist standards. But this may underplay the scope for the creation of self-limiting doctrine by courts operating on a common law model. Compare, for example, F Schauer, 'Precedent' (1989) 39 *Stanford Law Review* 571, 589 (the knowledge that decisions will become precedent is itself a constraint on judges' freedom) and see Eisenberg, *The Nature of the Common Law* (n 8), discussed below.

[15] P Sales, 'Judges and Legislature: Values into Law' (2012) *Cambridge Law Journal* 287.

[16] *Chapman v United Kingdom* (2001) 33 EHRR 18 [70]; see Sales, 'Strasbourg Jurisprudence' (n 3) 261.

[17] *Tyrer v United Kingdom* (1979-1980) 2 EHRR 1 [31]; see Sales 'Strasbourg Jurisprudence' (n 3) 256–57.

[18] D Beetham, *The Legitimation of Power* (Basingstoke, Palgrave, 1991).

[19] M Tushnet, *Taking the Constitution Away from the Courts* (Princeton, NJ, Princeton University Press, 1999) 133–35; Keith E Whittington, *Constitutional Construction: Divided Powers and Constitutional Meaning* (Cambridge, MA, Harvard University Press, 1999); Keith E Whittington, *Political Foundations of Judicial Supremacy: The Presidency, the Supreme Court and Constitutional Leadership in U.S. History* (n 12) (especially 102–03, emphasising that judges are subject to the same public opinion pressures as those affecting elected officials); Tom S Clark, *The Limits of Judicial Independence* (New York, Cambridge University Press, 2011) (especially 3, '. . . the most relevant constraining force on judicial power [of the US Supreme Court] is public support', and 7, 22); Stephen Breyer, *America's Supreme Court: Making Democracy Work* (Oxford, Oxford University Press, 2010); Jack M Balkin, *Constitutional Redemption: Political Faith in an Unjust World* (Cambridge, MA, Harvard University Press, 2011), especially ch 3. Also see John Gray, *False Dawn: The Delusions of Global Capitalism* (London, Granta Books, 2009

strating a concern not to allow any dissonance between its role and democratic resolution of important issues become too great. It is, for example, difficult to avoid the feeling that the crucial opinion of Chief Justice Roberts to uphold the constitutionality of President Obama's controversial health care reforms in *National Federation of Independent Business v Sebelius, Secretary of Health and Human Services*[20] was, underneath the doctrinal debate, motivated in part by a concern that to strike them down as unconstitutional could undermine the legitimacy of the Court's role. This is a stance which is easier for the US Supreme Court to adopt than the ECtHR, CJEU or United Kingdom Supreme Court. The US Court is embedded in a specific national political system while the ECtHR and CJEU are not. The US Court, legislature and the executive have a good and largely common understanding of their respective roles, grounded in their mutual action in carrying on politics together under a settled constitutional scheme. A subtle process of dialogue is possible between the political and judicial organs.

By contrast, the ECtHR and the CJEU stand outside specific national political systems. Focusing on the ECtHR, in a sense it legislates under the auspices of the ECHR for all 47 contracting states in the Council of Europe. It is not feasible for it to engage in a process of dialogue with the legislatures of all those states, which will adopt highly varied policy positions and will reflect the interests and demands of very disparate national populations. The ECtHR has to stand above the fray, in seeking to articulate common standards to be applied across all those states. It is not an active participant in a living, breathing, self-adjusting political system as a national supreme court can be. The situation and role of the CJEU is similar to that of the ECtHR, and it tends to follow the rulings of the ECtHR on human rights (a tendency which may be expected to become more pronounced as the CJEU applies the ECHR-inspired rights contained in the EU Charter of Fundamental Rights and when the EU becomes a party to the ECHR).

Although the United Kingdom Supreme Court is embedded in a set of specific national legal systems, it is in practice in a position closer to that of the ECtHR than to that of the US Supreme Court. Under the Human Rights Act domestic courts apply the Convention rights set out in the ECHR, and in doing so those courts (including the Supreme Court) follow the approach and doctrine laid down in the jurisprudence of the ECtHR.[21]

Where Convention rights apply, the domestic courts are subject to a strong obligation under section 3 of the Human Rights Act to read domestic legislation compatibly with them, wherever possible.[22] When it is not possible, Parliamentary sovereignty governs and the non-compatible legislation remains binding in law, with the court able only to grant a declaration of incompatibility under section 4 of the Act. However, in practice this almost invariably leads to reform of the law through the making of primary or subordinate legislation. So despite the formal position, a declaration of incompatibility is closer in effect to a

---

ed) 109: 'In truth, rights are never the bottom line in moral or political theory – or practice. They are conclusions, end-results of long chains of reasoning from commonly accepted premises. Rights have little authority or content in the absence of a common ethical life. They are conventions that are durable only when they express a moral consensus. When ethical disagreement is deep and wide an appeal to rights cannot resolve it. Indeed, it may make such conflict dangerously unmanageable'.

[20]   US Supreme Court judgment, 28 June 2012.

[21]   *Pinnock v Manchester City Council* [2011] UKSC 6; [2011] 2 AC 104; P Sales and R Ekins, 'Rights-Consistent Interpretation and the Human Rights Act 1998' (2011) 127 *Law Quarterly Review* 217; Sales, 'Strasbourg Jurisprudence' (n 3).

[22]   Sales and Ekins, 'Rights-Consistent Interpretation' (n 21).

power to strike down legislation than is sometimes thought.[23] Similarly, where the ECtHR gives a ruling against the Government, the Government is under an obligation under international law, backed up by diplomatic and enforcement sanctions applied by the Council of Europe and its contracting states, to legislate to change the offending domestic law.[24]

One effect of the position of the ECtHR, located outside any one national legal and political system, is that it seeks to set out at the level of articulated doctrine clear scope for democratic decision-making procedures at the national level to operate and have decisive effect. The ECtHR sets out common ground-rules applicable across Europe of acceptable political practice, sometimes (particularly in relation to requirements of equal treatment of women, racial groups and homosexuals) with strong substantive content, but usually allowing a significant margin of appreciation to contracting states. I discuss this in detail below.

The legal doctrine developed by the ECtHR also represents a reasonably clear choice between different competing conceptions of democracy, a liberal conception and a radical conception.[25] Liberal democratic ideas emphasise the effectiveness of democratic procedures in constraining the exercise of power and domination of the individual and in protecting individual rights. Radical democratic ideas emphasise more the value of self-determination by a homogeneous community. The ECtHR emphasises in its case law that the ECHR is intended to promote a pluralist, tolerant and broadminded democratic society.[26] As examined below, the margin of appreciation is treated as particularly narrow where disadvantaged or marginalised groups are discriminated against. This is all far more compatible with promotion of a liberal conception of democracy. This is unsurprising, given the origins of the ECHR against a background of resistance to fascism and communism.[27] Nonetheless, acceptance of a more communitarian, radical aspect of democracy emerges at points in the ECtHR's case law, in particular when dealing with highly sensitive issues of enforcement of cultural norms, where these do not jeopardise too greatly the primary values of equality and non-discrimination to which the ECtHR tends to give priority.[28] The Court also generally allows a wide margin of appreciation to a state in determining who should be treated as constituting part of the *demos* with a right of participation in democratic procedures.[29] In all cases, the ECtHR emphasises the importance for those recognised as part of the *demos* of their right of

---

[23] ibid 230; Aileen Kavanagh, *Constitutional Review under the UK Human Rights Act* (Cambridge, Cambridge University Press, 2009); also see Adrian Vermeule, 'The Atrophy of Constitutional Powers' (2012) 32 *Oxford Journal of Legal Studies* 421, 441–44.

[24] The only instance of the UK failing to do this is in relation to the decision of the Grand Chamber of the ECtHR on prisoner voting rights in *Hirst v United Kingdom (No 2)* (2006) 42 EHRR 41. But even here, despite strong statements by the Prime Minister, at the time of writing it remains unclear how the situation will be resolved.

[25] Using the typology summarised in D Miller, 'Democracy's Domain' (2009) 37 *Philosophy and Public Affairs* 201.

[26] See eg *Smith and Grady v United Kingdom* (1999) 29 EHRR 493 [87]; *Barabkevich v Russia* (2008) 47 EHRR 8.

[27] See Müller, *Contesting Democracy* (n 3).

[28] See eg *Müller v Switzerland* (1985) 13 EHRR 212; *A, B, C v Ireland* (2011) 53 EHRR 13, GC (Irish law prohibiting abortion found not to be incompatible with the Convention, particularly in view of the wide margin of appreciation to be afforded where a state legislates to enshrine its view on a fundamental moral value: see especially [222]–[233]); *Van de Heljden v Netherlands*, ECtHR, GC, judgment of 3 April 2012 [60] (wide margin of appreciation applies in relation to a topic which raises sensitive moral or ethical issues); *Lautsi v Italy* (2012) 54 EHRR 3, GC (display of the crucifix in Italian schools; see Ian Leigh and Rex Ahdar, 'Post-Secularism and the European Court of Human Rights: Or How God Never Really Went Away' (2012) *Modern Law Review* 1064); *Stubing v Germany* (2012) 55 EHRR 24 (prohibition of incest: state authorities are in the best position to make decisions on moral requirements and the necessity of any restriction to meet them: [59]–[60]).

[29] *Santoro v Italy* (2006) 42 EHRR 38 [54]; *Sevinger and Eman v Netherlands* (2008) 46 EHRR SE14 [15]; see also *Zdanoka v Latvia* (2007) 45 EHRR 17, GC [134]–[135]. It remains to be seen whether the Grand Chamber judgments in *Hirst* (n 24) and *Scoppola v Italy (No 3)*, ECtHR, GC, judgment of 22 May 2012, on prisoner voting rights will lead to a more general narrowing of the margin of appreciation in this area.

participation in democratic procedures, as an aspect of the democratic principles inherent in the ECHR.

In the same way that the doctrine of the margin of appreciation allows for the operation of democratic decision-making procedures in contracting states, it accommodates republican theories of joint deliberation on the common good[30] by allowing space in which decisive priority is given to the decisions which emerge from such deliberation. As with democratic theory, republican theory has its own darker, anti-liberal communitarian aspects[31] and here, also, the strong liberal strain in the ECHR and the case law of the ECtHR operates as a major constraint.

In relation to both democratic and republican theory, the ECHR and the ECtHR address a further major concern regarding the operation of legally enforceable human rights, namely the way in which they can undermine political virtues of compromise and negotiation.[32] There is a danger that, rather than seeking to negotiate and compromise over political issues, interested parties fall back on their claimed rights and seek to find a solution in their favour by litigation instead. Mary Ann Glendon, in her important book *Rights Talk*,[33] identified this concern in relation to the US legal system, while emphasising what is, in her view, the superiority of the formulation of rights in the ECHR, which in most cases allows considerable scope for balancing the public interest against individual interests. The margin of appreciation, which is an inherent part of that balancing framework, reinforces the scope for political negotiated compromise solutions to be recognised and accepted as compatible with Convention rights. However, the concern about the impact of enforceable rights on political culture cannot be wholly discounted in the ECHR system.[34] Some risk of affecting political culture is inevitably inherent in having an enforceable human rights instrument in place – indeed, is, in an important sense, the point of putting such an instrument in place.

III RECOGNITION OF DEMOCRATIC VALUES IN THE DRAFTING OF THE ECHR

In developing detailed human rights doctrine in the way it does, moulding it around respect for democratic values, the ECtHR is responding to clear cues in the text of the ECHR itself. The fourth recital in the Preamble to the Convention refers to the twin requirements of 'an effective political democracy' and 'observance of . . . human rights'.[35]

---

[30] P Pettit, *Republicanism: A Theory of Freedom and Government* (Oxford, Oxford University Press, 1999); Iseult Honohan and Jeremy Jennings, *Republicanism in Theory and Practice* (London, Routledge, 2006); J Waldron, 'Representative Lawmaking' (2009) 89 *Boston University Law Review* 335.

[31] Robert E Goodin, 'Folie Republicaine' (2003) *Annual Review of Political Science* 6:55–76.

[32] See eg Martti Koskenniemi, 'The Effect of Rights on Political Culture' in P Alston (ed), *The EU and Human Rights* (Oxford, Oxford University Press, 1999) ch 3; Waldron, 'Representative Lawmaking' (n 30); Sales, 'Strasbourg Jurisprudence' (n 3) 266; Sales, 'Judges and Legislature' (n 15). This effect is an example of the way in which behaviour may be affected by changing the balance between Exit and Voice in social systems: see the classic study by Albert O Hirschman, *Exit, Voice, and Loyalty: Responses to Decline in Firms, Organizations and States* (Cambridge, MA, Harvard University Press, 1970).

[33] Mary Ann Glendon, *Rights Talk: The Impoverishment of Political Discourse* (New York, The Free Press, 1991).

[34] The effect on political culture extends more widely than creating the possibility of litigation as an alternative to negotiation. An enforceable human rights instrument creates new incentives and disincentives in relation to the way in which consideration may be given to public issues by politicians in the political process: A Stone Sweet, *Governing with Judges: Constitutional Politics in Europe* (Oxford, Oxford University Press, 2000).

[35] See also P Sales, 'The General and the Particular: Parliament and the Courts under the Scheme of the European Convention on Human Rights' in M Andenas and D Fairgrieve (eds), *Tom Bingham and the Transformation of the Law* (Oxford, Oxford University Press, 2009) ch 12, 163–64.

The ECHR protects the democratic process directly – a specific right of participation in democratic life is incorporated into the ECHR through the right to vote in Article 3 of the First Protocol[36] and protection is provided against egregious forms of non-democratic political methods such as arbitrary arrest and imprisonment (Article 5). The ECHR also protects the democratic process by a penumbra of supporting rights related to freedom of speech and association (Articles 10 and 11).

A number of the provisions set out in the ECHR[37] expressly allow for justification of interferences with individual rights where 'necessary in a democratic society'. There is a vast case law on the application of this rubric.

As the ECtHR held in the early landmark case of *Kjeldsen v Denmark*,[38] at [53]: '. . . any interpretation of the rights and freedoms guaranteed [in the Convention] has to be consistent with the general spirit of the Convention, an instrument designed to maintain and promote the ideals and values of a democratic society.' This necessarily requires the courts to accord respect to decision-making by the democratic institutions of the state within their proper sphere.[39]

IV PROMOTION OF DEMOCRATIC VALUES THROUGH DOCTRINAL DEVELOPMENT IN THE CASE LAW OF THE ECTHR

Convention rights other than those which expressly permit derogation, where 'necessary in a democratic society', have been interpreted by the ECtHR to allow for modified application where that is proportionate to some legitimate public interest. Articles 6 and 14 are good examples of this, which I examine below. Protection or promotion of democratic values or the democratic decision-making process can supply important legitimate interests for the purposes of such analysis.

The ECtHR has identified certain general principles as underlying the whole of the Convention. It is unsurprising that they reflect democratic principles and a substantive view of what a democratic society should be. The Court states that the rule of law is a fundamental principle of democratic society, and is inherent in all the Articles of the ECHR.[40] Although some aspects of the rule of law idea are in tension with popular democratic decision-making,[41] the paradigm of the rule of law in a democratic state is that laws duly promulgated under democratic procedures should be properly enforced and capricious decision-making outside such norms avoided.[42]

---

[36] This provision is said to enshrine a characteristic principle of effective political democracy and is therefore to be regarded as of prime importance in the Convention system: *Selim Sadak v Turkey* (2003) 36 EHRR 23 [32]–[33].

[37] Articles 8 to 12.

[38] *Kjeldsen v Denmark* (1979-80) 1 EHRR 711.

[39] See eg *Hatton v United Kingdom* (2003) 37 EHRR 28 [97]: national authorities have direct democratic legitimacy; therefore, in matters of general policy on which opinions in a democratic society may differ widely, the role of the democratic policy-maker should be given special weight.

[40] *Iatridis v Greece* (1999) 30 EHRR 97 [58]; *Ukraine-Tyumen v Ukraine*, ECtHR, judgment of 22 November 2007 [49]; *Stere v Romania* (2007) 45 EHRR 6 [53].

[41] Depending on how substantive a view one takes of the concept of the rule of law: compare eg J Raz, 'The Rule of Law and its Virtue' (1977) 93 *Law Quarterly Review* 195 and Tom Bingham, *The Rule of Law* (London, Allen Lane, 2010) ch 7. See also Raymond Plant, *The Neo-liberal State* (Oxford, Oxford University Press, 2010) for an account, and critique, of substantive conceptions of the rule of law in neo-liberal theory.

[42] It is, for example, a principle which is fundamental to giving effect to decisions regarding what the law should be as enacted by a democratic legislature: see Tom D Campbell, *The Legal Theory of Ethical Positivism* (n 14) 7; J Waldron, *Law and Disagreement* (Oxford, Oxford University Press, 1999) 101–02; J Waldron, 'Can there be a Democratic Jurisprudence?' (2009) 58 *Emory Law Journal* 675; P Sales, 'Three Challenges to the Rule of Law

The ECtHR has also elaborated a substantive conception of 'law' for the purposes of the many provisions of the Convention which deploy the concept, which requires a reasonable degree of specificity and foreseeability in the formulation of the law to be applied in a given case.[43] This is a constraint on how the legislature may behave. But it also functions as a reminder to Parliament how it *should* behave, as a responsible legislature making law.

Another general principle which the ECtHR has identified as underlying the whole of the ECHR is the concept of a fair balance between the rights of the individual and the general interest of the community.[44] The application of Convention rights is informed by this general, rather abstract, background idea. It is an idea which provides scope for weight to be given to the democratic process as the process which often best captures in concrete form in a given setting a considered view of what the general interest of the community might be.[45]

The ECHR has been held to impose important substantive constraints on the form of political organisations and their objectives which will be treated as acceptable. Democracy is the only political model which is compatible with the Convention.[46] Although, in general, extensive toleration is required for political parties and public organisations of all descriptions, it is compatible with the Convention for political parties which advocate the implementation of a non-democratic political order, or which are prepared to use violent means to secure their ends, to be banned.[47] In addition, the ECtHR has specified the sort of democratic society which it regards as envisaged and to be promoted by the ECHR. As referred to above, it is a society which is pluralistic, tolerant and broadminded. This high level specification then informs the detailed interpretation of Convention rights in various contexts, such as the law on discrimination and on the extent to which free speech should be respected under Article 10. Particular importance is attached to protection of freedom of speech under Article 10 on topics of general public and, in particular, political interest, as an essential part of an effective and vibrant democracy.[48] One measure of the weight given by the ECtHR to the right under Article 10 is its extension to protect journalists' sources against disclosure.[49] Legal immunity for Members of Parliament for speech in Parliament is compatible with Article 6, justified by reference to the need to foster free debate in deliberation by the legislature.[50]

in the Modern English Legal System' in Richard Ekins (ed), *Modern Challenges to the Rule of Law* (Wellington, LexisNexis, 2011) ch 10, 190–92.

[43] *Sunday Times v United Kingdom* (1979-80) 2 EHRR 245 [49]; *Grande Oriente v Italy* (2002) 34 EHRR 22; *Colon v Netherlands* (2012) 55 EHRR SE5 [72].

[44] See eg *Sheffield and Horsham v United Kingdom* (1999) 27 EHRR 163 [52].

[45] See eg *Brown v Stott* [2003] 1 AC 681, 704.

[46] *Zdanoka v Latvia* (2007) 45 EHRR 17, GC [98].

[47] *Refah Partisi v Turkey* (2003) 37 EHRR 1, GC; *HADEP v Turkey* (2013) 56 EHRR 5; *Hizb Ut-Tahrir v Germany*, ECtHR, decision of 12 June 2012.

[48] *Bladet Tromsø v Norway* (2000) 29 EHRR 125; *Nilsen and Johnsen v Norway* (2000) 30 EHRR 878; *Tatar and Faber v Hungary*, ECtHR, judgment of 12 June 2012.

[49] *Goodwin v United Kingdom* (1996) 22 EHRR 123; *Tillack v Belgium* (2012) 55 EHRR 25.

[50] *A v United Kingdom* (2003) 36 EHRR 51 [77]; *Kart v Turkey* (2010) 51 EHRR 40, GC, [79]–[114]. However, in applying Article 6, the ECtHR is (unlike a domestic court) willing to question the basis for the immunity and suggests it will be subject to limits. In other areas, too, the ECtHR has adopted an approach unlike a domestic court constrained by notions of parliamentary privilege and Article IX of the Bill of Rights, in which it is willing to examine the quality of debate in the legislature, at least to check that there has been active substantive consideration of the issues at stake, when assessing whether a wide margin of appreciation should be accorded in relation to legislation passed by that body: see *Hirst* (n 24); *Sukhovetskyy v Ukraine* (2007) 44 EHRR 57 [65]–[67] (the ECtHR placing weight on the careful up-to-date scrutiny by the legislature); ; *Friend v United Kingdom* (2010) 50 EHRR SE6, [50]; and *Stubing* (n 28) [65]–[67] (the ECtHR placing weight on the fact that public policy objectives had been expressly endorsed by the democratic legislator). See Sales, 'The General and the Particular' (n 35) 178–80.

The ECHR may thus be seen as an instrument which allows for, and promotes, the idea of a liberal democracy which defends itself against non-democratic and illiberal political tendencies, rather than providing for a purely neutral conception of the role of the state. This is a vision of liberal democracy which, I would suggest, is similar to that advocated by Chantal Mouffe in her political writing.[51] The ECHR, as interpreted by the ECtHR, also operates to promote a strong defence of liberal, pluralistic values, robust public debate and an agonistic form of politics, again in line with the form of liberal democracy advocated by Mouffe.[52]

A further way in which the ECtHR in its case law affords respect for the principle of democracy is negative, in the caution the Court displays before finding the existence of implied positive obligations in Articles of the Convention. Rights become ever harder to stipulate in a manner which commands widespread uncontested support such as a court might feel able to treat as legitimising judicial enforcement the further one moves from a model of negative rights (where rights, such as a right not to be tortured, do not imply a need to ration scarce resources but can be claimed by all rights holders and the corresponding duties can be recognised and acted on by others) to a model which includes positive rights (since the prioritisation or rationing of resources required to meet such positive rights, in preference to other pressing needs, is contestable and tends to undermine the clarity of the link between rights and duties).[53] The ECtHR is conscious of the resource implications which may be inherent in a finding that an implied positive obligation exists in a Convention Article; observes that the knowledge of and decisions as to the allocation of resources are primarily a matter for the national authorities; and seeks to limit positive obligations within narrow parameters which do not involve an unreasonable burden on the state.[54] In this way, the Court seeks to leave issues of resource allocation primarily to state authorities, in line with democratic principle,[55] rather than taking too prominent a role in dictating priorities itself.

Moreover, even where positive obligations may be identified, in areas of sensitivity and political controversy they may lead only to procedural obligations to give active consideration to particular factors, rather than to a substantive outcome stipulated by the Court itself.[56] This is a tactic for reducing what might otherwise be an acute conflict between

---

[51] Chantal Mouffe, 'Carl Schmitt and the Paradox of Liberal Democracy' in Chantal Mouffe (ed), *The Challenge of Carl Schmitt* (London, Verso, 1999) ch 3; Mouffe, *The Return of the Political* (n 1) especially 31–32, 47–48, 65–66, 145–46, 151.

[52] Chantal Mouffe, *The Democratic Paradox* (London, Verso, 2000); Mouffe, *The Return of the Political* (n 1). See also Ian Shapiro, *The Real World of Democratic Theory* (Princeton, New Jersey, Princeton University Press, 2010) 271–72. Shapiro prefers 'competition to deliberation as a mechanism for keeping democracy honest.... Its animating impulse is the robust conflict of ideas about which Mill wrote so eloquently in the second chapter of *On Liberty*.'

[53] See eg the neo-liberal critique of positive rights discussed in Plant, *The Neo-liberal State* (n 41) ch 5.

[54] See eg *Osman v United Kingdom* (2000) 29 EHRR 245 [115]–[116] (positive obligation of protection of life under Article 2); *Özgür Gündem v Turkey* (2001) 31 EHRR 49 [43] (positive obligation to protect freedom of speech against harassment by third parties); and for Article 8, see *Rees v United Kingdom* (1986) 9 EHRR 56 [37]; *Evans v United Kingdom* (2008) 46 EHRR 36 [75]; *Goodwin v United Kingdom* (2002) 35 EHRR 18 [72]; *Botta v Italy* (1998) 26 EHRR 241 [33]–[35]; *Sentges v The Netherlands*, ECtHR, decision of 8 July 2003; and *Draon v France* (2006) 42 EHRR 40, GC, [105]–[108]. For commentary, see M Pitanen, 'Fair and Balanced Positive Obligations – Do They Exist?' (2012) *European Human Rights Law Review* 538.

[55] *cf R (Alconbury Developments Ltd) v Secretary of State for the Environment, Transport and the Regions* [2001] UKHL 23, [2003] 2 AC 295 [71] (Lord Hoffmann).

[56] See eg *Hatton* (n 39); *Draon* (n 54); *Novoseletskiy v Ukraine* (2006) 43 EHRR 53; *Evans v United Kingdom* (2008) 46 EHRR 34; and *Giacomelli v Italy* (2007) 45 EHRR 38 [80]–[84]; *cf W v United Kingdom* (1987) 10 EHRR 29 (right of participation of parent in relation to complex decision concerning access to their child in care). For a discussion of the interaction between democratic theory and court enforcement of procedural protections and substantive outcomes, with reference to experience in the USA, see Martin Shapiro, *Who Guards the Guardians? Judicial Control of Administration* (Athens, GA, University of Georgia Press, 1988) ch 1.

judicial decision-making and democratic principle and expectations which is familiar from contexts in which courts have to rule upon fundamental constitutional solidarity rights/ rights to welfare,[57] and with which the CJEU and domestic courts are likely to become increasingly familiar as they grapple with the new justiciable solidarity rights in the EU Charter of Fundamental Rights. The sister convention of the ECHR, the European Social Charter (1961), has had a markedly lesser impact on contracting states than the ECHR, which reflects both institutional factors (there is no court to develop doctrine) but also the greater pressure which implementation of such rights faces against the prevailing head-wind and force of democratic theory. Indeed, it may be argued that the success, by comparison, of the ECHR in becoming a bedrock of a common European public law has depended in large part on the ability of the ECtHR to develop doctrine which provides a broadly acceptable accommodation of democratic theory.

V EQUALITY: ARTICLE 14 (RIGHT AGAINST DISCRIMINATION)

Protection against discrimination is itself an interest in line with democratic theory, since the idea of one person, one vote has built into it an idea of equality of respect. Protection against discrimination, particularly on grounds of race, sex or sexual orientation, also reflects powerful currents in the liberal tradition. In line with this, the ECtHR's case law emphasises the narrow scope for differential treatment based on distinctions of certain suspect personal characteristics such as race,[58] sex[59] or sexual orientation.[60]

Article 14 will not be violated where a state accords differential treatment to people with different characteristics, though in a comparable situation, when it acts in a way proportionate to a legitimate public interest.[61] The margin of appreciation allowed is central to the assessment of proportionality. Even in relation to cases of differential treatment within the suspect categories, other factors may apply to broaden the margin of appreciation allowed to the contracting state. A leading judgment in this area is *Stec v United Kingdom*,[62] in which the Grand Chamber said this at [51]–[52]:

> 51. Article 14 does not prohibit a Member State from treating groups differently in order to correct 'factual inequalities' between them; indeed in certain circumstances a failure to attempt to correct inequality through different treatment may in itself give rise to a breach of the Article. A difference of treatment is, however, discriminatory if it has no objective and reasonable justification; in other words, if it does not pursue a legitimate aim or if there is not a reasonable relationship of proportionality between the means employed and the aim sought to be realised. The Contracting State enjoys a margin of appreciation in assessing whether and to what extent differences in otherwise similar situations justify a different treatment.
>
> 52. The scope of this margin will vary according to the circumstances, the subject-matter and the background. As a general rule, very weighty reasons would have to be put forward before the

---

[57] Malcolm Langford, *Social Rights Jurisprudence: Emerging Trends in International and Comparative Law* (Cambridge, Cambridge University Press, 2008); Sandra Fredman, 'New Horizons: Incorporating Socio-economic Rights in a British Bill of Rights' [2010] *Public Law* 297; C Gearty and V Mantouvalou, *Debating Social Rights* (Oxford, Hart Publishing, 2010).
[58] *DH v Czech Republic* (2008) 47 EHRR 3, GC.
[59] *Wessels-Bergervoet v Netherlands* (2004) 38 EHRR 37 [49].
[60] *EB v France* (2008) 47 EHRR 21 [91]; *Kozak v Poland* (2010) 51 EHRR 16 [92] and [99].
[61] *Belgian Linguistics Case (No 2)* (1968) 1 EHRR 252, 284; *Lithgow v United Kingdom* (1986) 8 EHRR 329.
[62] *Stec v United Kingdom* (2006) 43 EHRR 47.

Court could regard a difference in treatment based exclusively on the ground of sex as compatible with the Convention. On the other hand, a wide margin is usually allowed to the State under the Convention when it comes to general measures of economic or social strategy. Because of their direct knowledge of their society and its needs, the national authorities are in principle better placed than the international judge to appreciate what is in the public interest on social or economic grounds, and the Court will generally respect the legislature's policy choice unless it is 'manifestly without reasonable foundation'.

It is implicit in this that tax and social welfare spending decisions are regarded as matters particularly suitable for, and legitimated by, democratic decision-making procedures. In a taxation context, the Strasbourg case law confirms that the authorities enjoy a wide margin of appreciation.[63] Distribution pursuant to social welfare budgets depends on funds raised by taxation. The idea of no taxation without representation (and the related venerable principle of 'What touches all is to be approved by all',[64] as applied in modern conditions) implies that tax and major spending decisions should be made primarily according to democratic procedures.

VI THE MARGIN OF APPRECIATION

As is apparent from the discussion of the terrain of democracy and human rights above, the margin of appreciation is the most important of the mechanisms by which the ECtHR provides in fine detail for the accommodation of liberal human rights thinking and democratic ideology. It is a flexible adjustment mechanism, highly attuned to questions of legitimation. The width of the margin of appreciation narrows or expands depending on the strength of the individual interests at stake and the force of countervailing collective interests, as illustrated by the passage from the merits judgment in *Stec v United Kingdom* set out above.

The margin of appreciation is a doctrine of considerable sensitivity, which gives scope for the ECtHR (and domestic courts following the case law of the ECtHR) to allow space for national democratic decision-making to operate and be recognised. In this way it functions as a sort of pressure valve for the democratic forces referred to above, of a kind not otherwise available to the ECtHR as an extra-national court (unlike, say, the ability of the US Supreme Court to adjust doctrine over time to perceived public opinion within the single polity of which it is a part). At the same time, the flexibility inherent in the doctrine allows the ECtHR to adjust the intensity of supervision by reference to common European standards articulated by the Court, depending on its perception of the value of the individual rights at stake and the importance of uniform enforcement of such standards. It is not an exaggeration to say that in very many cases the critical part of the Court's analysis for deciding whether a measure infringes or is compatible with Convention rights is the part directed to deciding whether the margin of appreciation to be applied should be wide or narrow.

---

[63] See eg *National Federation of Self-Employed v United Kingdom* (App 7995/77) 15 DR 198; *National and Provincial Building Society* (1998) 25 EHRR 127 [79]–[80]; *Burden v United Kingdom* (2007) 44 EHRR 51 [54] and [60] (the case went on to the Grand Chamber – (2008) 47 EHRR 38 – which analysed it differently and did not have to address this issue).

[64] *Quod omnes tangit, ab omnibus approbari debet* or *quod omnes similiter tangit, ab omnibus comprobetur* (Justinian, C.5, 59, 5§2): see eg Brian Tierney, *Religion, Law and the Growth of Constitutional Thought 1150–1650* (Cambridge, Cambridge University Press, 1982).

From one perspective – the perspective of international law – the margin of appreciation balances the sovereignty of contracting states with their obligations under the ECHR.[65] But this perspective is increasingly being replaced by (or subsumed within) a view-point more internal to the constitutional position within contracting states, one based more explicitly on recognition of the importance of democracy (and hence of the importance of legislative and, to some degree, executive choice) within the Convention system. Understandably, in light of the position from which national courts operate the Convention rights, it is this latter perspective which has become the primary framework for domestic courts.[66] But it has also assumed far greater prominence in the case law of the ECtHR as well, reflecting the Court's increasing engagement with the detailed constitutional position within states as it examines the precise facts of particular cases before it in order to arrive at an acceptable balance of individual and public interests. The margin of appreciation will generally be found to be wide where the Court is examining a choice made by a democratically elected legislature in relation to a topic which is the subject of public debate and one on which opinions may reasonably differ in a democracy.[67] Similarly, where compliance with a Convention right depends on a balance being struck by the national authorities by reference to some consideration of the public interest, the ECtHR will often give particular weight to their view because they are best placed to assess and respond to the needs of society.[68] This is an approach which naturally gains force when looking at a decision made by a democratic, representative legislature. Commentators likewise emphasise the importance of democratic legitimacy as a factor which tends to widen the margin of appreciation to be allowed in respect of action by a contracting state.[69]

The way in which the margin of appreciation is applied by the Court creates an incentive for democratic institutions within a state actively to foster debate and consultation about complex or sensitive issues before arriving at a decision in relation to them; that is to say, an incentive actually to engage in the careful deliberative process which in theory is at the heart of the democratic enterprise. The ECtHR gives significant weight, in assessing the width of the margin of appreciation to be allowed, to careful efforts by national authorities to engage in public consultation on such issues.[70] The fact that an issue has been the subject of substantial public debate in the legislature and society similarly operates to expand the

---

[65] Ronald St J Macdonald, 'The Margin of Appreciation' in Ronald St J Macdonald, Franz Matscher and Herbert Petzold (eds), *The European System for the Protection of Human Rights* (Dordrecht, Martinus Nijhoff, 1993) 83.

[66] See eg *SRM Global Fund LLP v Commissioners of HM Treasury* [2009] EWCA 788, especially [57]–[59] and [73]–[78]; *AXA General Insurance Ltd v HM Advocate* [2011] UKSC 46, [2012] 1 AC 868; *R (S and KF) v Secretary of State for Justice* [2012] EWHC 1810 (Admin) [50]–[71]. *cf* Martti Koskenniemi, 'What Use for Sovereignty Today?' (2011) 1 *Asian Journal of International Law* 61, emphasising the current importance of the concept of sovereignty as a vessel for ideas of self-government and national autonomy.

[67] *Hatton* (n 39) [97]; *Draon* (n 54) [106]–[108].

[68] See eg *Schalk and Kopf v Austria* (2011) 53 EHRR 20, concerning complaints under Arts 8, 12 and 14 and Art 1 of the First Protocol regarding the failure of Austria to permit a same sex couple to marry (as distinct from entering into an officially recognised same sex partnership). The ECtHR held that Austrian law, protecting the traditional institution of the family, fell within Austria's margin of appreciation, with particular weight being given to the view of the national authorities because they are 'best placed to assess and respond to the needs of society' ([62]). See also *Catholic Care (Diocese of Leeds) v Charity Commission* [2012] UKUT 395 (TCC) [46].

[69] For a recent careful analysis of the concept of the margin of appreciation, see Andrew Legg, *The Margin of Appreciation in International Human Rights Law: Deference and Proportionality* (Oxford, Oxford University Press, 2012), especially ch 4 entitled 'Democracy and Participation'.

[70] See eg *Evans* (n 56) (consultation on legal regulation of IVF fertility treatment); *Animal Defenders International v United Kingdom*, GC, judgment of 22 April 2013 [108] and [114]–[116] (extensive and careful consultation on and review of restrictions on paid political advertising on television, including with express reference to relevant Convention rights).

width of the margin of appreciation.[71] Conversely, the margin of appreciation allowed will be reduced where a legislature has automatically, without careful consideration, enacted or re-enacted a law.[72] In order to operate this distinction of principle, the ECtHR is willing to examine the quality of debate in the legislature, at least to check that there has been active substantive consideration of the issues at stake, when assessing whether a wide margin of appreciation should be accorded in relation to legislation passed by that body.[73] If respect is to be accorded to the judgment made by a body other than the Court (eg a national legislature), the Court displays an increasingly evident desire to take into account the quality of consideration given to the issues by that body.[74] It may be a significant factor tending to widen the ambit of the margin of appreciation to be applied if the domestic authorities identify the conflicting rights and the need to ensure a fair balance between them (in particular when endorsed by a decision of national courts taken in the light of principles drawn from the ECtHR's established case law).[75] The ECtHR appears in this way to be in the course of creating a significant incentive for national authorities to give active and careful consideration to the complex or sensitive issues which may underlie legislative decisions affecting individuals' Convention rights, ie to operate the democratic process in a manner which democratic theory requires. Governments should foster public debate and legislatures should use their capacity to deliberate on issues, in order to secure an expansion of the margin of appreciation to be accorded to them. In a sense, they should use their powers of deliberation on the public interest so as to avoid the ECtHR stepping in to impose solutions of its own, and to reduce the risk of losing their own power to take an effective decision which cannot be impugned. In this indirect way, the case law of the ECtHR promotes an active democratic process.

The ECtHR seeks to articulate common European standards governing the parameters within which national authorities (in particular, national legislatures) may operate. Over time it has spelled out a range of factors which tend to increase the width of the margin of appreciation (and hence the space within which priority will be given to decisions taken by national democratic institutions) and, conversely, a range of factors which tend to narrow the margin of appreciation (and hence which expand the area within which the Court considers it will be legitimate for it to intervene).

Factors which increase the width of the margin include the sensitivity and complexity of the area governed by legislation,[76] where it relates to matters of social and economic

---

[71] *Hatton* (n 39); *Draon* (n 54); *Animal Defenders International* (n 70).

[72] This is an important strand of the reasoning of the ECtHR in *Hirst* (n 24) by which the Court concluded that the UK's exclusionary rules on prisoner voting rights violated the Convention (and the failure of the Government to bring forward amending legislation in the following five years led the ECtHR to lay down a timetable for introduction of amending legislation in *Greens and MT v United Kingdom* (2011) 53 EHRR 21: see [97] and [103]–[122]); and see *Goodwin* (n 54) [92]–[93] (failure by government and legislature to address the up-to-date position of trans-sexual persons resulted in the Government no longer being able to claim that differential treatment of such persons fell within the margin of appreciation, in contrast to previous cases) and *Lindheim v Norway*, judgment of 12 June 2012, [128]–[135] (the absence of specific assessment by the legislature whether leasehold reform legislation achieved a fair balance between lessors and lessees was a factor which tended to narrow the margin of appreciation, resulting in a finding of violation of Art 1 of Protocol 1).

[73] See *Hirst* (n 24); *Sukhovetskyy* (n 50) [65]–[67] (the ECtHR placing weight on the careful up-to-date scrutiny by the legislature); *Dickson v United Kingdom* (2008) 46 EHRR 41, GC, [79]–[83]; *Friend v United Kingdom* (n 50) [50]; *Stubing* (n 28); and *Animal Defenders International* (n 70) [108].

[74] See the review of the position in *Aksu v Turkey* (2013) 56 EHRR 4, GC, [62]–[67], and in *Animal Defenders International v United Kingdom* (n 70), [108] and [114]–[116]; also see Sales, "The General and the Particular" (n 35), 178-180.

[75] *Aksu* (n 74) [66]–[67]; *Animal Defenders International* (n 70) [114]–[116].

[76] *Odievre v France* (2004) 38 EHRR 43 [47]–[49].

policy,[77] where it is an area of general policy in relation to which opinions may reasonably differ in a democracy,[78] where the case raises sensitive moral or ethical issues,[79] where the legal approach calls for a balancing of interests and rights (including, in particular, Convention rights)[80] – particularly where the domestic authorities have identified the conflicting rights and the need to ensure a fair balance between them[81] – and the absence of a clear common approach across members of the Council of Europe.[82] Conversely, the existence of a common approach across Member States[83] or identified common international standards[84] may have the effect of narrowing the margin of appreciation.[85]

It is at this point that it is apposite to expand upon the idea that the ECtHR, through doctrinal development in its case law, has created a common law system of human rights in Europe. There is a strong parallel between the model of common law adjudication explained by Melvin Eisenberg in his book, *The Nature of the Common Law*,[86] and doctrinal development by the ECtHR, particularly in relation to its approach to the width of the margin of appreciation (which, in light of the 'living instrument' doctrine, may vary over time, much as common law rules may do, as the general European or international social context changes[87]). Consensus in the practice of European states or widely accepted norms of international law are forms of what Eisenberg calls 'social propositions'[88] (a sort of communal morality or set of expectations at state level) which figure in determining the rules which common law courts establish and how they are extended, restricted and applied. In the Convention system, as in a common law system, the law consists of the rules that would

---

[77] *James v United Kingdom* (1986) 8 EHRR 123 [46].

[78] *Hatton* (n 39) [97].

[79] *Van de Heljden* (n 28) [59]–[60].

[80] *Odievre* (n 76); *Evans* (n 56) [77]; *Dickson* (n 73) [77]–[79].

[81] *Aksu* (n 74) [66]–[67].

[82] *Rasmussen v Denmark* (1984) 7 EHRR 371 [40]–[41]; *Petrovic v Austria* (2001) 33 EHRR 14 [38]; *Odievre* (n 76); *Evans* (n 56); *cf A, B, C* (n 28) where common standards regarding abortion in other European states tended to narrow the margin of appreciation, but were not decisive because other factors tended to widen it: [222]–[238].

[83] *Kiyutin v Russia* (2011) 53 EHRR 26.

[84] When interpreting concepts in the ECHR, such as the meaning of degrading treatment in Art 3, as in *Tyrer* (n 17), or the meaning of the right to life in Art 2, as in *Vo v France* (2005) 40 EHRR 12, GC, [82], the ECtHR looks to identify whether there is any consensus in the domestic law or practice of Member States or any relevant development or trend in relevant international instruments which might supply an appropriate standard for judgment regarding the current meaning to be given to the rather open-ended Articles of the ECHR: see also *Marckx v Belgium* (1979-80) 2 EHRR 330[41]; *Goodwin* (n 54) [74] and [84]–[85]; *Bayatyan v Armenia* (2012) 54 EHRR 15,GC, [101]–[109]. Other examples of international instruments informing the interpretation of the ECHR include the UN Convention on the Rights of the Child (see *In re E (Children) (Abduction: Custody Appeal)* [2011] UKSC 27, [2011] 2 WLR 1326 [26]) and the Hague Convention on the Civil Aspects of International Child Abduction (see *Ignaccolo-Zenide v Romania* (2001) 31 EHRR 7 [102]–[103]). Further, when assessing the width of the margin of appreciation to be accorded to state authorities in a range of contexts, the identification of common European standards or a clear approach to the issue in other international instruments is a relevant factor as tending to narrow the margin of appreciation (or, if there is no consensus, as tending to widen it): see eg *Goodwin* (n 54); *Bayatyan v Armenia*; *Rasmussen v Denmark* (n 82); *Genovese v Malta*, ECtHR, judgment of 11 October 2011, [44]. The ECtHR will refer to international instruments even if not ratified by the respondent state, if they provide good evidence that there is common ground among modern societies: *Demir v Turkey* (2009) 48 EHRR 54 [65]ff.

[85] And see the examination of the topic in Legg, *The Margin of Appreciation in International Human Rights Law* (n 69).

[86] Eisenberg, *The Nature of the Common Law* (n 8). Grégoire Webber, for example, emphasises that because the abstract statement of rights under-determines their actual application, with time 'subjects and officials will look not to the bill of rights, but to the corpus of legal decisions to evaluate the lawfulness of disputed claims of rights': Grégoire Webber, 'Rights and the Rule of Law in the Balance' (2013) 129 *Law Quarterly Review* 399, 416–17.

[87] For a good example, see the history of narrowing of the margin of appreciation in relation to the treatment of transgendered individuals, eventually leading to a finding of violation of the Convention in *Goodwin* (n 54).

[88] ibid ch 4.

be generated at the present moment by application of the institutional principles that govern adjudication by the courts: doctrinal propositions are consistently applied and extended if they are substantially congruent with relevant social propositions, but may fall to be modified if they are not. As in a common law system, the ECtHR's function is to resolve disputes fairly by reference to articulated standards and to enrich the supply of legal rules in a manner which provides reasonable guidance to individuals, states and their legal advisers for the future.[89] Like a common law court, the ECtHR strives in its case law 'to satisfy three standards: social congruence, systemic consistency and doctrinal stability'.[90] Like the common law, the Convention legal system is comprehensive – it is founded on broad principles and can generate a legal answer to every question.[91] The ECtHR is acutely aware that it is not a representative or democratically accountable body, and so, like a common law court, accepts that 'The legitimacy of the judicial establishment of legal rules therefore depends in large part on the employment of a process of reasoning that begins with existing legal and social standards rather than those standards the court thinks best'.[92]

As referred to above, it is a general feature of the law laid down by the ECtHR (as with domestic public law) that the Court is alive to areas of particular political controversy and sensitivity and in those areas tends to shift from dictating substantive answers to the issues in question towards judging by reference to procedural standards designed to ensure the quality of debate within political institutions. An adverse ruling then tends to take the form, 'There was insufficient consideration to allow this result to stand', rather than the form, 'This result is inherently incompatible with Convention rights'. This is a move available to the ECtHR and domestic courts, additional to adjustment of the width of the margin of appreciation, to soften the conflict between decision-making by judges and decision-making by democratically accountable institutions.

If the ECtHR and domestic courts do retreat in this way, in more sensitive and complex areas, into a focus on procedural protection and the opportunity to participate in the decision-making process, rather than an insistence on determining substantive outcomes in such areas, it is possible that this may be combined in future with a more demanding standard of decision-making by national authorities, involving explicit reference to the Convention rights or interests in issue. This would represent a potentially significant shift in approach, away from the position arrived at after due consideration by the domestic courts.[93] It is also a shift which, I suggest, could impose too high a cost in terms of undermining existing normal patterns of political debate, negotiation and compromise in a democratic polity.

A more attractive alternative, which could be adopted at less cost to those practices, might be for the ECtHR to create an incentive for national authorities to structure their reasoning directly by reference to Convention rights (but in a way falling short of actually requiring them to do this), by widening the margin of appreciation which would be allowed to them when they do. The Court does seem to be moving towards this sort of approach in its recent case law.[94] If this approach takes root and is broadened into a general principle, it

---

[89]   ibid 4 and chs 2 and 3.

[90]   ibid 50.

[91]   ibid 159.

[92]   ibid 150. Reasoning by reference to such standards means they have power as a source of law independent of democratic legislative authority: see Sales, 'Judges and Legislature' (n 15).

[93]   *R (SB) v Denbigh High School* [2006] UKHL 15, [2007] 1 AC 100; *Belfast City Council v Miss Behavin' Ltd* [2007] UKHL 19, [2007] 1 WLR 1420; *R (S and KF)* (n 66) [72]–[73].

[94]   See in particular *Aksu* (n 74) [62]–[67].

might be an avenue whereby in future the ECtHR can foster a deeper penetration of respect for Convention rights within national legislatures, enhancing the incentives which already exist for politicians and legislatures to try to mimic court-type reasoning around fundamental rights when taking legislative decisions of their own.[95]

VII ARTICLE 6 (RIGHT OF ACCESS TO COURT) AND ADMINISTRATIVE LAW

Although the whole of the ECHR is infused with the tension between democratic and human rights thinking, or the tension between mechanisms of political decision-making/accountability and judicial decision-making, the tension comes into the foreground in the area of application of the civil limb of Article 6 (right to determination of 'civil rights' by an independent and impartial tribunal) to administrative decision-making.[96] Here, the legal doctrine developed by the ECtHR addresses in the context of the fine detail of administrative law an important aspect – the aspect of control of government and the executive – of the fundamental question, 'How far can judicial review go before it trespasses on the proper function of government and the legislature in a democracy?'[97] When is the ECHR to be taken to require administrative decisions to be taken by judges (independent and impartial tribunals), and when are they properly left for decision by organs subject to accountability through political processes? The courts have had to address afresh, this time through the lens of the ECHR, that 'segment of politics that concerns the relationship between administrative agencies and the courts that review them'.[98] Once again, a practical and concrete accommodation between human rights and democratic values is found in the approach towards which the courts applying the ECHR have moved over time.

The ECtHR, drawing on the civilian legal tradition, divides the legal field into criminal law, civil rights (broadly, private law rights) and public law. The third of these categories falls outside the scope of Article 6, and its requirement of determination by an independent and impartial tribunal.[99] At first, therefore, it seemed that in the field of Article 6, space would be preserved for decision-making by administrative and executive authorities, subject to political accountability and unaffected by significant judicial intrusion, by virtue of its non-application to decisions taken by such authorities under public law.

However, this basic picture was undermined by two developments. First, in cases where an administrative decision would in practice be determinative of the existence of or an ability to exercise private law rights, the ECtHR held that Article 6 did apply to govern the situation. An individual affected by such a decision is entitled to a determination of his

---

[95] See Stone Sweet, *Governing with Judges* (n 34) 140 ('In constitutional politics . . . actors can pursue their interests only through normative argument, and effective normative arguments can only be fashioned by reasoning through rule structures . . . interests are constantly reconstituted as legal discourse . . .'; under such politics a constitutional court will expect legislators to reason through the constitutional norms as the court does, so techniques of constitutional adjudication tend to diffuse: 'In the end, governing with judges also means governing like judges', 204); *cf* Sales, 'Strasbourg Jurisprudence' (n 3) 266.

[96] P Sales, 'The Civil Limb of ECHR, Article 6' [2005] *Judicial Review* 52.

[97] See Jonathan Sumption QC, 'Judicial and Political Decision-Making: The Uncertain Boundary' [2011] *Judicial Review* 301, 301.

[98] To use the words of Martin Shapiro, *Who Guards the Guardians?* (n 56) ix.

[99] See eg *Maaouia v France* (2001) 33 EHRR 42, GC, no application of Art 6 to deportation decision; *Ferrazzini v Italy* (2002) 34 EHRR 45, no application to tax proceedings; *Hirst v United Kingdom* (2003) 37 EHRR CD176, no application to claim for prisoners' voting rights; *Ramsahai v Netherlands* (2008) 46 EHRR 43, GC, [359]–[360], no application to decision whether to prosecute; and see *R (BB) v Special Immigration Appeals Commission* [2012] EWCA Civ 1499, [2013] 1 WLR 1568.

rights by an independent and impartial tribunal.[100] The second development was the expansion of the concept of 'civil rights' to encompass rights to benefits under public law social welfare schemes, provided they are stipulated in sufficiently concrete and definitive terms in the scheme itself.[101]

But it was quickly perceived that these extensions of Article 6, with the effect that relevant decisions should be taken by independent courts, could jeopardise established and well-recognised patterns of administrative decision-making and mechanisms of democratically grounded political accountability. As observed by Lord Bingham in one of the leading domestic authorities,[102] an expansive approach to the application of Article 6 in relation to administrative decisions has necessitated an adaptation of the ostensible unrestricted right to determination by a court, so as to avoid the over-judicialisation of administrative decision-making.

As regards the first development, the courts have spelled out a modification of the application of Article 6 in relation to administrative decisions, by contrast to its application in relation to the determination of private law rights between individuals. The requirement of determination by a court in the case of administrative decisions will be restricted to ensuring that the administrative authority has followed a fair procedure and has reached a decision which cannot be impugned as unreasonable (even if the court might not have come to that conclusion itself).[103] This is a composite approach to satisfaction of the requirements of Article 6: fair and reasonable decision-making by an administrative authority (which is part of, not independent of, the executive) combined with availability of judicial review before an independent court to ensure that the administrative authority has so acted. In this context, therefore, Article 6 requires review for compliance by the administrative authority with the rule of law, rather than that the court itself should take the critical decision of what should be done in the circumstances of the case. If the law provides for the administrative authority to have discretion in deciding how to proceed, the requirements of Article 6 will be satisfied provided the individual has an opportunity to challenge that authority's decision for compliance with the relevant legal standards. Hence, where an administrative decision determinative of some 'civil right' has been taken in a 'specialised area of law',[104] by an administrative authority which has adopted a procedure which is itself fair and where its conclusion is reasonable according to the ordinary standards of (domestic) judicial review, and there is the opportunity for the affected individual to apply to court for review by the court that these standards have been complied with, Article 6 will be satisfied.

---

[100] The important case for the inception of this development was *Ringeisen v Austria* (1971) 1 EHRR 455, in which Art 6 was held to apply in relation to a decision by a public authority whether to approve and render enforceable a contract for the sale of land.

[101] See eg *Salesi v Italy* (1998) 26 EHRR 187; *Menotti v Italy* (2002) 34 EHRR 48; *Stec v United Kingdom* (2005) 41 EHRR SE18, GC, admissibility decision, [47]–[48]; *Tsfayo v United Kingdom* (2009) 48 EHRR 18.

[102] *Runa Begum v Tower Hamlets LBC* [2003] UKHL 5, [2003] 2 AC 430 [5].

[103] See, in particular, *Bryan v United Kingdom* (1995) 21 EHRR 342; the very full analysis of the Strasbourg authorities in *R (Alconbury Developments Ltd) v Secretary of State for the Environment, Transport and the Regions* (n 55); *Runa Begum* (n 102); and *Tsfayo* (n 101). A complete absence of review by a court, even if only to check whether a decision of an expert regulatory authority is rational, will not be compatible with Art 6: *Capital Bank v Bulgaria* (2007) 44 EHRR 48.

[104] See *Bryan* (n 103) [47]; *Alatulkkila v Finland* (2006) 43 EHRR 34 [52]; also *Kingsley v United Kingdom* (2002) 35 EHRR 10, GC, [32] (approving [52]–[54] in the judgment of the Chamber); *cf* the arrival at a similar composite type approach in the USA in the period following the New Deal era: Shapiro, *Who Guards the Guardians?* (n 56) ch 2.

In relation to the second development, the ECtHR has been astute in limiting the concept of 'civil rights' in state welfare schemes to situations in which the right to public assistance is closely analogous to private law rights, such as under a contract, where an insistence on decisions by an independent court rather than an administrative authority appears to be fully legitimate in view of the importance for the individual of the right in question and the nature of the decision on which the existence or exercise of that right depends. So, for example, if receipt of some important welfare benefit depends upon findings of fact whether a particular factual condition stipulated in legislation has been satisfied, Article 6 will require a decision on that issue by an independent and impartial tribunal – the more limited form of Article 6 judicial review under the approach mapped out in *Bryan v United Kingdom* and *Alconbury* will not be acceptable.[105] However, there will usually not be determination of a 'civil right' if the administrative authorities taking the decision in question exercise a discretion.[106] This approach limits the scope for judicial interference with administrative decisions under the rubric of Article 6.

The law governing the situations in which the composite approach to satisfaction of Article 6 reviewed in *Alconbury* will be accepted is still in a state of development. In particular, the notion of a 'specialised area of law' – which is the phrase used in the Strasbourg authorities to describe the context in which the composite approach may be applied – does not provide helpful, concrete guidance. There are many specialised areas of law, and they are often applicable to govern the relationship between individuals in the field of private law in which Article 6 will require determination of disputes by an independent court without permitting application of the composite approach. I suggest that a clearer and more principled approach would involve marrying another aspect of the Article 6 jurisprudence (concerning right of access to a court) with more explicit reference to factors which may justify limiting the intrusion of judicial decision-making in particular areas, including in particular the importance of preserving political accountability in a democracy to secure democratic legitimacy for decisions, the ability of government to take account of a wider range of considerations and points of view (than a court in a two-party legal dispute) to fashion general measures for the common good[107] and the exercise of special areas of expertise within government and the executive.[108]

From an early stage the ECtHR identified within Article 6 an implied right of access to an independent court, which could however be subject to limits and restrictions if they were objectively justified.[109] A standard formulation has been developed to express the governing principle here: a limitation on the right of access to a court must not restrict or

---

[105] *Tsfayo* (n 101); *cf* the warning by Lord Hope against the threat of over-judicialisation of administrative welfare schemes in *Ali v Birmingham City Council* [2010] UKSC 8, [2010] AC 39 [55]. There is a problematic boundary between the two classes of case, where factual findings may be relevant to inform some discretionary decision. Where the factual issues cannot readily be separated from the need for an overall discretionary decision to be taken, it seems that the *Bryan/Alconbury* composite approach to satisfaction of Art 6 will apply: *Runa Begum* (n 102) [9] (Lord Bingham).

[106] See eg the recent statement of the position in *Boulois v Luxembourg* (2012) 55 EHRR 32 [90]–[94]: decisions about prison leave are discretionary and do not involve determination of a 'civil right'. Also see *Ladbrokes v Sweden* (2008) 47 EHRR SE10 (no 'civil right' to a gaming licence where the grant depends on wide discretion of the regulatory authorities rather than certain criteria capable of examination by a court).

[107] The problem of decision-making in a polycentric environment, as described by Lon Fuller in his essay, 'The Forms and Limits of Adjudication', re-printed in Kenneth I Winston, *The Principles of Social Order: Selected Essays of Lon. L Fuller* (revised edition, Oxford, Hart Publishing, 2001) 101–40.

[108] *cf Secretary of State for the Home Department v Rehman* [2003] 1 AC 153 [49]–[58] and [62] (Lord Hoffmann).

[109] *Golder v United Kingdom* (1975) 1 EHRR 524.

reduce access to a court so as to impair the essence of the right; any limitation must pursue a legitimate aim and be proportionate to that legitimate aim.[110] The *Alconbury* type of composite satisfaction of Article 6 can be elegantly integrated with this principle. Where a state provides only *Wednesbury*-style judicial review as a basis of challenge in relation to administrative decision-making, the limit upon an affected individual being able to appeal to the court to substitute its view on the merits and so determine the dispute between him and the administrative decision-making authority can be regarded as a form of restriction upon access to a court. Rather than being able to ask the court to determine the merits of the dispute between the individual and an administrative authority, the individual is only able to ask the court to determine whether he has been treated fairly and whether the administrative authority has acted lawfully and reached a rational conclusion.

Integrating the *Alconbury* type composite approach with the principle governing restrictions on access to a court would create a clearer scheme within which justification for application of such a composite approach could be offered and assessed. The 'specialised areas of law' in which the composite approach is regarded as acceptable are those in which there is some legitimate aim to be advanced in restricting intervention by a court to *Wednesbury*-style judicial review. The requirement that the administrative authority should follow a fair procedure is an aspect of ensuring that the restriction on access to decision-making by a court is kept within proportionate limits: if the administrative authority has not acted fairly in assessing the facts and making its decision, the justification for limiting review by the court is undermined. It would also be possible to articulate a sliding scale of intensity of review required, depending on the nature of the administrative decision and the strength of the justification for the administrative authority to decide without interference by a court.[111]

The domestic courts do offer explanations for the application of the *Alconbury* type composite approach which conform to this model and offer scope for further, more explicit development along these lines. For example, in *Runa Begum* Lord Hoffmann said that compliance with Article 6(1) may be met by 'something less than a full review' of the administrative decision by the court, having regard to 'democratic accountability, efficient administration and the sovereignty of Parliament'.[112]

The same is true of the ECtHR. In *Alatulkkila v Finland*, concerning measures taken which prevented the applicants exercising their civil rights to fish in certain areas in order to ensure the preservation of fish stocks, the ECtHR referred (at [52]) to 'specialised areas of law', in which judicial review by the courts is sufficient for the purposes of Article 6, as those involving 'the exercise of discretion involving a multitude of local factors inherent in the choice and implementation of policies' (by reference to planning cases such as *Bryan v*

---

[110] See eg *Ashingdane v United Kingdom* (1985) 7 EHRR 528 [57]. It seems that the rather imprecise notion of impairing the essence of the right is best regarded as a limited example of a case in which either no legitimate aim is pursued by the restriction in question or the restriction is excessively wide and disproportionate to any such aim. In *Fayed v United Kingdom* (1994) 18 EHRR 393, the ECtHR said that there could be more extensive limits on access to a court 'when regulation of activities in the public sphere is at stake' ([75]).

[111] One can perhaps see the beginnings of this sort of development in the ECtHR's case law under Art 5(4) (requirement of access to review by a court in cases of detention). In *E v Norway* (1990) 17 EHRR 30, concerning detention of a person of unsound mind on grounds of 'expediency', limited judicial review was found to be sufficient to comply with Art 5(4): see [50] and [59]–[60]. In *HL v United Kingdom* (2005) 40 EHRR 32, in a similar context, the ECtHR found that mere judicial review on ordinary *Wednesbury* principles would not comply with the ECHR, but that a more intensive form of review in the future in the light of the Human Rights Act 1998 would be likely to comply: [136]–[140].

[112] *Runa Begum* (n 102) [34] and [35].

United Kingdom) and involving 'important conflicting considerations and interests and, as in this case, a wider international context in the form of a co-operation agreement with a neighbouring state implicated in the environmental concerns in issue'. The Court held that the standard of review required by Article 6(1) in such a context was one in which the domestic court was capable of reviewing judgments made by the executive as to the necessity for and proportionality of the measure in question, ie 'in reaching the conclusion that it was necessary for safeguarding fish stocks'. The domestic court in that case had dismissed the proceedings on the basis that the decision 'is not based on manifestly incorrect application of the law or a (procedural) error that might have fundamentally affected the decision';[113] the ECtHR concluded that, notwithstanding the limited nature of the review conducted by the national court, there had been no violation of Article 6(1).

VIII CONCLUSION

The temptation when reviewing the impact of a fundamental rights instrument such as the ECHR upon the democratic arrangements in the United Kingdom, based on the sovereignty of Parliament, is to regard it as a simple constraint on otherwise unrestrained democratic political processes. That is part of the story,[114] but by no means the whole picture. The existence of judicially policed fundamental or constitutional rights can be argued to be increasingly important in itself for viable democracies to be maintained.[115] Moreover, the ECHR was itself created to foster democracy and western European democratic traditions, which included within them respect for human rights and the rule of law. The ECtHR has been active in creating legal doctrine based on the abstractly formulated Convention rights which is infused with democratic values and provides strong practical support for democratic practices. The legal rules developed under the ECHR carry within them an increasingly articulated vision of a particular kind of democracy – a democracy based on enforceable fundamental rights; liberal democracy rather than radical democracy; pluralistic, broad-minded and tolerant of differences; strongly focused on equal treatment; respectful of the private lives, choices and interests of its individual members in trying to maintain what the ECtHR regards as a fair balance between the individual and the general society of which they are part.

---

[113] See [22] of the ECtHR's judgment.

[114] See Sales, 'The General and the Particular' (n 35) 163–168.

[115] Compare Beetham, *The Legitimation of Power* (n 18): the main way the powerful maintain their legitimacy is by respecting the intrinsic limits set to their power by the rules and the underlying principles on which they are based: 'Legitimate power . . . is limited power,' and a feature of the modern world is the increasingly precise legal specification of powers (p 25); it is important for the viability of democracy that the losers in elections do not perceive defeat as involving irretrievable harm to their vital interests and therefore that they have confidence in the restraints governing the winners – so it is not surprising that the Westminster model of democracy, based on tacit conventions and a culture of self-restraint on the part of the winners, has not proved to be workable in other countries without a highly developed culture of that kind, and there has been a preference for more explicit legal controls and balancing of different centres of power (pp 147–48). But there may be an increased danger of such shared cultural understandings as are fundamental to the Westminster model in its purest form breaking down: see Daniel T Rodgers, *Age of Fracture* (Cambridge, MA, Harvard University Press, 2011). And for limitations on political power providing a foundation for its expansion and increase, see the discussion in Martin Loughlin, *Foundations of Public Law* (Oxford, Oxford University Press, 2010); also Chris Thornhill, *A Sociology of Constitutions: Constitutions and State Legitimacy in Historical-Sociological Perspective* (Cambridge, Cambridge University Press, 2011).

It is the legal doctrine created by the ECtHR and its case law which provides the link between these general conceptions and practical outcomes in cases, producing a concrete compromise between the democratic and liberal traditions in European political thought. The concept of the margin of appreciation is critical to this enterprise, as it is at the centre of the welding together of these two disparate traditions. The flexibility of the concept allows the ECtHR to fine tune the balance between judicial and democratic decision-making by reference to the precise facts and context of each case before it. In this way, the ECHR and the ECtHR constitute effective means by which the club of European states promote a mutually supporting, viable and concrete liberal democratic constitutional form which they can share.[116]

There are points of tension as this institutional framework and the concrete legal doctrine it generates come to be applied to and within the domestic legal order. As with the interface with other areas of domestic law,[117] the impact of the ECHR in the constitutional field is to strengthen some aspects of domestic law (eg protection for freedom of speech, increased judicial control of administrative action under Article 6) while tending to disrupt others (eg calling parliamentary privilege into question). Areas of traditional protection for democratic practices in domestic law are substantially endorsed, but are also modified in the way the underlying interests are refracted through the lens of the ECHR scheme of values. The recognition of similar values in the ECHR as in domestic law is not surprising, given the involvement of British lawyers in the drafting of Convention. Also unsurprising is the development and reflection back into domestic law of such values with a specific Convention twist, since the ECHR and ECtHR were intended to provide a set of ground rules for a common democratic constitutional form across Europe. At a time when the future of the Convention rights in the United Kingdom is being called in question, it should perhaps also be recalled that the success of the ECHR as a core part of the European public order can be regarded as a considerable achievement for the United Kingdom in spreading its legal and democratic values across Europe.

---

[116] Sales, 'Strasbourg Jurisprudence' (n 3) 266–67.
[117] See eg P Sales, 'Property and Human Rights: Protection, Expansion and Disruption' [2006] *Judicial Review* 141; and compare also the impact which the ECHR has had on criminal procedure: see P Roberts and J Hunter (eds), *Criminal Evidence and Human Rights: Reimagining Common Law Procedural Tradition* (Oxford, Hart Publishing, 2012); John Jackson and Sarah Summers, 'Confrontation with Strasbourg: UK and Swiss Approaches to Criminal Evidence' (2013) *Criminal Law Review* 114.

16

Politics, Law and Constitutional Moments in the UK

DAWN OLIVER

I INTRODUCTION

MUCH HAS BEEN written concerning the procedures that have brought about the many changes to the British constitution in the last 30 years or so, and how they could or should be improved. Rodney Brazier suggests a standing Constitutional Commission[1] to be responsible for keeping the constitution under review, and considering and reporting on possible reforms. Sir John Baker in his Maccabaean lecture of 2009, 'Our Unwritten Constitution' argues that, 'if there is to be constitutional reform, there ought to be some new mechanism, independent of government and of the House of Commons, to consider it as a connected whole'.[2] Robert Blackburn suggests that there should be rigorous processes of consultation before reforms are proposed, in line with the Government's own Code of Practice on Consultation of 2006, or that the Second Chamber should have an enhanced role in relation to the UK constitution.[3]

Committees in the two Houses of Parliament have also taken an interest in the process of reform. The House of Lords Constitution Committee's report on *The Process of Constitutional Change* recommended a range of procedures to improve the process;[4] the House of Commons Political and Constitutional Reform Committee's inquiry into 'Mapping the Path to Codifying – or not Codifying – the UK's Constitution' is considering process among other things. In its report, *Do We Need a Constitutional Convention for the UK?*,[5] that Committee accepted that there was 'a range of very different opinions' as to how issues raised by devolution should be approached, but its members were not unanimous about whether there was a need for further review of constitutional arrangements or whether a constitutional convention would be appropriate. The report suggested that the Government *consider* preparations for a UK-wide constitutional convention which should take into account the debate from pre-convention hearings in England.

---

[1] R Brazier, *Constitutional Reform: Reshaping the British Political System*, 3rd edn (Oxford, Oxford University Press, 2008).

[2] *Proceedings of the British Academy* (London, British Academy, 2010) vol 167, 115.

[3] R Blackburn, 'Constitutional Amendment in the UK' in X Contiades (ed), *Engineering Constitutional Change: A Comparative Perspective on Europe, Canada and the USA* (Abingdon, Routledge, 2012) 378–81.

[4] Constitution Committee, *The Process of Constitutional Change* (HL 2010–12, 177).

[5] Political and Constitutional Reform Committee, *Do We Need a Constitutional Convention for the UK?* Fourth Report (HC 2012–13, 371).

All of these proposals seek to regulate and even to minimise the part that party politics plays in constitutional reform.

The relationship between politics and constitutional law in the UK is complex. In the post-World War II period, there was a surge of enthusiasm for politics and scepticism about its relationship with law. Crick's *In Defence of Politics* epitomised[6] these attitudes on the political left. In 1977 Griffith argued in *The Politics of the Judiciary*[7] that judges were in practice political and conservative and not – as received wisdom had it – politically neutral. The implication of Griffith's argument was that politicians should be left to do politics without interference by the law or the courts. In 1978 Griffith memorably coined the phrase 'The Political Constitution',[8] arguing that it was right that political decisions were and should continue to be made by politicians, since they were elected and therefore dismissible; Griffith argued that it would be inappropriate for the courts to take politically controversial decisions, for instance about the balance between human rights and other public interests, because judges could not be dismissed.

But in the last 30 years or so more and more of the UK's constitutional arrangements have come to be based in law and thus subject to judicial supervision: devolution to Scotland, Wales and Northern Ireland, and the Human Rights Act 1998, inevitably entail that the courts are brought in to adjudicate on disputes of a controversial, often political, nature. For the most part they are trusted to do so impartially. Nowadays the general understanding is that many aspects of politics should be regulated so as to avoid undue short-termism and partisanship (for instance in relation to the making of public appointments, the collection and publication of national statistics, the fixing of the minimum lending rate, determination of fiscal policy[9]) and in particular that party politics should be kept out of constitutional reform. This, it is widely felt, ought to be undertaken in a non-partisan spirit and not in order to give an advantage to one political party or its supporters over others. So why, in practice, does – or does not – constitutional reform take place? These are the questions on which I shall focus in this chapter. For instance:

- What are the contexts in which constitutional changes take place?
- Why, how and by whom are changes effected?
- Why are some proposed changes not effected or effected only after a long delay?
- Why do some reforms, once enacted, endure, while others fail to gain broad public support?
- Why are some other possible reforms not made?

A Why and How Does Constitutional Reform Take Place?

We need to bear in mind the flexibility of the UK's unentrenched, unsettled[10] constitutional arrangements – something which Elliott has interestingly referred to as a 'mystery'[11]

---

[6] B Crick, *In Defence of Politics* (Gosport, Weidenfeld and Nicolson, 1962; Reading, Pelican, 1964; 2nd edn 1982).

[7] JAG Griffith, *The Politics of the Judiciary*, 5th edn (London, Fontana, 1997). The book was first published in 1977.

[8] JAG Griffith, 'The Political Constitution' (1979) 42 *Modern Law Review* 1.

[9] See D Oliver, 'The Politics Free Dimension to the UK Constitution' in M Qvortrup (ed), *The British Constitution: Continuity and Change* (Oxford, Hart Publishing, 2013).

[10] See N Walker, 'The Unsettled Constitution', the 2013 Public Law Journal lecture, to be published in 2013/2104 *Public Law*.

[11] See M Elliott, 'Interpretative Bills of Rights and the Mystery of the Unwritten Constitution' (2011) *New Zealand Law Review* 591.

– when asking why constitutional change does or does not take place, or why, once enacted, it does or does not settle comfortably into the system.

First we need to recognise that implementation of a reform may have been delayed for a range of reasons:

- the reform may have been against the interests of the government of the day;
- inertia on the part of government: other matters have priority; and
- lack of urgency.

My hypothesis is that sometimes, but by no means always, these obstacles to constitutional reform can only be overcome so that reform takes place and endures when the time is ripe,[12] ie if a 'key moment' in Wick's[13] words, or a constitutional moment, to borrow Ackerman's phrase,[14] has arrived: not only does such a moment allow a reform to take place, but once implemented it commonly becomes unthinkable that the reform would be reversed.

A number of factors will influence the arrival of ripe time. A newly elected government, having recently experienced the frustrations of opposition, may seize the opportunity to reform. There may be a scandal of some kind which finally persuades those in charge to reform. These are both highly political factors. There may have to be a strong shift in political and/or public opinion in favour of reform. Reforms that are uncontroversial but have been delayed may become urgent. (The delay in introducing legislation to change the rules of royal succession until the Duchess of Cambridge was pregnant is a topical example.[15]) A reform proposal may need an effective, non-party political 'Champion' if it is to gain sufficient momentum to be implemented by government and/or Parliament. These are not matters of process or procedure, but of social, legal and political culture – of dynamics. Unlike process and procedure, they cannot always be managed or engineered or manipulated by actors, normally politicians, in the reform process.

Although the phrase 'constitutional moment' in my title refers to Bruce Ackerman's discussions of 'transformative' changes brought about outside the normal constitutional amendment processes, I use it in relation to both large and relatively minor changes in the UK's constitutional arrangements. I suggest that not only the public at large (the focus of Ackerman's thesis), but politicians, individually or collectively, may experience their own transformative moments leading to constitutional change – as for example when reforms to House of Commons select committees were introduced in 1997 and 2010 (see below).

But reforms will not take place, or if enacted they may not settle comfortably into the constitutional landscape, if they do not 'fit' the political and legal systems and the cultures that go with them; for instance, if they challenge the legislative supremacy of Parliament, the doctrines of ministerial responsibility to Parliament, the primacy of the House of

---

[12] See FM Cornford, *Microcosmographia Academica, Being a Guide for the Young Academic Politician* (Cambridge, Bowes and Bowes, 1908) on the Principle of Unripe Time.

[13] See E Wicks, *The Evolution of a Constitution: Eight Key Moments in British Constitutional History* (Oxford, Hart Publishing, 2006).

[14] B Ackerman, *We the People* (Cambridge MA, Harvard University Press, 1991, 1998) vols 1 and 2. Ackerman's thesis is about major transformations in US constitutional arrangements, such as the abolition of slavery, the Fourteenth amendment and the New Deal. This is not the sense in which the phrase is used in this paper.

[15] It may become urgent to deal with the West Lothian Question if a government at Westminster depends for its majority on the votes of MPs for seats in Scotland, Wales or Northern Ireland: see Report of the Commission on the Consequences of Devolution for the House of Commons (The McKay Commission), March 2013, accessible at http://tmc.independent.gov.uk/wp-content/uploads/2013/03 for discussion of the issues and possible ways of dealing with them.

Commons, the independence of the judiciary, the need for accountability and transparency in government, and the public service principle. Nor will a reform settle if it flies in the face of public or political opinion. Election to the House of Lords is an example of a reform of doubtful 'fit'. The Human Rights Act is another. I consider in Part III why this is the case.

II CHANGES WHEN THE TIME IS RIPE

Ripe time has arrived in the last 30 years or more for a whole lot of previously resisted and controversial constitutional changes. And most of them have proved stable and gained popular acceptance so that it would be unthinkable to reverse them. Once they are in place they may develop organically, as indeed does every aspect of the UK Constitution. But no one seriously suggests that, for instance, select committee reforms, devolution, freedom of information, or the Constitutional Reform Act 2005 should be repealed. In the following brief case studies of some successful reforms, I explore the questions raised at the start of this chapter: in what contexts constitutional changes took place, why, how and by whom they were effected, why were some of them effected only after a long delay, and why they are stable whereas others, eg the Human Rights Act, are not.

A House of Commons Reforms 1979–2010

Just as significant sources of the UK's constitutional norms include Acts of Parliament, the law and custom of Parliament, judicial decisions, conventions, codes and other soft law documents, so significant constitutional reforms may take place through changes to these sources. The reforms to House of Commons select committees in 1979,[16] the early 2000s, and 2010[17] illustrate the point.[18] These changes, achieved by amendments to the standing orders of the Commons, produced, taken together, a greatly strengthened system of ministerial accountability to Parliament.

The 1979 reforms set up a comprehensive system of departmentally related select committees charged with examining the administration, expenditure and policy of departments. Initially the membership and chairs of these committees were in effect selected – and could be removed – by the party whips in the Commons. Their members were thus under considerable pressure not to go against their party's policies or to inquire into and report on matters which their parties would not welcome. But 1979 was only the first stage in a process, which continues, of parliamentary reform.

[16] See G Drewry, (ed), *The New Select Committees*, 2nd edn (Oxford, Clarendon Press, 1989). In brief, under the new system select committees were established to scrutinise the work of each government department.

[17] These reforms had been developed by the Public Administration Select Committee and the Select Committee on Reform of the House of Commons, chaired by Tony Wright MP before the 2010 election. See their report of the 24 November 2009, *Rebuilding the House* (HC 2008–09, 1117). In brief, the reforms provided for the chairs of select committees to be elected by the House and not by the whips as hitherto, and for members of the committees to be elected by their parties, the number of places for each party on each committee being determined by reference to the representation of the parties in the House. See R Kelly, 'Select Committees: Powers and Functions' in A Horne, G Drewry and D Oliver (eds), *Parliament and the Law* (Oxford, Hart Publishing, 2013). In March 2013 the Political and Constitutional Reform Committee of the House of Commons started an inquiry into 'Revisiting *Rebuilding the House*: The Impact of the Wright Reforms': see the Committee website at www.parliament.uk/pcrc.

[18] For general discussion of select committees and their reform, see Kelly (n 17).

Important additions to ministerial responsibility include the resolutions on ministerial responsibility passed by both Houses[19] in the wake of the publication of the *Report of the Inquiry into the Export of Defence Equipment and Dual-use Goods to Iraq and Related Prosecutions* (The Scott Report[20]) in which, among other things, serious weaknesses in the conventions of ministerial responsibility were revealed. These resolutions made it clear that the duty of ministers to account to Parliament was imposed by and owed to the two Houses and was not a favour granted by ministers to Parliament.

By contrast with the 1979 select committee reforms, the commitments of the newly elected Labour Government in 1997 to the reform of parliamentary procedure made slow progress. Plans for reform had not been fully developed in the previous Parliament. Soon after the election, the Government established a committee to 'consider how the practices and procedures of the House should be modernised, and to make recommendations thereon'. The Committee on Modernisation of the House of Commons worked to a time-table that meant that by the time their proposals were formulated, the Government had lost its opposition-minded attitudes and had converted to a pro-government view of the world – as always happens after a change of government. Some reforms of the hours and practices of the Commons were introduced during that period, largely under pressure from the Leader of the House, Robin Cooke MP, a committed parliamentarian and former Foreign Secretary, who devoted himself enthusiastically to the project to modernise the House of Commons. He was Leader of the House from 2001 until March 2003, when he resigned over the invasion of Iraq. During 2003 the reforms included the introduction of additional salaries for chairs of select committees; the select committees' core purposes were spelt out, and the Prime Minister agreed to meet the members of the Liaison Committee (formed of the chairs of select committees) twice a year.[21] After Cooke resigned, the impetus for reform under the Labour Government slackened.

After the change of government at the 2010 general election, a raft of important further reforms was introduced.[22] These provided for chairs of committees and committee members to be elected by backbenchers and for the introduction of a backbench business committee, thus loosening government control of parliamentary time and Parliament's agenda.[23] A commitment was made in the Coalition Agreement[24] to introduce a Business Committee in the third year of the Parliament – as of August 2013 this had not yet been done.

Let us look a little more closely at how these reforms to select committees and ministerial responsibility came about. The reforms of 1979 and the early 2000s were introduced by Leaders of the House, Norman St John Stevas in 1979 and Robin Cooke from 2001–03. Both were non-partisan in their roles as 'Champions' of the reforms, committed parliamentarians acting in a non-party spirit. The reforms themselves were non-partisan and they had the support of government. The pre-election Champion for the reforms of 2010 was Tony Wright MP, the energetic and charismatic chair of the Public Administration Select Committee in the 2005–10 Parliament, which, with the Liaison Committee, had

---

[19] HC Deb vol 292, 19 March 1997, cols 1046–47; HL Deb vol 579, 20 March 1997, cols 1055–62.

[20] Rt Hon Sir Richard Scott, *Report of the Inquiry into the Export of Defence Equipment and Dual-Use Goods to Iraq and Related Prosecutions* (HC 1995–96, 115).

[21] See Kelly (n 17).

[22] ibid.

[23] Similar reforms had been proposed but rejected in 2002: see Modernisation Committee, *Select Committees* (HC 2001–02, 224–I).

[24] *The Coalition: Our Programme for Government*, (Cabinet Office, 2010) ch 24, 27, available at www.gov.uk/publications/the-coalition-programme-for-government.

campaigned for reforms to improve the accountability of government to the House of Commons in a series of reports. (He did not stand for re-election in 2010.) He too was acting in a non-partisan spirit, despite the fact that he was a member of the governing party.

The immediate background to the formulation and eventual implementation of the 2010 reforms was the MPs' expenses scandal of 2008/09.[25] The reputation of MPs was very low: Wright was appointed to chair a new special ad hoc Commons committee to consider reforms; it published its report *Rebuilding the House*[26] shortly before the general election. 'Rebuilding' referred in part to rebuilding the reputation of the House after the damage done by that scandal. Thus the scandal was a transformative constitutional moment about the powers of backbenchers in relations with government.

This aspect of the 'constitutional moment' was experienced by MPs rather than by the electorate. It is not self-evident that the electorate, if asked, would have agreed that increasing the powers of MPs in their relations with the Government would be a natural or appropriate response to the expenses scandal. In both 1979 and 2010 the newly elected Government, having experienced powerlessness in holding government to account in opposition, and retaining the attitudes of opposition for a period after taking office, supported changes that would improve their ability to hold government to account: the time was ripe.

The reactions of the general public to the revelations about MPs' expenses mirrored those in the 'cash for questions' scandal of 1995 in which MPs were found to have accepted payments for putting down questions to ministers in Parliament. This had led to the formation of the Committee on Standards in Public Life: it produced a statement of the Seven Principles of Public Life: selflessness, integrity, objectivity, accountability, honesty, openness and leadership.[27] These principles were then adopted as part of the Code of Conduct for MPs in 1996, and revised in 2006.[28]

The 2009 scandal too led to the formation of a new institution, the Independent Parliamentary Standards Authority (IPSA), to take over the management of MPs' expenses and their salaries. After initial grumbling by MPs about this new system it appears to be settling into the constitutional landscape well. It is easy to imagine the uproar there would be if management of expenses were to be returned to MPs. A strong shift in political opinion, in the House of Commons and in government, favoured reform.

Thus, the 'constitutional moment' of the 2009 expenses scandal led to two quite separate, different reforms – the strengthening of the select committee system and a new MPs' expenses regime. Like the 'sleaze' scandal that led to the formation of the Committee on Standards in Public Life in 1995, the expenses scandal resulted in the articulation of deeply rooted and in reality uncontroversial (though forgotten) norms – for instance that those in public life should serve the public in preference to their own interests.

B Devolution to Scotland and Wales

The next set of reforms that involved ripe time, constitutional moments and a Champion were devolution to Scotland and Wales. Attempts to introduce devolution in Scotland and

---

[25] See Kelly (n 17).

[26] *Rebuilding the House* (n 17).

[27] *First Report of the Committee on Standards in Public Life* (Cm 2850, 1995). The seven principles have also been incorporated into the Ministerial Code and many other public sector codes.

[28] HC 351 (2005–06).

Wales in 1978 failed for lack of the required level of support in the referendums on the proposals. [29] Devolution then dropped down the political agenda for about 10 years. It resurfaced in the wake of the introduction by the Government at Westminster of the community charge – the 'poll tax' as it was called – in place of domestic rates north of the border in 1989. This arbitrary and unjust law was imposed by the UK Conservative Government on Scotland before being introduced in England and Wales in 1990. The opposition and civil disobedience that it caused led to its abolition and replacement by the council tax in 1993.[30] Experience of the poll tax created a strong shift in political and public opinion, a constitutional moment in Scotland, in favour of reform of the arrangements for the Government of Scotland.

The Labour Party then experienced its own transformative constitutional moment when its traditional support in Scotland started to drift towards the SNP: its conversion to devolution to Scotland was in part attributable to the threat from the SNP to the Labour vote in Scotland – on which a Labour government at Westminster might well have to rely if, as was entirely possible, it did not win a majority of seats in England at the next general election.

But a transformative shift in public or political opinion alone is unlikely to result in stable, successful constitutional change that comes to be accepted by the electorate. Preparation and constitutional fit (discussed below) and perhaps a Champion will also be required. And these were all part of the Scottish devolution process in the 1990s. By comparison with the position in 1978, in the run up to the Scotland Act 1998 the proposals for devolution had been carefully prepared and consulted on by the Scottish Constitutional Convention in which a wide range of civil society organisations participated (but not the SNP, which favoured independence, or the Conservative Party).[31] The Labour Party, in opposition since 1979, committed itself in its manifesto to devolution to Scotland on the lines proposed by the Constitutional Convention's document *Scotland's Parliament, Scotland's Right*, 1995. The newly elected Labour Government then proposed to adopt those proposals. This was put to a referendum in Scotland shortly after the election and won strong support both for a Scottish Parliament and for it to enjoy tax-raising powers. The recent election win and the referendum result meant that it would be difficult for the Conservative opposition in the House of Commons to be successful in opposing, amending or defeating the Scotland Bill, and the Bill was passed in 1998. The first elections to the new Scottish Parliament were held in 1999. This was the result of the model reform process that preceded the Act.

Since the Scotland Act 1998 support for increased powers for the Scottish Parliament and executive has grown; many of the claims were met in the Scotland Act 2012. Under pressure from the majority SNP Government in Edinburgh, an agreement (the Edinburgh Agreement) was reached between the UK Government and the Scottish executive on the holding of a referendum on independence on 18 September 2014 on the question 'Should

---

[29] The insufficient support for devolution in the 1978 referendum may have been due to the particular proposals for devolution that had been developed. The consultation process had not been as thorough as that in the 1990s.

[30] See D Butler and T Travers, *Failure in British Government: The Politics of the Poll Tax* (Oxford, Oxford University Press, 1994).

[31] The Constitution Unit at University College London also prepared thorough papers on the options for devolution and their implications. The Unit was formed by Robert Hazell in 1995 in advance of the Election of 1997, in the knowledge that Labour might win on a manifesto full of commitments to constitutional reform, but that the party was not in a position to prepare for those reforms appropriately. The Unit therefore produced a number of reports on the options for devolution (and many other proposed reforms). See www.ucl.ac.uk/constitution-unit/publications.

Scotland be an independent state?' The path is clear for negotiated independence for Scotland if the referendum result is positive. It is unthinkable that devolution would be repealed by the Westminster Parliament except to provide for Scottish independence.

Devolution to Wales has also settled well into the constitutional landscape, with additional powers to those granted by the Government of Wales Act 1998 having been granted in the Government of Wales Act 2006. But no strong constitutional moment preceded the 1998 Act. The majority for devolution in the referendum in Wales before the Act was passed was only 50.3 per cent of those who voted, and the turnout was only 51 per cent. There had not been widespread pressure for devolution in Wales. But, as the referendum result showed, the time was just about ripe. It is worth noting at this point that the result of the referendum on a new regional authority in the North East of England in November 2004 showed that there the time was not ripe. But the devolution arrangements that are currently in place fit the UK's evolving constitutional arrangements well, helped by the flexibility of agreements such as the Memorandums of Understanding between the UK Government and those in Wales, Scotland and Northern Ireland. However, they leave unresolved 'the English (and Welsh) Question': what part should MPs sitting for constituencies not in England or Wales play in the passing of legislation affecting only England or England and Wales? Resolution of that issue awaits a 'constitutional moment'.[32]

C Freedom of Information Act 2000

My third case study is the Freedom of Information Act 2000. The non-party Campaign for Freedom of Information, established in 1984, had campaigned for a Freedom of Information Act for many years before the 2000 Act was passed. The history of the implementation of the policy in legislation reflects the anti-Freedom of Information cultures of politicians in power and of civil servants.[33] A Freedom of Information Act had been promised in the election manifestos of the Labour Party a number of times before 1997. Eventually, as often happens, it was on a change of government after a general election that the process of establishing a Freedom of Information system for the UK became part of the governmental programme.[34]

James Cornford, Chair of the Campaign for Freedom of Information from 1984 to 1997, was appointed adviser to David Clark, Chancellor of the Duchy of Lancaster in the newly elected Labour Government: they were 'Champions' of the reform. Cornford prepared a proposal for a full blooded Freedom of Information Act in that year. However, many of the proposals in this document were rejected by Cabinet, and Clark resigned, taking Cornford with him. Thereafter, government proposals for Freedom of Information were watered down in what became the Freedom of Information Act 2000; and implementation of the Act was delayed, its provisions being phased in over the next five years. The time was slowly ripening. There was clearly no enthusiasm for the policy in government. Tony Blair, after he had resigned as Prime Minister, expressed the view that the Act had been a big mistake.

---

[32] See n 15.

[33] For an account of the history and of the Act, see P Birkinshaw, *Freedom of Information, The Law, the Practice and the Ideal*, 4th edn (Cambridge, Cambridge University Press, 2010) and 'Regulating Information' in J Jowell and D Oliver (eds), *The Changing Constitution*, 7th edn, (Oxford, Oxford University Press, 2011).

[34] John Smith, Leader of the Labour Party in opposition, had been keen on Freedom of Information, but he died before Labour came to power in 1997.

As of 2013 the Government is considering amending the Act, making access to information more difficult on grounds of cost. And yet it is unthinkable that the Act would be repealed. Freedom of Information enables the public to keep an eye on what public authorities do, and thus incentivises them to meet expectations that they will serve the general interest and not their own selfish or partisan ones. While Freedom of Information has not settled well into political and civil service cultures, it is an established feature of the constitutional landscape as far as the public and the press are concerned. It also 'fits' important constitutional principles of accountability.

D Constitutional Reform Act 2005

The Constitutional Reform Act created a new Supreme Court for the United Kingdom, altered the role of the Lord Chancellor, and established a new Judicial Appointments Commission. While none of these changes would now be reversed, though some may develop, they were controversial among judges and other lawyers at the time. The 'constitutional moment' that led to the Constitutional Reform Act 2005 was experienced by the Prime Minister, Tony Blair who became frustrated by the confrontations between his Lord Chancellor, Lord Irvine of Lairg and his Home Secretary David Blunkett. He announced in 2003, without any prior consultation outside government, that the office of Lord Chancellor was abolished. In due course the Constitutional Reform Act retained the office of Lord Chancellor (but without the judicial roles and presiding in the House of Lords), and included establishment of the Supreme Court (effective from 2009) and a new system for judicial appointments.[35] It was the failure of government to consult appropriately over these proposals that was responsible for most of the controversy: it generated a sense of profound suspicion of the Government's motives among judges and others, who saw the changes as undermining judicial independence and the rule of law. The proposed reforms had no non-partisan Champion in government or in Parliament.

Lord Woolf was Champion for the judges. He negotiated a Concordat between government and the judiciary and secured formal recognition in section 1 of the Act of the importance of the rule of law, and a statement of the importance of the independence of the judiciary.[36] However, it is clear that acceptance – and understanding – of the central importance of the rule of law in government, without the powerful and highly respected traditional office of Lord Chancellor, is weaker than it was. There would surely have been a row and possible resignation by a pre-reform Lord Chancellor over, for instance, the unwillingness of the Government to comply with the decision of the European Court of Human Rights (ECtHR) in the case of *Hirst v UK*[37] on votes for prisoners, discussed later in this chapter.

However, the storm about process having blown over, the Constitutional Reform Act 2005 does 'fit' the current constitutional landscape well. These changes will not be reversed,

---

[35] See A Le Sueur, 'From Appellate Committee to Supreme Court: A Narrative' in L Blom-Cooper, B Dickson and G Drewry (eds), *The Judicial House of Lords 1876-2009* (Oxford, Oxford University Press, 2009). See also www.guardian.co.uk/politics/2009/nov/01/lord-irvine-sacking-tony-blair.

[36] Section 1 provides that: This Act does not adversely affect (a) the existing constitutional principle of the rule of law, or (b) the Lord Chancellor's existing constitutional role in relation to that principle. Section 3(1) provides that 'The Lord Chancellor, other Ministers of the Crown and all with responsibility for matters relating to the judiciary or otherwise to the administration of justice must uphold the continued independence of the judiciary'.

[37] *Hirst v UK (No 2)* ECtHR Grand Chamber, no 74025/01, October 2005.

though they may be updated and developed from time to time. The time was ripe for change given the extremely anomalous position of the top court and the Lord Chancellor, especially in the light of case law of the ECtHR under Article 6 (right of access to an independent and impartial tribunal). But it took a highly political 'constitutional moment' to push it up the Government's agenda.

III WHAT IF A CHANGE DOES NOT 'FIT'?

There is no real likelihood that the changes discussed above would be reversed. They may lead on to further reforms, as has been the case in devolution to Scotland and Wales. They have settled firmly and relatively comfortably into the legal and political constitutional landscape. They fit.

But there remain two questions. First, why has it proved so difficult to reform the House of Lords? In my view it is because the present arrangements fit the legal and political system rather well, and an elected House of Lords would not do so. And secondly, what is the future of the Human Rights Act 1998? Again in my view although that Act fits our constitutional and legal arrangements and traditions rather well, it does not 'fit' the political or public culture so well, and this is why it has come under frequent criticism and review, not so much from lawyers as from politicians, the press and the public.

A The House of Lords

The issue of House of Lords reform has moved up and down the political agendas of all parties since the Parliament Act 1911. Most recently it fell down the agenda of all political parties when the House of Lords Reform Bill, though it passed second reading in the House of Commons in July 2012, was withdrawn when the House refused to agree a timetable for its passage.[38] Ballinger, in his discussion of the 'century of non-reform',[39] suggests that 'The principal reason for the lack of reform is that no government has been united in a commitment – whether of its own volition or necessity – to secure reform'.[40]

I suggest that a large part of the difficulty over Lords reform is constitutional 'fit'. As Ballinger states, an elected House of Lords would take away the lack of legitimacy which inhibits the present House from exercising its powers to the full.[41] From the point of view of both governments and the House of Commons, this lack of legitimacy is a very valuable piece of constitutional cultural capital. But to deal with the problem of an uninhibited second chamber by cutting down its powers at the same time as providing for its election to increase its legitimacy would look perverse. Ballinger adds: 'Reform . . . risks altering the balance of power between the Commons and the Lords, or between Parliament and the executive . . . there has been nothing to counter the unicameralist tendencies of the system of parliamentary responsible government.'[42]

---

[38] See *House of Commons Library Standard Note SN 06405, House of Lords Reform Bill 2012-13: Decision not to proceed.*
[39] C Ballinger, *The House of Lords 1911-2011. A Century of Non-Reform* (Oxford, Hart Publishing, 2012).
[40] ibid 219.
[41] ibid.
[42] ibid.

This point about unicameralism is important. States with bicameral parliaments are almost always federations. It is unusual for a non-federal state to have a second chamber. New Zealand abolished its second chamber (the Legislative Council) in 1950. So why does the UK remain bicameral, and why is the second chamber not elected? Surely the UK Parliament ought to be unicameral?

If the system in the UK were unicameral, the scrutiny and revision of Bills and draft Bills would be disastrously less well done than now. There would be a strong case for the establishment of an independent expert body to complement the Commons in the processing of Bills – perhaps a statutory Scrutiny and Revision Commission or Council of State to do the job now done in the Lords, examining and reporting to Parliament and the Government on matters such as the compatibility of the proposals with constitutional principles, technical and legal issues, the evidence base for the policy, and whether appropriate consultations have taken place before the introduction of the Bill or draft Bill.[43] Alternatively, or additionally, an independent, expert body could be granted the power to engage in post implementation scrutiny, perhaps a Supreme or Constitutional Court with power to strike down legislation or declare it to be 'unconstitutional'. It is because neither of these changes to the UK arrangements is needed at present, and it has not been proposed in political circles that either would be made if the House of Lords were elected, that the House of Lords 'fits' the operation of the British parliamentary system well, although it does not 'fit' the assumptions about 'democracy' that prevail in many circles.

To elaborate, much of what the current House of Lords does (as opposed to who are in it and how they get there) works well.[44] The House performs important and, in a liberal democracy, essential functions of scrutiny and revision of Bills and draft Bills, and inquiring into matters of public policy and interest. It does so effectively and authoritatively and normally in a non-partisan way. In this it complements and only seldom challenges the House of Commons in holding government – and note 'government', not the House of Commons – to account. The current arrangements maintain the primacy of the House of Commons, and do not cause policy paralysis of the 'fiscal cliff' kind that the USA experiences from time to time: that is the point of ensuring that one House, in which the Government has a majority, has primacy. The fact that the House of Lords lacks democratic legitimacy restrains it from exercising its powers of delay to the full save in exceptional circumstances and on exceptional grounds, which are often, though not always, of a 'constitutional'[45] rather than 'political'[46] nature. As the War Crimes Act 1991 and the Hunting Act 2004 demonstrate, the Parliament Acts generally provide an escape hatch for a government which has the support of the Commons when faced with refusal by the Lords to consent to a Bill. Overall, the relations between government and the second chamber owe a great deal to intangible culture and traditions rather than to law.

The specialist committees in the Lords – notably the Constitution Committee, the European Union Committee and it sub-committees, and the Delegated Powers and

---

[43] I have elaborated on this set of ideas in D Oliver, 'The Parliament Acts, the Constitution, the Rule of Law, and the Second Chamber' (2012) 33 *Statute Law Review* 1.

[44] See M Russell, *The Contemporary House of Lords. Westminster Bicameralism Revived* (Oxford, Oxford University Press, 2013).

[45] The House of Lords refused to consent to the War Crimes Act 1991 on the ground that it introduced criminal liability for acts that were not criminal at the time they were committed.

[46] The Hunting Act 2004 passed under the Parliament Acts, having been blocked by the House of Lords on largely political rather than 'constitutional' grounds, although the expected difficulties in its enforcement may be thought of as a constitutional point against it.

Regulatory Reform Committee – perform important, indeed some of them essential, functions which, if not performed by the second chamber would either not be performed at all, or would have to be transferred to another body – not the courts, not the House of Commons, but a statutory scrutiny and revision commission of some kind.

As for composition, the introduction of life peerages and the removal of most of the hereditary peers have provided the House with a range (but not much of a balance) of party representation and normally no government majority because of the presence of cross benchers, and a range of expertise: these factors enable the House to perform its functions well and with political sensitivity. These qualities would not be present in an elected House or in an appointed independent Constitutional Court or a Scrutiny and Revision Commission.

In sum, the aspects of the UK constitutional system that the House of Lords fits are:

1. The fact of an unwritten constitution and thus the absence of constitutional judicial review of legislation: therefore there need to be effective *intra*-parliamentary legislative procedures in place to minimise the risk that 'unconstitutional', unwise or imprudent legislation will be passed. The Lords and its Committees do these things well. 2. The relative weakness of party politics in the House of Lords due to the presence of independent members: this promotes non-partisan debates of the provisions in Bills and of government policy and secures that Bills are considered on their merits and not purely on the basis of whipping and party loyalty. 3. The maintenance of the primacy of the House of Commons.

Proposals for election to the House of Lords are based in part on inappropriate comparisons with other bicameral countries with written constitutions and constitutional courts, and upon misconceptions about the functions of the Lords and the nature of the institution. Election of all or most of the members of the second chamber would not 'fit' the system because they would undermine each of the above 'fits'. They would weaken the effectiveness of intra-parliamentary legislative scrutiny and revision of Bills because the elected members would lack the independence and experience which this function requires. The members would be more political because they would be elected: it is likely that the parties would choose candidates who had been active in their party, serving for instance in local authorities or in the devolved bodies. There would be fewer experts in Culture, Defence, Disability, Economics, EU matters, Foreign Affairs, Finance, Health, Human Rights, Law, Regulation and so on in an elected second chamber. The elected members of the House would feel it legitimate to challenge the primacy of the House of Commons; and public opinion would often no doubt agree.

I suggest that it is awareness not only in the House of Lords but also in the Commons and often in government circles of the poor 'fits' that elections to the House of Lords would produce that accounts for the failures of the efforts of successive governments to secure the passage of legislation for elections to the House. This is why there has not been, and in my mind it is most unlikely that there will be, a 'constitutional moment' for an elected House of Lords. If however such a moment were to arrive and if the second chamber were elected, this would in my view be a very unstable arrangement and would lead to further changes to the relationships between the two Houses and relationships with the Government, because of the loss of constitutional fit between the UK system and an elected second chamber.

However, a mini-moment may be imminent for reform to the present arrangements in the House of Lords. The issue of elections to the House will not be raised again before the general election in 2015, and it is in any event unlikely that a new government in 2015 would treat elections to the second chamber as a priority given the economic and other problems that will still face the country. But the second chamber is far too large and expensive; there is insufficient office accommodation for the active members; the number of members wishing to participate in debates means that their contributions are required to be so short as to undermine their effectiveness and impact; the inclusion of hereditary peers can no longer be justified; the working practices of the House should be reformed;[47] the appointment of life peers by exercise of unregulated prime ministerial patronage allows for the appointments of people lacking the expertise and experience which justify the House's existence and the return of favours to party supporters – and it allows for the uncontrolled increase in the size of the House; many members of the Lords contribute little or nothing to the important functions it and its committees perform; many of them attend only to draw their tax free daily allowances, a thoroughly disreputable practice.

So the House should be reformed.[48] The hereditary members should be removed. Arrangements need to be made for retirement from the House in order to reduce its size and cost. Appointments to the House should be made on merit according to statutory criteria to ensure that it contains people who can contribute to its valuable work. Allowances should reflect the contributions made to the business of the House by its part-time members. Reforms to working practices could include the establishment of a new legislative standards committee.[49] Many of these reforms could be made without legislation, for instance by changes to Standing Orders or the Prime Ministerial decision to establish an independent advisory committee on appointments to the House of Lords in 2000.[50]

If, as seems likely, a set of such reforms will not be made, and if instead more and more appointments were to be made by the Prime Minister in the exercise of his unregulated patronage, an Ackerman style 'transformative constitutional moment' in public opinion and opinion in the House of Commons may arrive. That may spur a government and the Commons to legislate for election, if necessary relying on the Parliament Acts to do so. What then? The new House will not fit. Members of the largely or wholly elected House will not scrutinise and revise Bills as well as the current House does: much worse, unscrutinised, unrevised legislation will be passed. There will be sterile deadlocks between the two Houses or rubber stamping of government Bills. The members will be more political – that will be the quality that attracts their parties to nominate them for election. And most significantly and damaging to the constitution, the primacy of the Commons will be undermined and with it effective, responsible government. I doubt if any Prime Minister would want these things to happen when there are so many other urgent calls on parliamentary time and political energy: that consideration may itself be a reason for the PM to hold back from flooding the House with lots of new life peers to secure a new party balance there.

A better alternative to election, if the other reforms suggested above are not made, would be for the House of Lords to be abolished and replaced by a new independent Scrutiny Commission established to carry out the functions referred to above and thus to 'fit' the system. But this is not the place to develop that idea.[51]

---

[47] See *Report of the Leader's Group on Working Practices* (HL 2010–2012, 136).
[48] See Russell (n 44).
[49] ibid.
[50] See discussion of some of these issues in HL Deb vol 743, 28 February 2013, cols 1165–83.
[51] See Oliver (n 43).

B The Human Rights Act 1998

The commitment of the Labour Party in opposition in the 1990s to a Bill of Rights that would incorporate the main provisions of the European Convention on Human Rights (ECHR) into UK law was in some respects surprising: the Party was traditionally sceptical about granting broad powers to interpret the law to judges, especially if to do so would inhibit political decision-making. It was the conversion of John Smith, the Leader of the Labour Party from 1992–94 to the cause of a Human Rights Act that resulted in Labour including the project in its election manifesto of 1997 as 'Bringing Rights Home'. This was in part a reaction against government policies under Conservative Prime Minister Margaret Thatcher from 1979 to 1990, for instance on industrial relations, which were felt to infringe trade unionists' and others' rights.[52] Smith was the first and highly respected politician Champion of a Bill of Rights. After Smith died and Tony Blair was elected Leader, the commitment to a Human Rights Act was retained. The experience of policies under the Conservative Government, particularly against the trade unions during and after the Miners' Strike of 1984/85, assisted the conversion. The embarrassment of the British Government at successive findings by the ECtHR that the UK was in breach of its obligations under the Convention provided a further reason for doing one's laundry at home.[53]

Proposals for the content of what became the Human Rights Act 1998 had been well prepared in the years running up to its enactment. Lord Wade and Lord Lester had each introduced Bills to 'incorporate' the main provisions of the ECHR in the House of Lords in previous years. These Bills had not progressed to the House of Commons, but experience had led to the refining of the proposed arrangements for incorporation. The joint Labour Liberal Democrat consultative committee report on Constitutional Reform of 1997[54] had laid the political foundations for support for the Bill in the Commons before the election of 1997. Lord Irvine, the Lord Chancellor in waiting during the Conservative Government of the 1990s, had consulted and formulated his proposals in advance of the election. He was its legal Champion during the passage of the Bill. In sum, in light of the thorough preparation of the Bill in advance of its introduction into Parliament, its Champions in the preceding years (John Smith and then Lord Irvine) and the political background which brought the Labour Party to favour a Bill of Rights, in 1997–98 the time seemed 'ripe'. But there was no contemporaneous *public* transformative constitutional moment in or around 1997; 'moments' had been experienced in the 1980s and 1990s, largely by politicians and lawyers rather than by the general public.

The Human Rights Act 1998 is a subtle piece of legislation which gives considerable direct and indirect effect to the Convention rights which the UK Government is required in international law to protect. It 'fits' the legal aspects of the British constitutional system well in its respect for the doctrine of parliamentary sovereignty, thus placing ultimate responsibility for compliance with the Convention as an international law obligation on the Government and Parliament – politicians – rather than on the courts. This approach is consistent with the tradition of 'the political constitution', so well highlighted by Griffith in his Chorley lecture of 1978.[55]

---

[52] See for instance K Ewing and C Gearty, *Freedom under Thatcher* (Oxford, Clarendon Press, 1990).

[53] M Zander, *A Bill of Rights?*, 4th edn (London, Sweet and Maxwell, 1996).

[54] See Appendix 2 to R Blackburn and R Plant (eds), *Constitutional Reform* (London, Longman, 1999) paras 17–23.

[55] 42 MLR 1.

But we all know that there are pressures for the Act to be repealed and/or replaced by a British Bill of Rights (and possibly Responsibilities). Part of the public and political resentment of the Human Rights Act is directed at the decisions of the ECtHR which the UK is obliged under the Convention to implement by bringing our law into line with the Convention. The protection that the Human Rights Act and the ECHR have offered to suspected terrorists, illegal immigrants, foreign criminals who have established a family life in the UK, prisoners, paedophiles and others, has been lambasted by the press, and this has added to political and public pressures to alter the law.[56] The implications of reluctance by the UK to fulfill its international law obligations to comply for other states seeking excuses for non-compliance are very serious: but they have not been taken seriously by our political class, or by our press.

At the time of writing, the Government – with a good deal of support in the House of Commons – is delaying steps to implement the decision of the ECtHR in the prisoners' voting case, *Hirst v UK*,[57] by publishing a draft Bill setting out options for complying with the *Hirst* decision, to be subjected to pre-legislative scrutiny by a Commons committee in due course – probably not before the general election in 2015: the issue is being kicked into the long grass.

From time to time, Conservative politicians call for the repeal of the Human Rights Act and its replacement by a British Bill of Rights. But unless the UK were to resile from the Convention, the country would continue to be bound to comply with it. And this would be the case even if a new British Bill of Rights made no mention of the Convention. Every now and again, politicians call for the UK to withdraw from the ECHR. This would not be a simple matter as it would affect the UK's relations both with the European Communities, and with devolved bodies in Scotland, Wales and Northern Ireland.[58]

It is clear that the Act has not achieved the settled acceptance among politicians and the general public that other constitutional reforms have enjoyed. The regrettable (to my mind) fact is that the Human Rights Act and the ECHR do not 'fit' the UK's political culture or many aspects of its public culture at all well: while the legislative supremacy of the UK Parliament is preserved under the Act, the fact that the country is a signatory to the ECHR means that the exercise of functions of a public nature by the Government and other public authorities incompatibly with Convention rights is unlawful.[59] If the Government (by making remedial orders under section 10 of the Act) or Parliament (by passing primary legislation) does not make our law compatible with the Convention, the UK – in effect the Government – is in breach of its international obligations. Thus, ministers and parliamentarians may feel 'bullied' into legislating for changes which they do not wish for: the issue of prisoners' votes after the ECtHR decision in *Hirst v UK* and the inability of the Government to deport suspected terrorist Abu Qatada brought these issues to the surface in 2012.[60] It is also the case that some members of the House of Commons assume that they are 'sovereign' in not being subject to any law: they have difficulty taking on board that as part of the system of government they ought, in accordance with common understandings of the rule of law,

---

[56] See discussion in A Horne and L Maer 'From the Human Rights Act to a Bill of Rights?' in A Horne, G Drewry and D Oliver, n 17 above.

[57] *Hirst v UK* (n 37).

[58] For discussion of the difficulties see C O'Cinneide, *Human Rights and the UK Constitution* (London, British Academy, 2012).

[59] Human Rights Act 1998, s 6(1).

[60] *A v UK 8139/09* [2012] ECHR 56.

to secure that the UK fulfils its international law obligations. The international rule of law[61] culture among some politicians in the UK is weak, largely through their ignorance and mis-understanding of the meanings of 'sovereign', but also because of arrogance brought about by the fact that they live in a Westminster village bubble.

The long and the short of it is that Human Rights Act and the ECHR simply do not 'fit' popular culture in the UK.

It has been suggested by many commentators[62] that there should have been wide consul-tation before the Human Rights Act was passed, and that the introduction of a new British Bill of Rights should be preceded by wide consultation in order to build up public support for it.[63] The assumptions in this set of views are that, had such a process taken place, the Human Rights Act would still have been passed in more or less its current form, and it would have been welcomed and adopted wholeheartedly by the press and the general pop-ulation; and that a new British Bill of Rights would also command public support if its passage was preceded by wide consultation. Personally I doubt that. Consultation does not of itself generate a transformative constitutional moment. The consensus seems to be that any new Bill of Rights should be 'Convention plus', 'Convention compliant', and not 'Convention minus'. In the absence of a 'moment', a fully participatory procedure before enactment of a British Bill of Rights would not guarantee that the press and sections of the general public would agree that suspected terrorists ought not to be deported to their home countries or the places they have fled from, even if faced with the likelihood of torture or of being convicted of offences on the basis of evidence acquired by torture in the country to which they were deported. I suspect, though I cannot prove it, that no amount of con-sultation, or referendums, would change the political and public culture of resentment and anger against prisoners, paedophiles and other such people. And in the absence of a historical cultural transformative moment – and there is no sign that such a moment is imminent – public dissatisfaction with the Human Rights Act cannot be countered. This is just a fact of life. So although a government with a majority in Parliament might be able to push through a new Bill of Rights which makes no mention of the ECHR but is compatible with it, the resulting new Act would not in my view command any more support than the present arrangements.

In any event a new 'British Bill of Rights' would be hard to formulate and then to pass, largely because it would almost certainly not 'fit' the legal and political systems in the UK as well as the Human Rights Act does. Some of the difficulties are demonstrated in the Commission on a Bill of Rights Report, *A UK Bill of Rights? – The Choice Before Us*, in 2012. For instance, reference to 'British' in such a Charter would not fit in Northern Ireland's divided communities, or in Scotland among those seeking independence. Scotland's legal system differs from that of England and Wales, so including the right to trial by jury in a British Bill of Rights might not 'fit' into the system in Scotland. There has not been the same level of concern in Scotland, Wales and Northern Ireland as there has been in the Westminster Parliament and the English press about the Human Rights Act: there would clearly be difficulties for political relations between the UK Government and the devolved bodies if the latter objected to the repeal of the Human Rights Act or to the terms of a

---

[61] See Tom Bingham, *The Rule of Law* (London, Allen and Lane, 2010) ch 10.

[62] See for instance Commission on a Bill of Rights, *A UK Bill of Rights? – The Choice Before Us* (London, Commission on a Bill of Rights, December 2012), available at www.justice.gov.uk/about/cbr/index.htm.

[63] See report of the Commission on a Bill of Rights (n 62); and JUSTICE, *A Bill of Rights for Britain: A Discussion Paper* (JUSTICE Constitution Project, 2007) 4.

BBoR.[64] It is not unthinkable that the Scottish Parliament would pass its own Bill of Rights if the Human Rights Act were repealed.

In sum, the root of the problems over the Human Rights Act is the fact that there has not been a 'transformative constitutional moment' in Britain, or at least in England and in the Westminster Parliament, that has shifted public *and* political opinion in favour of a Human Rights Act *of any kind*. In my view unless such a moment arrives, which seems unlikely, the Human Rights Act will continue to be unpopular with many politicians and the public, it will not be replaced by anything like a British Bill of Rights, and no amount of public consultation and engagement will change that. But the Human Rights Act will not be repealed. It will continue to fit the legal system and our international obligations rather well, and the 'lack of fit' with political pressures and public opinion will not be sufficient to produce a 'moment' for it to be repealed and/or replaced.

IV REFLECTIONS

Most recent constitutional reforms are stable in that they will not be reversed. Stable changes, once in place, are stable because they reflect political, legal or public opinion as it has developed, organically, over the years. So the substance of a proposed reform, whether it advances liberal democracy, whether it is inappropriately partisan, and so on, is important. To be durable a change must fit not only the legal system but the political and public culture. This is why the Human Rights Act has not taken root among the public and many politicians, especially in England.

But many factors stand in the way of constitutional reform – inertia on the part of government, lack of urgency, or the Government's reluctance to change things in ways that will make its own life more difficult. So sometimes, but by no means always, constitutional reforms can only take place and endure if countervailing considerations outweigh these factors. Some of the following may need to be present:

- A newly elected government, mindful of its experience in opposition, attaches more weight to the importance of effective opposition than a government that has settled in. A new government will have a weaker sense of the need to protect its own as opposed to the public's interests: House of Commons Select Committee reforms provide examples.
- A transformative constitutional moment is experienced by government or in Parliament or by the public and overcomes inertia: the MPs' expenses scandal, the Scott report on Arms to Iraq and the introduction of the poll tax in Scotland illustrate this point.
- A strong shift in public opinion in favour of reform takes place, either suddenly, for instance because of a scandal such as the MPs expenses one, or gradually over a period of time, for instance the case for moving the top court out of Parliament and the introduction of freedom of information.
- An effective, non-party-political 'Champion' emerges and enables change to take place, as has been the case with reform in the House of Commons.
- Delayed, uncontroversial reform may become urgent, for instance in relation to succession to the Crown.

---

[64] See for instance C O'Cinneide, 'Human Rights, Devolution and the Constrained Authority of the Westminster Parliament' (UK Constitutional Law Group Blog, 4 March 2013) available at http://ukconstitutionallaw.org.

In addition, the reform will need to 'fit' fundamental principles of our existing constitutional arrangements, such as:

- Constitutional arrangements, and their reform, should be non-partisan and promote the general interest.
- The legislative supremacy of Parliament is to be upheld.
- Individual ministerial responsibility to Parliament should be effective.
- The primacy of the House of Commons and the effective government that it promotes should be protected.
- Accountability and transparency in government should be enhanced.
- The independence of the judiciary and the maintenance of the rule of law should be maintained.
- The public service principle should not be breached.

This list is drawn only from the selection of constitutional reforms that have been discussed above. Additional principles would emerge from the study of other constitutional reforms. Sadly, at the moment the protection of the human rights of unpopular minorities is not one of these principles.

Because these principles are embedded in the cultures of the law and of politics, and in public opinion, there is a limit to the ability of government and other players to manage, engineer or manipulate these things. Consulting widely and appointing a Champion will not necessarily do the trick.

To return to the themes of this volume, the relationships between politics and law are deeply intertwined in the British constitution. If constitutional reforms are to be put in place and endure, the political and cultural *dynamics* must be right, the time must be ripe and the changes must fit; if not, it will either be impossible to make a reform, or a reform, once made, will be unstable.

17

Looking Back and Moving On

DAVID FELDMAN

I REFLECTING ON THEMES

IN CHAPTER ONE, I tried to set the essays in the book against a number of themes: different kinds of connection between politics and law as bodies of knowledge and experience and as types of discourse; law as a tool of political action; and the connections between different levels of government (international, national, sub-national) at which politics and law interact. Here, I return to those themes, and look forward to the next steps on the road to understanding the relationships.

The first point which seems to me to emerge strongly from the collection is the complexity of the relationships. Both law and politics are complex, of course. My friend and sometime colleague Professor Nigel Lowe, now of Cardiff University, used to say that law is complex because life is complex, but needless complexity should be avoided in legal exegesis. When one looks at the relationships between them, however, complexity is greatly increased by the different though overlapping functions they serve. They are not merely modes of discourse or scholarship. Each is embodied in institutions, and those who work in them have distinct ideals and needs, related to their roles, which can lead them to treat the ideas and ideals of law and of politics in divergent ways, and take different views of their relative importance. This clearly emerges from David Seymour's and Sir Michael Wood's anecdotal, yet illuminating, accounts of their work as government lawyers in chapters six and seven. As a result, government lawyers, imbued with legal ideals and functioning in a predominantly political environment, face special problems concerning their responsibilities to their employers (or clients), to the legal system (especially courts), and to the integrity of the law itself. Matthew Windsor's analysis in chapter eight of the ethical implications highlights the internal conflicts which such lawyers must either resolve for themselves or suppress.

Intuitively, it seems likely that lawyers who become politicians may face similar difficulty, although it may be that their decision to enter politics as their main career, so that they function thereafter principally as politicians rather than lawyers, makes it easier for them to treat the demands of politics as overriding the values of law when the two cannot be accommodated together. Yet the evidence of the lawyer-politicians who have contributed to this volume suggests that it is not that simple. The late Lord Rodger of Earlsferry, Sir Ross Cranston and David Howarth all see one of the tasks of lawyers in politics as being to uphold respect for the values of the rule of law among ministers, civil servants and parliamentarians. They express this in different ways, but Sir Ross Cranston and David Howarth are both concerned that the diminishing number of lawyers entering

Parliament may undermine understanding, and so appreciation, of legal values among those who make laws, with a consequential loss of quality in the law-making process and in the content of laws. This is quite apart from the risk of harming the quality of adjudication when, as they also point out, fewer judges and legal practitioners have experience and understanding of politics and the way politicians and civil servants think and work.

The second matter to which I would draw attention is the challenging nature of the task of harnessing law to achieve political aims. As Lord Rodger and Sir Stephen Laws make clear in chapters four and five, a Bill has to be drafted to give effect to policy (usually a government's policy), but it does not stop there. The drafter has to make it fit into all the fields of law which the policy touches. An apparently simple change may require many statutory schemes and institutional arrangements to be adjusted, and the drafter has to be aware of them all. Occasionally, the task is so daunting, and the institutional consequences so labyrinthine, that the change is, for practical purposes, legally impossible, at least within the time which a minister is prepared to allow. Professor Dawn Oliver gives an example in chapter 16: Mr Blair's decision in 2003 to abolish the office of Lord Chancellor would have affected so many institutions, processes and pieces of legislation, because of the many tasks which the Lord Chancellor performed, that it was impracticable.

Alongside the problem of 'fit', legal as well as constitutional (on which Professor Oliver concentrates), the nature of everyday party politics can lead to the making of law which is evanescent. Politics, at any rate in the UK, tends to be adversarial and short-sighted. Governments rarely think beyond the lifetime of the current Parliament. Forward planning therefore tends to be limited to a five-year horizon, which shortens progressively as the next election becomes closer. This means that a good deal of law-making is a matter of fiddling, often for the purpose of allowing a minister to generate publicity by announcing an initiative, whether or not it is likely to have any, or any long-term, impact. It is significant that most of the major innovations of constitutional principle made during the Labour governments of 1997–2010, which Professor Oliver discusses, were planned while Labour was in opposition during the early and middle 1990s. Once in government, the need to cope with rapidly developing events leaves little time for collective reflection and deliberative, evidence-based decision-making.

Perhaps this is to say no more than that politics is (or are) irreducibly political. Legal changes which flow from politics have to be forced or negotiated through Parliament. When they have far-reaching, constitutional significance, many interests need to be squared in order to make them acceptable. And there must be what Professor Oliver calls a 'constitutional moment' in order to make change chime harmoniously with prevailing political and social cultures. Even when a change appears to be inspired by constitutional principle, it may be actuated by political advantage.

The history of the Parliament Acts, discussed by Lord Norton and Dr Chris Ballinger in chapters 10 and 11, exemplifies this. The Liberal Government in 1911 needed the Parliament Act to force home rule for Ireland through Parliament, but that was a deeply divisive issue on which the House of Lords arguably had more public support than the Government. The House of Lords' rejection of the budget provided the *casus belli*, but the practical effects of the 1911 Act were, first, to allow the Government of Ireland Bill and the Welsh Church disestablishment legislation to pass, and, secondly, to change the political psychology and tactical balance within Parliament. Thenceforth the House of Lords could negotiate with the Government of the day, but as long as the Government commanded a majority in the House of Commons the shadow of the Parliament Act always loomed over the negotiation. As Daniel Greenberg and Dr Rhodri Walters demonstrate in chapters 12 and 13, the effect is that the main constraint on a government's ability to get its legislative programme through Parliament is time.

The story of the passing of the Parliament Act 1949 exemplifies this. As Dr Ballinger shows, the Labour Government needed the Act to shorten the time for which the House of Lords could delay legislation, in order to ensure that the Government could get its Iron and Steel Bill, nationalising those industries, through Parliament before a general election supervened. The effective power of the Lords over a government's legislation depends on the time left to a government before the end of a Parliament, and the amount and importance to a government of the rest of its programme. The political effect of this on the legislative process and on a government's ability to plan and manage its legislative programme is brought out clearly by Daniel Greenberg and Rhodri Walters.

Another feature of the interplay of party politics and law-making is the way that an individual minister may have a 'constitutional moment' in isolation from others and announce an initiative which, unknown to the minister, involves a constitutional upheaval. Particularly when that minister is the Prime Minister, the Government may find itself in a position where it would lose so much face if it were to back away from the idea entirely that a principled reason has to be found for pressing ahead with it. Mr Blair's announcement that the office of Lord Chancellor would be abolished, already mentioned, is an example. Whilst abolition proved unmanageable, an unforeseen consequence of the announcement was that the Government felt politically (though not emotionally) committed to the principles (rather than the short-term aims) underlying it, namely the separation of powers between the judiciary and the legislature and executive, and the independence of the judiciary. Supported by the desire to save face, the principles then took on a momentum which, in a relatively short time, led to the Constitutional Reform Act 2005, a new top court for the UK, a new independent system for appointing, managing and disciplining the judges, and a statutory obligation on ministers to uphold the rule of law and the independence of the judiciary. It is highly unlikely that Mr Blair contemplated any of that when he made his snap announcement.

The relationship between the stuff of politics and the stuff of law, then, is messy, and subject to the law of unintended consequences. People in one institution invest acts and statements by someone in a different institutional role with significance quite different from that which was originally intended, and things can happen which are both unexpected and largely unwanted. This is not because anything has really gone wrong. It is just the consequence of people having different ideas about what behaviour on the part of other people should be taken seriously. To some extent, contrasting institutional cultures, values and ambitions make this both inevitable and highly unpredictable.

A similar combination of inevitable but unplanned and unpredictable consequences afflicts relationships between states. Matthew Parish, however, denies in chapter 14 that this is due to the interaction of law and politics. Indeed, he challenges the idea that international law is law in a conventional sense. By presenting it in the light of international relations, he argues that state sovereignty remains a powerful phenomenon on the international plane, and that the supposed obligations of states to each other or to international organisations are, if anything, moral, not legal. This deprives public international 'law' of its normative heft. It is, as AV Dicey quipped, 'law which is not law'.[1] Yet it may be that this

---

[1] AV Dicey, *An Introduction to the Study of the Law of the Constitution*, 10th edn (edited by ECS Wade) (London, Macmillan, 1959) 22.

underestimates the significance of commitment to principles as an instrument of success-ful international relations. Just as national politicians can find that they have painted them-selves into a corner from which they cannot escape without giving legal force to principles which are not in their party or short-term interests, their postures on international stages may make it impossible for them to justify certain kinds of behaviour. One of the most shocking aspects of what happened in Abu Ghraib Prison was that prisoners were mistreated by US forces. The US Government's rhetoric when going to war in Iraq con-centrated on the misdeeds of Saddam Hussein's regime. It could not be seen to attempt to justify similar behaviour by its own troops. Attempts to protect the US's reputation by redefining torture to exclude waterboarding prisoners at Guantanamo Bay ultimately did more damage to the state's international standing than the waterboarding itself. Values, once invoked, become important standards for evaluating one's own conduct. A virtuous circle may develop, limited in scope and not necessarily long lasting, but nevertheless allowing legal values to influence political behaviour.

This process may also work in reverse. In chapter 15, Sir Philip Sales argues persuasively that the European Court of Human Rights, in its jurisprudence, has developed the values underpinning rights in the European Convention on Human Rights (ECHR) in ways which strengthen democracy. This happens in two ways. First, rights to freedom of speech, freedom of association, and electoral rights have been interpreted in ways which extend franchises, restrict discrimination between groups, liberalise political discourse, and tend to bolster the representativeness of legislatures within Council of Europe states. This often happens at the expense of governmental self-determination where politically dominant groups in a society want to freeze other groups or individuals out of politics, so govern-ments in these countries tend to present such decisions, which regulate their capacity for national self-determination, as an attack on democracy, which they confuse with self-determination. (For an example, we need look no further than the UK's foot-dragging response to decisions of the European Court of Human Rights about the voting rights of prisoners.) From an objective viewpoint, however, the judgments, if properly implemented within states, can be seen to advance the inclusiveness and so the legitimacy of political processes, improve their democratic credentials, and so enhance the democratic legitimacy of policies and laws which state agencies adopt and pursue.

Secondly, the Court has given normative substance to the idea of democracy contained in the formula, in several articles of the ECHR, requiring that any interference with rights under those articles be shown to be 'necessary in a democratic society'. The Court's adop-tion of pluralism, tolerance and broad-mindedness as hallmarks of a democratic society for this purpose recognises that democracy is not merely a matter of counting preferences; it makes normative demands of a society's culture, including but not limited to its political culture.[2] Again, to some extent this restricts the capacity of states' governments and legisla-tures for self-determination in the ways they organise the political structures of the state, but the idea of self-determination is not the same as democracy: if a state wants to be accepted as democratic, it has to make concessions to the rights of all its citizens in order that 'self' in 'self-determination' relates to the people, not just to some of them.

---

[2] *Handyside v UK* Series A no 24 (1976) 1 EHRR 737, §49.

II A CONCLUSION?

The various kinds of relationships and interactions between politics and the law, and between politicians and lawyers, and between different levels of governance, are dynamic and constantly shifting in response to events, ideas, ideals and agendas. It has been the achievement of the contributors to this collection to illuminate different facets of those relationships – personal and professional as well as institutional and ideological – in ways which make it easier to comprehend their vibrancy and negotiability as well as their principled importance. What seems to me to have emerged – and in this I am just a reader, reflecting on what they have written, rather than an original contributor – is that to understand the relationships we have to appreciate how different cultures co-exist in our world, and tend to push in divergent directions. The people who have to make things work as sensibly as possible have to cope with clashes of culture which sometimes lead to mutual misunderstanding or inability to engage with each other and with each other's arguments. People and institutions begin from different assumptions, have different aims, and are guided by different values and world views.

This understanding allows us to see that it is not surprising that political and legal efforts go wrong. The surprising thing is that they ever work at all. When they do, it is a result of people in all walks of life and government (nationally and internationally) being prepared to accommodate each other's eccentricities (as they are often seen). People daily show each other that respect for pluralism, the tolerance and the broad-mindedness that the European Court of Human Rights saw as key elements of democracy. They are needed because democracy and constitutions are not about securing agreement. They are concerned with managing disagreement.

Professor Oliver has powerfully argued for lawyers to appreciate the importance of social psychology, anthropology and other behavioural sciences in shaping constitutional ideas and behaviour.[3] Her analysis would indicate that there is a need for greater understanding of the way in which different political and legal groups see themselves, their cultures and their relationships. This volume may perhaps have made a small, unscientific contribution to that. The next step in enhancing understanding is, perhaps, for the approach to be extended, and made properly systematic and scientific.

---

[3] Dawn Oliver, 'Psychological Constitutionalism' [2010] *Cambridge Law Journal* 639–75.

Index